NEW TRANSLATION

OF

THE BOOK OF PSALMS

AND OF

THE PROVERBS,

WITH

INTRODUCTIONS, AND NOTES, CHIEFLY EXPLANATORY.

By GEORGE R. NOYES, D.D.,

HANCOCK PROFESSOR OF HEBREW, ETC., AND DEXTER LECTURER IN HARVARD UNIVERSITY.

FIFTH EDITION.

BOSTON:
AMERICAN UNITARIAN ASSOCIATION.
1874.

THE PSALMS.

INTRODUCTION.

I. General Character and Value of the Psalms.

The Book of Psalms has been styled by some of the German critics, in allusion to a portion of Grecian literature, The Hebrew Anthology; that is, a collection of the lyric, moral, historical, and elegiac poetry of the Hebrews. Regarded in this light alone, it presents a most interesting subject of literary taste and curiosity. Many of these psalms must have been composed some hundreds of years before the period which is commonly assigned to the origin of the Iliad of Homer. But it is not with them as with many of the productions of the classic Muse, of which the antiquity constitutes their greatest claim upon the attention of the scholar, and of which the subjects possess little or no interest for the world in its manhood. It was the privilege of the Hebrew bards to be employed upon subjects possessing an interest as enduring as the attributes of God and the nature of dependent man. Their poetry has the deep foundation of eternal truth. It comes, for the most part, in language the most glowing, from the very depths of the soul, rich in sentiments adapted to the soul's most urgent wants. Hence its living spirit, its immortal freshness. Hence its power of reaching the hearts of all men, in all countries and in all ages. Where, in the whole compass of literature, can one find more of the "thoughts that breathe and words that burn" than in the Hebrew Anthology? Then, too, what variety is there in the subjects of these ancient compositions! How diverse the states of heart and fortune that occasioned them! How various the strains of joy, sorrow, gratitude, love, hope, confidence, fear, remorse, and penitence, which come from the sacred lyre! There is scarcely a conceivable state of the human soul, in which one may not repair to the Psalter, as it were to a sympathizing friend.

What a sensation would be produced in the literary world by such a collection of poetry as is presented in the Book of Psalms, could it come recommended by the attraction of novelty! But the truth is, that, in general, the ear is accustomed to these admirable productions, before the mind can comprehend their meaning or feel their beauty; so that, in maturer life, it requires no inconsiderable effort to give them that attention which is necessary for the reception of the impressions they are adapted to impart.

Another obstacle to a proper estimate of the poetry of the Scriptures is the very imperfect translation, and wretched arrangement, in which it has been presented to English readers. Let the lover of poetry imagine what impressions he should receive from the odes of Collins or Gray, cut up into fragments like the verses in the common version of the Bible, and he may comprehend what injustice has been done to the Hebrew poets.

The compositions in the Book of Psalms are the productions of various authors and periods, belong to different species of poetry, and possess various degrees of poetic merit. While some of them present the fresh gushes of excited feeling, or the calmer expression of the sublimest sentiments, in the boldest language of poetry, others consist only of moral maxims artificially arranged in a sententious style, or of elaborate and imitative prayers and praises, prepared for the public worship of God.

The Psalms, says De Wette, are lyric poems. This is all that is implied in the name which they bear. Ψαλμός, from *ψάλλειν*, *chordas tangere*, *fidibus canere*, signifies *the music of a stringed instrument*, *the sound of the lyre;* then, a song sung to the music of the lyre. This word is used by the Alexandrian translators for the Hebrew מִזְמוֹר, as well as *ψάλλειν* for the verb זִמֵּר; but these Hebrew words, whatever may be their etymology, have the signification of song accompanied with music. *Psalter* (*ψαλτήριον*), the name which, in imitation of the Greeks, we give to the collection of Psalms, properly denotes *a stringed instrument;* and the appellation is to be understood in the same manner as when we give to a collection of lyric poems the title of *The Lyre.* The Jews call the Psalms תְּהִלִּים, *songs of praise*, and the collection סֵפֶר תְּהִלִּים, also, abbreviated, תִּלִּים, an appellation which applies to a part only of the Psalms. The term, מִזְמֹרִים or שִׁירִים, *songs*, *odes*, would be more correct.

The Psalms are lyric, in the proper sense; for with the Hebrews, as in the ancient world generally, song and music were connected, and the titles to most of the Psalms determine their connection with music, though in a manner which is often unintelligible to us. These compositions deserve, moreover, the name of lyric, on account of their character as works of taste. The essence of lyric poetry is the immediate expression of feeling; and feeling is the sphere to which most of the Psalms belong. Pain, sorrow, fear, hope, joy, confidence, gratitude, submission to God, every thing that moves and elevates the soul, is expressed in these hymns.

In the Psalms we have merely the remains of the lyric poetry of the Hebrews. The productions of this class were undoubtedly far more numerous than would seem to have been the case from these remains, and spread through a wider and more diversified field. The Psalter is chiefly composed of religious and devotional hymns; but it cannot be maintained, that the lyric poetry of the Hebrews was exclusively devoted to the service of religion and of public worship. The supposition is sufficiently contradicted by those invaluable examples of another species of lyric poetry, which are preserved in other parts of the Scriptures; such as David's elegy over Saul and Jonathan, the song at the well (Numb. xxi. 17), and especially the Song of Solomon, although the last belongs to a somewhat different branch of poetical composition. In the Book of Psalms itself, there is one production which possesses an altogether secular character, namely, Ps. xlv. For most of the hymns which are extant, we are indebted probably to the religious use to which they were consecrated, rather than to any common poetical sympathy; and hence so few secular songs have been preserved from destruction.

In respect to their contents and character, the Psalms have been classified in the following manner: * —

* See De Wette's Commentar über die Psalmen, p. 8. Biblical Repository for 1833, p. 448.

I. Hymns in praise of Jehovah. 1. Generally as God of nature and of man, Ps. viii., civ., cxlv. 2. As God of nature and of Israel, Ps. xix., xxix., xxxiii., lxv., xciii., cxxxv., cxxxvi., cxlvii., and others. 3. As God of Israel, Ps. xlvii., lxvi., lxvii., lxxv. 4. As the saviour and helper of Israel, Ps. xlvi., xlvii., xlviii., lxxv., lxxvi.; and of individuals, Ps. xviii., xxx., cxxxviii., and others.

II. National psalms, containing allusions to the ancient history of the Israelites, and to the relation of the people to Jehovah, Ps. lxxviii., cv., cvi., cxiv.

III. Psalms of Zion and of the temple, Ps. xv., xxiv., lxviii., lxxxi., lxxxvii., cxxxii., cxxxiv., cxxxv.

IV. Psalms relating to the king, Ps. ii., xx., xxi., xlv., lxxii., cx.

V. Psalms which contain complaints under affliction and the persecution of enemies, and prayers for succor; the most numerous class, comprising more than a third part of the whole collection. These psalms of complaint are, — 1. Personal, relating to the case of an individual, Ps. vii., xxii., lv., lvi., cix., and others. 2. National, Ps. xliv., lxxiv., lxxix., lxxx., cxxxvii., and others. 3. Personal and national at the same time, Ps. lxix., lxxvii., cii. From these divisions proceed still others. 4. General psalms of complaint, reflections on the wickedness of the world, Ps. x., xii., xiv., xxxvi. 5. Didactic psalms, respecting the condition of the pious and the godless, Ps. xxxvii., xlix., lxxiii. 6. Psalms of thanksgiving for deliverance from enemies, which also pass over into the first class, Ps. xxxiv., xl., and others.

VI. Religious and moral psalms. 1. Odes to Jehovah with special allusions, Ps. xc., cxxxix. 2. Expressions of religious conviction, hope, confidence, Ps. xxiii., xci., cxxi., cxxvii., cxxviii. 3. Expressions of religious experience, resolutions, &c., Ps. xlii., xliii., ci., cxxxi. 4. Development of religious or moral ideas, Ps. i., cxxxiii. 5. Didactic poems relating to religion, Ps. xxxii., l. 6. Collections of proverbs, in alphabetical order, Ps. cxix. The few which cannot be brought under any of the foregoing classes and divisions either constitute new ones by themselves, or possess an intermediate character.

It will be perceived, that, in this classification, proposed by De Wette, no place is assigned to psalms relating to the Messiah. This is in accordance with the opinion of the above-mentioned distinguished commentator, and others, who reject the doctrine of a double sense in the Scriptures, that there is not in the Book of Psalms any prediction relating to the Messiah. The question whether any, and, if any, how many, of the Psalms relate to the Messiah is attended with considerable difficulty. At first view, it would be natural to expect, that the lyrical productions of the Jewish poets, as well as the writings of the prophets, would contain allusions to the Messiah. But when we come to examine those which have been chiefly referred to as containing the Messianic hopes, such as the ii., xvi., xxii., xl., xlv., lxxii., cx., we seem to find, on the principles of historical interpretation which are applied to all other books, in some of them no predictions whatever, but only references to the past or the present; in others, only glowing anticipations, which seem to refer to the writer of the psalm, or to Jewish kings contemporary with him. The question can be decided only by a critical examination of each psalm. But it deserves consideration, whether Christ may not be said to have fulfilled what is written in the Psalms concerning him, when he *filled out*, or completed, what was valuable in the experience, or precious in the hopes, of David and other servants of God, which are the proper subjects of the Psalms.* His life and sufferings were analogous to theirs, but of a higher character and attended with more glorious results. It is well observed by Stanley, in connection with other valuable remarks on the subject, "The Psalter is especially prophetic of Christ, because, more than any other part of the ancient Scriptures, it enters into those truths of the spiritual life, of which he was the great revealer."† This view is confirmed by the interpretation of the Psalms which has generally prevailed in the Christian church. The ever-recurring remark of the common expositor is, "This psalm in part refers to David, and in part to Jesus Christ;" or, "This psalm is fulfilled in a lower sense in David, but in a higher and better sense in Christ." But the supposition that the psalm itself contained,

* See Int. to the Prophets, p. lxx.

† History of the Jewish Church, vol. ii. p. 161.

in the mind of the writer, more senses than one, seems to contradict all just views of the nature of language. In regard to some of the references* made to the Psalms by Paul and Peter, and the author of the Epistle to the Hebrews, it seems necessary to suppose that they were not inspired as critics and interpreters, but that they argued according to a mode of reasoning and of interpretation which they held in common with their contemporaries, but which cannot be regarded as valid at the present day.

Now, it is an indisputable fact, that the ancient Jews, without regard to any just laws of interpretation, without any regard to the connection in which words stand, and especially in pursuance of the typical or the allegorical method, applied hundreds of passages of the Old Testament to the Messiah, which no one in modern times can suppose to relate to him.† It would be singular, therefore, if we did not find traces of the same mode of applying Scriptural passages in the writers of the New Testament.

It is probable, that, in some cases, the reference in the New Testament to a passage in the Psalms is merely in the way of rhetorical illustration, or of *argumentum ex concessis;* for instance, in John xiii. 18; Matt. xxii, 44, &c. But this mode of explanation cannot be applied to such passages as Acts iv. 25, xiii. 33, and several in the Epistle to the Hebrews, without doing violence to language.

These observations are offered for the consideration of those, of whom I am one, who can find no psalm of which, in its primary sense, the Messiah is the exclusive subject. Of recent orthodox commentators, Tholuck finds only four, namely, Ps. ii., xlv., lxxii., and cx., containing a direct and literal reference to the Messiah. So also Hengstenberg applies to him only the same psalms. It seems to me that all four plainly indicate that they refer to kings actually living and reigning in the time of the writers. Nor is any thing ascribed to them, or hoped for them, which, when due allowance is made for the language of Oriental hyperbole, does not belong to the conception of a Jewish theocratic king, the vicegerent of Jehovah. As the ancient prophets, such as Isaiah, Jeremiah, Micah, &c., predict the Messiah in the char-

* Acts iv. 25; xiii. 33; Heb. i. 5, 6; x. 5, &c.

† See Schoettgen's Horæ Hebraicæ et Talmudicæ, passim.

acter of a perfect Jewish king, it follows, of course, that the representations of actual kings in the Psalms will resemble the Messianic predictions of the Prophets. But why some writers should exert their ingenuity to find predictions of a future Messiah, where there are none, it is difficult to say. If the predictions of a Messiah in the Old Testament are regarded as a miraculous attestation of the truth of Christianity, are not the plain and universally acknowledged predictions of a Messianic king in the writings of the prophets Isaiah, Micah, Jeremiah, Ezekiel, and Zechariah, enough for the purpose? Why multiply doubtful cases of Messianic predictions, when there are so many beyond doubt? Truly, it is cause for thankfulness, that God has laid the foundations of the Christian religion deeper than some of its friends imagine.

On the relation of the literature and history of the Jewish Commonwealth to the Christian dispensation, Dean Stanley * has a passage, which we cannot help citing for the benefit of those who cannot have access to his expensive work: "I may be allowed to express by an illustration the true mode of regarding this question. In the gardens of the Carthusian Convent, which the Dukes of Burgundy built near Dijon for the burial place of their race, is a beautiful monument, which alone of that splendid edifice escaped the ravages of the French Revolution. It consists of a group of prophets and kings from the Old Testament, each holding in his hand a scroll of mourning from his writings; each with his own individual costume and gesture and look; each distinguished from each by the most marked peculiarities of age and character, — absorbed in the thoughts of his own time and country. But above these figures is a circle of angels, as like each to each as the human figures are unlike. They too, as each overhangs and overlooks the prophet below him, are saddened with grief. But their expression of sorrow is far deeper and more intense than that of the prophets whose words they read. They see something in the prophetic sorrow, which the prophets themselves see not; they are lost in the contemplation of the Divine Passion, of which the ancient saints below them are but the unconscious and indirect exponents.

* Lectures on the Hist. of the Jewish Church, part ii. pp. xii.-xv.

"This exquisite mediæval monument, expressing, as it does, the instinctive feeling at once of the truthful artist and of the devout Christian, represents better than any words the sense of what we call, in theological language, 'the Types' of the Old Testament. The heroes and saints of old times, not in Judea only, — though there more frequently than in any other country, — are indeed 'types,' that is, 'likenesses,' in their sorrows of the Greatest of all sorrows, in their joys of the Greatest of all joys, in their goodness of the Greatest of all goodness, in their truth of the Greatest of all truths. This deep inward connection between the events of their own time and the crowning close of the history of their whole nation, — this gradual convergence towards the event which, by general acknowledgment, ranks chief in the annals of mankind, — is clear, not only to the all-searching Eye of Providence, but also to the eye of any who look above the stir and movement of earth. It is part, not only of the foreknowledge of God, but of the universal workings of human nature and human history. The angels see, though man sees not. The mind flies silently upwards from the earthly career of David or Isaiah or Ezekiel to those vaster and wider thoughts which they imperfectly represented. 'The rustic murmur' of Jerusalem was, although they knew it not, part of 'the great wave that echoes round the world.' It is a continuity recognized by the Philosophy of History no less than by Theology, — by Hegel even more closely than by Augustine. But the sorrow, the joy, the goodness, the truth of those ancient heroes is notwithstanding entirely their own. They are not mere machines or pictures. When they speak of their trials and difficulties, they speak of them as from their own experience. By studying them, with all the peculiarities of their time, we arrive at a profounder view of the truths and events to which their expressions and the story of their deeds may be applied in after-ages than if we regard them as the organs of sounds unintelligible to themselves, and with no bearing on their own period. Where there is a sentiment common to them and to Christian times, a word or act which breaks forth into the distant future, it will be reverently caught up by those who are on the watch for it, to whom it will speak words beyond their words, and thoughts beyond their thoughts. 'Did not our heart burn within us while He walked with us by the way, and while He opened to us the Scriptures?' But, even in the act of uttering these sentiments, they still remained encompassed with human, Jewish, Oriental peculiarities, which must not be explained away or softened down, for the sake of producing an appearance of uniformity which may be found in the Koran, but which it is hopeless to seek in the Bible; and which, if it were found there, would completely destroy the historical character of its contents. To refuse to see the first and direct application of their expressions to themselves is like an unwillingness — such as some simple and religious minds have felt — to acknowledge the existence, or to dwell on the topography, of the city of Jerusalem and the wilderness of Arabia, because those localities have been so long associated with the higher truths of spiritual religion."

The hearts of the pious for ages have felt the value of the Psalms as helps to devotion, and many have labored for expressions in which to set forth their praise. For its truth, as well as beauty, we quote the following description by Bishop Horne, who yet saw some things in them which modern views of interpretation will not permit us to find: —

"In them," says he, "we are instructed to conceive of the subjects of religion aright, and to express the different affections which, when so conceived of, they must excite in our minds. They are, for this purpose, adorned with the figures, and set off with all the graces, of poetry; and poetry itself is designed yet farther to be recommended by the charms of music thus consecrated to the service of God; that so delight may prepare the way for improvement, and pleasure become the handmaid of wisdom, while every turbulent passion is calmed by sacred melody, and the evil spirit is still dispossessed by the harp of the son of Jesse. This little volume, like the paradise of Eden, affords us in perfection, though in miniature, every thing that groweth elsewhere, — 'every tree that is pleasant to the sight, and good for food;' and above all, what was there lost, but is here restored, *the tree of life in the midst of the garden*. That which we read as matter of speculation in the other Scriptures is reduced to practice when we recite it in the Psalms; in those, faith and repentance are described, but in these they are acted: by a perusal of the former, we learn how others served God; but, by using the latter, we serve him ourselves."

"The hymns of David," says Milman, "excel no less in sublimity and tenderness of expression than in loftiness and purity of religious sentiment. In comparison with them, the sacred poetry of all other nations sinks into mediocrity. They have embodied so exquisitely the universal language of religious emotion, that (a few fierce and vindictive passages excepted, natural in the warrior-poet of a sterner age) they have entered, with unquestioned propriety, into the ritual of the holier and more perfect religion of Christ. The songs which cheered the solitude of the desert caves of Engedi, or resounded from the voice of the Hebrew people as they wound along the glens or the hill-sides of Judea, have been repeated for ages in almost every part of the habitable world, in the remotest islands of the ocean, among the forests of America, or the sands of Africa. How many human hearts have they softened, purified, exalted! Of how many wretched beings have they been the secret consolation! On how many communities have they drawn down the blessings of Divine Providence, by bringing the affections into unison with their deep devotional fervor!"

Luther, in his preface to the Psalter, has the following just remarks: "A human heart is like a ship on a wild sea, driven by high winds from the four quarters of the world. Here rush fear and anxiety on account of future calamity, there press affliction and sorrow, caused by present evil; here blow hope and confidence in future prosperity, there come security and joy in present good. These high winds teach a man to speak with earnestness, to open his heart, and pour out the bottom of it. For he who is in fear and distress speaks of trouble very differently from one who is in joy; and he who is in joy speaks of joy very differently from one who is in fear. It comes not from the heart, it is said, when a sad man laughs, or a joyful man weeps; that is, the bottom of his heart stands not open, and nothing comes forth. But what is the greater part of the Psalter but such earnest speech in the midst of high winds of every kind? Where do we find a sweeter voice of joy than in the psalms of thanksgiving and praise? There you look into the heart of all the holy as into a beautiful garden, — as into heaven itself. What delicate, sweet, and lovely flowers are there springing up of all manner of beautiful, joyous thoughts towards God and his goodness! On the other hand, where do you find more profound, mournful, pathetic expressions of sorrow than the plaintive psalms contain? There again you look into the heart of all the holy as into death, — yea, as into the pit of despair. How dark and gloomy is it there, in consequence of all manner of melancholy apprehension of God's displeasure! So also when the psalmists speak of fear or hope, they use such words, that no painter could so delineate, and no Cicero or eloquent orator so describe them."

We will add two passages more from the highly valuable work to which we have already referred: * —

"The Psalter has further become the Sacred Book of the world, in a sense belonging to no other part of the Biblical records. Not only does it hold its place in the liturgical services of the Jewish Church, not only was it used more than any other part of the Old Testament by the writers of the New, but it is in a special sense the peculiar inheritance of the Christian Church through all its different branches. 'From whatever point of view any Church hath contemplated the scheme of its doctrine, by whatever name they have thought good to designate themselves, and however bitterly opposed to each other in church government or observance of rites, — you will find them all, by harmonious and universal consent, adopting the Psalter as the outward form by which they shall express the inward feelings of the Christian life.' It was so in the earliest times. The Passover psalms were the 'Hymn' of the Last Supper. In the first centuries, psalms were sung at the Love-feasts, and formed the morning and evening hymns of the primitive Christians. 'Of the other Scriptures,' says Theodoret in the fifth century, 'the generality of men know next to nothing. But the Psalms you will find again and again repeated in private houses, in market-places, in streets, by those who have learned them by heart, and who soothe themselves by their divine melody.' 'When other parts of Scripture are used,' says St. Ambrose, 'there is such a noise of talking in the church, that you cannot hear what is said; but, when the Psalter is read, all are silent.

* Stanley: Lectures on the Hist. of the Jewish Church, ii. 162–4; 170–4.

They were sung by the ploughmen of Palestine, in the time of Jerome; by the boatmen of Gaul, in the time of Sidonius Apollinaris. In the most barbarous of churches, the Abyssinians treat the Psalter almost as an idol, and sing it through from end to end at every funeral. In the most Protestant of churches, — the Presbyterians of Scotland, the Nonconformists of England, — 'psalm-singing' has almost passed into a familiar description of their ritual. In the Churches of Rome and of England, they are daily recited, in proportions such as far exceed the reverence shown to any other portion of the Scriptures.

If we descend from churches to individuals, there is no one book which has played so large a part in the history of so many human souls. By the Psalms, Augustine was consoled on his conversion and on his death-bed. By the Psalms, Chrysostom, Athanasius, Savonarola, were cheered in persecution. With the words of a psalm, Polycarp, Columba, Hildebrand, Bernard, Francis of Assisi, Huss, Jerome of Prague, Columbus, Henry the Fifth, Edward the Sixth, Ximenes, Xavier, Melancthon, Jewell, breathed their last. So dear to Wallace in his wanderings was his Psalter, that during his execution he had it hung before him, and his eyes remained fixed upon it as the one consolation of his dying hours. The unhappy Darnley was soothed in the toils of his enemies by the 55th Psalm. The 68th Psalm cheered Cromwell's soldiers to victory at Dunbar. Locke, in his last days, bade his friend read the Psalms aloud; and it was whilst in rapt attention to their words that the stroke of death fell upon him. Lord Burleigh selected them out of the whole Bible as his special delight. They were the framework of the devotions and of the war-cries of Luther: they were the last words that fell on the ear of his imperial enemy, Charles the Fifth."

"But there are three points in which the Psalms stand unrivalled: —

"The first is the depth of personal expression and experience. There are doubtless occasions when the psalmist speaks as the organ of the nation. But he is for the most part alone with himself and with God. Each word is charged with the intensity of some grief or joy, known or unknown. If the doctrines of St. Paul derive half their force from their connection with his personal struggles, the doctrines of David also strike home and kindle a fire wherever they light, mainly because they are the sparks of the incandescence of a living human experience like our own. The patriarchs speak as the fathers of the chosen race; the prophets speak as its representatives and its guides. But the psalmist speaks as the mouthpiece of the individual soul, of the free, independent, solitary conscience of man everywhere.

"The second of these peculiarities is, what we may call in one word, the perfect naturalness of the Psalms. It appears, perhaps, most forcibly, in their exultant freedom and joyousness of heart. It is true, as Lord Bacon says, that, 'if you listen to David's harp, you will hear as many hearselike airs as carols;' yet still the carols are found there more than anywhere else. 'Rejoice in the Lord.' — 'Sing ye merrily.' — 'Make a cheerful noise.' — 'Take the psalm, bring hither the tabret, the merry harp, with the lute.' — 'O praise the Lord, for it is a good thing to sing praises unto our God.' — 'A joyful and pleasant thing it is to be thankful.' This, in fact, is the very meaning of the word 'psalm.' The one Hebrew word which is their very pith and marrow is 'hallelujah.' They express, if we may so say, the sacred duty of being happy. Be happy, cheerful, and thankful, as ever we can, we cannot go beyond the Psalms. They laugh, they shout, they cry, they scream for joy. There is a wild exhilaration which rings through them. They exult alike in the joy of battle, and in the calm of nature. They see God's goodness everywhere. They are not ashamed to confess it. The bright side of creation is everywhere uppermost; the dark, sentimental side is hardly ever seen. The fury of the thunder-storm, the roaring of the sea, are to them full of magnificence and delight. Like the Scottish poet in his childhood, at each successive peal they clap their hands in innocent pleasure. The affection for birds and beasts and plants, and sun and moon and stars, is like that which St. Francis of Assisi claimed for all these fellow-creatures of God, as his brothers and sisters. There have been those for whom, on this very account, in moments of weakness and depression, the Psalms have been too much; yet not the less is this vein of sacred merriment valuable in the universal mission of the chosen people. And the more so, because it grows out of another feeling in the Psalms, which has also jarred strangely on the minds of devout but narrow schools, 'the free and princely heart of innocence,' which to modern religion has often seemed to savor of self-righteousness and want of proper humility. The psalmist's bounding, buoyant hope, his fearless claim to be rewarded according to his righteous dealing, his confidence in his own integrity, no less than his agony over his own crimes; his passionate delight in the Law, not as a cruel enemy, but as the best of guides, sweeter than honey and the honeycomb,—these are not according to the requirements of Calvin, or even of Pascal: they are from a wholly different point of the celestial compass than that which inspired the Epistles to the Romans and Galatians. But they have not the less a truth of their own, a truth to nature, a truth to God, which the human heart will always recognize. The frank, unrestrained benediction on the upright, honest man, 'the noblest work of God,' with which the Psalter opens, is but the fitting prelude to the boundless generosity and prodigality of joy with which in its close it calls on 'every creature that breathes,' without stint or exception, to 'praise the Lord.' It may be that such expressions as these owe their first impulse, in part, to the new epoch of national prosperity and individual energy ushered in by David's reign; but they have swept the mind of the Jewish nation onward towards that mighty destiny which awaited it; and they have served, though at a retarded speed, to sweep on, ever since, the whole spirit of humanity in its upward course. 'The burning stream has flowed on, after the furnace itself has cooled.' As of the classic writers of Greece it has been well said, that they possess a charm quite independent of their genius, in the radiance of their brilliant and youthful beauty; so it may be said of the Psalms, that they possess a like charm, independent even of their depth of feeling or loftiness of doctrine. In their free and generous grace, the youthful, glorious David seems to live over again with a renewed vigor. 'All our fresh springs' are in him, and in his Psalter.

"These various peculiarities of the Psalms lead us, partly by way of contrast, partly by a close though hidden connection, to their main characteristic, which appears nowhere else in the Bible with equal force, unless it be in the life and words of Christ himself. The 'reason why the Psalms have found such constant favor in every portion of the Christian Church, while forms of doctrine and discourse have undergone such manifold changes in order to represent the changing spirit of the age, is this, that they address themselves to the simple, intuitive feelings of the renewed soul.' They represent 'the freshness of the soul's infancy, the love of the soul's childhood; and therefore are to the Christian what the love of parents, the sweet affections of home, and the clinging memory of infant scenes, are to men in general.'"

Perhaps the maledictions or imprecations, contained in some of the psalms, may appear inconsistent with the views which have been advanced. I am here willing to admit the unsoundness of some of the explanations which have been given of these imprecations. They cannot all, as has been supposed, be regarded as mere predictions or denunciations of the punishment which awaits evil-doers. Some of them, at least, are wishes or prayers. See Ps. cxxxvii. 8. But on this subject it should be remembered that—

I. Many prayers against enemies, contained in the Psalms, are equivalent to prayers for personal safety. They were composed by the head of the nation, in a state of war, when prayer for the destruction of enemies was equivalent to prayer for preservation and success. So Christian ministers are accustomed to pray for success for the arms of their country. So on our national festivals we are accustomed to thank God that he enabled our fathers to overcome their enemies. What is harsh, therefore, in prayers of this kind, is incidental to a state of warfare. This explanation will also apply to the psalms composed by David during his persecution by Saul. These prayers should never be used by private Christians with respect to personal enemies.

II. Another consideration is, that these prayers are expressed in the strong language of poetry; and that some of the particular thoughts and expressions, which are connected with the general subject of the prayer, result from an effort for poetic embellishment and effect, rather than from vindictiveness of feeling.

III. The imprecations which are not included in the classes above mentioned are extremely few. I shall not undertake to reconcile a part of Ps. lxix., cix., and cxxxvii., with the general spirit of even the Jewish religion, and far less with the spirit of Him who said, "Forgive, and ye shall be forgiven," and who spent his last breath in prayer for his murderers, — "Father, forgive them, for they know not what they do."

But is it strange that a human soul should be embittered by persecution so as occasionally to utter a sentiment inconsistent with the religion which it professes; that one, who had even spared the life of his deadly enemy when entirely in his power, should, under circumstances of great provocation, express personal feelings inconsistent with his own general character, and with the spirit of his religion? Why should not the *language* of David, as well as his *conduct*, be sometimes inconsistent with what is right? It must be remembered, too, that, in the Jewish religion, the duty of forgiveness had been less insisted on, because the age was not prepared to comprehend it. The law was our schoolmaster to bring us unto Christ. There are no imaginable circumstances in which Christians would be justifiable in using the language of the psalms above referred to, or similar language, in their addresses to the God and Father of our Lord Jesus Christ.

A writer in the Andover "Bibliotheca Sacra" * has undertaken, if we understand him, to maintain the absolute rectitude of all these imprecations, and their immediate inspiration by the Deity. But if this be so, then are Christian ministers in general very deficient in their duty, and there is far too little cursing in Christian pulpits. If the psalms in question are consistent with absolute rectitude, then our Saviour's precept to "bless them that curse us, and to pray FOR them that despitefully use us," cannot be; unless, indeed, to pray *for* our enemies be to pray that "iniquity may be added to their iniquity," "that they may be blotted out of the book of the living," "that there may be none to show them compassion, and none to pity their fatherless children," and that "their little ones may be taken and dashed against the stones."

It was not, I suppose, a want of common sense or of Christian feeling, but adherence to an unfounded theory of inspiration, that led the writer in the "Bibliotheca Sacra" to maintain a view apparently so inconsistent, not only with the precepts and spirit of Christ, but with the general feelings of the Christian Church.

* Vol. i. p. 102.

For the attempt to explain the imprecations of the Psalms as simple predictions, which has been made by interpreters from the time of Augustine* to the present day, shows the uncongeniality of such imprecations with the feelings of Christians. A recent Orthodox commentator on the Psalms, well known by some of his writings which have been translated in this country, adopts substantially the view which I have given of the subject. Having suggested every excuse for these imprecations of which the case admits, and especially having suggested whether some of them may not have been uttered as disinterested prayers for simple divine retribution, rather than as expressions of personal feeling and passion, he says: "If now the question be asked, whether in no case the unholy fire of personal anger mingled itself with the holy fire of the psalmist, we dare not maintain such a thing even of the apostles.† Whether in excited speech the anger be such as 'worketh not the righteousness of God,'‡ or such as that with which Christ himself was animated,§ may generally be known from the nature of the case; namely, when there is an evident satisfaction in being permitted to be the instrument of divine retribution, or when particular kinds of retribution are prayed for with evident pleasure, or when it is manifest that the representation of them is connected with delight on the part of the speaker. Thus Ps. cix. and lix. contain many expressions of a passionate character: Ps. cxlix. 7, 8; cxxxvii. 8, 9; lviii. 10; and xli. 10, may also have proceeded from a similar feeling. On other passages individual feeling may decide differently." ||

For all that is pure and wholesome in religion and morality, and adapted to promote peace and good-will among men, one would be glad to adduce all possible authority. But the solicitude to obtain a divine sanction for hating and cursing even enemies would be truly marvellous, did we not know to what extremes good men are sometimes led by attachment to theory.

* Opp., vol. v. Serm. 22. So Luther on Ps. lv.

† Acts xv. 39, xxiii. 3; Phil. iii. 2; Gal. v. 12.

‡ James i. 20.

§ Mark iii. 5.

|| Tholuck's Uebersetzung und Auslegung der Psalmen, Halle, 1843 p. lxiii.

II. Authors of the Psalms.

The opinion has long since been exploded, that David was the sole author of the Psalms. For the contents of some of them prove that they were written during the captivity at Babylon.

According to the Hebrew inscriptions, which are translated in the Common version of the Scriptures, and which form the Italic titles in the following translation, the authors of the Psalms are Moses, David, Solomon, Asaph, Heman, Ethan, and the sons of Korah.

But great uncertainty rests on these inscriptions, because several of them are inconsistent with the contents of the psalms to which they are prefixed. It is, indeed, not improbable that the name of the author was originally prefixed to his composition by his own hand. This is said to have been the practice of the Oriental poets from a very remote age, as it certainly was of several of the Hebrew prophets. If this were the case with respect to the Psalms, it is probable that many of the titles were lost in consequence of the use made of them in public worship, and that their place was afterwards partially supplied by uncertain tradition or mere conjecture. What is certain is, that many of the inscriptions are at undeniable variance with the contents of the psalms to which they are prefixed; and this fact tends to throw discredit on those with which the tenor of the composition sufficiently agrees. In the Septuagint and Syriac versions, the titles in many instances vary from the Hebrew.

To David the Hebrew titles ascribe seventy-three psalms, — according to some editions, seventy-four. Of these, many contain positive internal evidence of the accuracy of their titles. From his fame as a player upon the harp when he was invited to play before Saul, from his appellation of "the sweet psalmist of Israel," and from the tradition of antiquity, there can be no doubt that he was the author of most of those which are ascribed to him, and of some which have no title. But several of the psalms which bear David's name cannot be his, as they contain allusions to the Babylonian captivity, and similar events belonging to a later age, besides occasional Chaldaisms.

"The inscriptions indicating the authorship of David," says Eichhorn, "cannot be all right; not, however, on account of the greatness of the number ascribed to him. Who knows not, that, as a shepherd and in a private station, David knew no truer friend than his harp; and that, when a king, he gloried in his songs more than in his crown? The whole course of his life, whether joyous or sorrowful, he introduced into his compositions. Who, then, can be surprised at the number of psalms of lamentation which come under his name? Who ever suffered more, or more variously, or more undeservedly, than David? From the condition of a shepherd he raised himself to the throne. Through what hosts of enviers and enemies must he have pressed before he reached it! More than once was he obliged to flee from the javelin of Saul with his harp in his hand; what wonder, then, that it sounded his terrors? How often was he compelled to rove through the wilderness to avoid the persecution of one who should have loved and protected him, as a member of his house and successor to his throne! And when these dangers were past, long was it before the dangers of his life were past. Ishbosheth contended with him as a rival aspirant for the throne; and, until the whole royal family was extinct, he never felt himself at rest. Then he engaged, with various success, in war with the neighboring kings, from Egypt to the Euphrates; and at last, after so many victories, he was destined to find his most dangerous enemy in the person of his own son, the rebellious Absalom. Amid so many and bitter calamities, the number of his poetic sighs and lamentations is not a matter of surprise. Besides, is it at all probable that the brief chronicles of the Hebrews make us acquainted with all his domestic afflictions through the whole course of his life? These, however, are not less hard to be borne than public calamities." *

The characteristics of David's poetry are said, by the same distinguished critic, to be loveliness and deep feeling. With him agrees so good a judge of poetry as the author of "The Pleasures of Hope." "His traits of inspiration are lovely and touching, rather than daring and astonishing. His voice, as a worshipper, has a penetrating accent of human sensibility, varying from plaintive melancholy to luxuriant gladness, and even rising to ecstatic

* Einleitung in das Alte Test., § 622.

rapture. In grief, 'his heart is melted like wax, and deep answers to deep, whilst the waters of affliction pass over him;' or his soul is led to the green pastures by the quiet waters, or his religious confidence pours forth the metaphors of a warrior, in rich and exulting succession. 'The Lord is my rock, and my fortress, and my deliverer, — my God, my strength, in whom I will trust, — my buckler, and the horn of my salvation, and my high tower.' Some of the sacred writers may excite the imagination more powerfully than David, but none of them appeal more interestingly to the heart. Nor is it in tragic so much as in joyous expression, that I conceive the power of his genius to consist. Its most inspired aspect appears to present itself, when he looks abroad upon the universe with the eye of a poet, and with the breast of a glad and grateful worshipper. When he looks up to the starry firmament, his soul assimilates to the splendor and serenity which he contemplates. This lofty but bland spirit of devotion reigns in the eighth and in the nineteenth psalm. But, above all, it expands itself in the hundred and fourth into a minute and diversified picture of the creation. Verse after verse in that psalm leads on the mind through the various objects of nature as through a mighty landscape; and the atmosphere of the scene is colored, not with a dim or mystic, but with a clear and warm, light of religious feeling. He spreads his sympathies over the face of the world, and rejoices in the power and goodness of its protecting Deity. The impression of that exquisite ode dilates the heart with a pleasure too instinctive and simple to be described."

To Moses only one psalm is ascribed, namely, the ninetieth. In this beautiful elegy there is nothing absolutely inconsistent with the supposition, that he was the author of it. Most critics, however, have supposed it to savor of a later age. Grotius remarks, "that it was not composed by him, but adapted by the author to the circumstances and feelings of Moses, containing sentiments which he might have expressed." The writers of the Talmud ascribe the ten psalms following the ninetieth to Moses; but they do this upon the wholly unfounded supposition, that those psalms which have no title are to be attributed to the author whose name occurs in the next preceding title. The ninety-ninth certainly could not have been written by him, since it contains the name of the prophet Samuel, who was not born till nearly three hundred years after the death of Moses.

Twelve psalms, namely, Ps. l. and lxxiii.–lxxxiii., are ascribed to ASAPH, a celebrated Levite, and chief of the choirs of Israel in the time of David (1 Chron. xvi. 4, 5). That he was a poet, and composed as well as sung, is evident from 2 Chron. xxix. 30: "Moreover Hezekiah the king and the princes commanded the Levites to sing praise unto the Lord with the words of David, and of Asaph the seer." But he could have been the author of but a small portion of these twelve psalms. Ps. lxxiv., lxxvii., lxxix., lxxx., indisputably belong to the times of the captivity; and several of the rest have with good reason been referred to the same period. They may, however, have been written by a later poet of the same name. Eichhorn, Rosenmüller, and De Wette are of opinion, that, of all the psalms ascribed to Asaph, the contemporary of David, only the fiftieth is decidedly his. This, however, is enough to place him in the number of poets of the very first order. It is marked by a deeper vein of thought and a loftier tone of sentiment than any of the compositions of David. In Asaph, the poet and the philosopher are combined. "He was," says Eichhorn, "one of those ancient wise men who felt the insufficiency of external religious usages, and urged the necessity of cultivating virtue and purity of mind." It may well be asserted of him, as of the scribe in the New Testament, who said that for a man to love God with all the heart, and with all the understanding, and with all the soul, and with all the strength, and to love his neighbor as himself, was more than all the whole burnt-offerings and sacrifices, — that *he was not far from the kingdom of God.*

Eleven psalms, the forty-second and forty-third being supposed to be one psalm, — namely, Ps. xlii.–xlix., and lxxxiv., lxxxv., lxxxvii., and lxxxviii., — are ascribed to the SONS OF KORAH, a Levitical family of singers (1 Chron. vi.). In consequence of the ambiguity of the Hebrew preposition, it has been doubted whether the inscription is intended to designate them as the authors of these psalms, or only as the musicians who were to perform them in the temple. The preposition, however, is the same that denotes authorship in the case of those psalms which are ascribed to David. Heman the Ezrahite, whose name occurs in the title of one of these psalms, may have been one of the sons or descendants of Korah; or the mention of him in the inscription may have arisen from the amalgamation of contradictory titles. The titles were probably given them by some one who had learned from tradition, that they were the productions of the sons of Korah, but had not been informed of the names of their respective authors. It is probable that only a few of the most distinguished sons of Korah were concerned in their production. Whatever may be the true explanation of their inscriptions, it is almost universally conceded that the psalms in question were not written by David. In style they differ materially from his. Whoever was their author, they are not unworthy of Asaph. No psalms in the whole collection possess a more permanent interest. None indicate a richer imagination or a more powerful inspiration. None breathe a bolder, freer spirit of enthusiasm, or contain more sublime and affecting sentiments. Most of them, especially Ps. xlii., xlvi., and lxxxiv., belong to that order of compositions, which, having once passed through the mind, are never forgotten; and which are most remembered in seasons when much that passes for poetry, being weighed in the balance, is found lighter than vanity.

In the Hebrew titles, the eighty-eighth psalm is ascribed to Heman, and the eighty-ninth to Ethan, both called Ezrahites. The persons intended were, probably, Levitical singers in the time of David, — mentioned in 1 Chron. vi. 33, 44. But there can be little doubt that the titles are wrong, and that these psalms belong to a later age than that of David.

To Solomon only two of the psalms are inscribed, namely, the seventy-second and one hundred twenty-seventh. But these could scarcely have been written by him. It has been suggested, that his name was prefixed to the latter, merely because the first verse mentions the building of *a house*, which the author of the title supposed to refer to the temple. Of the seventy-second he seems to be the subject, rather than the author. It is not improbable, however, that some of the psalms were written by Solomon, since, in 1 Kings iv. 32, he is said to have written one thousand and five songs.

The remaining fifty-one psalms have, in the Hebrew, no titles indicating their authors. And, from what has been said of the Hebrew inscriptions, it follows that the authors of more than half of the psalms are unknown to us. As to the inscriptions which are added in the ancient versions, they are evidently the conjectures of editors and copyists. Modern interpreters, also, have exercised their sagacity in assigning authors to the anonymous psalms. Some suppose that many of them belong to the age of the Maccabees. I see no improbability in the supposition that some of them did. The book of Daniel was added to the canon after that time; and, in all ages, religious poets are impelled to express their feelings in hymns. But I have not thought it allowable to indulge in, or to follow, mere conjectures.

III. Titles of the Psalms.

Besides the names of the authors, some of the titles indicate the species of the composition; some, the occasion and subject of it; some refer to the leader of the choir of singers; some, to the musical instrument to be used; and some, to the tune to which the psalm was to be sung. Respecting the origin and antiquity of these titles, the opinion of Rosenmüller is as plausible as any that has been offered.

"I doubt not that all the psalms once had a title containing the name of the author, and in some instances the occasion of the composition, as was the custom of the Arabic, Syriac, and Hebrew poets. But those titles which relate to the air, or the instrument to which the psalm was to be sung, appear to have proceeded from those who, at various periods, made use of the psalms for public worship. Thus, in 2 Sam. xxii., which contains the eighteenth psalm, there is in the title no mention of the leader of the music. The use of the psalms in public worship affords a reason for the mutilation or loss of the more ancient inscriptions, which mentioned the name of the author and the occasion and subject of the psalm. Those who collected the psalms at different periods undertook to supply the deficiency of titles from their own judgment or fancy, without a due regard to manuscripts, or to the tenor of the psalm. Not a few seem to have been added by commentators, copyists, and even readers. This is proved by the Greek, Syriac, Arabic, Latin, and even by some Hebrew manuscripts. In many cases, probably, a conjecture, placed by a reader in the margin of a manuscript, was in course of time introduced into the text. Hence it may be seen how it happens that many of the psalms are at variance with their titles, and could not have been written by the author to whom they are assigned. We conclude, therefore, that all the Hebrew titles are not to be rashly rejected, nor indiscriminately received. But, with the help of sound criticism and interpretation, we must distinguish those which were given by the poet from those which were added by a later hand."

To indicate the species of composition with respect to the sentiment, the metre, or the music to which it was adapted, the Hebrew terms *Mismor*, *Shir*, *Shir-Mismor*, *Mismor-Shir*, *Maschil*, *Michtam*, *Shiggaion*, and *Shir-Hammachaloth* are used.

With the exception of the last term, it is doubtful whether it can be ascertained in what respects these titles differ, and still more doubtful, whether there are words in English to express their difference. What is certain is, that they all denote a species of psalm, with respect to the sentiment, the measure, or the music. I have thought it better to translate all of them by the next generic term which is applicable to all of them, rather than to puzzle the English reader with the Hebrew terms *Michtam* and *Maschil*, or the barbarous English *psalm-song* or *song-psalm*.*

The title *Maschil* is very probably derived from the verb signifying *to be wise*, and hence translated by some critics a *didactic* psalm. It occurs as the title of thirteen psalms. But several of those to which it is prefixed have not the character commonly understood by didactic, and it is not prefixed to some that have

* See Dr. Geddes's Version.

that character. Thus it is prefixed to Ps. lv., lxxxviii., and cxlii., and not to the fiftieth.

Michtam is sometimes translated *golden*, but it is difficult to perceive any peculiar excellence in the six psalms — namely, Ps. xvi., lvi., lvii., lviii., lix., lx. — to which it is prefixed, which should gain for them the distinguished epithet of *golden*. According to modern taste, there are many others far more deserving of this appellation. The same objection may be made to the supposition, that they derive their appellation from their being hung up in the temple in golden letters, like the *Moallacat* in the temple at Mecca. Besides that there is no evidence of such a Hebrew custom, what is there in these six psalms which should give them such a distinction above the rest? On the whole, there seems to be no more probable derivation of the word than that which makes it denote *writing*, that is, *composition, psalm;* מִכְתָּם, by a change of the labials ם and ב being written for מִכְתָּב, which occurs in Isa. xxxviii. 9, in the title of a song.

The hundred and forty-fifth is called *Tehillah*, "Praise;" and so excellent was this psalm always accounted by the Jews, that the title of the whole book of Psalms, *Sephir Tehillim*, "The Book of Praises," was taken from it. The Jews used to say, "He cannot fail of being an inhabitant of the heavenly Canaan, who repeats this psalm three times a day."

Some suppose *Shiggaion* to denote *a song of lamentation*. But this is very uncertain.

Fifteen psalms, cxx.–cxxxiv., are entitled *Shir-Hammachaloth*, literally, *Song of steps* or *of ascents;* in the common version, *Song of degrees*. By some they are termed *Odes of ascension*, or *Pilgrim songs*, and are supposed to have derived their name from the circumstance, that they were sung when the people went up to worship in Jerusalem, at the annual festivals. *To go up* to Jerusalem was a common expression with reference to journeys to the metropolis. Thus, our Saviour says, "Behold, we go up to Jerusalem." It is supposed that they travelled in the Oriental manner, not single, but in companies, and chanted these psalms by the way. Ps. cxx. and cxxiii., however, do not seem suitable for such an occasion.

Others suppose them to refer to the return from the captivity.

that return being styled an ascent or going up (Ez. vii. 9). To this supposition it is objected, that Ps. cxxii. 1 speaks of going up to the house of the Lord, which of course was in ruins when they were returning from the captivity.

Others suppose the term *steps* to refer to a peculiarity in the structure of some of these psalms, according to which a sentiment or expression of the preceding verse is introduced and carried forward in the next, so that there shall be a sort of *climax*, or *ascending series* of similar sentiments. Thus, Ps. cxxi.: —

"I lift up mine eyes to the hills:
Whence cometh *my help?*
My help cometh from Jehovah,
Who made heaven and earth.
He will not suffer thy foot to stumble,
Thy guardian *doth not slumber.*
Behold! the *guardian of Israel*
Doth neither *slumber nor sleep*," &c.

But this peculiarity is found in only a few of the psalms to which the title is prefixed.

Michaelis has intimated, that the word *steps* may have reference to a particular species of metre, and denote something like *feet* in English. He refers to the poetry of the Syrians, in which one species is distinguished by the term denoting *steps*. But what the metre is, cannot be ascertained.

Luther, Hammond, and others suppose the word to be a musical term, denoting that these psalms are to be sung in a higher tone of voice or key.

Other parts of the titles denote the air or tune to which the psalm is to be sung, by referring to the first words or to the name of psalms which are now lost. See Ps. lvii., lviii., lix. Others relate to the instruments of music, the choir of singers, and the leader, as may be understood from the translation and the notes.

In this connection we may say a word of the term *Selah*. Its signification is extremely doubtful. But its use is very generally admitted to have been that of a musical sign for the direction of the singers. But whether it denotes a pause, or slowness of time, or a change of tune, or a repeat, equivalent to the Italian *Da capo*, or a rest for the vocal performers, whilst the musicians were alone to be heard, critics are divided in opinion. The last seems the most probable opinion, namely, that the term denotes *silence!* or *pause!* and that its use was to direct the singers who chanted the notes of the psalm *to pause a little,* while the instruments played an interlude or symphony. The meaning of other titles is given in the Translation.

IV. The Collection of the Psalms, and their Division into Books.

The psalms appear to have been collected at different times and by different persons. This is manifest from the division into five books, which is certainly as ancient as the Septuagint version. For this version contains the doxologies which are placed at the end of the first four books, Ps. xli. 13, lxxii. 18–20, lxxxix. 52, cvi. 48. The cause of this division, says Jahn, may be gathered from the character of the psalms contained in each book. Almost all the psalms of the first book are the work of David. In the second, there are twenty-two of David, one of Asaph, and eight anonymous, ascribed to the Korahites. The third contains one, the eighty-sixth, ascribed to David, and this doubtful; the remainder are partly Asaph's, partly the work of an uncertain author, and partly anonymous. Two only in the fourth book are ascribed to David, and one, the ninetieth, to Moses; the others being anonymous. In the fifth, fifteen are assigned to David, one is ascribed conjecturally to Solomon, and the rest are anonymous. These five books of the Psalms, therefore, are evidently so many different collections, following each other in the order in which they were made. The first person who began the collection put together the psalms of David; the second, those psalms of David which it was still in his power to glean, admitting a few others; the third had no psalms of David in view, and when he wished to join his own collection to the former, he added the note at the end of the second book, "Here end the psalms of David, the son of Jesse" (lxxii. 20). The fourth collected anonymous psalms, and therefore his book exhibits only one of Moses, the ninetieth; and two of David, the hundred and first and the hundred and third, the latter of which, however, is certainly not his. The last made a collection of whatever sacred poems he could gather: he has, therefore, fifteen of David, and thirty anonymous. This view of the subject readily accounts for the fact, that some psalms contained in an earlier collection again occur in a later, as the fourteenth and fifty-third, the fifty-seventh and hundred and eighth.

The age and the authors of these collections it is impossible to ascertain. But, as in the first collection, as well as in the rest, there are some psalms which appear to have been written during the captivity, we may conclude that no one of them was made till the time of the captivity. Some of the others must have been made at different times after the return from Babylon. The last two books are supposed by several critics of eminence to contain psalms referring even to the times of the Maccabees.

"We must," says De Wette,* "suppose that the collection of the Psalms was made gradually. There is a prevailing want of order in it; pieces of like character are not brought together; songs of David are found scattered in all the five books; those of Asaph are separated as widely from each other as those of the Korahites, &c. But again, in the midst of this disorder, we remark a certain order: the majority of David's psalms stand together, Ps. iii.–xli. It is so also with the songs of the Korahites, of Asaph, and the songs of degrees; a circumstance which evinces that they have been brought together from many separate collections. In this view, we may also account for the fact, that one psalm occurs twice. Ps. xiv. is the same with Ps. liii. But less satisfactorily does this account for the recurrence of separate portions of psalms, as in the case of Ps. lxx. and Ps. cviii.

"It is as little possible for us to know who were the authors of the several particular collections, as who was the compiler of the whole. It cannot be true, as many suppose, that David himself prepared the first collection; because among the first psalms there appear several of an altogether later date, as Ps. xiv., xliv., xlv., xlvi., xlviii. Besides, David would hardly have given himself the honorable appellation of "servant of Jehovah," which is annexed to his name in two of the titles, Ps. xviii., xxxvi. Even Carpzov looked upon the first collection as a private undertaking.*

* As translated in the "Biblical Repository" for 1833, p. 464.

The age of these collections may be determined with greater certainty. The first two (Ps. i.–lxxii.) cannot have been completed until after the captivity, since pieces are found in them which belong to the period of the captivity (Ps. xiv., xliv., xlv.); but the collection of the whole was certainly not finished until a considerable time afterwards, though it must have been completed before the translation of Jesus Sirac., 130 B.C.,—as early as which the collection of Psalms was probably translated into Greek. As it respects the design of the collection of the psalms, it may be remarked, that they who suppose it was made in behalf of the musical service of the temple entertain too limited views of the object;† besides that this supposition is irreconcilable with the fact of its having probably originated from private collections. A religious use, however, was undoubtedly the aim by which the collectors were guided, at least in general. Ps. xlv., which is so entirely secular, must be considered as an accidental exception, unless we are indebted for its insertion to the allegorical method of interpretation, which may also have been the means of preserving from destruction the Song of Solomon.

"In the mode of dividing and numbering the several psalms, the Hebrew manuscripts, and the Seventy and Vulgate, occasionally differ from the printed Hebrew text. In many manuscripts, the first psalm is numbered with the second, and, in like manner, the forty-second with the forty-third, and the one hundred and sixteenth with the one hundred and seventeenth. On the other hand, a new psalm is commenced with Ps. cxviii. 5; indeed, Ps. cxviii. is divided in some manuscripts into three psalms. The Seventy also formerly numbered the first psalm with the second; and they still differ, in common with the Vulgate, from the ordinary method of enumeration, after the tenth psalm; inasmuch as they join together psalms ninth and tenth, and thus fall one number or psalm behind the Hebrew text, as far as to the one hundred and forty-seventh psalm, which they separate into two, and thus return back once more to the old enumeration. They also unite Ps. cxiv. with Ps. cxv., but immediately afterwards divide Ps. cxvi. into two, so that this difference is cancelled on the spot. It is

* Introd. ad Libr. Can., &c., part ii. p. 107.

† Comp. Eichhorn, § 626.

necessary to be acquainted with this different mode of numbering, because the Fathers quote by it. The Seventy have besides an apocryphal psalm (cli.) on the victory of David over Goliah."

V. Means of understanding the Psalms.

In order that the Psalms may be understood in the fulness of their meaning, beauty, and spirit, the most important directions to an English reader are these three: —

1. Gain some knowledge of Jewish antiquities. Be so familiar with the history, the manners and customs, the climate and scenery, and the modes of thinking and feeling, of the Hebrews, that you may receive such impressions from the sacred poetry as would be received by an enlightened inhabitant of ancient Jerusalem. "It is not enough," says Bishop Lowth, "to be acquainted with the language of this people, their manners, discipline, rites, and ceremonies; we must even investigate their inmost sentiments, the manner and connection of their thoughts; in one word, we must see all things with their eyes, estimate all things by their opinions. We must endeavor as much as possible to read Hebrew as the Hebrews would have read it." For this object, they who have less taste for the simple and immethodical narrative of the sacred historians may be referred to the more elaborate, but popular and interesting, "History of the Jews" by Milman. For consultation, every one who wishes to understand his Bible should own Jahn's "Biblical Archæology," which has been translated in this country.

2. In addition to a general knowledge of the Jewish history and antiquities, it is of great use to ascertain the subject, the occasion, and the author of the psalm. It is true that these points can rarely be discovered with any considerable degree of certainty. Many of the captions prefixed to the psalms in this translation must be regarded in the light of theories or conjectures. As such, however, they may be regarded as useful. We may be more able to comprehend the sentiment and feel the spirit of a psalm, if we

only assign to it an occasion similar to that for which it was composed. At best, however, as has been remarked by Bishop Lowth, "much of the harmony, propriety, and elegance of the sacred poetry must pass unperceived by us, who can only form distant conjectures of the general design, but are totally ignorant of the particular application." The following remarks of Michaelis are also highly deserving of consideration: "There are some," says he, "who undertake to explain the psalms from the historical parts of Scripture, as if every occurrence were known to them, and as if nothing had occurred during the reign of David which was not committed to writing. This, however, considering the extreme brevity of the sacred history, and the number and magnitude of the facts which it relates, must of course be very far from the truth. The causes and motives of many wars are not at all adverted to; the battles that are related are few, and those the principal. Who can doubt, though ever so inexperienced in military affairs, that many things occurred, which are not mentioned, between the desertion of Jerusalem by David, and that famous battle which extinguished the rebellion of Absalom? They who will not allow that they are ignorant of a great part of the Jewish history will be apt to explain more of the psalms upon the same principle, and as relating to the same facts, than they ought; whence the poetry will appear tame and languid, abounding in words, but with little variety of description or sentiment.

"Others have recourse to mystical interpretations, or convert those historical passages which they do not understand into prophecies. Into none of these errors would mankind have fallen but through the persuasion, that the whole history of the Jews was minutely detailed to them, and that there were no circumstances with which they were unacquainted."

3. It is of the utmost consequence to attend to the characteristics of the language and structure of Hebrew poetry. In order to avoid important errors, the reader of Hebrew poetry must especially keep in mind one of its features, by which it is distinguished from the poetry of the Western world, — namely, its boldness in the use of figurative and metaphorical language.

Many mistakes have arisen from interpreting the language of Eastern hyperbole in too strict a sense. As an instance of the kind of language to which I refer, I may mention the eighteenth psalm, from verse ninth to the eighteenth. The simple fact, that God aided David and the Israelites in battle, is the foundation of this magnificent description. The Supreme Being is represented as interposing in the midst of a tempest, and the tempest itself is described in language extremely hyperbolical. Compare Hab. iii. 3, &c.

As an instance of error arising from the neglect of this characteristic of Hebrew poetry, it may be mentioned that several learned critics have gravely undertaken to explain what habitation David could provide for Jehovah in a single day; that is, before he literally "gave sleep to his eyes, or slumber to his eyelids." From inattention to the same thing, Ps. li. 5 has been made to convey a meaning at war with the attributes of God, with common sense, and with other portions of the sacred volume.

In regard to the construction of Hebrew poetry, so far as *quantity* is concerned, we are entirely ignorant. It is true, that now and then a scholar has arisen who thought he could perceive the measures of Greek and Latin verse in the productions of the Hebrew poets. Josephus, too, speaks of the trimeters and pentameters of David. St. Jerome also observes, "If any one doubt that the Hebrews employed similar measures to those of Horace, Pindar, Alcæus, and Sappho, let him read Philo, Josephus, Origen, and Eusebius, and find by their testimony whether my assertion be true." But the ears of a vast majority of Hebrew scholars have not been able to detect any such measures in Hebrew poetry, nor to distinguish it from prose, so far as mere sound or quantity is concerned. That, in the ancient mode of pronouncing the Hebrew language, such measures existed, it is not necessary to deny. But, if the ears of ninety-nine in a hundred are to be trusted, it is impossible to discover them.*

What is obvious in the sacred poetry is a division into lines of

* For a good view of this subject, see the "Introduction to De Wette's Commentary on the Psalms," and the works to which he refers. A translation of it may be found in the "Biblical Repository" for July, 1833.

nearly equal length, or containing nearly the same number of syllables, two of which lines generally form a verse, or complete a sentence. In several compositions, the initial letters of the successive lines or stanzas follow the order of the letters of the Hebrew alphabet. This is the case with seven of the psalms, four chapters of the Lamentations of Jeremiah, and the last chapter of Proverbs, from the tenth verse to the end.

But the most important feature in the construction of Hebrew verse is as obvious in a translation as in the original. It is what may be called *a rhythm of sentiment.* A period is divided into members, generally two, but sometimes more, which, as it were, balance each other by thought corresponding to thought in repetition, in amplification, in reply, or in contrast.

This feature of Hebrew poetry is called *parallelism.* The illustration of it constitutes the great merit of Dr. Lowth. A more complete view of its varieties has been given by De Wette in his "Introduction to the Psalms," the greater part of which I shall transcribe.*

But the examples I give, of course, in the language of my own Translation.

The Hebrew rhythm — namely, the parallelism of members — is nothing more nor less than a rhythmical proportion, and that of the simplest sort, between the larger sections or members of a period; the smaller being neglected. Nothing is more simple than the symmetry, the proportion, between two parts of a whole: the proportion between several begins to require more ingenuity and calculation. Thus, the relation between parallel lines is the simplest that we can conceive to exist between different lines; the triangle, the square, already begin to be more complex, and the circle is the most perfect of all figures. It might also be remarked, that every period consisting of two propositions forms a whole, and suffices for a full expression of the voice and satisfying of the ear; while a single proposition is insufficient for either. The breast is still elevated, the ear continues to listen, and yet there is nothing more to be said, nothing more to be heard. In fact, the parallelism of members seems to be a

* See the translation in "Biblical Repository" for 1833, p. 494, and following.

fundamental law of rhythm. It obviously lies at the foundation of the rhyme, where one verse is made to answer to the other. The more complicated forms of rhyme, in the stanza, sonnet, &c., were invented at a comparatively later period: but even in these the law of parallelism may still be detected; at least, the *ottave rime* and the sonnet naturally fall into two divisions, each answering to the other.* In like manner, the relation of the hexameter and pentameter is that of parallelism; and even the lyric strophes admit, perhaps, of being referred to the same form. The relation of the strophe, antistrophe, and epode, on the contrary, already indicates the transposition of the parallelism to the more perfect form of the triangle.

But in what does the parallelism of members in the Hebrew poetry consist, and how is it indicated? Here we must forget all the demands which might be made by the delicate, musical ear of the Greeks, so sensitive to the measure of time; or by that of the moderns, so partial to similitude of sound. The Hebrew has neither the one nor the other. His rhythm belonged more to the thought than to the outward form and sound; and he therefore indicated his rhythmical divisions by the divisions of the thought, and the proportion of the rhythmical propositions by that of the subject-matter.

The following circumstances contributed, perhaps, in some measure, to the formation of this rhythm of thought. The Hebrew, and whoever like him stands at that point of intellectual cultivation where the mind is in a condition to seize only certain general and simple relations of things, is fond of presenting his ideas and feelings in short sentences: these sentences are connected with each other in a manner which possesses but little variety, usually according to the law of resemblance and contrast (a law which readily presents itself to the observing understanding), and for the most part only in couplets, because the combination of several sentences implies already the notice of a greater variety of relations. This speaking in short sentences is still further favored by the impassioned tone of the speaker; for, in the

* In the former, the two concluding verses are parallel to the first six, and in the second there is the same relation between the first eight and the last six verses.

fulness and glow of inspiration and internal feeling, the words are slow to adapt themselves to the thought, the speaker struggles with language, and wrests from it nothing but single short expressions. A peculiar fondness is manifested in this style of speaking for tautology and comparison. There is a want of versatility and variety of expression, and yet there is a wish to express one's self fully, and to present the subject in various points of light; hence the same thing is often repeated in synonymous expressions and figures. Now, if a person who speaks in this way is disposed to introduce into his discourse a regular rhythm, a proportion between the several propositions presents itself as a ready expedient, whose original law will be that of resemblance and contrast, — the law by which, in other cases, one proposition is arranged with another.

After these remarks, nothing will appear more natural than the following form of discourse (Job vii. 1–3) : —

> "Is there not a war-service for man on the earth?
> Are not his days as the days of a hireling?
> As a servant panteth for the shade,
> And as a hireling looketh for his wages,
> So am I made to possess months of affliction,
> And wearisome nights are appointed for me."

> "The earth is the Lord's, and all that is therein;
> The world, and they who inhabit it.
> For he hath founded it upon the seas,
> And established it upon the floods."
>
> Ps. xxiv. 1. 2, —

where each thought is twice expressed, and after each such repetition there is a pause.

But the parallelism of members is of different kinds. In the first place, it differs according to the different laws of the association of thoughts.* The two principal laws of resemblance and contrast or antithesis produce the *synonymous* and *antithetic* parallelism, according to the terminology of Lowth; a third is founded simply upon a resemblance in the form of construction and progression of the thoughts, and this we may call with Lowth

* This is the basis of the classification of parallelism given by Lowth, Lect. XIX.

the *synthetic* parallelism. With the synonymous parallelism belongs also the *identical*, or the repetition with suspense; for example (Job xviii. 13): —

"His limbs are consumed,
Yea, his limbs are devoured by the first-born of death."

Under the term "synonymous" is included also comparison, subordination, &c. But, as we are concerned at present chiefly with the rhythmical form, we shall venture upon another classification, and only retain the logical arrangement in the minor divisions.

I. Thought is represented by words: hence it will frequently happen, where there is a perfect resemblance or antithesis of thoughts, that the *words will be equal*, at least in their number; and sometimes, on account of the similar construction and position of the words, there will also be a certain resemblance of sound. This we may call the *original*, perfect kind of parallelism of members, which coincides with metre and rhyme, yet without being the same with them. Such is the kind of parallelism in which the song of Lamech is composed (Gen. iv. 23). The translation can present nothing more than the equality in the number and position of the words: the rhyme must be omitted: —

"Adah and Zillah, hear my voice!
Ye wives of Lamech, mark my speech!
For I have slain a man for my wound,
And a young man — for my hurt.
If Cain was avenged sevenfold,
Then Lamech — seventy times seven."

Here all is nearly equal, except the places marked with a dash, where the words must be supplied from the preceding member. Similar examples of rhyme occur in Ps. viii. 5; xxv. 4; lxxxv. 11; cvi. 5.* For more, see Schindler † and Leutwein.

* The references are to the verses as numbered in the Hebrew Bible, in which the inscriptions in the Psalms to "the leader of the music," &c., are numbered as one verse; and in which the numbering of other verses varies a little from that of the English version.

† Tract. de Accent. Hebr., p. 81, seq.

Verses similar in their termination, but unequal in the number of their words, and without exact parallelism of thought, occur in the following passage (Job x. 17): —

> "Thou renewest thy witnesses against me,
> And increasest thine anger toward me:
> New hosts continually rise up against me."

Equality in the number of words, together with exact proportion of thought, is a case of frequent occurrence in Job; for example (chap. vi. 5): —

> "Doth the wild ass bray in the midst of grass,
> Or loweth the ox over his fodder?"

Comp. chap. vi. 23; viii. 2.

We have an example of equality in words, with antithesis of thought (Ps. xx. 9): —

> "They stumble and fall,
> But we stand and are erect."

Comp. Isa. lxv. 13.

Also in the synthetic parallelism, equality in the number of words sometimes occurs; for example (Ps. xix. 8): —

> "The law of the Lord is perfect, reviving the soul;
> The precepts of the Lord are sure, making wise the simple."

For many examples of this case, in which the number of words is equal, see Leutwein, p. 64, seq.

II. But this external proportion of words is not the essential part of the parallelism of members. It may be adopted, it is true, as a rule, that the number of words is about equal, especially in certain books, as the Proverbs of Solomon and Job; but in the Psalms a great inequality prevails. This inequality is of different kinds, as follows: —

1. The *simple unequal* parallelism, in which one of the members is too short, compared with the other; for example (Ps. lxviii. 33): —

> "Ye kingdoms of the earth, sing unto God;
> Sing praises to the Lord."

This construction frequently produces a grand effect; for example, Ps. xxxvii. 13, xlviii. 5; Job xiv. 14, where the conciseness of expression adds in one case to the vividness of the thought; in the other, to its emphasis.

Yet in these examples the inequality seems to have arisen from the brevity of the thought: it fell naturally into these words, and the poet let it pass. Hence, it is still not inconceivable that there might have been a metre. *We* also sometimes sacrifice metre to conciseness of thought, to emphasis, to a pause.

2. But a still more frequent kind of unequal parallelism — viz., the *complex* — admits not of this explanation. It consists in this, that either (*a*) the first member, or (*b*) the second member, is composed of two propositions, so that a complex member corresponds to a simple one. This structure arises whenever, in addition to the principal parallelism of thought, another subordinate parallelism presents itself to the poet in the full flow of his thoughts and feelings; hence we most frequently meet with it in lively, impassioned passages. It occurs more rarely in the book of Job, commonly in the speeches of Job himself, which sometimes rise to the lofty lyric style; but it is frequently to be met with in the Psalms. Hence there are also different kinds of parallelism, according to the logical connection of the propositions: —

א) The synonymous; for example (Ps. xxxvi. 7): —

> " Thy righteousness is like the high mountains;
> Thy judgments are a great deep;
> Thou, O Lord! preservest man and beast."

(Job x. 1): —

> " I am weary of my life;
> I will let loose within me my complaint;
> I will speak in the bitterness of my soul."

Comp. Job iii. 5, vii. 11; Ps. cxii. 10.

ב) The antithetic (Ps. xv. 4): —

> " In whose eyes a vile person is contemned;
> But who honoreth them that fear the Lord;
> Who sweareth to his own hurt, and changeth not."

Comp. Job x. 15; Ps. xlix. 11.

ג) The synthetic (Ps. xv. 5): —

"He that lendeth not his money for interest,
And taketh not a bribe against the innocent, —
He that doeth these things shall never fall."

Comp. Job x. 17, xx. 26; Ps. xxii. 25, xiv. 7, xviii. 31.

3. Sometimes the simple member is disproportionably small, so that the inequality is still more striking; for example (Ps. xl. 10):

"I have proclaimed thy righteousness in the great congregation,
Lo, I have not restrained my lips,
O Lord! thou knowest."

Sometimes a noble effect is thus produced; for example (Ps. xci. 7): —

"A thousand shall fall by thy side,
And ten thousand at thy right hand;
But thee it shall not touch."

Comp. Cant. vi. 4.

Frequently there is a parallelism in each several proposition and member; for example (Ps. lxix. 21): —

"Reproach hath broken my heart, and I am full of heaviness;
I look for pity, but there is none;
For comforters, but find none."

Here belongs also Ps. lxix. 5: —

"More numerous than the hairs of my head are they who hate me without reason;
Mighty are they who seek to destroy me, being my enemies without cause:
I must restore what I took not away."

4. Sometimes the complex member is increased to three or four propositions; for example (Ps. i. 3): —

"He is like a tree planted by streams of water,
That bringeth forth its fruit in its season,
Whose leaves also do not wither;
All that he doeth shall prosper."

Comp. Ps. lxv. 10; lxviii. 31; lxxxviii. 6. This form is particularly frequent in the prophets, who, approaching, as they generally do, nearer to prose, often allow the parallelism to flow almost into a free, prosaic diction. Members with three propositions occur in Amos i. 5, ii. 14; Mic. v. 4. Indeed, no less than four propositions sometimes form one member, and with a grand effect; for example (Amos iv. 13): —

"For, behold, he formed the mountains and created the wind;
He declareth to man what is his thought;
He maketh the morning darkness,
And walketh upon the high places of the earth:
Jehovah, God of Hosts, is his name."

5. Instead of the full subordinate parallelism, we sometimes find only a short clause or supplement, for the most part in the second member; for example (Ps. xxiii. 3): —

"He reviveth my spirit;
He leadeth me in the paths of safety,
For his name's sake."

Comp. Ps. v. 3; xxvii. 11, 12, &c.

In these forms of parallelism, the proportion is apparently destroyed; but it is not so, provided we suppose it to consist, not in the number of the words and extent of the period, but in the thoughts. The relation between two thoughts remains essentially the same, although one of them may be more fully developed than the other. As it does not depend in the least upon the measure of the words, a considerable inequality in these makes no difference. It were well if we could but always forget, what was unknown to the Hebrew, the rule which requires a measure of time in rhythm.

III. Out of the parallelism which is rendered unequal by the complexity of one of the members, there arises, in the case of a still greater fulness of thought, another, in which the equality is restored by both members becoming complex. Here richness of matter is combined with perfect proportion of form. The modes of combination are again the same, and accordingly we meet with the same species of parallelism: —

א) The synonymous; for example (Ps. xxxi. 11): —

"For my life is wasted with sorrow,
And my years with sighing;
My strength faileth by reason of my affliction,
And my bones are consumed on account of all my enemies"

Sometimes the members have an alternate correspondence; for example (Ps. xl. 17): —

" But let all who seek thee
Be glad and rejoice in thee;
Let those who love thy protection
Ever say, — 'The Lord be praised.' "

Comp. Ps. xxxv. 26, xxxvii. 14; Cant. v. 3; Ps. lxxix. 2; Mic. i. 4.

ב) The antithetic; for example (Ps. xxx. 6): —

" For his anger endureth but a moment,
But his favor through life;
In the evening sorrow may be a guest,
But joy cometh in the morning."

Comp. Ps. lv. 22.

Sometimes there is an alternate correspondence in the antithesis (Ps. xliv. 3): —

" With thine own hand didst thou drive out the nations,
And plant our fathers;
Thou didst destroy the nations,
And cause our fathers to flourish."

Comp. Isa. liv. 10.

ג) There are also instances of this double parallelism with the synthetic structure; for example (Cant. ii. 3): —

" As the apple-tree among the trees of the forest,
So is my beloved among the sons;
In his shadow I love to sit down,
And his fruit is sweet to my taste."

" As high as are the heavens above the earth,
So great is his mercy to them that fear him;
As far as the east is from the west,
So far hath he removed our transgressions from us."
Ps. ciii. 11, 12.

This species of double parallelism occurs with peculiar frequency in the prophets: comp. Am. i. 2, iii. 4 seq., iv. 4 seq., ix. 2 seq.; Mic. i. 4 seq., iii. 6 seq.; Nah. i. 1, ii. 1 seq.; Hab. i. 13, 16. Indeed, they were not satisfied with the latitude of this form, but gave to one of the members, or even to both, more than two propositions, and sometimes as many as four; for example (Hab. iii. 17): —

> "For the fig-tree shall not blossom,
> And there shall be no fruit upon the vine;
> The produce of the olive shall fail,
> And the fields shall yield no food;
> The flocks shall be cut off from the folds,
> And there shall be no herd in the stalls."

Comp. Amos ii. 9, v. 5, vii. 17; Mic. ii. 13, vii. 3; Hab. ii. 5, iii. 17.

In the better poets these subordinate propositions are short; in the other, long, which occasions a sort of dragging; for example, Zeph. iii. 19, 20.

Sometimes there are triplet parallelisms, both of the synonymous and synthetic class. Thus: —

> "The floods, O Lord, lift up,
> The floods lift up their voice,
> The floods lift up their roaring!
> Mightier than the voice of many waters,
> Yea, than the mighty waves of the sea,
> Is the Lord in his lofty habitation."
>
> Ps. xciii. 3, 4.

> "Thy thunder roared in the whirlwind;
> Thy lightning illumined the world;
> The earth trembled and shook.
> Thy way was through the sea,
> And thy path through great waters,
> And thy footsteps could not be found."
>
> Ps. lxxvii. 18, 19.

IV. But we should entertain too narrow a view of the parallelism of members, if we supposed it to consist exclusively in the proportion of the thoughts. For how could we dispose of the numerous passages where this is entirely wanting, — where the thoughts are found to correspond to each other neither by their resemblance, nor by antithesis, nor by synthesis? The parallelism of members assumed further a *simply external rhythmical* form, such as rhyme is. Originally, and according to rule, it was expressed in the matter; but next it left its impression as a distinct form, even where the matter did not correspond to it. The proportion grew habitual, and hence greater freedom and license in the thoughts were sometimes tolerated; besides, the constant recurrence of resemblance and antithesis would have been tedious both to poet and hearer. This species of parallelism we shall call the *rhythmical*, because it consists simply in the form of the period. Examples of it occur in all the kinds.*

1) With the number of the words nearly equal; for example (Ps. xix. 12): —

> "By them also is thy servant warned,
> And in keeping of them there is great reward."

2) With striking inequality in the number of the words; for example (Ps. xxx. 3): —

> "O Jehovah, my God!
> I called upon thee, and thou hast healed me."

3) With a double and a simple member; for example (Ps. xiv. 7): —

> "Oh that salvation for Israel would come out of Zion!
> When the Lord bringeth back the captives of his people,
> Then shall Jacob rejoice, and Israel be glad."

It is deserving of remark, how the rhythmical parallelism makes good its place where three parallel thoughts occur, and there is no internal ground for dividing them into exactly two members; for example (Ps. i. 1): —

> "Happy the man that walketh not in the counsel of the unrighteous,
> Nor standeth in the way of sinners,
> Nor sitteth in the seat of scoffers."

4) With two double members; for example (Ps. xxxi. 23): —

> "I said in my distress,
> I am cut off from before thine eyes;
> But thou didst hear the voice of my supplication,
> When I cried unto thee."

When the members of this rhythmical parallelism are more than double, which is sometimes the case, it approaches very near to prose: it is too loose a form to retain an exuberant matter

* It is highly important to distinguish this sort of parallelism, in order to avoid the mistakes which have so frequently arisen from the abuse of the parallelism of members as an exegetical help.

without passing over into the prosaic style. With good poets this is rarely the case, but it sometimes occurs; for example, Am. vi. 10: with the later and less correct, it happens more frequently; for example, Mal. i. 6; Zech. xiii. 3, x. 6; Zeph. iii. 8. The length of the members contributes in a special manner to destroy the rhythmical form. But, while this form of parallelism brings us to the utmost limits of the province of rhythm, it also settles the question, that the parallelism of members is really a rhythmical form, which there would be room to doubt, if we had nothing but parallelism of thoughts.

The simply rhythmical parallelism holds the most prominent place in the Lamentations of Jeremiah. Here the parallelism of thoughts is to be reckoned almost among the exceptions; and, when it does occur, it is, for the most part, the subordinate parallelism of a member by itself: in general, the rhythm alone predominates, and that, too, with a regularity which is rare among Hebrew poets, producing here a suitable effect; namely, monotony of complaint. The following orders of rhythm may be traced in the Lamentations.* In chapters first and second, the verses consist of three members, the first two of which constitute one parallel, and stand over against the third as the second parallel. Each member has besides a cæsura, which coincides with the sense and the accent. Still, however, we are sometimes under the necessity of abandoning the accents, because they follow the sense; while the rhythm is independent of the sense. According to the accents, the first parallel is sometimes simple (for example, chap. ii. 6), yet without a valid logical ground. The periods in chap. i. 7, and chap. ii. 19, are distinguished by having four members. It is remarkable that the length of these verses should so greatly exceed those which elsewhere occur in Hebrew poetry. Lowth is of the opinion that these long verses are adapted to lamentation, and it must be acknowledged that they do have a tendency to produce a certain impression of melancholy. Chap. iii. has only verses of one member, without parallelism; but this one member is rhythmically divided in such a manner as to produce, if not a complete rhythmical parallelism, yet a supplementary clause which conduces to repose. Here again the accents sometimes stand in the

* Comp. Lowth, Prælect. XXII. p. 257, seq.

way; for example, chap. iii. 3, where כל הרום is not enough to form a supplementary clause. Tiphcha, also, sometimes changes place with Zakeph Katon, although the rhythmical cæsura is always the same. Perhaps, however, every three verses are to be considered as a rhythmical whole, since they are connected by having the same initial letters. Chap. v. is of the same structure with chap. iii., except that it has a real short rhythmical parallelism; which, however, the authors of the accents did not consider as complete, and therefore have not separated with Athnach. Chap. iv. has double parallelism, but, for the most part, simply rhythmical.

We must notice one more exception in Hebrew rhythm. There sometimes occur separate propositions of a single member, almost always introduced with design, since the poet lingers upon the thought: we may conceive it to be accompanied with a long pause; for example, Ps. xxiii. 1; xxv. 1. Here the poet indicates, as it were, the tone and character of the song; and, after a pause, again collects himself. Cant. vii. 6 is beautiful:—

"How fair, how pleasant art thou, love, in delights!"

where the poet loses himself, as it were, in the contemplation of beauty. In Job x. 22 the voice sinks with two parallel clauses beautifully to repose.

"In this peculiar conformation or parallelism of the sentences," says Lowth, "I apprehend a considerable part of the Hebrew metre to consist, though it is not improbable that some regard was also paid to the numbers and feet. But of this particular we have at present so little information, that it is utterly impossible to determine whether it were modulated by the ear alone, or according to any settled or definite rules of prosody."

"The nervous simplicity and conciseness of the Hebrew muse," says the poet Campbell, "prevent this parallelism from degenerating into monotony. In repeating the same idea in different words, she seems as if displaying a fine opal, that discovers fresh beauty in every new light to which it is turned. Her amplifications of a given thought are like the echoes of a solemn melody,—her repetitions of it, like the landscape reflected in the stream; and, whilst her questions and responses give a lifelike effect to her compositions, they remind us of the alternate voices in public devotion, to which they were manifestly adapted."

The parallelism affords an important aid in interpretation; for sometimes the meaning of one member of a verse is clear, where that of the other is ambiguous. Thus the new translation of Ps. xxiv. 4 is confirmed by the parallelism, though it does not depend upon it. In Ps. lv. 15, —

> "May sudden death seize upon them!
> May they go down to the underworld alive!"

the second line is no doubt intended to be synonymous with the first, and is completely explained by it.

What goes beyond this simple rhythm, in the rhythmical art of the Hebrews, amounts to but little. Here belongs, —

1. The artificial arrangement of the alphabetical psalms. Thus Ps. xxv., xxxiv., xxxvii., cxi., cxii., cxix., cxlv.; Prov. xxxi. 10, seq. The Lamentations of Jeremiah, with the exception of the last chapter, are alphabetically arranged by the initial letters of the verses, and this in different ways. Commonly each verse begins with a new letter; in Ps. xxxvii., however, only every other verse, though with interruption and change; in Ps. cxix. and Lam. iii., there are alphabetical strophes, as it were, — that is, a series of verses have the same initial letters; in Ps. cxi., cxii., the half-verses are alphabetically arranged. This arrangement answers for us the valuable purposes of proving the existence of the parallelism of members, and of confirming the system of accentuation in the division of verses and half-verses, respecting which we might otherwise have our doubts, as well as respecting the whole law of parallelism. The alphabetical arrangement is supposed by many* to have been intended to assist the memory. Michaelis, indeed, was of the opinion, that it was employed in the first place in the funeral dirge as an aid to the mourners, and afterwards employed on other occasions. Lowth supposes that the alphabetic poetry "was confined altogether to those compositions which consisted of detached maxims, or sentiments without any express order or connection." I consider the alphabetic

* As Lowth, pp. 29, 259; and Michaelis on Lowth, p. 562, ed. Rosenm.

arrangement as a contrivance of the rhythmical art, an offspring of the later vitiated taste. When the spirit of poetry is flown, men cling to the lifeless body, the rhythmical form; and seek to supply its absence by this. In truth, nearly all the alphabetical compositions are remarkable for the want of connection (which I regard as the consequence, instead of the cause, of the alphabetical construction), for common thoughts, coldness and languor of feeling, and a low and occasionally mechanical phraseology. The thirty-seventh psalm, which is the most free in its alphabetical arrangement, is perhaps alone to be excepted from this censure, and in truth is one of the best didactic poems of the Hebrews. The Lamentations are, indeed, possessed of considerable merit in their way, but still betray an unpoetic period and degenerated taste.

In many of the alphabetic pieces, we observe certain irregularities and deficiencies, which many (as Capell) have incorrectly imputed to the transcribers, who were the least exposed to commit mistakes in these compositions, since they were confined by the peculiar arrangement itself. In Ps. xxv. two verses begin with א, none with ב; yet the word אֱלֹהַי in the second verse (like the interjection of the Greek tragedians ῴμοι) might not have been included in the verse, or (as Bengel conjectures) might have been written in the margin, in which case the following בְּךָ would restore the alphabetical order. Also in this, and in Ps. xxxiv., the ו is wanting; perhaps it should be restored by the ו in the beginning of the second hemistich of the verse commencing with ה; and so also, perhaps, the ק, which is wanting in the seventeenth verse of the former psalm, should be replaced by the ק in מְצוּקוֹתַי, at the beginning of the second hemistich. On the other hand, two verses begin with ר, and after the last letter, ת, follows another פ. This last we find also at the close of the thirty-fourth psalm. Michaelis supposes the פ is counted twice, on account of its double pronunciation, as Pe and Fe. Hasse* erected upon it a *paleographical* hypothesis peculiar to himself, which is hardly capable of being sustained, and gives no satisfactory explanation of the phenomenon to be explained.

* Eichhorn's Allg. Bibl., viii. p. 42, seq.

According to this, the concluding פ, with a softer pronunciation, takes the place of the Φ in the Greek alphabet. The conjecture of Bengel is no better, who supposes that ו and פ both sprung out of the Phœnician Vau and Fau, and that the latter stands for the former; then the supernumerary verse with פ must come in the place of ו.* Rosenmüller (1st edit.) considers both verses as the additions of a later hand, by which these psalms were prepared for the public service. But this could not be the case in respect to Ps. xxxiv. at least, as the last verse is necessary to the concluding of the whole: the conclusion of the twenty-fifth psalm is also very appropriate, and cannot well be dispensed with. In Ps. xxxvii., צ precedes פ, ע is wanting, and צ is repeated. Bengel accounts for this not unsatisfactorily from the interchangeable use of צ and ע in Chaldee. Others resort for help to criticism. The thirty-ninth verse begins with וּתְשׁוּעַת, where perhaps the ו was not regarded. In Ps. cxlv., the verse with נ is wanting, which, according to Michaelis, has fallen out of the text. In Lam. ii., iii., iv., פ precedes ע, which Bengel explains in the same manner as the simliar fact in Ps. xxxvii. The order only is different: it was the custom to place letters of a similar sound together.

Perhaps all these irregularities are to be ascribed to the negligence and unskilfulness of the poets, as we impute to the same causes the many harsh and inelegant rhymes of our older ecclesiastical poets. The hypothesis of Bengel, that of many alphabetical psalms we have only the first imperfect sketch, amounts to nearly the same thing. The occurrence of the same irregularities in Ps. xxv. and xxxiv. proves their relation to each other; and the circumstance, that פדה, *to redeem*, forms the conclusion of both, may be regarded as a characteristic trait in these popular elegiac psalms (for such I esteem them), as the later Jews in their oppression were always hoping for redemption.

2. We find in the Hebrew poetry the first beginnings of a complex rhythmical structure, similar to our strophes. In Ps. xlii., xliii., an odd verse (refrain) forms the conclusion of a greater

* Another explanation of this irregularity is given by Vogel in Capelli Crit., i. p. 123.

rhythmical period. Something of the same kind, though not complete, occurs in Ps. cvii., where verses 1–9, 10–16, 17–32, are separated by a nearly similar conclusion. The prophecies Isa. ix. 7—x. 4 and Am. i. 2—ii. 16 are upon the same plan. Gesenius (on Isaiah) supposes that the same kind of refrain is to be found in a part of Solomon's Song. There is a singular specimen of art in Ps. xlix., where the thirteenth and twenty-first verses are word for word alike, except that by the change of a single letter, יָלִין in the one becomes יָבִין in the other, so that a different sense is produced where the sound is entirely similar.

3. The *rhythm by gradation*, in the psalms of degrees, is a remarkable form. It consists in this, that the thought or expression of a preceding verse is resumed and carried forward in the next; for example (Ps. cxxi.): —

"I lift up mine eyes to the hills:
Whence *cometh my help?*
My help cometh from the Lord,
Who made heaven and earth.
He will not suffer thy foot to stumble;
Thy guardian *doth not slumber.*
Behold! *the guardian* of Israel
Doth neither *slumber nor sleep.*
The Lord is *thy guardian;*
The Lord is thy shade at thy right hand.
The sun shall not smite thee by day,
Nor the moon by night.
The Lord *will preserve* thee from all evil;
He *will preserve* thy life.
The Lord *will preserve* thee, when thou goest out, and when thou comest in,
From this time forth for evermore."

Gesenius has pointed out the same arrangement in the song of Deborah, and in Isa. xxvi., where verses 5, 6, read thus: —

"The lofty city he *hath laid low,*
He hath laid her low to the ground;
He hath levelled her with the dust.
The foot shall trample upon her,
The feet of the poor, the steps of the needy."

A form somewhat similar to this in modern poetry is the *triolet;* but it differs in making the whole composition turn upon one principal thought.

The question whether the psalms were sung by choirs may be distinctly answered in the affirmative, so far as it regards the Temple psalms, and all that were destined for the public service. It is still the custom in the synagogue for the assembly to respond as a choir to the chant of the chorister; and Miriam, with her women, formed an alternate chorus (Ex. xv.). By supposing many of the psalms to have been sung in this way, we shall perceive in them a greater degree of propriety, spirit, and grandeur. Thus in that of which every other line is, "For his mercy endureth for ever," the repetition of these words might have had an excellent effect when sung by way of response to a choir which sung the other line: though, to a mere reader, such repetition may appear tedious. Ps. xxiv., cxxxv., cl., and others, are evidently adapted to the same mode of performance. But it by no means follows that we must divide the psalms themselves into choruses, as Nachtigall, Kuinoel, and others, have done in their translations: it is probable that the chorus simply repeated.* But even were this not the case, yet this division is a matter of too much uncertainty to be safely attempted. It is very doubtful whether the singing was alternate or responsive in all cases where there is a change of the person speaking; for the Orientals are extremely fond of such a change of the person speaking even in poems which are not sung.†

In what way song was connected with the dance, it is impossible to determine. Few of the psalms which we now possess probably ever had any connection with the dance. Songs like that of the women upon David's victory were performed dancing: it could hardly be the case, however, that the two performances were so connected as to resemble the music and dance of modern times. The dance, perhaps, consisted for the most part of certain figures, which were executed by the files of dancers, chiefly in circles, as the Hebrew name מָחוֹל seems to indicate; and the

* Such is the present custom in the East. The chorus repeats the melody in a lower key. See Niebuhr's Travels, i. 176.

† Comp. Jahn, Einleit. ins Alte Test., ii. 723.

step, if not perfectly artless, was free and without rule.* In this case, the dance of the Hebrews was the same in relation to other modes of dancing, as was their rhythm compared with the rhythm of other nations.

The last direction in regard to the mode of using the psalms may be given in the language of Dr. Hammond, citing the opinion of the ancient fathers.

"Form thy spirit by the affection of the psalm, saith St. Augustine. If it be the affection of love, enkindle that within thy breast, that thou mayest not speak against thy sense and knowledge and conscience when thou sayest, 'I will love thee, O Lord, my strength!' If it be an affection of fear, impress that on thy soul, and be not thyself an insensible anvil to such strokes of divine poetry, which thou chantest out to others, 'Oh, consider this, ye that forget God, lest he pluck you away, and there be none to deliver you.' If it be an affection of desire which the psalmist in a holy transportation expresseth, let the same breathe in thee; accounting, as St. Chrysostom minds thee on Ps. xlii., that, when thou recitest these words, 'Like as the hart desireth the water-brooks, so longeth my soul after thee, O God!' thou hast sealed a covenant, betrothed and engaged thy soul to God, and must never have a coldness or indifferency to him hereafter. If it be the affection of gratitude, let thy soul be lifted up in praises: come with affections this way inflamed, sensible of the weight of mercies of all kinds, spiritual and temporal, with all the enhancements that the seasonable application thereof to the extremities of thy wants can add to thy preservations and pardons and joys; or else the reciting the hallelujahs will be a most ridiculous piece of pageantry. And so likewise for the petitory part of the psalms, let us be always in a posture ready for them, with our spirits minutely prepared to dart them up to heaven. And, whatever the affection be, let the heart do what the words signify."

* Such is still the manner of the female dancers of the East. One of them takes the lead, *extemporizing* the steps and movement, which the others imitate, following in a circle. See Niebuhr's Travels, i. 184; Lady Montague's Letters, Let. 30. For other authorities, see Jahn's Bibl. Archæol., i. 1, 405.

THE translator leaves the principles and views which governed him in his labors to be inferred from the work itself. In one particular, however, some may be at a loss to know the reason for the translation which I adopt. I refer to the name of the Supreme Being, JEHOVAH. As it is a proper name, and not a mere appellative, like the terms God and Lord, perhaps the strict rules of interpretation require that it should be always translated by the same term. But as the same great Being is denoted, whether his name be translated THE LORD, or JEHOVAH, I have thought it best, in many cases, not to alter the name to which the feelings of the devout have been so long accustomed. Where I have used "the Lord" instead of "Jehovah," I have put the former in capital letters. The same rule has been adopted in translating the Proverbs. The word "Jehovah" is now very seldom used in prayers or in hymns, and, of course, cannot have those devout feelings connected with it which belong to appellations of the Supreme Being which are habitually used. In some cases, however, the proper name of the Supreme Being — JEHOVAH — has a significance which does not belong to any of the generic terms by which he is denoted. In every case where any positive reason whatever exists for retaining the proper name, I have retained it. In all the other books of the Old Testament which I have translated, I have used the proper name, Jehovah, for the corresponding Hebrew word.

In this edition, I have carefully revised the translation by a new comparison of it with the original, and the aid of some English and German versions; viz., those of Hengstenberg, Hupfeld, Hitzig, Wellbeloved, and Alexander, which I had not seen when the former editions were printed. I have consulted them on the more obscure and difficult passages, and sometimes with advantage. I have also added a number of pages to the Introduction, and some explanatory notes, which, without materially increasing the size of the volume, will, I hope, add to its value.

CAMBRIDGE, June 28, 1866.

THE PSALMS.

BOOK I.

PSALM I.

The happiness of the righteous and the misery of the wicked.

1 HAPPY the man who walketh not in the counsel of the unrighteous,
Nor standeth in the way of sinners,
Nor sitteth in the seat of scoffers;
2 But whose delight is in the law of the LORD,
And who meditateth on his precepts day and night.
3 He is like a tree planted by streams of water,
That bringeth forth its fruit in its season,
Whose leaves also do not wither:
All that he doeth shall prosper.
4 Not so the unrighteous;
They are like chaff, which the wind driveth away.
5 Therefore the wicked shall not stand in judgment,
Nor sinners in the assembly of the just.
6 For the LORD knoweth the way of the righteous,
But the way of the wicked leadeth to ruin.

PSALM II.

Vain attempts of the nations against the king anointed by God.

1 WHY do the heathen rage,
And the nations meditate a vain thing?
2 Why do the kings of the earth rise up,
And the princes combine together,
Against Jehovah, and against his anointed king?

3 "Let us break their bonds asunder;
Let us cast away from us their fetters!"
4 He that sitteth in heaven will laugh;
The Lord will have them in derision.
5 Then shall he speak to them in his wrath,
And confound them in his hot displeasure.
6 "I myself have anointed my king,
Upon Zion, my holy hill."
7 I will declare the decree of Jehovah:
He hath said to me, "Thou art my son;
This day I have begotten thee.
8 Ask of me, and I will give thee the nations for thine inheritance,
And the ends of the earth for thy possession.
9 Thou shalt break them with a rod of iron;
Thou shalt dash them in pieces like a potter's vessel."
10 Be wise, therefore, O ye kings!
Be admonished, ye rulers of the earth!
11 Be subject to Jehovah with awe,
And fear with trembling!
12 Kiss the son, lest He be angry, and ye perish in your way;
For soon shall his wrath be kindled.
Happy are all they who seek refuge in him.

PSALM III.

Trust in God in a time of distress.

A Psalm of David, when he fled from his son Absalom.

1 How many, O LORD, are mine enemies!
How many are they who rise up against me!
2 How many are they who say of me,
"There is no help for him with God"! [Pause.]
3 But thou, O LORD! art my shield,
My glory, and the lifter-up of my head.
4 I call upon the LORD with my voice,
And he heareth me from his holy hill. [Pause.]
5 I lay me down and sleep;
I awake, for the LORD sustaineth me.

6 I will not fear the ten thousands of people
Who on every side set themselves against me.
7 Arise, O LORD! Save me, O my God!
For thou smitest the cheek of all my enemies;
Thou breakest the teeth of the wicked.
8 Deliverance cometh from the LORD:
May thy blessing be with thy people! [Pause.]

PSALM IV.

A prayer for deliverance from enemies; with a remonstrance to them, and expressions of confidence in Divine aid. It may, with the last psalm, have been occasioned by the rebellion of Absalom. But it is rather remarkable that there is no particular allusion to the affecting circumstance of David's own son being at the head of it.

For the leader of the music; to be accompanied with stringed instruments A psalm of David.

1 HEAR me, when I call, O God of my righteousness!
Thou hast helped me, when I was in trouble, —
Have pity upon me, and hear my prayer!
2 How long, O men! will ye dishonor my dignity?
How long will ye love vanity, and seek disappointment?
[Pause.]
3 Know ye that the LORD hath exalted one that is devoted to him;
The LORD will hear, when I call upon him.
4 Stand in awe, and sin no more;
Commune with your hearts upon your beds, and desist!
[Pause.]
5 Offer sacrifices of righteousness,
And put your trust in the LORD!
6 There are many who say, Who will show us any good?
LORD, lift thou up the light of thy countenance upon us!
7 Thou puttest gladness into my heart,
Greater than theirs, when their corn and wine are abundant.
8 I will lay me down in peace, and sleep;
For thou alone, O LORD! makest me dwell in safety.

PSALM V.

Prayer of a pious man for aid against impious, deceitful, and sanguinary enemies. It may be referred to the rebellion of Absalom, or to the persecution of David in the court of Saul.

For the leader of the music; to be accompanied with wind instruments. A psalm of David.

1 GIVE ear to my words, O LORD;
Have regard to my cry!
2 Listen to the voice of my supplication, my King and my God!
For to thee do I address my prayer.
3 In the morning shalt thou hear my voice, O LORD!
In the morning will I address my prayer to thee, and look for help.
4 For thou art not a God that hath pleasure in wickedness;
The unrighteous man dwelleth not with thee.
5 The haughty shall not stand in thy sight;
Thou hatest all that do iniquity.
6 Thou destroyest them that speak falsehood;
The man of blood and deceit the LORD abhorreth.
7 But I, through thy great goodness, will come to thy house;
In thy fear will I worship at thy holy temple.
8 Lead me, O LORD! in thy righteousness, because of mine enemies;
Make thy path straight before my face!
9 For in their mouth there is no truth;
Their heart is malignity;
Their throat is an open sepulchre;
They flatter with their tongue.
10 Requite them, O God!
Let them be confounded in their devices;
Cast them out for the multitude of their transgressions;
For against thee have they rebelled!
11 But let all, that put their trust in thee, rejoice;
Let them ever shout for joy, because thou defendest them;
Let them, that love thy name, be joyful in thee!
12 For thou, O LORD! dost bless the righteous;
With favor dost thou encompass him, as with a shield.

PSALM VI.

A prayer of one in great distress.

For the leader of the music; to be accompanied with stringed instruments; to the octave. A psalm of David.

1 O LORD! rebuke me not in thine anger;
Chasten me not in thy hot displeasure!
2 Have pity upon me, O LORD! for I am weak;
Heal me, O LORD! for my bones tremble!
3 My soul, also, is sore troubled;
And thou, O LORD! how long — ?
4 Return, O LORD! and deliver me;
Oh, save me according to thy mercy!
5 For in death no praise is given to thee;
In the underworld who can give thee thanks?
6 I am weary with my groaning;
All the night I make my bed to swim,
And drench my couch with my tears.
7 Mine eye is wasted with grief;
It hath become old because of all my enemies.
8 Depart from me, all ye that do iniquity;
For the LORD heareth the voice of my weeping.
9 The LORD heareth my supplication;
The LORD accepteth my prayer.
10 All my enemies shall be ashamed and utterly confounded;
They shall be turned back, and put to shame suddenly.

PSALM VII.

Prayer against an enemy, or, perhaps, against enemies in general.

A psalm of David, which he sang to Jehovah, on account of the reproaches of Cush the Benjamite.

1 O JEHOVAH, my God! to thee do I look for help;
Save me from them that persecute me, and deliver me!
2 Lest mine enemy tear me like a lion;
Lest he rend me in pieces, while there is none to help.

3 O Jehovah, my God! if I have done this, —
If there be iniquity upon my hands,
4 If I have rendered evil to my friend,
Or have despoiled him that without cause is mine enemy, —
5 Let my adversary pursue and take me;
Let him trample me to the ground,
And lay me prostrate in the dust! [Pause.]
6 Arise, O LORD! in thine anger;
Lift thyself up against the rage of mine enemies;
Awake for me, ordain judgment!
7 Let the assembly of the nations compass thee about,
And on their account return to the height!
8 The LORD judgeth the nations;
Judge me, O LORD! according to my righteousness,
And requite me according to my integrity!
9 Oh, let the wickedness of the wicked be at an end;
But establish the righteous!
For the righteous God trieth the heart and the reins.
10 My shield is with God,
Who saveth the upright in heart.
11 God is a righteous judge,
And a God who is angry every day.
12 If he do not desist, He sharpeneth his sword;
He bendeth his bow, and maketh it ready;
13 He prepareth for him the instruments of death;
He shooteth his burning arrows.
14 Behold, he travailed with iniquity,
And conceived mischief,
But hath brought forth disappointment!
15 He made a pit and digged it,
And is fallen into the ditch which he made.
16 His mischief returneth upon his own head,
And his violence cometh down upon his own skull.
17 I will praise the LORD according to his righteousness;
I will sing praise to the name of the LORD most high.

PSALM VIII.

The greatness of the Creator, and his goodness to man.

For the leader of the music; to be accompanied with the gittith. A psalm of David.

1 O JEHOVAH, our Lord!
How excellent is thy name in all the earth!
Thou hast set thy glory above the heavens.
2 Out of the mouths of babes and sucklings hast thou ordained praise,
To put thine adversaries to shame,
And to silence the enemy and avenger.
3 When I consider thy heavens, the work of thy fingers,
The moon and the stars which thou hast ordained:
4 What is man, that thou art mindful of him,
And the son of man, that thou carest for him?
5 Yet thou hast made him little lower than God;
Thou hast crowned him with glory and honor.
6 Thou hast given him dominion over the works of thy hands;
Thou hast put all things under his feet, —
7 All sheep and oxen,
Yea, and the beasts of the forest;
8 The birds of the air, and the fishes of the sea,
And whatever passeth through the paths of the deep.
9 O Jehovah, our Lord,
How excellent is thy name in all the earth!

PSALM IX.

A thanksgiving ode for victory and deliverance from enemies; with prayers for future help. Supposed to have been composed after the wars mentioned in 2 Samuel, chap. viii.

For the leader of the music; to be sung in the manner or with the voice of maidens. To the Benites, or to Ben. A psalm of David.

1 I WILL praise thee, O LORD! with my whole heart;
I will show forth all thy marvellous works.
2 I will be glad and rejoice in thee;
I will sing praise to thy name, O thou Most High!

3 All my enemies are turned back;
They fall and perish at thy presence.
4 For thou dost defend my right and my cause;
Thou sittest upon the throne, a righteous judge.
5 Thou rebukest the nations;
Thou destroyest the wicked;
Thou blottest out their name for evermore!
6 The enemy is fallen, — a desolation for ever!
Thou, O LORD! hast destroyed their cities;
Their memory itself hath perished!
7 The LORD reigneth for ever;
He hath prepared his throne for judgment.
8 He judgeth the world in righteousness;
He administereth judgment to the nations with uprightness.
9 Yea, the LORD is a refuge for the oppressed;
A refuge in times of trouble.
10 They who know thy name put their trust in thee;
For thou, O LORD! forsakest not them that seek thee!
11 Sing praises to the LORD, who reigneth in Zion;
Declare his doings among the people!
12 As the avenger of blood, he remembereth the distressed;
He forgetteth not their complaint.
13 "Have pity upon me, [said I,] O LORD!
Look upon my affliction through them that hate me;
Lift me up from the gates of death:
14 That I may show forth all thy praise in the gates of the daughter of Zion;
That I may rejoice in salvation by thee."
15 The nations have sunk into the pit which they made;
In the net, which they hid, is their own foot taken.
16 Thus it is known that the LORD executeth judgment;
The wicked are ensnared in the work of their own hands.
[Stringed instruments. Pause.]
17 The wicked shall be driven into the underworld;
Yea, all the nations that forget God.
18 For the poor shall not always be forgotten;
The hopes of the afflicted shall not perish for ever.
19 Arise, O LORD! Let not man prevail;
Let the nations be judged by thee!
20 Strike terror into them, O LORD!
Let the nations know that they are but men! [Pause.]

PSALM X.

A prayer against impious, deceitful, and blood-thirsty enemies.

1 WHY standest thou afar off, O LORD?
Why hidest thou thyself in times of trouble?
2 Through the haughtiness of the wicked the poor are in distress;
They are caught in the wiles which are contrived for them.
3 The wicked boasteth of his heart's desire;
The rapacious renounceth and contemneth Jehovah.
4 The wicked [saith] in his haughtiness, "He careth not!"
All his thoughts are, "There is no God."
5 His course is always prosperous;
Far in the heights are thy judgments from him;
As for all his enemies, he puffeth at them.
6 He saith in his heart, "I shall never fall;
I shall never be in adversity."
7 His mouth is full of perjury, deceit, and oppression;
Mischief and injustice are upon his tongue.
8 He sitteth in the lurking-places of the villages;
In secret places doth he murder the innocent;
His eyes are secretly fixed upon the poor.
9 He secretly lieth in wait, like a lion in a thicket;
He lieth in wait to seize upon the helpless;
He catcheth the poor, drawing him into his net.
10 He croucheth, and lowereth himself,
And the wretched fall into his paws.
11 He saith in his heart, "God doth forget;
He hideth his face; he doth never see it."
12 Arise, O LORD! O God, lift up thine hand;
Forget not the distressed!
13 Wherefore doth the wicked contemn God,
And say in his heart, "He careth not for it"?
14 Thou dost see it; yea, thou beholdest malice and oppression,
And markest it upon thy hand!
The poor committeth himself to thee;
Thou art the helper of the fatherless.

15 Break thou the arm of the unjust and wicked man;
Seek out his wickedness, till thou canst find none!
16 Jehovah is king for ever and ever;
The gentiles shall perish out of his land.
17 Thou, O LORD! wilt hear the desires of the distressed;
Thou wilt strengthen their hearts;
Thou wilt lend a listening ear!
18 Thou wilt maintain the cause of the fatherless and the oppressed,
That henceforth none may be driven from the land.

PSALM XI.

An expression of trust in God, as a security from the plots and assaults of enemies.

For the leader of the music. A psalm of David.

1 IN the LORD do I put my trust. Why say ye to me,
"Flee, like a bird, to your mountain?
2 For, lo! the wicked bend their bow;
They make ready their arrows on the string,
To shoot in secret at the upright in heart.
3 If the pillars be broken down,
What can the righteous do?"
4 The LORD is in his holy palace;
The LORD's throne is in heaven;
His eyes behold, his eyelids prove the children of men.
5 The LORD trieth the righteous;
But the wicked, and the lover of violence, his soul hateth.
6 Upon the wicked he will rain lightning;
Fire and brimstone and a burning wind shall be the portion of their cup.
7 For the LORD is righteous; he loveth righteousness;
The upright shall see his face.

PSALM XII.

A prayer for protection against calumniating foes.

For the leader of the music; to the octave. A psalm of David.

1 HELP, LORD; for the godly man ceaseth;
The faithful are failing among men.
2 They speak falsehood one to another;
With flattering lips, with a double heart, do they speak.
3 May the LORD destroy all flattering lips,
And the tongue which speaketh proud things!
4 Who say, "With our tongues will we prevail;
Our lips are our reliance;
Who is lord over us?"
5 For the oppression of the poor and the sighing of the wretched,
Now will I stand up, saith the LORD;
I will set in safety him whom they puff at.
6 The words of the LORD are pure;
Like silver purified in a furnace on the earth,
Seven times refined.
7 Thou, O LORD! wilt watch over them;
Thou wilt preserve them from this generation for ever.
8 The wicked walk on every side,
When the vilest of men are exalted.

PSALM XIII.

Supplication for deliverance from enemies, and confidence of obtaining it.

For the leader of the music. A psalm of David.

1 How long, O LORD! wilt thou forget me for ever?
How long wilt thou hide thy face from me?
2 How long shall I have anxiety in my soul for ever,
And sorrow in my heart all the day?
How long shall my enemy be exalted over me?
3 Look down and hear me, O LORD, my God!
Enlighten my eyes, lest I sleep the sleep of death;

4 Lest my enemy say, "I have prevailed against him!"
Lest my adversaries rejoice, when I am fallen.
5 Yet will I trust in thy goodness;
My heart shall rejoice in thy salvation;
6 I will sing to the LORD, that he hath dealt kindly with me.

PSALM XIV.

The complaint of a pious man in exile concerning the wickedness of men, and supplication for the restoration of the Israelites from captivity.

For the leader of the music. A psalm of David.

1 THE fool saith in his heart, "There is no God."
They are corrupt; abominable are their doings;
There is none that doeth good.
2 Jehovah looketh down from heaven upon the children of men,
To see if there are any that have understanding,
That have regard to God.
3 They are all gone out of the way; together are they corrupt;
There is none that doeth good — no, not one.
4 Shall not the evil-doers be requited,
Who devour my people like bread,
And call not upon Jehovah?
5 Yea, then shall they be in great fear;
For Jehovah is with the race of the righteous.
6 Ye would put to shame the counsel of the poor;
But Jehovah is their refuge.
7 Oh that salvation for Israel would come out of Zion!
When Jehovah bringeth back the captives of his people,
Then shall Jacob rejoice, and Israel be glad.

PSALM XV.

The qualifications of an acceptable worshipper. This psalm may have been composed when David removed the ark to the tabernacle on Mount Zion; 2 Samuel, chap. vi.

A psalm of David.

1 LORD, who shall abide at thy tabernacle?
Who shall dwell upon thy holy hill?
2 He that walketh uprightly, and doeth righteousness,
And speaketh the truth from his heart;
3 He that slandereth not with his tongue,
That doeth no injury to his neighbor,
And uttereth no reproach against his neighbor;
4 In whose eyes a vile person is contemned;
But who honoreth them that fear the LORD;
Who sweareth to his own hurt, and changeth not;
5 He that lendeth not his money for interest,
And taketh not a bribe against the innocent:
He that doeth these things shall never be moved.

PSALM XVI.

The person who is the subject of this psalm expresses his entire dependence upon God, his gratitude for Divine goodness, his satisfaction with the condition assigned him, and his firm hopes of future protection and favor.

A psalm of David.

1 PRESERVE me, O God! for to thee do I look for help.
2 I have said to Jehovah, Thou art my Lord;
I have no happiness beyond thee!
3 The holy that are in the land, and the excellent, —
In them is all my delight.
4 They who hasten after other gods shall have multiplied sorrows;
Their drink-offerings of blood I will not offer,
Nor will I take their names upon my lips.
5 Jehovah is my portion and my cup;
Thou wilt maintain my lot!

6 My portion hath fallen to me in pleasant places;
Yea, I have a goodly inheritance.
7 I will bless the LORD, who careth for me;
Yea, in the night my heart admonisheth me.
8 I set the LORD before me at all times;
Since he is at my right hand, I shall not fall.
9 Therefore my heart is glad, and my spirit rejoiceth;
Yea, my flesh dwelleth in security.
10 For thou wilt not give me up to the underworld;
Nor wilt thou suffer thy holy one to see the pit.
11 Thou wilt show me the path of life;
In thy presence is fulness of joy;
At thy right hand are pleasures for evermore.

PSALM XVII.

A prayer for help against impious enemies; together with expressions of confidence in the favor of God.

A psalm of David.

1 HEAR the righteous cause, O LORD!
Attend to my cry;
Give ear to my prayer from lips without deceit!
2 May my sentence come forth from thy presence;
May thine eyes behold uprightness!
3 Provest thou my heart, visitest thou me in the night,
Triest thou me like gold, thou shalt find nothing!
4 My thoughts do not vary from my lips.
As to the deeds of men,
Through the word of thy lips I have kept me from the paths of the destroyer.
5 Support my steps in thy paths,
That my feet may not slip!
6 I call upon thee, O God! for thou wilt hear me;
Incline thine ear to me, and listen to my prayer!
7 Show forth thy loving-kindness, O thou that savest by thy right hand
Them that seek refuge in thee from their adversaries!
8 Guard me as the apple of the eye;
Hide me under the shadow of thy wings

9 From the wicked who assault me,
From my deadly enemies who compass me about!
10 They shut up their hard heart;
With their mouth they speak haughtily.
11 They encompass us in all our steps;
They fix their eyes upon us, that they may cast us on the ground.
12 They are like a lion, eager for his prey;
Like a young lion, lurking in secret places.
13 Arise, O LORD! disappoint them, cast them down!
Deliver me from the wicked by thy sword,
14 From men, by thy hand, O LORD! from men of the world,
Whose portion is in life; whom thou loadest with thy treasure;
Whose children have enough, and leave their superfluity to their children.
15 But I through righteousness shall see thy face;
I shall be satisfied with the revival of thy countenance.

PSALM XVIII.

For the leader of the music. A psalm of David, the servant of the Lord, who spake to the Lord the words of this song, in the day that the Lord delivered him from the hand of all his enemies, and from the hand of Saul: And he said,—

1 I LOVE thee, O LORD, my strength!
2 Jehovah is my rock, my fortress, and my deliverer;
My God, my strength, in whom I trust;
My shield, my strong defence, and my high tower.
3 I called upon the LORD, who is worthy to be praised,
And was delivered from my enemies.
4 The snares of death encompassed me;
The floods of destruction filled me with dismay;
5 The snares of the underworld surrounded me,
And the nets of death seized upon me.
6 In my distress I called upon the LORD,
And cried unto my God;
He heard my voice from his palace,
And my cry came before him into his ears.

7 Then the earth quaked and trembled;
The foundations of the mountains rocked and were shaken,
Because his wrath was kindled.
8 A smoke went up from his nostrils,
And fire from his mouth devoured;
Burning coals shot forth from him.
9 He bowed the heavens, and came down;
And darkness was under his feet;
10 And he rode upon a cherub, and did fly;
Yea, he did fly upon the wings of the wind.
11 And he made darkness his covering;
His pavilion round about him was dark waters and thick clouds of the skies.
12 At the brightness before him, his thick clouds passed away;
Then came hailstones and coals of fire.
13 The LORD also thundered from heaven,
And the Most High uttered his voice,
Amid hailstones and coals of fire.
14 He sent forth his arrows, and scattered them;
Continual lightnings, and discomfited them.
15 Then the channels of the deep were seen,
And the foundations of the earth were laid bare
At thy rebuke, O LORD!
At the blast of the breath of thy nostrils.
16 He stretched forth his hand from above; he took me,
And drew me out of deep waters.
17 He delivered me from my strong enemy;
From my adversaries, who were too powerful for me.
18 They fell upon me in the day of my calamity;
But the LORD was my stay.
19 He brought me forth into a large place;
He delivered me, because he delighted in me.
20 The LORD hath rewarded me according to my righteousness;
According to the cleanness of my hands hath he recompensed me.
21 For I have kept the ways of the LORD,
And have not wickedly departed from my God.
22 For all his laws were in my sight;
I did not put away his statutes from me.
23 I was upright before him,
And kept myself from iniquity.

24 Therefore hath the LORD rewarded me according to my righteousness,
According to the cleanness of my hands before his eyes.
25 To the merciful thou showest thyself merciful;
To the upright thou showest thyself upright;
26 To the pure thou showest thyself pure,
And to the perverse thou showest thyself perverse.
27 For thou savest the afflicted people,
But the haughty countenance thou bringest down.
28 Thou causest my lamp to shine;
Jehovah, my God, enlighteneth my darkness.
29 For through thee I have broken through troops;
Through my God I have leaped over walls.
30 The ways of God are just and true;
His word is pure, tried in the fire;
He is a shield to all who put their trust in him.
31 Who, then, is God, save Jehovah?
And who is a rock, save our God?
32 It is God that girded me with strength,
And made my way plain.
33 He made my feet like the hind's,
And set me in my high places;
34 He taught my hands to war,
So that my arm bent the bow of brass.
35 Thou gavest me the shield of thy protection;
Thy right hand held me up,
And thy goodness made me great.
36 Thou didst make a wide path for my steps,
So that my feet did not stumble.
37 I pursued my enemies and overtook them,
And turned not back till I had destroyed them.
38 I smote them, so that they could not rise;
They fell under my feet.
39 Thou didst gird me with strength for the battle;
Thou didst cast down my adversaries under me.
40 Thou didst cause my enemies to turn their backs,
So that I destroyed them that hated me.
41 They cried, but there was none to help;
To Jehovah, but he answered them not.
42 I beat them small, like dust before the wind;
I cast them out as the dirt of the streets.

43 Thou hast delivered me from the assaults of the nations;
Thou hast made me the head of the kingdoms.
Nations whom I knew not serve me;
44 They who have only heard of me obey me;
Yea, men of a strange land submit themselves to me;
45 Men of a strange land fade away, like a leaf,
And come trembling from their strongholds.
46 Jehovah is the living God; blessed be my rock;
Exalted be the God of my salvation!
47 It is God who hath given me vengeance,
And subdued the nations under me;
48 He delivered me from my enemies;
Yea, thou hast lifted me up above my adversaries;
Thou hast saved me from the violent man!
49 Therefore I will give thanks to thee, O LORD! among the nations,
And sing praises to thy name.
50 Great deliverance giveth he to his king,
And showeth mercy to his anointed, —
To David and to his posterity for ever.

PSALM XIX.

The glory of God manifested in the material creation, and in the law given to man. Prayer for forgiveness and deliverance from temptation.

For the leader of the music. A psalm of David.

1 THE heavens declare the glory of God;
The firmament showeth forth the work of his hands.
2 Day uttereth instruction unto day,
And night showeth knowledge unto night.
3 They have no speech nor language,
And their voice is not heard;
4 Yet their sound goeth forth to all the earth,
And their words to the ends of the world.
In them hath he set a tabernacle for the sun,
5 Which cometh forth like a bridegroom from his chamber,
And rejoiceth, like a strong man, to run his course.

6 He goeth forth from the extremity of heaven,
And maketh his circuit to the end of it;
And nothing is hid from his heat.
7 The law of the LORD is perfect, reviving the soul;
The precepts of the LORD are sure, making wise the simple;
8 The statutes of the LORD are right, rejoicing the heart;
The commandments of the LORD are pure, enlightening the eyes;
9 The fear of the LORD is clean, enduring for ever;
The judgments of the LORD are true and righteous altogether.
10 More precious are they than gold; yea, than much fine gold;
Sweeter than honey and the honeycomb.
11 By them also is thy servant warned,
And in keeping of them there is great reward.
12 Who knoweth his own offences?
Oh, cleanse thou me from secret faults!
13 Keep back also thy servant from presumptuous sins;
Let them not have dominion over me!
Then shall I be upright;
I shall not be polluted with gross transgression.
14 May the words of my mouth and the meditation of my heart
Be acceptable in thy sight,
O LORD, my strength and my redeemer!

PSALM XX.

Prayer of a people for their king going to war. It may have been composed when David was going to war with the Syrians. 2 Samuel, chap. viii.–x.

For the leader of the music. A psalm of David.

1 MAY Jehovah hear thee in the day of trouble;
May the name of the God of Jacob defend thee!
2 May he send thee help from his sanctuary,
And strengthen thee out of Zion!
3 May he have regard to all thine offerings,
And accept thy burnt sacrifice! [Pause.]

4 May he grant thee thy heart's desire,
And fulfil all thy purposes!
5 We will rejoice in thy protection,
And in the name of our God will we set up our banners,
When Jehovah hath fulfilled all thy petitions.
6 Now I know that Jehovah helpeth his anointed;
That he heareth him from his holy heaven,
And aideth him with the saving strength of his right hand.
7 Some glory in chariots, and some in horses,
But we in the name of Jehovah our God.
8 They stumble and fall,
But we stand and are erect.
9 The LORD save the king!
May he hear us when we call!

PSALM XXI.

Triumphal song of a people for the victories of their king.

For the leader of the music. A psalm of David.

1 THE king rejoiceth in thy strength, O LORD!
Yea, he doth greatly exult in thy protection.
2 Thou hast given him his heart's desire,
And hast not denied him the request of his lips. [Pause.]
3 Yea, thou hast met him with rich blessings,
Thou hast placed a crown of pure gold upon his head.
4 He asked life of thee; thou gavest it him;
Even long life, enduring for ever.
5 Great is his glory through thine aid;
Honor and majesty hast thou laid upon him.
6 Thou hast made him blessed for evermore;
Thou hast made him glad with the joy of thy countenance.
7 For the king trusteth in the LORD;
And through the goodness of the Most High he shall never fall.
8 Thy hand shall overtake all thine enemies;
Thy right hand shall overtake them that hate thee.
9 Thou wilt make them like a burning oven in the time of thine anger;
Jehovah shall swallow them up in his wrath,
And the fire shall devour them.

10 Their offspring shalt thou destroy from the earth,
And their posterity from the sons of men.
11 For they spread a net of mischief against thee;
They devised plots against thee, but they did not prevail.
12 Therefore thou wilt cause them to turn their backs;
Thou wilt make ready thine arrows upon the strings against them.
13 Exalt thyself, O LORD! by thy strength!
So will we sing, and praise thy mighty deeds.

PSALM XXII.

A prayer of one in deep distress on account of his enemies; together with expressions of confidence in Divine aid, and hopes of future prosperity, and of the extension of the knowledge and worship of God.

For the leader of the music. To the tune of "The hind of the morning." A psalm of David.

1 MY God, my God! why hast thou forsaken me?
Why so far from mine aid, and from the words of my cry?
2 O my God! I cry during the day, but thou hearest not;
In the night also, but I have no rest.
3 And yet thou art holy,
Dwelling amid the praises of Israel!
4 Our fathers trusted in thee;
They trusted, and thou didst save them.
5 They called upon thee, and were delivered;
They trusted in thee, and were not put to shame.
6 But I am a worm, and not a man;
The reproach of men, and the scorn of the people.
7 All who see me scoff at me;
They open wide the lips; they shake the head.
8 "He trusted in the LORD, let him help him;
Let him deliver him, since he delighted in him!"
9 Surely thou art he that didst bring me into the world;
Thou didst make me lie secure upon my mother's breast!
10 Upon thee have I cast myself from my birth;
Thou hast been my God from my earliest breath!
11 Oh, be not far from me, for trouble is near;
For there is none to help!

12 Many bulls surround me;
Strong bulls of Bashan close me in on every side.
13 They open their mouths wide against me,
Like a ravening and roaring lion.
14 I am poured out like water,
And all my bones are out of joint;
My heart is become like wax;
It melteth in my bosom.
15 My strength is dried up like an earthen vessel,
And my tongue cleaveth to my jaws;
Thou hast brought me to the dust of death!
16 For dogs have surrounded me;
Bands of evil-doers have encompassed me, —
Like lions my hands and my feet.
17 I can count all my bones;
They gaze, and feast their eyes upon me.
18 They divide my garments among them,
And for my vesture they cast lots.
19 But be not thou far from me, O LORD!
O my strength! make haste to mine aid!
20 Deliver my life from the sword;
My blood from the power of the dog;
21 Save me from the lion's mouth;
Shield me from the horns of the buffaloes!
22 I will proclaim thy name to my brethren;
In the midst of the congregation will I praise thee.
23 Praise him, ye worshippers of Jehovah!
Extol him, all ye race of Jacob,
And fear him, all ye race of Israel!
24 For he hath not despised nor abhorred the misery of the afflicted,
Nor hath he hid his face from him;
But when he cried unto him, he heard.
25 My praise shall be of thee in the great congregation;
I will pay my vows before them that fear him!
26 The afflicted shall eat, and be satisfied;
They that seek the LORD shall praise him;
Your hearts shall be glad for ever and ever!
27 All the ends of the earth shall remember, and turn to Jehovah;
All the families of the nations shall worship before thee!

28 For the kingdom is Jehovah's;
He is the governor of the nations.
29 All the rich of the earth shall eat and worship;
Before him shall they also bow, who are going down to the dust,
Who cannot keep themselves alive.
30 The future generation shall serve him;
The race which is to come shall hear of Jehovah.
31 They shall come, and declare his righteousness;
His mighty deeds to the people that shall be born.

PSALM XXIII.

God our shepherd.

A psalm of David.

1 The Lord is my shepherd: I shall not want.
2 He maketh me to lie down in green pastures;
He leadeth me beside the still waters.
3 He reviveth my soul;
He leadeth me in paths of safety,
For his name's sake.
4 When I walk through a valley of deathlike shade,
I fear no evil; for thou art with me;
Thy crook and thy staff, they comfort me.
5 Thou preparest a table before me
In the presence of mine enemies.
Thou anointest my head with oil;
My cup runneth over.
6 Surely goodness and mercy shall follow me all the days of my life,
And I shall dwell in the house of the Lord for ever.

PSALM XXIV.

Hymn to Jehovah, occasioned by the introduction of the ark of the covenant into the tabernacle, or temple.

A psalm of David.

1 THE earth is the LORD'S, and all that is therein;
The world, and they who inhabit it.
2 For he hath founded it upon the seas,
And established it upon the floods.
3 Who shall ascend the hill of the LORD?
And who shall stand in his holy place?
4 He that hath clean hands and a pure heart;
Who hath not inclined his soul to falsehood,
Nor sworn deceitfully.
5 He shall receive a blessing from the LORD,
And favor from the God of his salvation.
6 This is the race of them that seek him;
They that seek thy face are Jacob. [Pause.]
7 Lift up your heads, O ye gates!
Lift yourselves up, ye everlasting doors,
That the king of glory may come in!
8 "Who is this king of glory?"
Jehovah, strong and mighty;
Jehovah, mighty in battle.
9 Lift up your heads, O ye gates!
Lift yourselves up, ye everlasting doors,
That the king of glory may enter in!
10 "Who is this king of glory?"
Jehovah, God of hosts, he is the king of glory. [Pause.]

PSALM XXV.

A prayer for deliverance from enemies, for instruction in duty, for Divine forgiveness, and for a distressed nation.

A psalm of David.

1 To thee, O LORD! do I lift up my soul.
2 O my God! I trust in thee; let me not be put to shame!
Let not my enemies triumph over me!
3 Yea, none that hope in thee shall be put to shame:
They shall be put to shame who wickedly forsake thee.

4 Cause me to know thy ways, O LORD!
Teach me thy paths!
5 Lead me in thy truth, and teach me!
For thou art the God from whom cometh my help;
In thee do I trust at all times!
6 Remember thy loving-kindness, O LORD! and thy tender mercy,
Which thou hast exercised of old!
7 Remember not the faults and transgressions of my youth!
According to thy mercy remember thou me,
For thy goodness' sake, O LORD!
8 Good and righteous is the LORD;
Therefore showeth he to sinners the way.
9 The humble he guideth in his statutes,
And the humble he teacheth his way.
10 All the doings of the LORD are mercy and truth
To those who keep his covenant and his precepts.
11 For thy name's sake, O LORD,
Pardon my iniquity; for it is great!
12 Who is the man that feareth the LORD?
Him doth he show the way which he should choose.
13 He shall himself dwell in prosperity,
And his offspring shall inherit the land.
14 The friendship of the LORD is with them that fear him,
And he will teach them his covenant.
15 Mine eyes are ever directed to the LORD,
For he will pluck my feet from the net.
16 Look upon me, and pity me;
For I am desolate and afflicted!
17 Lighten the sorrows of my heart,
And deliver me from my troubles!
18 Look upon my affliction and distress,
And forgive all my sins!
19 Consider how many are my enemies,
And with what violence they hate me!
20 Guard thou my life, and deliver me!
Let me not be put to shame, for I have trusted in thee!
21 Let integrity and uprightness preserve me,
For on thee do I rest my hope!
22 Redeem Israel, O God! from all his troubles!

PSALM XXVI.

A prayer for deliverance from distress, with protestations of the righteousness of him who offers it. It is commonly supposed to relate to the persecution of David by Saul.

A psalm of David.

1 Be thou my judge, O Lord! for I have walked in uprightness.
I have put my trust in the Lord, therefore shall I not fall.
2 Examine me, O Lord! and prove me;
Try my reins and my heart!
3 For thy kindness is ever before my eyes,
And I walk in thy truth.
4 I sit not with men of falsehood,
And go not in company with dissemblers.
5 I hate the assembly of evil-doers,
And do not sit with the wicked.
6 I wash my hands in innocence,
And go around thine altar, O Lord!
7 To utter the voice of thanksgiving,
And tell of all thy wondrous works.
8 O Lord! I love the habitation of thy house,
The place where thine honor dwelleth!
9 Gather not my breath with sinners,
Nor my life with men of blood,
10 In whose hands is mischief,
And whose right hands are full of bribes!
11 But as for me, I walk in my integrity;
Oh, redeem me, and be merciful to me!
12 My feet tread in a straight path;
In the congregation will I bless the Lord.

PSALM XXVII.

A pious man in distress expresses his confidence in God, and his earnest desire for his temple. He then prays for relief in his desolate condition, and trusts that he shall obtain it. This psalm may have been composed on the same occasion as the last.

A psalm of David.

1 THE LORD is my light and my salvation;
Whom shall I fear?
The LORD is the shield of my life;
Of whom shall I be afraid?
2 When the wicked came upon me to devour me,
Even my persecutors and enemies, they stumbled and fell.
3 Though a host should encamp against me, my heart shall not fear;
Though war should rise against me, yet will I be confident.
4 One thing have I desired of the LORD; that do I yet seek;
That I may dwell in the house of the LORD all the days of my life,
To behold the grace of the LORD,
And to gaze upon his temple.
5 For in the day of trouble he will hide me in his pavilion;
Yea, in the secret place of his tabernacle will he shelter me;
He will set me upon a rock.
6 Yea, already doth he lift my head above my enemies, who are around me;
Therefore in his tabernacle will I offer sacrifices with the sound of trumpets;
I will sing, yea, with instruments of music I will give praise to the LORD.
7 Hear my voice, O LORD! when I cry unto thee;
Have pity upon me, and answer me!
8 When I think of thy precept, "Seek ye my face!"
Thy face, LORD, do I seek.
9 O hide not thou thy face from me;
Cast not thy servant away in displeasure!
Thou hast been my help, do not leave me;
Do not forsake me, O God, my helper!
10 For my father and my mother have forsaken me;
But the LORD will take me up.

11 Teach me thy way, O LORD!
And lead me in the right path, because of my enemies!
12 Give me not up to the will of my adversaries!
For false witnesses have risen up against me,
And such as breathe out injustice.
13 I trust that I shall see the goodness of the LORD
In the land of the living. Hope thou in the LORD!
14 Be of good courage; let thy heart be strong;
Hope thou in the LORD!

PSALM XXVIII.

Prayer for aid, and for the punishment of enemies, with strong hopes of being heard.

A psalm of David.

1 To thee do I cry, O LORD! O my rock! be not silent
to me,
Lest, if thou answer me not, I become like those who go
down to the pit!
2 Hear the voice of my supplication, when I cry unto thee,
When I lift up my hands to thy most holy sanctuary!
3 Draw me not away with the impious, and with evil-doers,
Who speak peace to their neighbors, while mischief is in
their hearts!
4 Give them according to their deeds, and the wickedness
of their doings;
Give them according to the work of their hands;
Render to them their desert!
5 For they regard not the doings of the LORD, nor the work
of his hands;
Therefore will he destroy them, and not again build
them up.
6 Praised be the LORD, for he hath heard the voice of my
supplications!
7 The LORD is my strength and my shield;
My heart trusteth in him, and he helpeth me
Therefore doth my heart exult,
And in my song I will praise him.

8 Jehovah is the strength of his people;
He is the protecting shield of his anointed.
9 Save thy people, and bless thine inheritance;
Feed them also, and build them up for ever!

PSALM XXIX.

The glory of God, as manifested in a thunder-storm.

A psalm of David.

1 GIVE to Jehovah, O ye sons of God!
Give to Jehovah glory and praise!
2 Give to Jehovah the glory due to his name;
Worship Jehovah in holy attire!
3 The voice of Jehovah is heard above the waters;
The God of glory thundereth, —
Jehovah above the great waters.
4 The voice of Jehovah is powerful;
The voice of Jehovah is full of majesty;
5 The voice of Jehovah breaketh the cedars;
Yea, Jehovah breaketh the cedars of Lebanon;
6 Yea, he maketh them to leap like a calf, —
Lebanon and Sirion like a young buffalo.
7 The voice of Jehovah divideth the flames of fire.
8 The voice of Jehovah maketh the wilderness tremble;
Yea, Jehovah maketh the wilderness of Kadesh tremble.
9 The voice of Jehovah maketh the hinds bring forth,
And layeth bare the forests;
While, in his palace, every one declareth his glory.
10 Jehovah sitteth above the flood;
Yea, Jehovah sitteth king for ever.
11 Jehovah will give strength to his people;
Jehovah will bless his people with peace.

PSALM XXX.

A song of thanksgiving for deliverance from distress.

A psalm of David. To the air of songs for the dedication of a house.

1 I WILL extol thee, O LORD! for thou hast lifted me up,
And hast not suffered my enemies to rejoice over me.
2 O Jehovah, my God!
I called upon thee, and thou hast healed me!
3 O LORD! thou hast raised me up from the underworld;
Thou hast kept me alive, that I should not go down to the pit!
4 Sing unto the LORD, O ye his servants!
And praise his holy name!
5 For his anger endureth but a moment,
But his favor through life;
In the evening sorrow may be a guest,
But joy cometh in the morning.
6 I said in my prosperity, "I shall never be moved!"
7 Thou, O LORD! by thy favor, hast made my mountain to stand strong;
Thou didst hide thy face, and I was troubled!
8 I cried unto thee, O LORD!
To the LORD I made supplication:
9 "What will my blood profit thee, that I should go down to the pit?
Can dust praise thee? Can it declare thy faithfulness?
10 Hear, O LORD! and have pity upon me!
Be thou, O LORD! my helper!"
11 Thou didst turn my mourning into dancing;
Thou didst loose my sackcloth, and gird me with gladness.
12 Therefore I will sing praise to thee, and not be silent;
O Jehovah, my God! I will give thanks to thee for ever!

PSALM XXXI.

A prayer for deliverance, in the confident hope of being heard.

For the leader of the music. A psalm of David.

1 In thee, O Lord! do I trust; let me never be put to shame;
According to thy goodness deliver me!
2 Bow down thine ear to me; help me speedily!
Be to me a strong rock, a high fortress, for my deliverance
3 For thou art my rock and my high fortress;
Be thou also my guide, and lead me, for thy name's sake!
4 Draw me out of the net which they have secretly laid for me,
For thou art my strength!
5 Into thy hand I commit my life;
Thou wilt deliver me, O Lord, thou God of truth!
6 I hate those who regard lying vanities,
And put my trust in the Lord.
7 I will be glad and rejoice in thy mercy,
That thou hast looked upon my trouble,
And hast had regard to my distress;
8 That thou hast not given me up to the hands of my enemies,
But hast set my feet in a wide place.
9 Have mercy upon me, O Lord! for I am in trouble!
My face is consumed with grief;
Yea, my spirit and my body.
10 For my life is wasted with sorrow,
And my years with sighing;
My strength faileth by reason of my affliction,
And my bones are consumed on account of all my enemies.
11 I have become the scorn of my neighbors,
And the terror of my acquaintance;
They who see me abroad flee from me.
12 I am forgotten like a dead man out of mind;
I am like a broken vessel.
13 I hear the slander of many; fear is on every side;
For they take counsel together against me;
They devise to take away my life.

14 But I trust in thee, O Jehovah!
I say, "Thou art my God!"
15 My destiny is in thy hand;
Deliver me from the power of my enemies and persecutors!
16 Let thy face shine upon thy servant,
And save me through thy mercy!
17 Let me not be put to shame, O LORD! for I have called upon thee;
Let the wicked be put to shame;
Let them be silenced in the grave!
18 Let lying lips be put to silence,
Which speak proud things against the righteous,
With haughtiness and contempt!
19 O how great is thy goodness, which thou treasurest up for them that fear thee;
Which thou showest to them that trust in thee, before the sons of men!
20 Thou hidest them in the secret place of thy presence from the machinations of men;
Thou shelterest them in thy pavilion from the violence of tongues.
21 Praised be the LORD; for he hath shown me his wonderful kindness,
As in a fortified city!
22 I said in my distress,
"I am cut off from before thine eyes;"
But thou didst hear the voice of my supplication,
When I cried unto thee.
23 O love the LORD, all ye his servants;
For the LORD preserveth the faithful,
And requiteth the proud in full measure!
24 Be of good courage; let your hearts be strong,
All ye who trust in the LORD!

PSALM XXXII.

The happiness of him whose sins are forgiven. This psalm is commonly supposed to express the feelings of David after his reproof by Nathan the prophet. See 2 Samuel, chap. xii.

A psalm of David.

1 HAPPY is he whose transgression is forgiven, whose sin is pardoned!
2 Happy the man to whom the LORD imputeth not iniquity,
And in whose spirit there is no guile!
3 While I kept silence, my bones were wasted,
By reason of my groaning all the day long.
4 For day and night thy hand was heavy upon me;
My moisture dried up, as in summer's drought.
5 At length I acknowledged to thee my sin,
And did not hide my iniquity.
I said, "I will confess my transgression to the LORD;"
And thou forgavest the iniquity of my sin! [Pause.]
6 Therefore shall every pious man pray to thee, while thou mayst be found;
Surely the floods of great waters shall not come near him.
7 Thou art my hiding-place; thou preservest me from trouble;
Thou compassest me about with songs of deliverance. [Pause.]
8 I will instruct thee, and show thee the way thou shouldst go;
I will give thee counsel, and keep mine eye upon thee.
9 Be ye not like the horse and the mule, which have no understanding,
Whose mouths must be pressed with the bridle and curb,
Because they will not come near thee!
10 The wicked hath many sorrows;
But he that trusteth in the LORD is encompassed with mercies.
11 Rejoice in the LORD, and be glad, ye righteous;
Shout for joy, all ye that are upright in heart!

PSALM XXXIII.

A hymn to Jehovah as the creator and governor of the world, and the special protector of the Jewish nation.

1 Rejoice, O ye righteous, in the Lord!
For praise becometh the upright.
2 Praise the Lord with the harp;
Sing to him with the ten-stringed psaltery!
3 Sing to him a new song;
Play skilfully amid the sound of trumpets!
4 For the word of the Lord is right,
And all his acts are faithful.
5 He loveth justice and equity;
The earth is full of the goodness of the Lord.
6 By the word of the Lord were the heavens made,
And all the hosts of them by the breath of his mouth.
7 He gathereth the waters of the sea, as a heap;
He layeth up the deep in storehouses.
8 Let all the earth fear the Lord;
Let all the inhabitants of the world stand in awe of him!
9 For he spake, and it was done;
He commanded, and it stood fast.
10 The Lord bringeth the devices of the nations to nothing;
He frustrateth the designs of kingdoms.
11 The purposes of the Lord stand for ever;
The designs of his heart, to all generations.
12 Happy the nation whose God is Jehovah;
The people whom he hath chosen for his inheritance.
13 The Lord looketh down from heaven;
He beholdeth all the children of men;
14 From his dwelling-place he beholdeth all the inhabitants of the earth, —
15 He that formed the hearts of all,
And observeth all their works.
16 A king is not saved by the number of his forces,
Nor a hero by the greatness of his strength.
17 The horse is a vain thing for safety,
Nor can he deliver his master by his great strength.
18 Behold, the eye of the Lord is upon them that fear him, —

Upon them that trust in his goodness;
19 To save them from the power of death,
And keep them alive in famine.
20 The hope of our souls is in the LORD;
He is our help and our shield.
21 Yea, in him doth our heart rejoice;
In his holy name we have confidence.
22 May thy goodness be upon us, O LORD!
According as we trust in thee!

PSALM XXXIV.

Thanksgiving for deliverance from distress, and a description of the happiness of the good and the misery of the wicked.

A psalm of David, when he feigned himself mad before Abimelech, who drove him away, and he departed.

1 I WILL bless the LORD at all times;
His praise shall continually be in my mouth.
2 In the LORD doth my soul boast;
Let the afflicted hear, and rejoice!
3 O magnify the LORD with me,
And let us exalt his name together!
4 I sought the LORD, and he heard me,
And delivered me from all my fears.
5 Look up to him, and ye shall have light;
Your faces shall never be ashamed.
6 This afflicted man cried, and the LORD heard,
And saved him from all his troubles.
7 The angels of the LORD encamp around those who fear him,
And deliver them.
8 O taste, and see how good is the LORD!
Happy the man who trusteth in him!
9 O fear the LORD, ye his servants!
For to those who fear him there shall be no want.
10 Young lions want, and suffer hunger;
But they who fear the LORD want no good thing.
11 Come, ye children, hearken to me!
I will teach you the fear of the LORD.

12 Who is he that loveth life,
And desireth many days, in which he may see good?
13 Guard well thy tongue from evil,
And thy lips from speaking guile!
14 Depart from evil, and do good;
Seek peace, and pursue it!
15 The eyes of the LORD are upon the righteous,
And his ears are open to their cry.
16 But the face of the LORD is against evil-doers,
To cut off their remembrance from the earth.
17 The righteous cry, and the LORD heareth,
And delivereth them from all their troubles.
18 The LORD is near to them that are of a broken heart,
And saveth such as are of a contrite spirit.
19 Many are the afflictions of the righteous;
But the LORD delivereth him from them all.
20 He guardeth all his bones;
Not one of them shall be broken.
21 Calamity destroyeth the wicked,
And they who hate the righteous suffer for it.
22 The LORD redeemeth the life of his servants,
And none that put their trust in him will suffer for it.

PSALM XXXV.

A prayer for help against enemies; commonly supposed to relate to the persecution of David by Saul and his courtiers.

A psalm of David.

1 CONTEND, O LORD! with them that contend with me!
Fight against them that fight against me!
2 Take hold of shield and buckler,
And stand up for my help!
3 Draw forth the spear and the axe against my persecutors;
Say to me, "I am thy salvation."
4 May they be confounded and put to shame, who seek my life;
May they be turned back with disgrace, who devise my hurt!

5 May they be like dust before the wind;
May the angel of the LORD drive them!
6 May their way be dark and slippery,
And may the angel of the LORD pursue them!
7 For without cause they have laid for me a snare;
Without cause they have digged for me a pit.
8 May unforeseen destruction come upon them!
May the snare which they have laid lay hold on themselves,
And may they fall into destruction!
9 Then shall my soul rejoice in the LORD;
It shall exult in his protection.
10 All my bones shall say, Who, O LORD! is like thee,
Who dost rescue the afflicted from the oppressor,
The afflicted and destitute from the spoiler?
11 False witnesses have risen up;
They charge me with that which has not entered my mind.
12 They repay me evil for good;
They cause bereavement to my soul.
13 And yet I, during their sickness, clothed myself with sackcloth,
And afflicted myself with fasting;
And my prayer was turned to my bosom.
14 I behaved myself as if he had been my friend or brother;
I bowed down in sadness, as one mourning for his mother.
15 But at my fall they rejoice, and gather themselves together;
Revilers whom I know not assemble themselves against me;
They tear me without ceasing.
16 With base men who mock for their bread,
They gnash at me with their teeth.
17 How long, O LORD! wilt thou look on?
O rescue my life from the destruction they plot for me;
My precious life from these young lions!
18 I will thank thee in the great assembly;
Before a numerous people I will praise thee.
19 Let not them that are my enemies wrongfully triumph over me;
Let them not wink with the eye, who hate me without cause!

20 For they speak not peace;
They devise deceit against them that are quiet in the land.
21 Yea, they open their mouths wide against me;
They say, "Aha, aha! our eye seeth it."
22 Thou seest it, O LORD! be not silent!
O LORD! be not far from me!
23 Arouse thyself; awake for my defence!
My God and my Lord, awake to my cause!
24 Judge me according to thy righteousness, O Jehovah, my God!
Let them not triumph over me!
25 Let them not say in their hearts, "Aha! we have our wish!"
Let them not say, "We have swallowed him up!"
26 May they all be confounded and brought to shame,
Who rejoice at my calamity!
May they be clothed with ignominy and disgrace,
Who exalt themselves against me!
27 Let them shout for joy, and be glad,
Who favor my righteous cause;
Let them ever say, "The LORD be praised,
Who delighteth in the prosperity of his servant!"
28 So shall my tongue speak of thy righteousness,
And daily repeat thy praise.

PSALM XXXVI.

Complaint of the wickedness of men; description of the goodness of God; prayer for help.

For the leader of the music. A psalm of David, the servant of the Lord.

1 To speak of the ungodliness of the wicked is in my heart:
He hath no fear of God before his eyes.
2 For he flattereth himself in his own eyes,
Till his iniquity is found out and hated.
3 The words of his mouth are iniquity and deceit;
He neglecteth to be wise and to do good.

4 He deviseth mischief upon his bed;
He persevereth in an evil way;
He abhorreth not sin.
5 Thy goodness, O LORD! reacheth to the heavens,
And thy faithfulness to the clouds;
6 Thy righteousness is like the high mountains;
Thy judgments are a great deep;
Thou, O LORD! preservest man and beast!
7 How precious is thy loving-kindness, O God!
Yea, the sons of men seek refuge under the shadow of thy wings.
8 They are satisfied with the abundance of thy house,
And thou causest them to drink of the full stream of thy pleasures.
9 For with thee is the fountain of life;
Through thy light we see light.
10 O continue thy loving-kindness to them that know thee,
And thy favor to the upright in heart!
11 Let not the foot of the proud come upon me,
Nor the hand of the wicked remove me!
12 Lo! already are the workers of iniquity fallen;
They are cast down; they are unable to rise!

PSALM XXXVII.

A didactic psalm on the rewards of the righteous and the punishment of the wicked.

A psalm of David.

1 BE not thou angry on account of the wicked,
Nor be envious of those who do iniquity.
2 For soon shall they be cut down like grass,
And wither like the green herb.
3 Trust in the LORD, and do good;
Abide in the land, and delight in faithfulness.
4 Place thy delight in the LORD,
And he will give thee thy heart's desires.
5 Commit thy way to the LORD;
Trust in him, and he will give thee success!

6 He will cause thy justice to shine forth like the light,
And thy righteousness like the noonday's brightness.
7 Hope thou patiently on the LORD,
And in him place thy trust!
Be not angry on account of the prosperous,—
On account of him that deviseth deceit!
8 Cease from anger; give not way to wrath;
Be not provoked, so as to do evil!
9 For evil-doers shall be rooted out;
But they who trust in the LORD, they shall inherit the land.
10 Yet a little while, and the wicked shall be no more;
Thou mayst look for his place, and he will not be found.
11 But the meek shall inherit the land,
And delight themselves in the fulness of prosperity.
12 The wicked man plotteth against the just,
And gnasheth at him with his teeth.
13 The Lord laugheth at him;
For he seeth that his day is coming.
14 The wicked draw the sword,
And bend their bow,
To cast down the afflicted and the needy,
And to slay the upright.
15 Their swords shall enter their own hearts,
And their bows shall be broken in pieces.
16 Better is the little of the righteous man
Than the great abundance of the wicked;
17 For the arms of the wicked shall be broken,
But the LORD will uphold the righteous.
18 The LORD careth for the life of the upright,
And their inheritance shall endure for ever.
19 They shall not be ashamed in the evil time,
And in the days of famine they shall have enough.
20 But the wicked shall perish;
Yea, the enemies of the LORD shall be consumed, like the glory of the fields;
They shall be consumed into smoke.
21 The wicked borroweth, and repayeth not;
But the righteous is merciful and bountiful.
22 For they who are blessed by God shall inherit the land,
And they who are cursed by him shall be rooted out.

23 The steps of the good man are directed by the LORD;
He delighteth himself in his way.
24 Though he fall, he shall not be utterly cast down,
For the LORD holdeth him by the hand.
25 I have been young, and now am old;
Yet have I not seen the righteous forsaken,
Nor his offspring begging bread.
26 He is ever merciful and lendeth,
And his offspring shall be blessed.
27 Depart from evil, and do good;
So thou shalt dwell in the land for ever.
28 For the LORD loveth righteousness,
And forsaketh not his servants;
They are preserved for ever;
But the posterity of the wicked shall be rooted out.
29 The righteous shall inherit the land,
And shall dwell therein for ever.
30 The mouth of the righteous uttereth wisdom,
And his tongue speaketh what is right.
31 The law of his God is in his heart;
His footsteps shall not slip.
32 The wicked watcheth the righteous,
And seeketh to slay him;
33 The Lord will not leave him in his hand,
Nor suffer him to be condemned, when he is judged.
34 Trust in the LORD, and keep his way,
And he will exalt thee to the possession of the land,
Whilst thou shalt see the destruction of the wicked!
35 I have seen a wicked man in great power,
And spreading himself like a green cedar;
36 But he passed away, and, lo! he was no more;
Yea, I sought him, but he was not found.
37 Mark the righteous man, and behold the upright,
That posterity is to the man of peace!
38 But transgressors will all be destroyed;
The posterity of the wicked shall be rooted out.
39 The salvation of the just is from the LORD.
He is their strength in the time of trouble.
40 The LORD will help and deliver them;
He will deliver them from their enemies, and save them,
Because they trust in him.

PSALM XXXVIII.

A prayer of one in deep affliction. It may have been occasioned by the affair of Bathsheba, or by some other offence of David.

A psalm of David. To bring to remembrance.

1 O LORD! rebuke me not in thy wrath,
Nor chasten me in thy hot displeasure!
2 For thine arrows have deeply pierced me,
And thy hand hath been heavy upon me.
3 There is no soundness in my flesh, because of thine anger;
Nor rest in my bones, because of my sin.
4 For my iniquities have gone over my head;
Like a heavy burden, they are more than I can bear.
5 My wounds putrefy and are loathsome on account of my folly.
6 I am bent; I am bowed down greatly;
I go mourning all the day long.
7 For my loins are full of burning heat,
And there is no soundness in my flesh.
8 I am weakened and bruised exceedingly;
I roar by reason of the disquietude of my heart.
9 O Lord! thou knowest all my desire,
And my groaning is not hidden from thee!
10 My heart panteth; my strength faileth me;
The very light of my eyes is gone from me.
11 My friends and acquaintance keep aloof from my woe,
And my kinsmen stand afar off:
12 While they who seek my life lay snares for me;
They who seek my hurt threaten destruction,
And meditate deceit all the day long.
13 But I, like a deaf man, hear not;
And, like a dumb man, open not my mouth.
14 I am like one who heareth nothing,
And in whose mouth is no reply.
15 For in thee, O LORD! do I put my trust;
Thou wilt hear, O Lord, my God!
16 For I have prayed, "Let them not rejoice over me;
Let them not exult at the slipping of my feet!"
17 For I am ready to fall,
And my pain doth never leave me;

18 For I confess my iniquity,
And am troubled on account of my sin.
19 But my enemies flourish and are strong;
They who hate me without cause are multiplied.
20 They who repay good with evil are my enemies,
Because I follow that which is good.
21 Forsake me not, O LORD!
O my God! be not far from me!
22 Make haste to mine aid, O Lord, my salvation!

PSALM XXXIX.

Complaints of one in affliction respecting the shortness and vanity of human life, with expressions of submission, and prayer for relief.

A psalm of David. For the leader of the music of the Jeduthunites.

1 I SAID, I will take heed to my ways,
That I may not sin with my tongue;
I will keep my mouth with a bridle,
While the wicked is before me.
2 I was dumb with silence; I spake not even what was good;
But my pain was increased.
3 My heart was hot within me;
In my anguish the fire burst forth,
And I spake with my tongue:
4 LORD, make me to know mine end,
And the number of my days,
That I may know how frail I am!
5 Behold, thou hast made my days as a hand-breadth,
And my life is as nothing before thee;
Yea, every man in his firmest state is altogether vanity.
[Pause.]
6 Surely every man walketh in a vain show;
Surely he disquieteth himself in vain;
He heapeth up riches, and knoweth not who shall gather them.
7 What, then, O Lord! is my hope?
My hope is in thee!
8 Deliver me from all my transgressions;
Let me not be the reproach of scoffers!

9 Yet I am dumb; I open not my mouth;
For thou hast done it!
10 But remove from me thine infliction;
For I am perishing by the blow of thine hand.
11 When thou with rebukes dost chasten man for iniquity,
Thou causest his glory to waste away like a moth!
Surely every man is vanity.
12 Hear my prayer, O LORD!
Give ear to my cry;
Be not silent at my tears!
For I am but a stranger with thee,
A sojourner, as all my fathers were.
13 O spare me, that I may recover strength,
Before I go away, and be no more!

PSALM XL.

Thanksgiving for past favors, resolutions of obedience to the Divine will, and prayer for continued mercy.

For the leader of the music. A psalm of David.

1 I TRUSTED steadfastly in the LORD,
And he listened, and heard my cry.
2 He drew me out of a horrible pit,
Out of the miry clay;
He set my feet upon a rock,
And made my steps firm.
3 He hath put into my mouth a new song,
A song of praise to our God.
Many shall see, and fear,
And put their trust in the LORD.
4 Happy the man who maketh the LORD his trust,
And resorteth not to men of pride and falsehood!
5 Many, O LORD, my God! are the wonderful works which thou hast done;
Many have been thy gracious purposes towards us;
None can be compared to thee!
Would I declare and rehearse them, they are more than can be numbered.

6 In sacrifice and oblation thou hast no pleasure;
Mine ears thou hast opened;
Burnt-offering and sin-offering thou requirest not.
7 Therefore I said, "Lo, I come;
In the scroll of the book it is prescribed to me;
8 O my God! to do thy will is my delight,
And thy law dwelleth in my heart!"
9 I have proclaimed thy righteousness in the great assembly,
Lo, I have not restrained my lips,
O LORD! thou knowest!
10 I hide not thy justice in my heart;
I declare thy faithfulness and thy salvation;
I conceal not thy mercy and truth from the great assembly.
11 Withdraw not from me thy tender mercies, O LORD!
May thy loving-kindness and thy truth continually preserve me!
12 For evils without number have encompassed me;
My iniquities have overtaken me;
I cannot see the end of them;
They are more than the hairs of my head,
And my heart dieth within me.
13 May it please thee, O LORD! to deliver me!
O LORD! make haste to mine aid!
14 May they all be confounded and covered with shame
Who seek to take away my life!
Let them be driven back with disgrace
Who desire to do me injury!
15 Let them be overwhelmed with confusion
Who cry out to me, Aha! aha!
16 But let all who seek thee
Be glad and rejoice in thee!
Let those who love thy protection
Ever say, "Great is Jehovah!"
17 I am poor and afflicted, yet the Lord thinketh upon me;
Thou art my help and my deliverer;
My God! make no delay!

PSALM XLI.

Prayer of one in affliction, whose enemies desired and plotted his destruction.

For the leader of the music. A psalm of David.

1 HAPPY is he who hath regard to the poor!
The LORD will deliver him in time of trouble.
2 The LORD will preserve him, and keep him alive;
He shall be happy on the earth;
Thou wilt not give him up to the will of his enemies!
3 The LORD will strengthen him upon the bed of disease;
All his bed thou wilt change in his sickness.
4 I said, O LORD! be merciful to me!
Heal me, for I have sinned against thee!
5 My enemies speak evil of me:
"When will he die, and his name perish?"
6 If one come to see me, he speaketh falsehood;
His heart gathereth malice;
When he goeth abroad, he uttereth it.
7 All that hate me whisper together against me;
Against me do they devise mischief:
8 "A deadly disease cleaveth fast unto him;
He lieth down, and he shall never arise!"
9 Yea, my familiar friend in whom I trusted, who did eat
of my bread, —
He hath lifted up his heel against me.
10 But do thou, O LORD! have pity upon me;
Raise me up, that I may requite them!
11 By this I know that thou favorest me,
Because my enemy doth not triumph over me.
12 As for me, thou wilt uphold me in my integrity;
Thou wilt set me before thy face for ever!

13 *Praised be Jehovah, the God of Israel,*
From everlasting to everlasting. Amen! Amen!

BOOK II.

PSALM XLII., XLIII.

The aspirations of an afflicted exile after the temple and worship of God.

For the leader of the music. A song of the sons of Korah.

1 As the hart panteth for the water-brooks,
So panteth my soul for thee, O God!
2 My soul thirsteth for God, the living God:
When shall I come, and appear before God?
3 My tears have been my food day and night,
While they say to me continually, "Where is thy God?"
4 When I think of it, I pour out my soul in grief;
How I once walked with the multitude,
Walked slowly with them to the house of God,
Amid sounds of joy and praise with the festive multitude!
5 Why art thou cast down, O my soul?
And why art thou disquieted within me?
Hope thou in God; for I shall yet praise him,
Him, my deliverer and my God!
6 My soul is cast down within me,
While I remember thee from the land of Jordan and Hermon,
From the mountain Mizar.
7 Deep calleth for deep at the noise of thy waterfalls;
All thy waves and billows have gone over me!
8 Once the LORD commanded his kindness by day,
And by night his praise was with me, —
Thanksgiving to the God of my life.
9 Now I say to God, my rock, Why hast thou forgotten me?
Why go I mourning on account of the oppression of the enemy?

10 Like the crushing of my bones are the reproaches of the enemy,
While they say to me continually, "Where is thy God?"
11 Why art thou cast down, O my soul?
And why art thou disquieted within me?
Hope thou in God; for I shall yet praise him,
Him, my deliverer and my God!
1 Judge me, O God! and defend my cause against a merciless nation!
Deliver me from unjust and deceitful men!
2 Thou art the God of my refuge: why dost thou cast me off?
Why go I mourning on account of the oppression of the enemy?
3 O send forth thy light and thy truth; let them guide me;
Let them lead me to thy holy mountain, and to thy dwelling-place!
4 Then will I go to the altar of God,
To the God of my joy and exultation;
Yea, upon the harp will I praise thee, O God, my God!
5 Why art thou cast down, O my soul?
And why art thou disquieted within me?
Hope thou in God; for I shall yet praise him,
Him, my deliverer and my God!

PSALM XLIV.

Prayer of a pious Israelite for the relief of his oppressed and persecuted nation.

For the leader of the music. A psalm of the sons of Korah.

1 O God! we have heard with our ears,
Our fathers have told us,
What deeds thou didst in their days,
In the days of old.
2 With thine own hand didst thou drive out the nations,
And plant our fathers;
Thou didst destroy the nations,
And cause our fathers to flourish.

3 For not by their own swords did they gain possession of the land,
Nor did their own arms give them victory;
But thy right hand, and thine arm, and the light of thy countenance;
For thou didst favor them!
4 Thou art my king, O God!
O send deliverance to Jacob!
5 Through thee we may cast down our enemies;
Through thy name we may trample upon our adversaries!
6 I trust not in my bow,
Nor can my sword save me.
7 But it is thou only who savest us from our enemies,
And puttest to shame those who hate us!
8 In God will we glory continually;
Yea, we will praise thy name for ever! [Pause.]
9 Yet now thou hast cast us off, and put us to shame;
Thou goest not forth with our armies.
10 Thou makest us turn back from the enemy,
And they who hate us make our goods their prey.
11 Thou makest us like sheep destined for food,
And scatterest us among the nations.
12 Thou sellest thy people for nought,
And increasest not thy wealth by their price.
13 Thou makest us a reproach to our neighbors,
A scorn and a derision to those who are around us.
14 Thou makest us a byword among the nations,
And causest the people to shake their heads at us.
15 My ignominy is continually before me,
And shame covereth my face,
16 On account of the voice of the scoffer and the reviler,
And on account of the enemy and the avenger.
17 All this hath come upon us;
Yet have we not forgotten thee,
Nor have we been false to thy covenant.
18 Our hearts have not wandered from thee,
Nor have our feet gone out of thy path;
19 Though thou hast crushed us in a land of jackals,
And covered us with thick darkness.
20 If we had forgotten the name of our God,
Or stretched forth our hands to a strange God,

21 Surely God would search it out;
For he knoweth the secrets of the heart.
22 But for thy sake we are killed all the day;
We are counted as sheep for the slaughter.
23 Awake! why sleepest thou, O Lord?
Arise! cast us not off for ever!
24 Wherefore dost thou hide thy face,
And forget our affliction and oppression?
25 Our soul is bowed down to the dust;
Our body cleaveth to the earth.
26 Arise, O thou, our strength!
And deliver us, for thy mercy's sake!

PSALM XLV.

The praises of a king.

For the leader of the music. To be accompanied with the Shoshannim. A song of loveliness by the sons of Korah.

1 My heart is overflowing with a good matter;
I will address my work to the king:
May my tongue be like the pen of a ready writer!
2 Thou art the fairest of the sons of men;
Grace is poured upon thy lips;
For God hath blessed thee for ever!
3 Gird thy sword to thy thigh, thou hero!—
Thy glory and ornament!
4 In thy glorious array ride forth victoriously,
On account of truth and mildness and justice;
And thy right hand shall teach thee terrible things!
5 Thine arrows are sharp;
Nations shall fall before thee;
They shall pierce the hearts of the king's enemies.
6 Thy throne is God's for ever and ever;
The sceptre of thy kingdom is a sceptre of equity!
7 Thou lovest righteousness, and hatest iniquity;
Therefore hath God, thy God, anointed thee
With the oil of gladness above thy fellows!

8 All thy garments are myrrh, aloes, and cassia;
From ivory palaces stringed instruments delight thee.
9 Daughters of kings are among thy chosen women;
On the right hand stands the queen
In gold of Ophir.
10 Listen, O daughter! consider, and incline thine ear;
Forget thy people and thy father's house!
11 For the king is captivated with thy beauty;
He is now thy lord; honor thou him!
12 So shall the daughter of Tyre seek thy favor with gifts,
The rich among the people.
13 All glorious is the king's daughter in her apartment;
Her robe is embroidered with gold.
14 In variegated garments shall she be led to the king;
The virgin companions that follow her shall be brought unto thee.
15 With gladness and rejoicing shall they be brought;
They shall enter the king's palace.
16 Instead of thy fathers shall be thy children,
Whom thou shalt make princes through all the land.
17 I will make thy name memorable throughout all generations;
So shall the nations praise thee for ever and ever!

PSALM XLVI.

Thanksgiving for victory over enemies, and trust in God as a national refuge and defence.

For the leader of the music. Of, or for, the sons of Korah. To be sung in the manner, or with the voice, of virgins.

1 God is our refuge and strength;
An ever present help in trouble.
2 Therefore will we not fear, though the earth be changed;
Though the mountains tremble in the heart of the sea;
3 Though its waters roar and be troubled,
And the mountains shake with the swelling thereof.
[Pause.]
4 A river with its streams shall make glad the city of God,
The holy dwelling-place of the Most High.

5 God is the midst of her; she shall not be moved;
God will help her, and that full early.
6 The nations raged; kingdoms were moved;
He uttered his voice, the earth melted.
7 The LORD of hosts is with us;
The God of Jacob is our refuge. [Pause.]
8 Come, behold the doings of the LORD;
What desolations he hath made in the earth!
9 He causeth wars to cease to the end of the earth;
He hath broken the bow, and snapped the spear asunder,
And burned the chariots in fire.
10 "Desist, and know that I am God;
I will be exalted among the nations, I will be exalted throughout the earth!"
11 The LORD of hosts is with us;
The God of Jacob is our refuge.

PSALM XLVII.

A hymn of thanksgiving to Jehovah, as the giver of victory to the Israelites.

For the leader of the music. A psalm of the sons of Korah.

1 O CLAP your hands, all ye nations!
Shout unto God with the voice of triumph!
2 For terrible is Jehovah, the Most High,
The great king over all the earth.
3 He hath subdued nations under us,
And kingdoms under our feet;
4 He hath chosen for us an inheritance,
The glory of Jacob, whom he loved. [Pause.]
5 God goeth up with a shout;
Jehovah with the sound of the trumpet.
6 Sing praises to God, sing praises!
Sing praises to our king, sing praises!
7 For God is king of all the earth;
Sing to him hymns of praise!
8 God reigneth over the nations;
God sitteth upon his holy throne.

9 The princes of the nations gather themselves together
To the people of the God of Abraham;
For the mighty of the earth belong to God;
He is supremely exalted.

PSALM XLVIII.

A hymn of thanksgiving for the deliverance of Jerusalem from invading enemies.

A psalm of the sons of Korah.

1 GREAT is Jehovah, and greatly to be praised
In the city of our God, upon his holy mountain.
2 Beautiful in its elevation is Mount Zion,
The joy of the whole earth;
The joy of the farthest North is the city of the great king;
3 In her palaces God is known as a refuge.
4 For, lo! kings were assembled against it;
They passed away together.
5 As soon as they saw, they were astonished;
They were confounded, and hasted away.
6 There terror seized upon them,—
Pain, as of a woman in travail;
7 As when the east wind breaketh in pieces
The ships of Tarshish.
8 As we have heard, so have we seen
In the city of the LORD of hosts, in the city of our God;
God will establish it for ever. [Pause.]
9 We think of thy loving-kindness, O God!
In the midst of thy temple!
10 As thy name, O God! so thy praise, extendeth to the ends of the earth;
Thy right hand is full of righteousness.
11 Mount Zion rejoiceth,
The daughters of Judah exult,
On account of thy righteous judgments.
12 Go round about Zion; number her towers;
13 Mark well her bulwarks; count her palaces;
That ye may tell it to the next generation!
14 For this God is our God for ever and ever;
He will be our guide unto death.

PSALM XLIX.

The condition of the righteous and the wicked. The rich oppressor not to be envied. The comfort of the righteous, when they are oppressed, in the consideration that God is their friend.

For the leader of the music. A psalm of the sons of Korah.

1 Hear this, all ye nations;
Give ear, all ye inhabitants of the world;
2 Both high and low, rich and poor alike!
3 My mouth shall speak wisdom,
And the meditation of my mind shall be understanding.
4 I will incline mine ear to a poem;
I will utter my song upon the harp.
5 Why should I fear in the days of adversity,
When the iniquity of my adversaries encompasseth me;
6 They who trust in their riches,
And glory in the greatness of their wealth?
7 No one can redeem his brother from death,
Nor give a ransom for him to God,
8 That he should live to eternity,
And not see the pit.
9 Too costly is the redemption of his life,
And he giveth it up for ever.
10 For he seeth that wise men die,
As well as the foolish and the ignorant;
They perish alike,
And leave their wealth to others.
11 They imagine that their houses will endure for ever,
And their dwelling-places from generation to generation:
Men celebrate their names on the earth.
12 Yet man, who is in honor, abideth not;
He is like the beasts that perish.
13 Such is the way which is their confidence!
And they who come after them approve their maxims.
[Pause.]
14 Like sheep they are cast into the underworld;
Death shall feed upon them;
And the upright shall soon trample upon them.
Their form shall be consumed in the underworld,
And they shall no more have a dwelling-place.

15 But God will redeem my life from the underworld;
Yea, he will take me under his care. [Pause.]
16 Be not thou afraid, when one becometh rich;
When the glory of his house is increased!
17 For, when he dieth, he will carry nothing away;
His glory will not descend after him.
18 Though in his life he thought himself happy, —
Though men praised thee, while thou wast in prosperity, —
19 Yet shalt thou go to the dwelling-place of thy fathers,
Who never more shall see the light!
20 The man who is in honor, but without understanding,
Is like the beasts that perish.

PSALM L.

The true way of serving God; or, outward forms of no avail without internal rectitude.

A psalm of Asaph.

1 THE mighty God, Jehovah, speaketh, and calleth the earth,
From the rising of the sun to its going down.
2 Out of Zion, the perfection of beauty,
God shineth forth.
3 Our God cometh, and will not be silent;
Before him is a devouring fire,
And around him a raging tempest.
4 He calleth to the heavens on high,
And to the earth, while he judgeth his people:
5 "Gather together before me my godly ones,
Who have made a covenant with me by sacrifice!"
6 (And the heavens shall declare his righteousness,
For it is God himself that is judge.) [Pause.]
7 "Hear, O my people, and I will speak!
O Israel, and I will testify against thee!
For I am God, thine own God.
8 I reprove thee not on account of thy sacrifices;
For thy burnt-offerings are ever before me.
9 I will take no bullock from thy house,
Nor he-goat from thy folds;

10 For all the beasts of the forest are mine,
And the cattle on a thousand hills.
11 I know all the birds of the mountains,
And the wild beasts of the field are before me.
12 If I were hungry, I would not tell thee;
For the world is mine, and all that is therein.
13 Do I eat the flesh of bulls,
Or drink the blood of goats?
14 Offer to God thanksgiving,
And pay thy vows to the Most High!
15 Then call upon me in the day of trouble:
I will deliver thee, and thou shalt glorify me!"
16 And to the wicked God saith,
"To what purpose dost thou talk of my statutes?
And why hast thou my laws upon thy lips?—
17 Thou, who hatest instruction
And castest my words behind thee!
18 When thou seest a thief, thou art in friendship with him,
And hast fellowship with adulterers.
19 Thou lettest loose thy mouth to evil,
And thy tongue frameth deceit;
20 Thou sittest and speakest against thy brother;
Thou slanderest thine own mother's son.
21 These things hast thou done, and I kept silence,
Hence thou thoughtest that I was altogether like thyself:
But I will reprove thee, and set it in order before thine
eyes.
22 Mark this, ye that forget God,
Lest I tear you in pieces, and none deliver you!
23 Whoso offereth praise honoreth me;
And to him who hath regard to his ways
Will I show salvation from God."

PSALM LI.

A prayer for forgiveness of sins.

For the leader of the music. A psalm of David, when Nathan the prophet came unto him, after his intercourse with Bathsheba.

1 Be gracious unto me, O God! according to thy loving kindness;
According to the greatness of thy mercy, blot out my transgressions!
2 Wash me thoroughly from my iniquity,
And cleanse me from my sin!
3 For I acknowledge my transgressions,
And my sin is ever before me.
4 Against thee, thee only, have I sinned,
And in thy sight have I done evil;
So that thou art just in thy sentence,
And righteous in thy judgment.
5 Behold! I was born in iniquity,
And in sin did my mother conceive me.
6 Behold! thou desirest truth in the heart;
So teach me wisdom in my inmost soul!
7 Purge me with hyssop, until I be clean;
Wash me, until I be whiter than snow!
8 Make me to hear joy and gladness,
So that the bones which thou hast broken may rejoice!
9 Hide thy face from my sins,
And blot out all my iniquities!
10 Create within me a clean heart, O God!
Renew within me a steadfast spirit!
11 Cast me not away from thy presence,
And take not thy holy spirit from me!
12 Restore to me the joy of thy protection,
And strengthen me with a willing spirit!
13 Then will I teach thy ways to transgressors,
And sinners shall be converted to thee.
14 Deliver me from the guilt of blood, O God, the God of my salvation!
That my tongue may sing aloud of thy goodness!
15 O Lord! open thou my lips,
That my mouth may show forth thy praise!

16 For thou desirest not sacrifice, else would I give it;
Thou delightest not in burnt-offerings.
17 The sacrifice which God loveth is a broken spirit;
A broken and contrite heart, O God! thou wilt not despise!
18 Do good to Zion according to thy mercy;
Build up the walls of Jerusalem!
19 Then shalt thou be pleased with sacrifices of righteousness,
With burnt-offerings and complete offerings;
Then shall bullocks be offered upon thine altar.

PSALM LII.

Remonstrance against a proud and malignant enemy, and prediction of his downfall.

For the leader of the music. A psalm of David, when Doeg, the Edomite, came and told Saul, and said to him, David is come to the house of Abimelech.

1 Why gloriest thou in mischief, thou man of violence?
The goodness of God yet continueth daily.
2 Thy tongue deviseth mischief,
Like a sharp razor, thou contriver of deceit!
3 Thou lovest evil more than good,
And to lie more than to speak truth. [Pause.]
4 Thou lovest all devouring words,
O thou deceitful tongue!
5 Thee also shall God utterly destroy!
He shall seize thee, and tear thee from thy dwelling-place,
And uproot thee from the land of the living. [Pause.]
6 The righteous shall see and fear,
And shall laugh at him.
7 "Behold the man that made not God his strength,
But trusted in the abundance of his riches,
And placed his strength in his wickedness!"
8 But I shall be like a green olive-tree in the house of God;
I will trust in the goodness of God for ever and ever.
9 I will praise thee for ever for what thou hast done;
I will trust in thy name, because it is good,
Before the eyes of thy godly ones!

PSALM LIII.

Complaint of the wickedness of men; uttered, probably, by one living under severe oppression in a foreign land, whither he had been carried captive.

For the leader of the music. To be sung on wind instruments. A psalm of David.

1 THE fool saith in his heart, "There is no God!"
They are corrupt; their doings are abominable;
There is none that doeth good.
2 God looketh down from heaven upon the children of men,
To see if there are any that have understanding,
That have regard to God.
3 They are all gone astray; together are they corrupt;
There is none that doeth good, no, not one.
4 Shall not the evil-doers be requited,
Who eat up my people like bread,
And call not upon God?
5 Yea! fear shall come upon them,
Where no fear is;
For God will scatter the bones of him that encampeth against thee;
Thou shalt put them to shame, for God despiseth them!
6 O that salvation for Israel would come out of Zion!
When God bringeth back the captives of his people,
Jacob shall rejoice, and Israel be glad.

PSALM LIV.

A prayer against enemies.

For the leader of the music. To be sung on stringed instruments. A psalm of David, when the Ziphites came and said to Saul, Doth not David hide himself with us?

1 SAVE me, O God! by thy name,
And by thy strength defend my cause!
2 O God! hear my prayer,
Give ear to the words of my mouth!
3 For enemies have risen up against me,
And oppressors seek my life;
They have not set God before their eyes. [Pause.]

4 Behold! God is my helper;
The Lord is the support of my life.
5 He will repay evil to my enemies;
For thy truth's sake, O God! cut them off!
6 With a willing heart will I sacrifice to thee;
I will praise thy name, O LORD! for it is good;
7 For thou hast delivered me from all trouble,
So that my eye hath looked with joy upon my enemies!

PSALM LV.

A prayer against enemies, especially against a treacherous friend.

For the leader of the music. To be sung on stringed instruments. A psalm of David.

1 GIVE ear to my prayer, O God!
Hide not thyself from my supplication!
2 Attend unto me, and hear me!
I wander about mourning and wailing,
3 On account of the clamors of the enemy,
On account of the violence of the wicked.
For they bring evil upon me,
And in wrath set themselves against me.
4 My heart trembleth in my bosom,
And the terrors of death have fallen upon me.
5 Fear and trembling have seized me,
And horror hath overwhelmed me.
6 Then I say, O that I had wings like a dove!
For then would I fly away, and be at rest.
7 Behold, I would wander far away,
And take up my abode in a wilderness. [Pause.]
8 I would hasten away to a shelter
From the rushing wind and tempest.
9 Confound, O Lord! divide their counsels!
For I behold violence and strife in the city.
10 Day and night do these go about its walls;
In the midst of it are iniquity and mischief.
11 Wickedness is in the midst of it;
Oppression and fraud depart not from its streets.

12 It was not an enemy that reviled me,
Then I could have borne it;
Nor one that hated me, who rose up against me;
From him I could have hid myself.
13 But it was thou, a man my equal,
My friend, and my acquaintance.
14 We held sweet converse together,
And walked to the house of God in company.
15 May sudden death seize upon them!
May they go down to the underworld alive!
For wickedness is in their dwellings, in the midst of them.
16 As for me, I will call upon God,
And Jehovah will save me.
17 At evening, at morn, and at noon I mourn and sigh,
And he will hear my voice.
18 He will deliver me in peace from my conflict;
For many have risen up against me.
19 God will hear me, and bring them down, —
He that hath been judge of old. [Pause.]
Because they have no changes,
Therefore they fear not God.
20 They lift up their hands against their friend,
And break their covenant with him.
21 Their speech was softer than butter,
But war was in their heart;
Their words were smoother than oil,
Yet were they drawn swords.
22 "Cast thy burden upon the LORD, and he will sustain thee;
He will never suffer the righteous to fall!"
23 Yea, thou, O God! wilt bring them down into the lowest pit!
Bloody and deceitful men shall not live out half their days.
But I will trust in thee!

PSALM LVI.

A prayer for help by one surrounded by enemies.

For the leader of the music. To be sung to the tune of "The dumb dove among strangers." A psalm of David, when the Philistines took him in Gath.

1 HAVE pity upon me, O God! for man panteth for my life;
My adversary daily oppresseth me!
2 Mine enemies daily pant for my life,
And many are they who war proudly against me.
3 When I am in fear,
I will put my trust in thee!
4 Through God shall I praise his word;
In God do I put my trust; I will not fear;
What can flesh do to me?
5 Every day they wrest my words;
All their thoughts are against me for evil.
6 They gather themselves together, they hide themselves, they watch my steps,
Lying in wait for my life.
7 Shall they escape by their iniquity?
In thine anger cast down the people, O God!
8 Count thou my wanderings;
Put my tears into thy bottle!
Are they not recorded in thy book?
9 When I cry to thee, my enemies shall turn back;
This I know, that God is for me.
10 Through God shall I praise his word;
I shall glory in the promise of Jehovah.
11 In God do I put my trust; I will not fear:
What can man do to me?
12 Thy vows are upon me, O God!
I will render praises to thee!
13 For thou hast delivered me from death,
Yea, my feet from falling,
That I may walk before God in the light of the living.

PSALM LVII.

For the leader of the music. To be sung to the tune of "Do not destroy." A psalm of David, when he fled from Saul in the cave.

1 Have pity upon me, O God! have pity upon me,
For in thee doth my soul seek refuge!
Yea, in the shadow of thy wings do I take shelter,
Until these calamities be overpast!
2 I call upon God the Most High,
Upon God, who performeth all things for me;
3 He will send from heaven, and save me;
He will put to shame him that panteth for my life; [Pause.]
God will send forth his mercy and his truth.
4 My life is in the midst of lions;
I dwell among them that breathe out fire;
Among men whose teeth are spears and arrows,
And whose tongue is a sharp sword.
5 Exalt thyself, O God! above the heavens,
And thy glory above all the earth!
6 They have prepared a net for my steps;
My soul is bowed down;
They have digged a pit before me,
But into it they have themselves fallen.
7 My heart is strengthened, O God! my heart is strengthened!
I will sing, and give thanks.
8 Awake, my soul! awake, psaltery and harp!
I will wake with the early dawn.
9 I will praise thee, O Lord! among the nations;
I will sing to thee among the kingdoms!
10 For thy mercy reacheth to the heavens,
And thy truth to the clouds!
11 Exalt thyself, O God! above the heavens,
And thy glory above all the earth!

PSALM LVIII.

An invective against wicked rulers. Prayers and hopes for their destruction.

For the leader of the music. To the tune of "Do not destroy." A psalm of David.

1 Do ye, indeed, administer justice faithfully, ye mighty ones?
Do ye judge with uprightness, ye sons of men?
2 Nay, in your hearts ye contrive iniquity;
Your hands weigh out violence in the land!
3 The wicked are estranged, from their very birth;
The liars go astray as soon as they are born.
4 They have poison, like the poison of a serpent;
Like the deaf adder's, which stoppeth her ear;
5 Which listeneth not to the voice of the charmer,
And of the sorcerer, skilful in incantations.
6 Break their teeth, O God! in their mouths!
Break out the great teeth of the lions, O Lord!
7 May they melt like waters, which flow away;
May their arrows, when they aim them, be as if cut in pieces!
8 May they be like the snail, which melteth away as it goeth;
Like the abortion of a woman, that seeth not the sun!
9 Before your pots feel the heat of the thorns,
Whether fresh, or burning, may they be blown away!
10 The righteous shall rejoice, when he seeth such vengeance;
He shall bathe his feet in the blood of the wicked.
11 Then shall men say, "Truly there is a reward for the righteous!
Truly there is a God who is judge upon the earth!"

PSALM LIX.

The contents of this psalm seem much better suited to a case of invasion from heathen enemies, than to the case referred to in the Hebrew inscription. See ver. 5.

For the leader of the music. To the tune of "Do not destroy." A psalm of David, when Saul sent, and they watched the house to kill him.

1 DELIVER me from my enemies, O my God!
Defend me from them that rise up against me!
2 Deliver me from the doers of iniquity,
And save me from men of blood!
3 For, lo! they lie in wait for my life;
The mighty are gathered against me,
Without any offence or fault of mine, O LORD!
4 Without any offence of mine, they run and prepare themselves;
Awake to help me, and behold!
5 Do thou, O Jehovah, God of hosts, God of Israel,
Awake to punish all the nations!
Show no mercy to any wicked transgressors! [Pause.]
6 Let them return at evening,
Let them howl like dogs,
And go round about the city!
7 Behold! with their mouths they belch out malice;
Swords are upon their lips;
"For who," say they, "will hear?"
8 Yet thou, O LORD! wilt laugh at them;
Thou wilt hold all the nations in derision!
9 O my Strength! to thee will I look!
For God is my defence;
10 My God will come to meet me with his mercy;
God will cause me to look with joy upon my enemies.
11 Slay them not, lest my people forget;
Scatter them by thy power, and cast them down,
O Lord, our shield!
12 The word of their lips is the sin of their mouth;
Let them be overtaken in their pride,
For the curses and the falsehood which they utter!

13 Consume them in thy wrath; consume them that they be no more,
That they may know that God ruleth in Jacob,
Even to the ends of the earth! [Pause.]
14 Let them return at evening,
Let them howl like dogs,
And go round about the city!
15 Let them wander about for food,
When they have passed the night unsatisfied!
16 But I will sing of thy power;
Yea, in the morning will I sing aloud of thy mercy;
For thou hast been my defence,
My refuge in the day of my distress.
17 To thee, O my Strength! will I sing!
For God is my defence; a God of mercy to me.

PSALM LX.

Prayer for success, and hopes of victory and conquest in a very disastrous state of public affairs.

For the leader of the music; upon the Shushan-Eduth; a psalm of David for instruction; when he was at strife with the Syrians of Mesopotamia, and the Syrians of Zoba; when Joab returned, and smote twelve thousand Edomites in the valley of Salt.

1 O God! thou hast forsaken us; thou hast broken us in pieces;
Thou hast been angry! O revive us again!
2 Thou hast made the land tremble; thou hast rent it;
O heal its breaches, for it tottereth!
3 Thou hast caused thy people to see hard things;
Thou hast made us drink the wine of reeling.
4 Lift up a banner for them that fear thee,
For the sake of thy faithfulness, that they may escape!
5 That thy beloved may be delivered,
Save with thy right hand, and answer me!
6 God promiseth in his holiness; I will rejoice;
I shall yet divide Shechem,
And measure out the valley of Succoth.

7 Gilead shall be mine, and mine Manasseh;
Ephraim shall be my helmet,
And Judah my sceptre;
8 Moab shall be my wash-bowl;
Upon Edom shall I cast my shoe;
I shall triumph over Philistia!
9 Who will bring me to the strong city?
Who will lead me into Edom?
10 Wilt not thou, O God! who didst forsake us,
And didst not go forth with our armies?
11 Give us thine aid in our distress,
For vain is the help of man!
12 Through God we shall do valiantly;
For he will tread down our enemies.

PSALM LXI.

A prayer of an exile for help, for restoration to his native land, and for the health and prosperity of the king.

For the leader of the music. To be sung upon stringed instruments. A psalm of David.

1 HEAR my cry, O God!
Attend to my prayer!
2 From the extremity of the land I cry unto thee in deep sorrow of heart;
Lead me to the rock that is high above me!
3 For thou art my refuge,
My strong tower against the enemy.
4 I shall dwell in thy tabernacle for ever;
I will seek refuge under the covert of thy wings.
5 For thou, O God! wilt hear my vows,
And give me the inheritance of those who fear thy name.
6 O prolong the life of the king!
May his years extend through many generations!
7 May he reign for ever before God!
Grant that mercy and truth may preserve him!
8 So will I sing praise to thy name for ever;
I will daily perform my vows.

PSALM LXII.

Trust in God in circumstances of distress.

For the leader of the music of the Jeduthunites. A psalm of David.

1 TRULY my soul resteth on God alone;
From him cometh my deliverance!
2 He alone is my rock and my salvation;
He is my safeguard, I shall not wholly fall!
3 How long will ye continue to assault a single man?
How long will ye all seek to destroy me,
Like a bending wall, or a tottering fence?
4 They study how to cast me down from my eminence;
They delight in falsehood;
They bless with their mouths, but in their hearts they curse.
5 My soul, rest thou on God alone,
For from him cometh my hope!
6 He alone is my rock and my salvation;
He is my safeguard,—I shall not fall.
7 From God cometh my help and my glory:
My strong rock, my refuge, is God.
8 Trust in him at all times, ye people!
Pour out your hearts before him!
God is our refuge!
9 Truly men of low degree are vanity,
And men of high degree are a lie;
Placed in the balance,
They are all lighter than vanity.
10 Trust not in extortion;
Place no vain hopes in rapine!
If riches increase, set not your heart upon them!
11 Once hath God promised, twice have I heard it,
That power belongeth unto God.
12 To thee also, O Lord! belongeth mercy;
For thou dost render to every man according to his work!

PSALM LXIII.

Aspirations after God, and confidence in his protection. Supposed to have reference to the circumstances of David during the rebellion of Absalom.

A psalm of David, when he was in the wilderness of Judah.

1 O God! thou art my God! earnestly do I seek thee!
My soul thirsteth, my flesh longeth for thee,
In a dry, thirsty land, where is no water!
2 Thus I look toward thee in thy sanctuary,
To behold thy power and thy glory!
3 For thy loving-kindness is better than life;
Therefore my lips shall praise thee!
4 Thus will I bless thee, while I live;
In thy name will I lift up my hands!
5 My soul shall be satisfied as with marrow and fatness,
And with joyful lips my mouth shall praise thee,
6 When I think of thee upon my bed,
And meditate on thee in the night-watches.
7 For thou art my help,
And in the shadow of thy wings I rejoice.
8 My soul cleaveth to thee;
Thy right hand holdeth me up.
9 While they who seek to destroy my life
Shall themselves go down into the depths of the earth.
10 They shall be given up to the sword,
And be a portion for jackals.
11 But the king shall rejoice in God;
All that swear by him shall be honored;
But the mouth of liars shall be stopped.

PSALM LXIV.

Prayer for protection from enemies. Supposed to refer to David's calumniators in the court of Saul, or during the rebellion of Absalom.

For the leader of the music. A psalm of David.

1 HEAR my voice, O God! when I pray!
Preserve my life from the terrors of the enemy!
2 Hide me from the assembly of the wicked,—
From the brawling crowd of evil-doers!
3 For like a sword they sharpen their tongues,
Like arrows they aim their poisoned words,
4 To shoot in secret at the upright;
Suddenly do they shoot at him without fear.
5 They prepare themselves for an evil deed;
They commune of laying secret snares:
"Who," say they, "will see them?"
6 They meditate crimes: "We have finished," say they, "our plans!"
The heart and bosom of every one of them are deep.
7 But God will shoot an arrow at them;
Suddenly shall they be wounded.
8 Thus their own tongues shall bring them down;
All who see them will flee away.
9 Then will all men stand in awe,
And declare what God hath done,
And attentively consider his work.
10 The righteous shall rejoice, and trust in the LORD;
All the upright in heart shall glory.

PSALM LXV.

Trust in the power and goodness of God.

For the leader of the music. A psalm of David.

1 To thee belongeth trust, to thee praise, O God in Zion!
And to thee shall the vow be performed!
2 O Thou that hearest prayer!
To thee shall all flesh come!

3 My iniquities are heavy upon me;
But thou wilt forgive our transgressions!
4 Happy is he whom thou choosest,
And bringest near thee to dwell in thy courts!
May we be satisfied with the blessings of thy house,
Thy holy temple!
5 By wonderful deeds dost thou answer us in thy goodness,
O God, our salvation!
Who art the confidence of all the ends of the earth,
And of the most distant seas!
6 Thou makest fast the mountains by thy power,
Being girded with strength!
7 Thou stillest the roar of the sea,
The roar of its waves,
And the tumult of the nations.
8 They who dwell in the ends of the earth are awed by thy signs;
Thou makest the outgoings of the morning and of the evening to rejoice!
9 Thou visitest the earth and waterest it;
Thou enrichest it exceedingly;
The river of God is full of water.
Thou suppliest the earth with corn,
When thou hast thus prepared it.
10 Thou waterest its furrows,
And breakest down its ridges;
Thou makest it soft with showers,
And blessest its increase.
11 Thou crownest the year with thy goodness;
Thy footsteps drop fruitfulness;
12 They drop it upon the pastures of the wilderness,
And the hills are girded with gladness.
13 The pastures are clothed with flocks,
And the valleys are covered with corn;
They shout, yea, they sing for joy.

PSALM LXVI.

Thanksgiving to God after deliverance from great distress.

For the leader of the music. A psalm.

1 SHOUT joyfully unto God, all ye lands!
2 Sing ye the honor of his name;
Make his praise glorious!
3 Say unto God, How terrible are thy doings!
Through the greatness of thy power thine enemies are suppliants to thee!
4 Let all the earth worship thee;
Let it sing praise to thee, let it sing praise to thy name! [Pause.]
5 Come, behold the works of God!
How terrible his doings among the sons of men!
6 He turned the sea into dry land;
They went through the deep on foot;
Then we rejoiced in him.
7 By his power he ruleth for ever;
His eyes are fixed upon the nations;
Let not the rebellious exalt themselves! [Pause.]
8 O bless our God, ye nations,
And make the voice of his praise to be heard!
9 It is he who preserveth our lives,
And suffereth not our feet to stumble.
10 Thou hast, indeed, proved us, O God!
Thou hast tried us as silver is tried.
11 Thou broughtest us into a snare,
And didst lay a heavy burden upon our backs;
12 Thou didst cause men to ride upon our heads,
And we have gone through fire and water:
But thou hast brought us to a place of abundance.
13 I will go into thy house with burnt-offerings;
I will pay thee my vows, —
14 The vows which my lips uttered,
Which my mouth promised in my trouble.
15 Burnt sacrifices of fatlings will I offer to thee with the fat of rams;
Bullocks, with he-goats, will I sacrifice to thee. [Pause.]

16 Come and hear, all ye who fear God,
And I will relate what he hath done for me!
17 I called upon him with my mouth,
And praise is now upon my tongue.
18 If I had meditated wickedness in my heart,
The Lord would not have heard me:
19 But surely God hath heard me;
He hath had regard to the voice of my supplication.
20 Blessed be God, who did not reject my prayer,
Nor withhold his mercy from me!

PSALM LXVII.

A hymn of praise.

For the leader of the music. To be sung on stringed instruments. A psalm.

1 O GOD! be merciful to us, and bless us,
And cause thy face to shine upon us! [Pause.]
2 That thy doings may be known on earth,
And thy saving power to all the nations.
3 Let the nations praise thee, O God!
Yea, let all the nations praise thee!
4 Let all the nations be glad, and shout for joy!
For justly dost thou judge the people,
And govern the nations on the earth.
5 Let the nations praise thee, O God!
Yea, let all the nations praise thee!
6 For the earth hath yielded her increase,
And God, our God, hath blessed us.
7 May God continue to bless us,
And may all the ends of the earth fear him!

PSALM LXVIII.

A triumphal ode, on the occasion of the removal of the ark to Mount Zion.

For the leader of the music. A psalm of David.

1 Let God arise, and his enemies are scattered,
And they who hate him flee before him!
2 As smoke is dispersed, so thou dispersest them;
As wax melteth before the fire,
So perish the wicked before the face of God.
3 But the righteous are glad and rejoice in his presence,
Yea, they exult exceedingly.
4 Sing unto God; sing praises to his name!
Prepare a way for him who rideth through the desert!
Jehovah is his name; be joyful in his presence!
5 The father of the fatherless, and the protector of the widow,
Is God in his holy habitation.
6 God causeth the forsaken to dwell in houses;
He leadeth forth to prosperity them that are bound;
But the rebellious shall dwell in a barren land.
7 O God! when thou didst go before thy people,
When thou didst march through the wilderness, [Pause.]
8 The earth quaked, and the heavens dropped at the presence of God;
This Sinai trembled at the presence of God, the God of Israel.
9 Thou, O God! didst send a plentiful rain;
Thou didst strengthen thy wearied inheritance.
10 Thy people established themselves in the land;
Thou, O God! in thy goodness, didst prepare it for the needy!
11 The Lord gave the song of victory
Of the maidens publishing glad tidings to the mighty host.
12 "The kings with their armies have fled, — have fled!
And the matron at home divideth the spoil.
13 Truly ye may repose yourselves in the stalls,
Like the wings of a dove covered with silver,
And her feathers with shining gold."

14 When the Most High destroyed the kings in the land,
It was white [with their bones] like Salmon.
15 Ye lofty hills, ye hills of Bashan,
Ye many-topped hills, ye hills of Bashan,
16 Why frown ye, ye many-topped hills,
At the hill in which God is pleased to dwell,
In which Jehovah will dwell for ever?
17 The chariots of God are myriads, yea, thousands of thousands;
The Lord is in the midst of them, as upon Sinai, in the sanctuary.
18 Thou hast ascended on high,
Thou hast led captive the vanquished,
Thou hast received gifts among men,
Even the rebellious, that here thou mightst dwell, O LORD God!
19 Praised be the Lord daily!
When we are heavy-laden, the Mighty One is our help.
20 Our God is a God of salvation;
From the Lord Jehovah cometh deliverance from death.
21 But God smiteth the head of his enemies,
Even the hairy crowns of those who go on in their iniquity.
22 "I will bring them back," saith the Lord, "from Bashan;
I will bring them back from the deep sea;
23 That thy foot may be dipped in their blood,
That thy dogs may drink the blood of thine enemies."
24 We have seen thy procession, O God!
The procession of my God, my king, to his sanctuary!
25 The singers go before, the minstrels follow,
Amidst damsels playing on timbrels.
26 Praise ye God in your assemblies;
Praise the Lord, all ye from the fountain of Israel!
27 Here is Benjamin, the youngest, and his leaders;
The chiefs of Judah, and their band;
The chiefs of Zebulon, and the chiefs of Naphtali.
28 Thy God has ordained thy strength, [O Israel!]
Show forth thy might, O God! thou who hast wrought for us!
29 Because of thy temple in Jerusalem
Shall kings bring presents to thee.

30 Rebuke the wild beast of the reeds,
The multitude of bulls with the calves of the nations,
So that they shall cast themselves down with masses of silver;
Scatter thou the nations that delight in war!
31 Princes shall come out of Egypt;
Ethiopia shall haste with outstretched hands to God.
32 Ye kingdoms of the earth, sing unto God;
Sing praises to Jehovah;
33 To him who rideth upon the ancient heaven of heavens!
Behold, he uttereth his voice, his mighty voice!
34 Give glory to God,
Whose majesty is in Israel, and whose might is in the clouds!
35 Terrible art thou, O God! from thy sanctuary!
The God of Israel giveth strength and power to his people.
Praised be God!

PSALM LXIX.

Prayer for aid against enemies. Hope of deliverance, and of return from exile.

For the leader of the music. Upon the Shoshannim. A psalm of David.

1 SAVE me, O God!
For the waters press in to my very life!
2 I sink in deep mire, where is no standing;
I have come into deep waters, and the waves flow over me.
3 I am weary with crying; my throat is parched;
Mine eyes are wasted, while I wait for my God.
4 More numerous than the hairs of my head are they who hate me without reason;
Mighty are they who seek to destroy me, being my enemies without cause:
I must restore what I took not away.
5 O God! thou knowest my offences,
And my sins are not hidden from thee!
6 Let not them that trust in thee through me be put to shame,
O Lord Jehovah, God of hosts!
Let not them that seek thee through me be confounded,
O God of Israel!

7 For on account of thee do I suffer reproach,
And shame covereth my face!
8 I am become a stranger to my brothers;
Yea, an alien to my mother's sons.
9 For zeal for thy house consumeth me,
And the reproaches of them that reproach thee fall upon me.
10 When I weep and fast,
That is made my reproach;
11 When I clothe myself in sackcloth,
Then I become their by-word.
12 They who sit in the gate speak against me,
And I am become the song of drunkards.
13 Yet will I address my prayer to thee, O LORD!
May it be in an acceptable time according to thy great goodness!
Hear, O God! and afford me thy sure help!
14 Save me from the mire, and let me not sink;
May I be delivered from my enemies, — from the deep waters!
15 Let not the water-flood overflow me;
Let not the deep swallow me up,
And let not the pit close her mouth upon me!
16 Hear me, O LORD! since great is thy loving-kindness;
According to the abundance of thy tender mercies look upon me!
17 Hide not thy face from thy servant;
I am greatly distressed, O make haste to mine aid!
18 Draw near to me, and redeem my life;
Deliver me because of my enemies!
19 Thou knowest my reproach, and dishonor, and shame;
All my adversaries are in thy view!
20 Reproach hath broken my heart, and I am full of heaviness;
I look for pity, but there is none;
For comforters, but find none.
21 For my food they give me gall,
And in my thirst they give me vinegar to drink.
22 May their table be to them a snare;
May it be a trap to them, while they are at ease!
23 May their eyes be darkened, that they may not see;
And cause their loins continually to shake!

24 Pour out upon them thine indignation,
And may the heat of thine anger overtake them!
25 Let their habitation be desolate,
And let none dwell in their tents!
26 For they persecute those whom thou hast smitten,
And talk of the pain of those whom thou hast wounded.
27 Add iniquity to their iniquity,
And let them never come into thy favor!
28 Let them be blotted out of the book of the living;
Let not their names be written with the righteous!
29 But I am poor, and sorrowful:
May thine aid, O God! set me on high!
30 Then I will praise the name of God in a song;
I will give glory to him with thanksgiving.
31 More pleasing shall this be to the LORD
Than a full-horned and full-hoofed bullock.
32 The afflicted shall see, and rejoice;
The hearts of them that fear God shall be revived.
33 For the LORD heareth the poor,
And despiseth not his people in their bonds.
34 Let the heaven and the earth praise him;
The sea, and all that move therein!
35 For God will save Zion, and will build the cities of Judah,
That they may dwell therein, and possess it.
36 Yea, the posterity of his servants shall possess it,
And they that love him shall dwell therein.

PSALM LXX.

This psalm is a repetition of the last five verses of the fortieth psalm, with some slight variations.

For the leader of the music. A psalm of David, for remembrance.

1 MAKE haste, O God! to deliver me,
O LORD! come speedily to mine aid!
2 May they all be confounded, and covered with shame,
Who seek to take my life!
May they be driven back with disgrace
Who desire to do me injury!

3 May they be turned back with shame
Who cry out to me, "Aha! aha!"
4 But let all who seek thee be glad and rejoice in thee!
Let them that love thy protection ever say,
"May God be praised!"
5 But I am poor and needy;
O God! hasten to mine aid!
Thou art my help and my deliverer,
O LORD! make no delay!

PSALM LXXI.

Prayer for assistance against enemies, and hope of deliverance. Commonly supposed to have been composed by David in his old age, during the rebellion of Absalom.

1 IN thee, O LORD! do I put my trust!
Let me never be put to shame!
2 In thy goodness deliver and rescue me;
Incline thine ear to me, and save me!
3 Be thou the rock of my abode, where I may continually resort!
Thou hast granted me deliverance;
For thou art my rock and my fortress!
4 Save me, O my God! from the hand of the wicked,—
From the hand of the unjust and cruel!
5 For thou art my hope, O Lord Jehovah!
Thou hast been my trust from my youth!
6 Upon thee have I leaned from my birth;
From my earliest breath thou hast been my support;
My song hath been continually of thee!
7 I am a wonder to many,
But thou art my strong refuge.
8 Let my mouth be filled with thy praise;
Yea, all the day long, with thy glory.
9 Cast me not off in mine old age;
Forsake me not, when my strength faileth!
10 For my enemies speak against me,
And they who lay wait for my life consult together:
11 "God," say they, "hath forsaken him;
Pursue and seize him; for he hath none to deliver him!"

12 O God! be not far from me!
Come speedily to mine aid, O my God!
13 Let them perish with shame who are my enemies;
Let them be covered with contempt and dishonor who seek my hurt!
14 But I will hope continually;
I shall yet praise thee more and more.
15 My mouth shall speak of thy goodness,—
Of thy sure protection all the day long;
For thy mercies are more than I can number.
16 I will celebrate thy mighty deeds, O Lord Jehovah!
I will make mention of thy goodness, of thine only!
17 O God! thou hast taught me from my youth,
And thus far have I declared thy wondrous deeds;
18 And now, when I am old and gray-headed,
O God! forsake me not,
Until I make known thine arm to the next generation,—
Thy mighty power to all that are to come!
19 For thy goodness, O God! reacheth to the heavens;
Wonderful things doest thou!
O God! who is like unto thee?
20 Thou hast suffered us to see great and grievous troubles;
Thou wilt again give us life,
And wilt bring us back from the depths of the earth!
21 Thou wilt increase my greatness;
Thou wilt again comfort me!
22 Then will I praise thee with the psaltery;
Even thy faithfulness, O my God!
To thee will I sing with the harp,
O Holy One of Israel!
23 My lips shall rejoice, when I sing to thee;
And my soul, which thou hast redeemed from death;
24 My tongue also shall continually speak of thy righteousness:
For all who seek my hurt are brought to shame and confounded.

PSALM LXXII.

Prayer for a righteous and prosperous reign for a king. The Hebrew title of this psalm is ambiguous, admitting of the translation *Of* or *For* Solomon. It is, perhaps, most probable that it was prefixed by some one who supposed Solomon to be the subject, rather than the author, of the psalm.

For Solomon.

1 To the king, O God! give thy justice,
And to the son of a king thy righteousness!
2 Yea! he shall judge thy people with equity,
And thine oppressed ones with justice.
3 For the mountains shall bring forth peace to the people,
And the hills, through righteousness.
4 He shall defend the oppressed of the people;
He shall save the needy,
And break in pieces the oppressor.
5 They shall fear thee as long as the sun and moon shall endure,
From generation to generation.
6 He shall be like rain descending on the mown field, —
Like showers which water the earth.
7 In his days shall the righteous flourish,
And great shall be their prosperity, as long as the moon shall endure.
8 He shall have dominion from sea to sea,
And from the river to the ends of the earth.
9 They that dwell in the desert shall bow before him,
And his enemies shall lick the dust.
10 The kings of Tarshish and of the isles shall bring presents;
The kings of Sheba and Seba shall offer gifts;
11 Yea, all kings shall fall down before him;
All nations shall serve him.
12 For he shall deliver the poor who crieth for aid,
And the oppressed who hath no helper.
13 He shall spare the weak and needy,
And save the lives of the poor.
14 He shall redeem them from deceit and violence,
And their blood shall be precious in his sight.

15 He shall prosper, and to him shall be given of the gold of Sheba;
Prayer also shall be made for him continually,
And daily shall he be praised.
16 There shall be an abundance of corn in the land;
Its fruit shall shake like Lebanon, even on the tops of the mountains;
And they of the cities shall flourish as the grass of the earth.
17 His name shall endure for ever;
His name shall be continued as long as the sun.
By him shall men bless themselves;
All nations shall call him blessed.

18 *Praised be God, Jehovah, the God of Israel,*
Who alone doeth wonderful things!
19 *Praised be his glorious name for ever!*
May his glory fill the whole earth! Amen, Amen!

20 *Here end the psalms of David, the son of Jesse.*

BOOK III.

PSALM LXXIII.

A meditation on the ways of Providence in the distribution of happiness and misery, or in appointing the condition of the wicked and of the righteous. The subject is similar to that of Ps. xxxvii., xxxix., and xlix., and of the book of Job.

A psalm of Asaph.

1 TRULY God is good to Israel, —
To those who are pure in heart.
2 Yet my feet almost gave way;
My steps had well nigh slipped:
3 For I was envious of the proud,
When I saw the prosperity of the wicked.
4 For they have no pains even to their death;
Their bodies are in full health.
5 They have not the woes of other men,
Neither are they smitten like other men.
6 Therefore pride encircleth their neck as a collar;
Violence covereth them as a garment.
7 From their bosom issueth their iniquity;
The designs of their hearts burst forth.
8 They mock, and speak of malicious oppression;
Their words are haughty;
9 They stretch forth their mouth to the heavens,
And their tongue goeth through the earth;
10 Therefore his people walk in their ways,
And there drink from full fountains.
11 And they say, "How doth God know?
How can there be knowledge with the Most High?"
12 Behold these are the ungodly!
Yet they are ever prosperous; they heap up riches.

13 Verily I have cleansed my heart in vain;
In vain have I washed my hands in innocence.
14 For every day have I been smitten;
Every morn have I been chastened.
15 If I should resolve to speak like them,
Surely I should be treacherous to the family of thy children.
16 So, when I studied to know this,
It was painful to my eyes;
17 Until I went into the sanctuaries of God,
And considered what was their end.
18 Behold! thou hast set them on slippery places;
Thou castest them down into unseen pits.
19 How are they brought to desolation in a moment,
And utterly consumed with sudden destruction!
20 As a dream when one awaketh,
Thou, O Lord! when thou awakest, wilt make their vain show a derision.
21 When my heart was vexed
And I was pierced in my reins,
22 Then was I stupid and without understanding;
I was like one of the brutes before thee.
23 Yet am I ever under thy care;
By my right hand thou dost hold me up.
24 Thou wilt guide me with thy counsel,
And at last receive me in glory.
25 Whom have I in heaven but thee,
And whom on earth do I love in comparison with thee?
26 Though my flesh and my heart fail,
God is the strength of my heart, and my portion for ever.
27 For, lo! they who are far from thee perish;
Thou destroyest all who estrange themselves from thee.
28 But it is good for me to draw near to God;
I put my trust in the Lord Jehovah,
That I may declare all thy works.

PSALM LXXIV.

Prayer on account of the desolation of the temple, and other grievous afflictions of the Hebrew nation.

A psalm of Asaph.

1 O God! why hast thou cast us off for ever?
Why doth thine anger smoke against the flock of thy pasture?
2 Remember the people which thou didst purchase of old;
Thine own inheritance, which thou didst redeem;
That Mount Zion, where thou once didst dwell!
3 Hasten thy steps to those utter desolations!
Every thing in the sanctuary hath the enemy abused!
4 Thine enemies roar in the place of thine assemblies;
Their own symbols have they set up for signs.
5 They appear like those who raise the axe against a thicket;
6 They have broken down the carved work of thy temple with axes and hammers;
7 They have cast fire into thy sanctuary;
They have profaned, and cast to the ground, the dwelling-place of thy name.
8 They said in their hearts, "Let us destroy them all together!"
They have burned all God's places of assembly in the land.
9 We no longer see our signs;
There is no prophet among us,
Nor any one that knoweth how long this desolation shall endure.
10 How long, O God! shall the adversary revile?
Shall the enemy blaspheme thy name for ever?
11 Why withdrawest thou thy hand, even thy right hand?
Take it from thy bosom, and destroy!
12 Yet God was our king of old,
Working salvation in the midst of the earth.
13 Thou didst divide the sea by thy power;
Thou didst crush the heads of the sea-monsters in the waters.
14 Thou didst break in pieces the head of the crocodile;
Thou gavest him for food to the inhabitants of the desert.

15 Thou didst cleave forth the fountain and the stream;
Thou didst dry up perennial rivers.
16 Thine is the day, and thine the night;
Thou didst prepare the light and the sun.
17 Thou didst establish all the boundaries of the earth;
Thou didst make summer and winter.
18 O remember that the enemy hath reviled Jehovah;
That an impious people hath blasphemed thy name!
19 Give not up the life of thy turtle-dove to the wild beast;
Forget not for ever thine afflicted people!
20 Have regard to thy covenant!
For all the dark places of the land are full of the abodes of cruelty.
21 O let not the afflicted go away ashamed!
Let the poor and needy praise thy name!
22 Arise, O God! maintain thy cause!
Remember how the impious revileth thee daily!
23 Forget not the clamor of thine adversaries, —
The noise of thine enemies, which continually increaseth!

PSALM LXXV.

Thanksgiving in view of deliverance from enemies. This psalm contains no indication of the time of its composition, except that it resembles those which were composed in the later ages of the kingdom.

For the leader of the music. To the tune of "Do not destroy." A psalm of Asaph.

1 We give thanks to thee, O God! we give thanks to thee, and near is thy name;
Men shall declare thy wondrous deeds!
2 "When I see my time,
Then will I judge with equity.
3 The earth trembleth, and all her inhabitants;
But I uphold her pillars."
4 I say to the proud, Behave not proudly!
To the wicked, Lift not up your horn!
5 Lift not up your horn on high,
And speak not with a stiff neck!

6 For promotion cometh neither from the east, nor from the
west, nor from the south;
7 But it is God that judgeth;
He putteth down one, and setteth up another.
8 For in the hand of the LORD there is a cup;
The wine is foaming and full of spices,
And of it he poureth out;
Even to the dregs shall all the wicked of the earth drink it.
9 Therefore I will extol him for ever;
I will sing praise to the God of Jacob.
10 "I will bring down all the power of the wicked;
But the righteous shall lift up their heads."

PSALM LXXVI.

Thanksgiving for victory over powerful enemies. This psalm probably belongs to the same age with the preceding.

For the leader of the music. Upon stringed instruments. A psalm of Asaph.

1 IN Judah is God known;
Great is his name in Israel.
2 In Jerusalem is his tabernacle,
And in Zion his dwelling-place.
3 There brake he the lightning of the bow,
The shield, the sword, and all the weapons of battle.
4 More glorious and excellent art thou
Than those mountains of robbers!
5 Spoiled are the stout-hearted;
They sank into their sleep;
The hands of the mighty were powerless.
6 Before thy rebuke, O God of Jacob!
Fell chariot and horseman into a deep sleep!
7 Thou, thou, O God! art terrible!
Who can stand before thee in thine anger?
8 Thou didst cause judgment to be heard from heaven;
The earth trembled and was still,
9 When God arose to judgment,
To save all the oppressed of the earth!

10 The wrath of man shall praise thee,
When thou girdest on the whole of thy wrath!
11 Make and perform vows to Jehovah, your God!
Let all that dwell around him bring gifts to the terrible One,
12 Who casteth down the pride of princes,
Who is terrible to the kings of the earth!

PSALM LXXVII.

Prayer in a season of great public calamity. Consolation and hope derived from meditation upon former favors of God to the nation.

For the leader of the music of the Jeduthunites. A psalm of Asaph.

1 I CALL upon God; I cry aloud for help;
I call upon God, that he would hear me!
2 In the day of my trouble I seek the Lord;
In the night is my hand stretched forth continually;
My soul refuseth to be comforted.
3 I remember God, and am disquieted;
I think of him, and my spirit is overwhelmed.
4 Thou keepest mine eyelids from closing;
I am distressed, so that I cannot speak!
5 I think of the days of old, —
The years of ancient times.
6 I call to remembrance my songs in the night;
I meditate in my heart,
And my spirit inquireth:
7 Will the Lord be angry for ever?
Will he be favorable no more?
8 Is his mercy utterly withdrawn for ever?
Doth his promise fail from generation to generation?
9 Hath God forgotten to be gracious?
Hath he in anger shut up his compassion?
10 Then I say, "This is mine affliction,
A change in the right hand of the Most High."
11 I remember the deeds of Jehovah;
I think of thy wonders of old.
12 I meditate on all thy works,
And talk of thy doings.

13 Thy ways, O God! are holy!
Who so great a god as our God?
14 Thou art a God who doest wonders;
Thou hast manifested thy power among the nations.
15 With thy strong arm thou didst redeem thy people, —
The sons of Jacob and Joseph.
16 The waters saw thee, O God!
The waters saw thee, and feared,
And the deep trembled.
17 The clouds poured out water,
The skies sent forth thunder,
And thine arrows flew.
18 Thy thunder roared in the whirlwind;
Thy lightning illumined the world;
The earth trembled and shook.
19 Thy way was through the sea,
And thy path through great waters;
And thy footsteps could not be found.
20 Thou didst lead thy people like a flock,
By the hands of Moses and Aaron.

PSALM LXXVIII.

Admonition to keep God's commandments, drawn from his former dealings toward the nation of Israel.

A psalm of Asaph.

1 Give ear, O my people, to my instruction!
Incline your ears to the words of my mouth!
2 I will open my mouth in a psalm;
I will utter sayings of ancient times.
3 What we have heard and learned,
And our fathers have told us,
4 We will not hide from their children;
Showing to the generation to come the praises of Jehovah,
His might, and the wonders he hath wrought.
5 For he appointed statutes in Jacob,
And established a law in Israel,
Which he commanded our fathers
To make known to their children;

6 So that the generation to come might know them;
The children, which should be born, and rise up,
Who should declare them to their children;
7 That they might put their trust in God,
And not forget his deeds,
But keep his commandments;
8 And might not be, like their forefathers,
A stubborn and rebellious generation,—
A generation whose heart was not fixed upon God,
And whose spirit was not steadfast toward the Almighty.
9 The children of Ephraim were like armed bowmen,
Who turn their backs in the day of battle.
10 They kept not the covenant of God,
And refused to walk in his law;
11 And forgot his mighty deeds,
And the wonders he had shown them.
12 Marvellous things did he in the sight of their fathers,
In the land of Egypt, in the field of Zoan.
13 He divided the sea, and caused them to pass through;
Yea, he made the waters to stand as a heap.
14 By day he led them by a cloud,
And all the night by a light of fire.
15 He clave the rocks in the wilderness,
And gave them drink, as from the great deep.
16 From the rock he brought flowing streams,
And made water to run down like rivers.
17 Yet still they sinned against him,
And provoked the Most High in the desert.
18 They tempted God in their hearts,
By asking food for their delight.
19 Yea, they spake against God, and said,
"Can God spread a table in the wilderness?
20 Behold! he smote the rock, and the water flowed,
And streams gushed forth:
Is he also able to give bread?
Can he provide flesh for his people?"
21 When, therefore, the LORD heard this, he was wroth:
So a fire was kindled against Jacob,
And anger arose against Israel,
22 Because they believed not in God,
And trusted not in his aid.

23 Yet he had commanded the clouds above,
And had opened the doors of heaven;
24 And had rained down upon them manna for food,
And had given them the corn of heaven.
25 Every one ate the food of princes;
He sent them bread to the full.
26 Then he caused a strong wind to blow in the heavens,
And by his power he brought a south wind;
27 He rained down flesh upon them as dust,
And feathered fowls as the sand of the sea.
28 He caused them to fall in the midst of their camp,
Round about their habitations.
29 So they did eat, and were filled;
For he gave them their own desire.
30 Their desire was not yet satisfied,
And their meat was yet in their mouths,
31 When the wrath of God came upon them,
And slew their strong men,
And smote down the chosen men of Israel.
32 For all this they sinned still,
And put no trust in his wondrous works.
33 Therefore he consumed their days in vanity,
And their years in sudden destruction.
34 When he slew them, they sought him;
They returned, and sought earnestly for God;
35 And remembered that God was their rock,
And the Most High their redeemer.
36 But they only flattered him with their mouths,
And spake falsely to him with their tongues.
37 For their hearts were not true to him,
Nor were they steadfast in his covenant.
38 Yet, being full of compassion, he forgave their iniquity,
And would not utterly destroy them;
Often he restrained his indignation,
And stirred not up all his anger.
39 He remembered that they were but flesh, —
A breath, that passeth and cometh not back.
40 How often did they provoke him in the wilderness!
How often did they anger him in the desert!
41 Again and again they tempted God,
And offended the Holy One of Israel.

42 They remembered not his hand,
Nor the day when he delivered them from the enemy;
43 What signs he had wrought in Egypt,
And what wonders in the fields of Zoan.
44 He turned their rivers into blood,
So that they could not drink of their streams.
45 He sent amongst them flies, which devoured them,
And frogs, which destroyed them.
46 He gave also their fruits to the caterpillar,
And their labor to the locust.
47 He destroyed their vines with hail,
And their sycamore-trees with frost.
48 He also gave up their cattle to hail,
And their flocks to hot thunderbolts.
49 He sent against them the fierceness of his anger,
Wrath, indignation, and woe, —
A host of angels of evil.
50 He made a way for his anger,
He spared them not from death,
But gave up their lives to the pestilence.
51 He smote all the firstborn in Egypt;
The first-fruits of their strength in the tents of Ham.
52 But he led forth his own people like sheep,
And guided them like a flock in the wilderness.
53 He led them on safely, so that they feared not,
While the sea overwhelmed their enemies.
54 He brought them to his own sacred border,
Even to this mountain which his right hand had gained.
55 He cast out the nations before them, [ance,
And divided their land by a measuring-line, as an inherit-
And caused the tribes of Israel to dwell in their tents.
56 Yet they tempted and provoked God, the Most High,
And kept not his statutes;
57 Like their fathers they were faithless, and turned back;
They turned aside, like a deceitful bow.
58 They provoked his anger by their high places,
And stirred up his jealousy by their graven images.
59 God saw this, and was wroth,
And greatly abhorred Israel;
60 So that he forsook the habitation at Shiloh,
The tabernacle where he dwelt among men,

61 And delivered his strength into captivity,
And his glory into the hand of the enemy.
62 His own people he gave up to the sword,
And was wroth with his own inheritance.
63 Fire consumed their young men,
And their maidens did not bewail them.
64 Their priests fell by the sword,
And their widows made no lamentation.
65 But at length the Lord awaked as from sleep,
As a hero who had been overpowered by wine;
66 He smote his enemies, and drove them back,
And covered them with everlasting disgrace.
67 Yet he rejected the tents of Joseph,
And chose not the tribe of Ephraim;
68 But chose the tribe of Judah,
The Mount Zion which he loved;
69 Where he built, like the heavens, his sanctuary;
Like the earth, which he hath established for ever.
70 And he chose David, his servant,
And took him from the sheepfolds;
71 From tending the suckling ewes he brought him
To feed Jacob his people,
And Israel his inheritance.
72 He fed them with an upright heart,
And guided them with skilful hands.

PSALM LXXIX.

Lamentation for the desolation of the city and the temple.

A psalm of Asaph.

1 O God! the nations have come into thine inheritance;
They have polluted thy holy temple;
They have made Jerusalem a heap of ruins!
2 They have given the dead bodies of thy servants to be food for the birds of heaven,
The flesh of thy holy ones to the wild beasts of the earth!
3 Their blood have they shed like water around Jerusalem,
And there was none to bury them!

4 We have become the reproach of our neighbors, —
The scorn and derision of those around us.
5 How long, O LORD! wilt thou be angry for ever?
How long shall thy jealousy burn like fire?
6 Pour out thy wrath on the nations which acknowledge thee not,
And on the kingdoms which call not upon thy name!
7 For they have devoured Jacob,
And laid waste his dwelling-place.
8 O remember not against us former iniquities;
Let thy tender mercy speedily succor us,
9 For we are brought very low!
Help us, O God of our salvation! for the honor of thy name;
For thy name's sake save us, and forgive our iniquities!
10 Why should the nations say, "Where is their God?"
May the revenging of the blood of thy servants, which hath been shed,
Be manifested among the nations before our eyes!
11 Let the cry of the prisoner come before thee!
According to the greatness of thy power preserve those that are appointed to die!
12 And return sevenfold into our neighbors' bosoms
The reproach with which they have reproached thee, O Lord!
13 So shall we, thy people, and the flock of thy pasture,
Give thanks to thee for ever,
And show forth thy praise to all generations.

PSALM LXXX.

Prayer for deliverance in a time of great national calamity.

For the leader of the music. Upon the Shushan-Eduth. A psalm of Asaph.

1 GIVE ear, O Shepherd of Israel!
Thou who leadest Joseph like a flock,
Thou who sittest between the cherubs, shine forth!
2 Before Ephraim and Benjamin and Manasseh, stir up thy strength,
And come and save us!

3 Bring us back, O God!
And cause thy face to shine, that we may be saved!
4 O LORD, God of hosts!
How long wilt thou be angry against the prayer of thy people?
5 For thou causest them to eat the bread of tears,
And givest them tears to drink, in full measure.
6 Thou hast made us the object of strife to our neighbors,
And our enemies hold us in derision.
7 Bring us back, O God of hosts!
And cause thy face to shine that we may be saved!
8 Thou didst bring a vine out of Egypt;
Thou didst expel the nations, and plant it.
9 Thou didst prepare a place for it;
It spread its roots, and filled the land.
10 The mountains were covered with its shade,
And its branches were like the cedars of God.
11 It sent out its boughs to the sea,
And its branches to the river.
12 Why hast thou now broken down its hedges,
So that all who pass by do pluck from it?
13 The boar from the wood doth waste it,
And the wild beast of the forest doth devour it.
14 O God of hosts! return, we beseech thee,
Look down from heaven, and behold,
And have regard to this vine!
15 Protect what thy right hand planted;
The branch which thou madest strong for thyself!
16 It is burnt with fire; it is cut down;
Under thy rebuke they perish.
17 May thy hand be over the man of thy right hand,
The man whom thou madest strong for thyself!
18 So will we no more turn back from thee:
Revive us, and upon thy name alone will we call!
19 Bring us back, O LORD, God of hosts!
And cause thy face to shine, that we may be saved!

PSALM LXXXI.

Exhortation to religious obedience. Adapted to the celebration of the feast of Tabernacles, or, as some suppose, of the Passover. See Levit. xxiii. 4, &c., and 33, &c.

For the leader of the music. On the Gittith. A psalm of Asaph.

1 SING joyfully to God, our strength!
Shout with gladness to the God of Jacob!
2 Raise a song, and strike the timbrel,
The sweet-sounding harp, and the psaltery!
3 Blow the trumpet at the new moon;
At the full moon, also, on our festal day!
4 For this is a statute for Israel,
A law of the God of Jacob;
5 He appointed it as a memorial in Joseph,
When he went out of the land of Egypt,
Where he heard a language which he knew not.
6 "I relieved [said he] thy shoulders from their burden;
Thy hands were removed from the hod.
7 Thou didst call in trouble, and I delivered thee;
In the secret place of thunder I answered thee;
I proved thee at the waters of Meribah. [Pause.]
8 Hear, O my people! and I will admonish thee!
O Israel! that thou wouldst hearken to me!
9 Let there be no strange god within thee,
Nor worship thou any foreign god!
10 I, Jehovah, am thy God,
Who brought thee out of the land of Egypt:
Open wide thy mouth, and I will fill it!
11 But my people would not listen to my voice,
And Israel would not hearken to me.
12 So I gave them up to the obstinacy of their hearts,
And they walked according to their own devices.
13 "O that my people had hearkened to me!
That Israel had walked in my ways!
14 Soon would I have brought low their enemies,
And turned my hand against their adversaries.
15 The haters of Jehovah should have become suppliants to them,
And their prosperity should have endured for ever.
16 With the finest of the wheat I would have fed them,
And with honey out of the rock would I have satisfied them."

PSALM LXXXII.

Against unjust Jewish magistrates; or, against tyrannical foreign kings, who oppressed the Jewish nation.

A psalm of Asaph.

1 God standeth in God's assembly,
He judgeth in the midst of the gods.
2 "How long will ye judge unjustly,
And favor the cause of the wicked? [Pause.]
3 Defend the poor and the fatherless;
Do justice to the wretched and the needy!
4 Deliver the poor and the destitute;
Save them from the hand of the wicked!
5 They are without knowledge and without understanding;
They walk in darkness:
Therefore all the foundations of the land are shaken.
6 I have said, Ye are gods,
And all of you children of the Most High;
7 But ye shall die like men,
And fall like the rest of the princes."
8 Arise, O God! judge the earth!
For all the nations are thy possession.

PSALM LXXXIII.

Prayer against the enemies of the Jewish nation; commonly supposed to have been composed in the days of Jehoshaphat, when a combination of the neighboring kings was formed against Judah.

A psalm of Asaph.

1 O God! keep not silence!
Hold not thy peace, and be not still, O God!
2 For, lo! thine enemies roar,
And they who hate thee lift up their heads.
3 For they form secret plots against thy people,
And consult together against thy chosen ones.

4 "Come," say they, "let us blot them out from the number of the nations,
That the name of Israel may no more be remembered!"
5 With one consent they consult together,
Against thee do they form a league, —
6 The tents of Edom and the Ishmaelites,
Of Moab and the Hagarenes,
7 Gebal and Ammon and Amalek,
The Philistines, with the inhabitants of Tyre.
8 The Assyrians also are joined with them;
They lend their strength to the children of Lot.
9 Do to them as to the Midianites,
As to Sisera, as to Jabin at the brook Kison,
10 Who perished at Endor,
And were trampled like dung to the earth.
11 Make their chiefs like Oreb and Zeeb;
Yea, all their princes as Zeba and Zalmunna!
12 Who say, "Let us seize on God's habitations!"
13 Make them, O my God! like whirling chaff;
Like stubble before the wind!
14 As fire consumeth the forest,
And as flame setteth the mountains in a blaze,
15 So pursue them with thy tempest,
And terrify them with thy storm!
16 Cover their faces with shame,
That they may seek thy name, O LORD!
17 Let them be confounded!
Yea, let them be put to shame, and perish!
18 That they may know that thy name alone is Jehovah;
That thou art the Most High over all the earth.

PSALM LXXXIV.

Aspirations after the worship of God in the sanctuary.

For the leader of the music. On the Gittith. A psalm of the sons of Korah.

1 How lovely are thy tabernacles, O LORD of hosts!
2 My soul longeth, yea, fainteth, for the courts of the LORD;
My heart and my flesh cry aloud for the living God.
3 The very sparrow findeth an abode,
And the swallow a nest, where they may lay their young,
By thine altars, O LORD of hosts,
My king and my God!
4 Happy they who dwell in thy house,
Who are continually praising thee! [Pause.]
5 Happy the man whose glory is in thee,
In whose heart are the ways [to Jerusalem]!
6 Passing through the valley of Baca, they make it a fountain;
And the early rain covereth it with blessings.
7 They go on from strength to strength;
Every one of them appeareth before God in Zion.
8 Hear my prayer, O LORD, God of hosts!
Give ear, O God of Jacob! [Pause.]
9 Look down, O God! our shield,
And behold the face of thine anointed!
10 For a day spent in thy courts is better than a thousand:
I would rather stand on the threshold of the house of my God,
Than dwell in the tents of wickedness.
11 For the LORD God is a sun and a shield;
The LORD giveth grace and glory;
No good thing doth he withhold
From them that walk uprightly.
12 O LORD of hosts!
Happy the man who trusteth in thee!

PSALM LXXXV.

A prayer for the establishment and prosperity of the Jewish nation after their return from captivity.

For the leader of the music. A psalm of the sons of Korah.

1 O LORD! thou hast been favorable to thy land;
Thou hast brought back the captives of Jacob;
2 Thou didst forgive the iniquity of thy people,
And cover all their sins! [Pause.]
3 Thou didst take away all thy displeasure,
And abate the fierceness of thy wrath.
4 Restore us, O God of our salvation!
And let thine anger towards us cease!
5 Wilt thou be angry with us for ever?
Wilt thou continue thy wrath from generation to generation?
6 Wilt thou not revive us again,
That thy people may rejoice in thee?
7 Show us thy compassion, O LORD!
And grant us thy salvation!
8 I will hear what God the LORD will speak:
Truly he will speak peace to his people, and to his servants;
Only let them not turn again to folly!
9 Yea, his salvation is near to those who fear him,
That glory may dwell in our land.
10 Mercy and truth shall meet together,
Righteousness and peace shall kiss each other;
11 Truth shall spring out of the earth;
Righteousness shall look down from heaven.
12 Yea, Jehovah will give prosperity,
And our land shall yield her increase.
13 Righteousness shall go before him,
And set us in the way of his steps.

PSALM LXXXVI.

This psalm corresponds very well with its title. There are numerous seasons in the life of David to which it will apply.

A prayer of David.

1 INCLINE thine ear, O LORD! and hear me,
For I am poor and distressed!
2 Preserve my life, for I am devoted to thee!
Save, O thou my God! thy servant who trusteth in thee!
3 Have pity upon me, O Lord!
For to thee do I cry daily!
4 Revive the soul of thy servant,
For to thee, O Lord! do I lift up my soul!
5 For thou, Lord, art good, and ready to forgive;
Yea, rich in mercy to all that call upon thee!
6 Give ear, O LORD! to my prayer,
And attend to the voice of my supplication!
7 In the day of my trouble I call upon thee,
For thou dost answer me!
8 Among the gods there is none like thee, O Lord!
And there are no works like thy works!
9 All the nations which thou hast made must come and worship before thee, O Lord!
And glorify thy name!
10 For great art thou, and wondrous are thy works;
Thou alone art God!
11 Teach me, O LORD! thy way,
That I may walk in thy truth;
Unite all my heart to fear thy name!
12 I will praise thee, O Lord, my God! with my whole heart;
I will give glory to thy name for ever!
13 For thy kindness to me hath been great;
Thou hast delivered me from the depths of the underworld!
14 O God! the proud have risen against me;
Bands of cruel men seek my life,
And set not thee before their eyes.
15 But thou, O Lord! art a God full of compassion and kindness,
Long-suffering, rich in mercy and truth!

Look upon me, and have compassion upon me!
Give thy strength to thy servant,
And save the son of thy handmaid!
17 Show me a token for good,
That my enemies may see it and be confounded;
Because thou, O LORD! helpest and comfortest me!

PSALM LXXXVII.

The glory of Zion, as the source and centre of the religion of the world.

A psalm of the sons of Korah.

1 HIS foundation is in the holy mountains;
2 Jehovah loveth the gates of Zion
More than all the dwellings of Jacob.
3 Glorious things are said of thee,
O city of God! [Pause.]
4 "I name Egypt and Babylon among them that know me;
Behold! Philistia, Tyre, and Ethiopia, —
They also were born there."
5 And of Zion it shall be said,
"Men of every nation were born there,
And the Most High hath established her."
6 Jehovah, when he numbereth the nations, shall write,
"These were born there!" [Pause.]
7 Singers as well as dancers, —
All my springs are in thee!

PSALM LXXXVIII.

Prayer of one in deep and various distress.

A psalm of the sons of Korah. For the leader of the music. Upon wind instruments. A psalm of Heman, the Ezrahite.

1 O LORD, God of my salvation!
To thee do I cry by day,
And by night is my prayer before thee!
2 Let my supplication come before thee;
Incline thine ear to my cry!

3 For my soul is full of misery,
And my life draweth near to the underworld.
4 I am counted with those who are going down to the pit;
I am like one who hath no strength.
5 I am left to myself among the dead,
Like the slain who lie in the grave,
Whom thou no more rememberest,
And who are cut off from thy [protecting] hand.
6 Thou hast placed me in a deep pit,
In a dark and deep abyss.
7 Thy wrath presseth hard upon me,
And thou afflictest me with all thy waves! [Pause.]
8 Thou hast put mine acquaintances far from me,
Yea, thou hast made me their abhorrence:
I am shut up, and cannot go forth.
9 Mine eyes languish by reason of my affliction.
I call upon thee daily, O LORD!
To thee do I stretch out my hands!
10 Canst thou show wonders to the dead?
Shall the dead arise, and praise thee? [Pause.]
11 Shall thy goodness be declared in the grave,
Or thy faithfulness in the place of corruption?
12 Shall thy wonders be known in the dark,
And thy justice in the land of forgetfulness?
13 To thee do I cry, O LORD!
In the morning doth my cry come before thee.
14 Why, O LORD! dost thou cast me off?
Why hidest thou thy face from me?
15 I have been afflicted and languishing from my youth;
I suffer thy terrors, and am distracted.
16 Thy fierce wrath overwhelmeth me;
Thy terrors utterly destroy me.
17 They surround me daily like water;
They compass me about together.
18 Lover and friend hast thou put far from me;
My acquaintances are withdrawn from my sight.

PSALM LXXXIX.

Prayer for the race and kingdom of David.

A psalm of Ethan, the Ezrahite.

1 I WILL sing of the mercies of the LORD for ever;
With my mouth will I make known thy faithfulness to all generations!
2 For I know that thy mercy endureth for ever;
Thou hast established thy truth like the heavens.
3 "I have made a covenant with my chosen;
I have sworn to David, my servant:
4 Thy family I will establish for ever,
And build up thy throne to all generations." [Pause.]
5 The heavens shall praise thy wonders, O LORD!
And the assembly of the holy ones thy truth!
6 Who in the heavens can be compared to Jehovah?
Who is like Jehovah among the sons of God?
7 A God greatly to be feared in the assembly of the holy ones,
And to be had in reverence above all who are around him?
8 O Jehovah, God of hosts!
Who is mighty like thee, O Jehovah?
And thy faithfulness is round about thee.
9 Thou rulest the raging of the sea;
When the waves thereof rise, thou stillest them!
10 Thou didst break Rahab in pieces, as one that is slain;
Thou didst scatter thine enemies with thy mighty arm.
11 The heavens are thine; thine also is the earth;
The world and all that is therein, thou didst found them.
12 The North and the South were created by thee;
Tabor and Hermon rejoice in thy name.
13 Thine is a mighty arm;
Strong is thy hand, and high thy right hand.
14 Justice and equity are the foundation of thy throne;
Mercy and truth go before thy face.
15 Happy the people that know the trumpet's sound!
They walk, O LORD! in the light of thy countenance;
16 In thy name they daily rejoice,
And in thy righteousness they glory!

17 For thou art the glory of their strength;
Yea, through thy favor our horn exalteth itself!
18 For from Jehovah is our shield,
And from the Holy One of Israel is our king.
19 Once thou spakest in a vision to thy holy one,
And saidst, — "I have laid help on one that is mighty;
I have exalted one chosen from the people;
20 I have found David, my servant;
With my holy oil have I anointed him.
21 With him shall my hand be established,
And my arm shall strengthen him.
22 The enemy shall not have power over him,
Nor shall the unrighteous man oppress him.
23 For I will beat down his foes before him,
And overthrow them that hate him.
24 My faithfulness and mercy shall be with him,
And through my name shall his horn be exalted.
25 I will extend his hand to the sea,
And his right hand to the rivers.
26 He shall say to me, 'Thou art my father,
My God, and the rock of my salvation!'
27 I will also make him my first-born,
Highest of the kings of the earth.
28 My mercy I will continue to him for ever;
My covenant with him shall be steadfast.
29 I will make his family to endure for ever;
And his throne shall be as lasting as the heavens.
30 Should his children forsake my law,
And walk not in my statutes,
31 Should they break my commandments,
And observe not my precepts,
32 I will punish their transgressions with a rod,
And their iniquity with stripes.
33 But my kindness will I not withdraw from him,
Nor suffer my faithfulness to fail.
34 I will not break my covenant,
Nor alter what hath gone from my lips.
35 Once have I sworn in my holiness,
That I will not be false unto David.
36 His family shall endure for ever,
And his throne as the sun before me.

37 It shall be established for ever like the moon;
Like the faithful witness in the sky."
38 But now thou forsakest and abhorrest,
And art angry with, thine anointed.
39 Thou hast made void the covenant with thy servant;
Thou hast cast his crown to the ground.
40 Thou hast broken down all his hedges;
Thou hast brought his strongholds to ruin.
41 All who pass by plunder him;
He is a reproach to his neighbors.
42 Thou hast lifted up the right hand of his enemies;
Thou hast made all his adversaries to rejoice.
43 Yea, thou hast turned the edge of his sword,
And made him unable to stand in battle.
44 Thou hast brought his glory to an end,
And hast cast down his throne to the ground.
45 Thou hast shortened the days of his youth;
Thou hast covered him with shame.
46 How long, O LORD! wilt thou hide thyself for ever?
How long shall thine anger burn like fire?
47 Remember how short is my life,
To what frailty thou hast created all men!
48 What man liveth, and seeth not death?
Who can deliver himself from the underworld?
49 Where, Lord, is thy former loving-kindness
Which thou didst swear to David in thy truth?
50 Remember, O Lord! the reproach of thy servants,
How I bear in my bosom the taunts of all the many nations,
51 With which thine enemies have reproached me, O LORD!
With which they have reproached the footsteps of thine anointed!

52 *Praised be Jehovah for ever!*
Amen, yea, amen!

BOOK IV.

PSALM XC.

The eternity of God, and the frailty of man. Prayer for divine mercy and forbearance.

A prayer of Moses, the man of God.

1 LORD! thou hast been our dwelling-place
In all generations!
2 Before the mountains were brought forth,
Or ever thou hadst formed the earth and the world,
Even from everlasting to everlasting thou art God!
3 But man thou turnest again to dust,
And sayst, "Return, ye children of men!"
4 For a thousand years are, in thy sight,
As yesterday when it is past,
And as a watch in the night.
5 Thou carriest him away as with a flood;
He is a dream;
In the morning he springeth up like grass,
6 Which flourisheth and shooteth up in the morning,
And in the evening is cut down, and withered.
7 For we are consumed by thine anger,
And by thy wrath are we destroyed.
8 Thou settest our iniquities before thee,
Our secret sins in the light of thy countenance.
9 By reason of thine anger all our days vanish away;
We spend our years like a thought.
10 The days of our life are threescore years and ten,
And, by reason of strength, may be fourscore years:
Yet is the pride of them weariness and sorrow;
For it vanisheth swiftly, and we fly away.

11 Yet who attendeth to the power of thine anger?
Who with due reverence regardeth thine indignation?
12 Teach us so to number our days,
That we may apply our hearts to wisdom!
13 Desist, O LORD! How long—?
Have compassion upon thy servants!
14 Satisfy us speedily with thy mercy,
That we may rejoice and be glad all our days!
15 Make us glad according to the time in which thou hast
afflicted us;
According to the years in which we have seen adversity!
16 Let thy deeds be known to thy servants,
And thy glory to their children!
17 Let the favor of the LORD our God be upon us,
And establish for us the work of our hands;
Yea, the work of our hands, establish thou it!

PSALM XCI.

The safety and happiness of him who puts his trust in God.

1 HE who sitteth under the shelter of the Most High
Maketh his abode in the shadow of the Almighty.
2 I say to the LORD, Thou art my refuge and my fortress;
My God, in whom I trust.
3 Surely he will deliver thee from the snare of the fowler,
And from the wasting pestilence;
4 He will cover thee with his feathers,
And under his wings shalt thou find refuge;
His faithfulness shall be thy shield and buckler.
5 Thou shalt not be afraid of the terror of the night,
Nor of the arrow that flieth by day;
6 Nor of the pestilence that walketh in darkness,
Nor of the plague that destroyeth at noonday.
7 A thousand shall fall by thy side,
And ten thousand at thy right hand;
But thee it shall not touch.
8 Thou shalt only behold with thine eyes,
And see the recompense of the wicked.

9 Because thou hast made the LORD thy refuge,
And the Most High thy habitation,
10 No evil shall befall thee,
Nor any plague come near thy dwelling.
11 For he will give his angels charge over thee,
To guard thee in all thy ways.
12 They shall bear thee up in their hands,
Lest thou dash thy foot against a stone.
13 Thou shalt tread upon the lion and the adder;
The young lion and the dragon shalt thou trample under foot.
14 "Because he loveth me, I will deliver him;
I will set him on high, because he knoweth my name.
15 When he calleth upon me, I will answer him;
I will be with him in trouble;
I will deliver him, and bring him to honor.
16 With long life will I satisfy him,
And show him my salvation."

PSALM XCII.

Praise to God, as the righteous governor of the world.

A psalm for the Sabbath-day.

1 It is a good thing to give thanks to the LORD,
And to sing praises to thy name, O Most High!
2 To show forth thy loving-kindness in the morning,
And thy faithfulness every night,
3 Upon the ten-stringed instrument and the lute,
Upon the harp with a solemn sound.
4 For thou, LORD, hast made me glad by thy doings;
In the works of thy hands I greatly rejoice!
5 How great are thy works, O LORD!
How deep thy purposes!
6 But the unwise man knoweth not this,
And the fool understandeth it not.
7 When the wicked spring up like grass,
And all who practise iniquity flourish,
It is but to be destroyed for ever!

8 Thou, O LORD! art for ever exalted!
9 For, lo! thine enemies, O LORD!
For, lo! thine enemies perish,
And dispersed are all who do iniquity!
10 But my horn thou exaltest like the buffalo's;
I am anointed with fresh oil.
11 Mine eye hath gazed with joy upon mine enemies;
Mine ears have heard with joy of my wicked adversaries.
12 The righteous shall flourish like the palm-tree;
They shall grow up like the cedars of Lebanon;
13 Planted in the house of the LORD,
They shall flourish in the courts of our God.
14 Even in old age they bring forth fruit;
They are green, and full of sap;
15 To show that the LORD, my rock, is upright,
That there is no unrighteousness in him.

PSALM XCIII.

Praise of God as eternal king, the controller of all nature, and the protector of his people.

1 JEHOVAH reigneth; he is clothed with majesty;
Jehovah is clothed with majesty, and girded with strength;
Therefore the earth standeth firm, and cannot be moved.
2 Thy throne was established of old;
Thou art from everlasting!
3 The floods, O LORD! lift up,
The floods lift up their voice;
The floods lift up their roaring!
4 Mightier than the voice of many waters,
Yea, than the mighty waves of the sea,
Is the LORD in his lofty habitation.
5 Thy promises are most sure;
Holiness becometh thy house, O LORD! for ever!

PSALM XCIV.

Prayer for the punishment of the oppressors of the Jewish nation.

1 O LORD! thou God of vengeance!
O thou God of vengeance! shine forth!
2 Rouse thyself, thou judge of the earth!
Render a recompense to the proud!
3 How long, O LORD! shall the wicked,
How long shall the wicked triumph?
4 How long shall their lips pour forth insolence?
How long shall all the evil-doers boast?
5 O LORD! they trample upon thy people,
And oppress thine inheritance!
6 They slay the widow, and the stranger,
And murder the fatherless;
7 And they say, "The LORD doth not see,
The God of Jacob doth not regard!"
8 Be instructed, ye most stupid of mankind!
O when, ye fools, will ye be wise?
9 He that planted the ear, shall he not hear?
He that formed the eye, shall he not see?
10 He that chastiseth nations, shall not he punish?
He that teacheth man knowledge, shall not he know?
11 The LORD knoweth the thoughts of men,
That they are vanity.
12 Happy the man, O LORD! whom thou correctest,
Whom by thy teaching thou makest wise;
13 To give him peace in the days of adversity,
Until a pit be digged for the wicked!
14 For the LORD will not forsake his people,
Nor abandon his own inheritance.
15 For judgment shall return to justice,
And all the upright in heart shall follow it.
16 Who will rise up for me against the wicked?
Who will stand up for me against the evil-doers?
17 If the LORD had not been my help,
I had well nigh dwelt in the land of silence.
18 When I think that my foot is slipping,
Thy goodness, O LORD! holdeth me up.

19 In the multitude of anxieties within me,
Thy consolations revive my soul.
20 Shall with thee be allied the throne of iniquity,
Which deviseth mischief against law?
21 They band together against the life of the righteous,
And condemn innocent blood.
22 But the LORD is my fortress,
And my God the rock of my refuge.
23 He will bring upon them their own iniquity;
Yea, through their own wickedness he will cut them off;
Yea, the LORD, our God, will cut them off.

PSALM XCV.

Exhortation to praise and obey God.

1 O COME, let us sing to the LORD;
Let us raise a voice of joy to the rock of our salvation!
2 Let us come into his presence with thanksgiving,
And sing joyfully to him with psalms!
3 For Jehovah is a great God;
Yea, a great king over all gods.
4 In his hands are the depths of the earth;
His also are the heights of the mountains.
5 The sea is his, and he made it;
The dry land also his hands formed.
6 O come, let us worship and bow down!
Let us kneel before the LORD, our maker!
7 For he is our God,
And we are the people of his pasture and the flock of his hand.
O that ye would now hear his voice!
8 "Harden not your hearts as at Meribah [the strife],
As in the day of temptation [Massah] in the wilderness,
9 Where your fathers tempted me
And tried me, although they had seen my works.
10 Forty years was I offended with that generation:
And I said, 'They are a people of a perverse heart,
And who have no regard to my ways.'
11 Therefore I sware, in my wrath,
That they should not enter into my rest."

PSALM XCVI.

Exhortation to the praise and worship of God. This psalm is, with some slight variations, a part of that contained in 1 Chron., chap. xvi., and said to have been composed by David on the occasion of the translation of the ark to Mount Zion. See 1 Chron. xvi. 7, 23–33.

1 O SING to Jehovah a new song;
Sing to Jehovah, all the earth!
2 Sing to Jehovah; praise his name,
Show forth his salvation from day to day!
3 Proclaim his glory among the nations,
His wonders among all people!
4 For Jehovah is great, and greatly to be praised;
He is to be feared above all gods.
5 For all the gods of the nations are idols;
But Jehovah made the heavens.
6 Honor and majesty are before him;
Glory and beauty are in his holy abode.
7 Give to Jehovah, ye tribes of the people,
Give to Jehovah glory and praise!
8 Give to Jehovah the glory due to his name;
Bring an offering, and come into his courts!
9 O worship Jehovah in holy attire!
Tremble before him, all the earth!
10 Say among the nations, Jehovah is king;
The world shall stand firm; it shall not be moved;
He will judge the nations in righteousness.
11 Let the heavens be glad, and the earth rejoice;
Let the sea roar, and the fulness thereof;
12 Let the fields be joyful, with all that is therein;
Let all the trees of the forest rejoice
13 Before Jehovah! for he cometh,
He cometh to judge the earth!
He will judge the world with justice,
And the nations with faithfulness.

PSALM XCVII.

Praise to God as the supreme ruler, the punisher of the idolatrous enemies of the Jews, and the rewarder of his worshippers. This psalm was probably occasioned by some victory gained by the Jews.

1 THE LORD reigneth, let the earth rejoice!
Let the multitude of isles be glad!
2 Clouds and darkness are round about him;
Justice and equity are the foundation of his throne.
3 Before him goeth a fire,
Which burneth up his enemies around.
4 His lightnings illumine the world;
The earth beholdeth and trembleth.
5 The mountains melt like wax at the presence of the LORD,
At the presence of the Lord of the whole earth.
6 The heavens declare his righteousness,
And all nations behold his glory.
7 Confounded be they who worship graven images,
Who glory in idols!
To him, all ye gods, bow down!
8 Zion hath heard, and is glad,
And the daughters of Judah exult
On account of thy judgments, O LORD!
9 For thou, O LORD! art most high above all the earth;
Thou art far exalted above all gods!
10 Ye that love the LORD, hate evil!
He preserveth the lives of his servants,
And delivereth them from the hand of the wicked.
11 Light is sown for the righteous,
And joy for the upright in heart.
12 Rejoice, O ye righteous, in the LORD,
And praise his holy name!

PSALM XCVIII.

A psalm of praise to God for his mighty deeds for his people.

A psalm.

1 SING to the LORD a new song;
For he hath done marvellous things;
His own right hand and his holy arm have gotten him the victory!
2 The LORD hath made known his salvation;
His righteousness hath he manifested in the sight of the nations.
3 He hath remembered his mercy and truth toward the house of Israel,
And all the ends of the earth have seen the salvation of our God.
4 Shout unto the LORD, all the earth!
Break forth into joy, and exult, and sing!
5 Sing to the LORD with the harp,
With the harp, and the voice of song!
6 With clarions, and the sound of trumpets,
Make a joyful noise before the LORD the King!
7 Let the sea roar, and the fulness thereof;
The world, and they that dwell therein;
8 Let the rivers clap their hands,
And the mountains rejoice together
9 Before the LORD! for he cometh to judge the earth!
With righteousness will he judge the world,
And the nations with equity.

PSALM XCIX.

Hymn of praise with reference to God's goodness to his people in ancient times.

1 THE LORD reigneth, let the nations tremble!
He sitteth between the cherubs, let the earth quake!
2 Great is the LORD upon Zion;
He is exalted over all the nations.

3 Let men praise thy great and terrible name!
It is holy.
4 Let them declare the glory of the King who loveth justice!
Thou hast established equity;
Thou dost execute justice in Jacob!
5 Exalt ye Jehovah, our God,
And bow yourselves down at his footstool!
He is holy.
6 Moses and Aaron, with his priests,
And Samuel, who called upon his name, —
They called upon the LORD, and he answered them.
7 He spake to them in the cloudy pillar;
They kept his commandments,
And the ordinances which he gave them.
8 Thou, O LORD, our God! didst answer them;
Thou wast to them a forgiving God,
Though thou didst punish their transgressions!
9 Exalt the LORD, our God,
And worship at his holy mountain!
For the LORD, our God, is holy.

PSALM C.

Exhortation to praise God.

A psalm of praise.

1 RAISE a voice of joy unto the LORD, all ye lands!
2 Serve the LORD with gladness;
Come before his presence with rejoicing!
3 Know ye that Jehovah is God!
It is he that made us, and we are his,
His people, and the flock of his pasture.
4 Enter into his gates with thanksgiving,
And his courts with praise;
Be thankful to him, and bless his name!
5 For the LORD is good; his mercy is everlasting;
And his truth endureth to all generations.

PSALM CI.

Resolution of a king to govern with justice. This psalm is supposed to have been composed by David, when he removed the ark to Mount Zion.

A psalm of David.

1 I WILL sing of mercy and justice;
To thee, O LORD! will I sing!
2 I will have regard to the way of uprightness:
When thou shalt come to me,
I will walk within my house with an upright heart.
3 I will set no wicked thing before mine eyes;
I hate the work of evil-doers;
It shall not cleave to me.
4 The perverse in heart shall be far from me;
I will not know a wicked person.
5 Whoso slandereth his neighbor in secret, him will I cut off;
Him that hath a haughty look and a proud heart I will not endure.
6 Mine eyes shall be upon the faithful of the land, that they may dwell with me;
He that walketh in the way of uprightness shall serve me.
7 He who practiseth deceit shall not dwell in my house;
He who telleth lies shall not remain in my sight.
8 Every morning will I destroy the wicked of the land,
That I may cut off all evil-doers from the city of the LORD.

PSALM CII.

Prayer in affliction and for restoration from captivity. This psalm was undoubtedly composed in the time of the captivity, and probably near the close of it, when hopes were cherished of a restoration.

A prayer of the afflicted, when in deep distress he poureth out his complaint before the Lord.

1 HEAR my prayer, O LORD!
And let my cry come unto thee!
2 Hide not thy face from me in the day of my trouble;
Incline thine ear to me when I call;
Answer me speedily!

3 For my life is consumed like smoke,
And my bones burn like a brand.
4 My heart is smitten and withered like grass;
Yea, I forget to eat my bread.
5 By reason of my sighing, my bones cleave to my skin;
6 I am like the pelican of the wilderness;
I am like an owl amid ruins.
7 I am sleepless;
I am like a solitary bird upon the house-top.
8 All the day long my enemies reproach me;
They who rage against me curse by me.
9 For I eat ashes like bread,
And mingle my drink with tears,
10 On account of thine indignation and thy wrath;
For thou hast lifted me up and cast me down!
11 My life is like a declining shadow,
And I wither like grass.
12 But thou, O LORD! endurest for ever,
And thy name from generation to generation!
13 Thou wilt arise and have pity upon Zion,
For the time to favor her, yea, the set time, is come.
14 For thy servants take pleasure in her stones;
Yea, they have a regard for her dust.
15 Then shall the nations fear the name of Jehovah,
And all the kings of the earth thy glory.
16 For Jehovah will build up Zion;
He will appear in his glory.
17 He will regard the prayer of the destitute,
And not despise their supplication.
18 This shall be written for the generation to come,
That the people to be born may praise Jehovah.
19 For he looketh down from his holy height,
From heaven doth he cast his eye upon the earth,
20 To listen to the sighs of the prisoner,
To release those that are doomed to death;
21 That they may declare the name of Jehovah in Zion,
And his praise in Jerusalem,
22 When the nations are assembled together,
And the kingdoms to serve Jehovah.
23 He hath weakened my strength on the way,
He hath shortened my days.

24 I say, O my God! take me not away in the midst of my
days!
Thy years endure through all generations.
25 Of old hast thou laid the foundations of the earth,
And the heavens are the work of thy hands;
26 They shall perish, but thou shalt endure;
Yea, all of them shall wax old like a garment;
As a vesture shalt thou change them,
And they shall be changed;
27 But thou art the same,
And thy years have no end.
28 The children of thy servants shall dwell securely,
And their posterity shall be established before thee.

PSALM CIII.

Praise to God for his righteousness and mercy, especially towards his people

A psalm of David.

1 BLESS the LORD, O my soul!
And all that is within me, bless his holy name!
2 Bless the LORD, O my soul!
And forget not all his benefits!
3 Who forgiveth all thine iniquities;
Who healeth all thy diseases;
4 Who redeemeth thy life from the grave;
Who crowneth thee with loving-kindness and tender mercies;
5 Who satisfieth thine old age with good,
So that thy youth is renewed like the eagle's.
6 The LORD executeth justice
And equity for all the oppressed.
7 He made known his ways to Moses,
His doings to the children of Israel.
8 The LORD is merciful and kind,
Slow to anger and rich in mercy.
9 He doth not always chide,
Nor doth he keep his anger for ever.
10 He hath not dealt with us according to our sins,
Nor requited us according to our iniquities.

11 As high as are the heavens above the earth,
So great is his mercy to them that fear him.
12 As far as the east is from the west,
So far hath he removed our transgressions from us.
13 Even as a father pitieth his children,
So the LORD pitieth them that fear him.
14 For he knoweth our frame,
He remembereth that we are dust.
15 As for man, his days are as grass;
As a flower of the field, so he flourisheth.
16 The wind passeth over it, and it is gone;
And its place shall know it no more.
17 But the mercy of the LORD is from everlasting to everlasting to them that fear him,
And his righteousness to children's children,
18 To such as keep his covenant,
And remember his commandments to do them.
19 The LORD hath established his throne in the heavens,
And his kingdom ruleth over all.
20 Bless the LORD, ye his angels,
Ye mighty ones who do his commands,
Hearkening to the voice of his word!
21 Bless the LORD, all ye his hosts;
Ye, his ministers, who do his pleasure!
22 Bless the LORD, all his works,
In all places of his dominion!
Bless the LORD, O my soul!

PSALM CIV.

The power and goodness of God, as displayed in the works of creation and providence.

1 BLESS the LORD, O my soul!
O LORD, my God! thou art very great!
Thou art clothed with glory and majesty!
2 He covereth himself with light as with a garment;
He spreadeth out the heavens like a curtain;
3 He layeth the beams of his chambers in the waters;
He maketh the clouds his chariot;
He rideth upon the wings of the wind.

4 He maketh the winds his messengers,
The flaming lightnings his ministers.
5 He established the earth on its foundations;
It shall not be removed for ever.
6 Thou didst cover it with the deep as with a garment;
The waters stood above the mountains!
7 At thy rebuke they fled;
At the voice of thy thunder they hasted away.
8 The mountains rose, the valleys sank,
In the place which thou didst appoint for them.
9 Thou hast established a bound which the waters may not pass,
That they may not return, and cover the earth.
10 He sendeth forth the springs in brooks;
They run among the mountains;
11 They give drink to all the beasts of the forest;
In them the wild asses quench their thirst.
12 About them the birds of heaven have their habitation;
They sing among the branches.
13 He watereth the hills from his chambers;
The earth is satisfied with the fruit of thy works!
14 He causeth grass to spring up for cattle,
And herbage for the service of man,
To bring forth food out of the earth,
15 And wine that gladdeneth the heart of man,
Making his face to shine more than oil,
And bread that strengtheneth man's heart.
16 The trees of the LORD are full of sap,
The cedars of Lebanon, which he hath planted;
17 There the birds build their nests;
In the cypresses the stork hath her abode.
18 The high hills are a refuge for the wild goats,
And the rocks for the conies.
19 He appointed the moon to mark seasons;
The sun knoweth when to go down.
20 Thou makest darkness, and it is night,
When all the beasts of the forest go forth!
21 The young lions roar for prey,
And seek their food from God.
22 When the sun ariseth, they withdraw themselves,
And lie down in their dens.

23 Man goeth forth to his work,
And to his labor, until the evening.
24 O LORD! how manifold are thy works!
In wisdom hast thou made them all!
The earth is full of thy riches!
25 Lo! this great and wide sea!
In it are moving creatures without number,
Animals small and great.
26 There go the ships;
There is the leviathan, which thou hast made to play therein.
27 All these wait on thee
To give them their food in due season.
28 Thou givest it to them, they gather it;
Thou openest thine hand, they are satisfied with good.
29 Thou hidest thy face, they are confounded;
Thou takest away their breath, they die,
And return to the dust.
30 Thou sendest forth thy spirit, they are created,
And thou renewest the face of the earth.

31 The glory of the LORD shall endure for ever;
The LORD shall rejoice in his works;
32 He looketh on the earth, and it trembleth;
He toucheth the hills, and they smoke.
33 I will sing to the LORD as long as I live,
I will sing praise to my God while I have my being.
34 May my meditation be acceptable to him!
I will rejoice in the LORD.
35 May sinners perish from the earth,
And the wicked be no more!
Bless the LORD, O my soul!
Praise ye the LORD!

PSALM CV.

Commemoration of God's faithfulness and goodness to the nation of Israel from the earliest period of their history. The first fifteen verses of this psalm are a part of David's hymn on the removal of the ark to Zion, contained in 1 Chron. xvi. 8–22.

1 O GIVE thanks unto the LORD;
Call upon his name;
Make known his deeds among the people!
2 Sing unto him; sing psalms unto him;
Tell ye of all his wondrous works!
3 Glory ye in his holy name;
Let the hearts of them that seek the LORD rejoice!
4 Seek the LORD, and his majesty;
Seek his face continually!
5 Remember the wonders he hath wrought,
His miracles and the judgments of his mouth,
6 Ye offspring of Abraham his servant,
Ye children of Jacob his chosen!
7 Jehovah, he is our God,
His judgments are over all the earth.
8 He remembereth his covenant for ever,
And the promise to a thousand generations;
9 The covenant which he made with Abraham,
And the oath which he gave to Isaac;
10 Which he confirmed to Jacob for a decree,
And to Israel for an everlasting covenant.
11 "To thee," said he, "will I give the land of Canaan
For the lot of your inheritance."
12 When they were yet few in number,
Very few, and strangers in the land;
13 When they went from nation to nation,
From one kingdom to another people,
14 He suffered no man to oppress them;
Yea, he rebuked kings for their sakes.
15 "Touch not," said he, "mine anointed,
And do my prophets no harm!"

16 Again, when he commanded a famine in the land,
And broke the whole staff of bread,

17 He sent a man before them;
Joseph was sold as a slave.
18 His feet they hurt with fetters;
He was bound in chains of iron;
19 Until his prediction came to pass,
And the word of the LORD proved him.
20 Then the king sent, and loosed him;
The ruler of nations, and set him free;
21 He made him governor of his house,
And lord of all his possessions;
22 To bind his princes at his pleasure,
And teach his counsellors wisdom.

23 Israel also came into Egypt,
And Jacob sojourned in the land of Ham;
24 Where God increased his people greatly,
And made them stronger than their enemies.
25 He turned their hearts to hate his people,
And form devices against his servants.
26 Then sent he Moses his servant,
And Aaron, whom he had chosen.
27 They showed his signs among them,
And his wonders in the land of Ham.
28 He sent darkness upon them, and made it dark;
And they did not disobey his word.
29 He turned their waters into blood,
And caused their fish to die.
30 Their land brought forth frogs in abundance,
Even in the chambers of their kings.
31 He spake, and there came flies,
And lice in all their coasts.
32 Instead of rain he gave them hail,
And flaming fire in their land.
33 He smote also their vines and fig-trees,
And broke the trees of their coasts.
34 He spake, and the locusts came,
Destructive locusts without number,
35 Which ate up all the herbage in their land,
And devoured the fruits of their fields.
36 Then he smote all the first-born in their land,
The first-fruits of all their strength.

37 He led forth his people with silver and gold;
Nor was there one feeble person in all their tribes.
38 Egypt was glad when they departed,
For their terror had fallen upon them.

39 He spread out a cloud for a covering,
And fire to give light by night.
40 They asked, and he brought quails,
And satisfied them with the bread of heaven.
41 He opened the rock, and the waters gushed forth,
And ran in the dry places like a river.
42 For he remembered his holy promise,
Which he had made to Abraham his servant;
43 And he led forth his people with joy,
And his chosen with gladness.
44 He gave to them the lands of the nations,
And they inherited the labor of the peoples;
45 That they might observe his statutes,
And obey his laws.
Praise ye the LORD!

PSALM CVI.

Commemoration of the national sins of the Jews throughout their history, and of God's mercies to them. This is evidently a psalm of the captivity. See verses 46, 47.

1 PRAISE ye the LORD!
O give thanks to the LORD, for he is good;
For his mercy endureth for ever!
2 Who can utter the mighty deeds of the LORD?
Who can show forth all his praise?
3 Happy are they who have regard to justice,
Who practise righteousness at all times!
4 Remember me, O LORD! with the favor promised to thy people;
O visit me with thy salvation!
5 That I may see the prosperity of thy chosen,
That I may rejoice in the joy of thy people,
That I may glory with thine inheritance!

6 We have sinned with our fathers;
We have committed iniquity; we have done wickedly.
7 Our fathers in Egypt did not regard thy wonders;
They remembered not the multitude of thy mercies;
But rebelled at the sea, the Red sea.
8 Yet he saved them for his own name's sake,
That he might make his mighty power to be known.
9 He rebuked the Red sea, and it was dried up,
And he led them through the deep as through a desert.
10 He saved them from the hand of him that hated them,
And redeemed them from the hand of the enemy.
11 The waters covered their enemies;
There was not one of them left.
12 Then believed they his words,
And sang his praise.
13 But they soon forgot his deeds,
And waited not for his counsel.
14 They gave way to appetite in the wilderness,
And tempted God in the desert;
15 And he gave them their request,
But sent upon them leanness.
16 They also envied Moses in the camp,
And Aaron, the holy one of the LORD.
17 Then the earth opened, and swallowed up Dathan,
And covered the company of Abiram,
18 And a fire was kindled in their company;
The flames burned up the wicked.

19 They made a calf in Horeb,
And worshipped a molten image;
20 They changed their God of glory
Into the image of a grass-eating ox.
21 They forgot God, their saviour,
Who had done such great things in Egypt,
22 Such wonders in the land of Ham,
Such terrible things at the Red sea.
23 Then he said that he would destroy them;
Had not Moses, his chosen, stood before him in the breach,
To turn away his wrath, that he might not destroy them.
24 They also despised the pleasant land,
And believed not his word;

25 But murmured in their tents,
And would not hearken to the voice of the LORD.
26 Then he lifted up his hand against them,
And swore that he would make them fall in the wilderness;
27 That he would overthrow their descendants among the nations,
And scatter them in the lands.
28 They also gave themselves to the worship of Baal-peor,
And ate sacrifices offered to lifeless idols.
29 Thus they provoked his anger by their practices,
And a plague broke in upon them.
30 Then stood up Phinehas, and executed judgment,
And the plague was stayed.
31 And this was counted to him for righteousness,
To all generations for ever.
32 They provoked him also at the waters of Meribah [strife],
And evil befell Moses on their account.
33 For they provoked his spirit,
So that he spake inconsiderately with his lips.
34 They did not destroy the nations,
As Jehovah had commanded them.
35 They mingled themselves with the peoples,
And learned their practices.
36 They even worshipped their idols,
Which became to them a snare.
37 Their sons and their daughters they sacrificed to demons,
38 And shed innocent blood,
The blood of their own sons and daughters,
Whom they sacrificed to the idols of Canaan;
And the land was polluted with blood.
39 Thus they defiled themselves with their works,
And played the harlot with their practices.
40 Then burned the anger of the LORD against his people,
So that he abhorred his own inheritance.
41 And he gave them into the hand of the nations,
And they who hated them ruled over them.
42 Their enemies oppressed them,
And they were bowed down under their hand.
43 Many times did he deliver them;
But they provoked him by their devices,
And they were brought low for their iniquities.

44 Yet, when he heard their cries,
He had regard to their affliction;
45 He remembered his covenant with them,
And repented according to the greatness of his mercy,
46 And caused them to find pity
Among all that carried them captive.
47 Save us, O Jehovah, our God! and gather us from among the nations,
That we may give thanks to thy holy name,
And glory in thy praise!

48 *Blessed be Jehovah, the God of Israel,*
From everlasting to everlasting!
And let all the people say, Amen!
Praise ye Jehovah!

BOOK V.

PSALM CVII.

The goodness of God to various classes of men, in delivering them from calamities of various kinds. This psalm appears from its contents to have been composed some time after the return from the Babylonish captivity.

1 O GIVE thanks to the LORD, for he is good;
For his mercy endureth for ever!
2 Let the redeemed of the LORD say it,
Whom he hath redeemed from the hand of the enemy;
3 Whom he hath gathered from the lands,
From the east, the west, the north, and the south.
4 They were wandering in the wilderness, in a desert,
They found no way to a city to dwell in.
5 They were hungry and thirsty,
And their souls fainted within them.
6 Then they cried to the LORD in their trouble,
And he delivered them out of their distress.
7 He led them in a straight way,
Till they came to a city where they might dwell.
8 O let them praise the LORD for his goodness,
For his wonderful works to the children of men!
9 For he satisfieth the thirsty,
And the hungry he filleth with good.
10 They dwelt in darkness and the shadow of death,
Being bound in affliction and iron;
11 Because they disobeyed the commands of God,
And contemned the will of the Most High;
12 Their hearts he brought down by hardship;
They fell down, and there was none to help.
13 But they cried to the LORD in their trouble,
And he saved them out of their distresses;

14 He brought them out of darkness and the shadow of death,
And brake their bands asunder.
15 O let them praise the LORD for his goodness,
For his wonderful works to the children of men!
16 For he hath broken the gates of brass,
And cut the bars of iron asunder.

17 The foolish, because of their transgressions,
And because of their iniquities, were afflicted;
18 They abhorred all kinds of food;
They were near to the gates of death.
19 Then they cried to the LORD in their trouble,
And he delivered them out of their distresses;
20 He sent his word, and healed them,
And saved them from their destruction.
21 O let them praise the LORD for his goodness,
For his wonderful works to the children of men!
22 Let them offer the sacrifices of thanksgiving,
And declare his works with joy!

23 They who go down to the sea in ships,
And do business in great waters,
24 These see the works of the LORD,
And his wonders in the deep.
25 He commandeth, and raiseth the stormy wind,
Which lifteth high the waves.
26 They mount up to the heavens,
They sink down to the depths,
Their soul melteth with distress;
27 They reel and stagger like a drunken man,
And all their skill is vain.
28 Then they cry to the LORD in their trouble,
And he saveth them out of their distresses;
29 He turneth the storm into a calm,
And the waves are hushed;
30 Then they rejoice that they are still,
And he bringeth them to their desired haven.
31 O let them praise the LORD for his goodness,
For his wonderful works to the children of men!
32 Let them extol him in the congregation of the people,
And praise him in the assembly of the elders!

33 He turneth rivers into a desert,
And springs of water into dry ground;
34 A fruitful land into barrenness,
For the wickedness of them that dwell therein.
35 He turneth the desert into a lake of water,
And dry ground into springs of water;
36 And there he causeth the hungry to dwell,
And they build a city for a dwelling-place,
37 And sow fields and plant vineyards,
Which yield a fruitful increase.
38 He blesseth them, so that they multiply greatly,
And suffereth not their cattle to decrease.
39 When they are diminished and brought low
By oppression, affliction, and sorrow,
40 He poureth contempt upon princes,
And causeth them to wander in a pathless wilderness;
41 But he raiseth the poor from their affliction,
And increaseth their families like a flock.
42 The righteous see it and rejoice,
And all iniquity shutteth her mouth.
43 Whoso is wise, let him observe this,
And have regard to the loving-kindness of the LORD!

PSALM CVIII.

Prayer for deliverance from enemies; expression of assurance of it. This psalm is composed of parts of two other psalms; namely, Ps. lvii. 7–11, and Ps. lx. 5–12. It has been conjectured that it was compiled for some public occasion in the later period of the Jewish nation.

A psalm of David.

1 O GOD! my heart is strengthened!
I will sing and give thanks.
2 Awake, my soul! awake, my psaltery and harp!
I will wake with the early dawn.
3 I will praise thee, O LORD! among the nations;
I will sing to thee among the peoples!
4 For thy mercy reacheth to the heavens,
And thy truth above the clouds.
5 Exalt thyself, O God! above the heavens,
And thy glory above all the earth!

6 That thy beloved ones may be delivered,
Save with thy right hand, and answer me!
7 God promiseth in his holiness; I will rejoice
I shall yet divide Shechem,
And measure out the valley of Succoth;
8 Gilead shall be mine, and mine Manasseh;
Ephraim shall be my helmet,
And Judah my sceptre.
9 Moab shall be my washbowl;
Upon Edom shall I cast my shoe;
I shall triumph over Philistia.
10 Who will bring me to the strong city?
Who will lead me into Edom?
11 Wilt not thou, O God! who didst forsake us,
Who didst not go forth with our armies?
12 Give us thine aid in our distress,
For vain is the help of man!
13 Through God we shall do valiantly;
For he will tread down our enemies.

PSALM CIX.

Prayer against enemies.

For the leader of the music. A psalm of David.

1 O God of my praise! be not silent!
2 For the mouths of the wicked and the deceitful are opened against me;
They speak against me with a lying tongue.
3 They assault me on every side with words of hatred;
They fight against me without a cause.
4 For my love they are my adversaries:
But I give myself unto prayer.
5 They repay me evil for good,
And hatred for love.
6 Set thou a wicked man over him,
And let an adversary stand at his right hand!
7 When he is judged, may he be condemned,
And may his prayer be a crime!

8 May his days be few,
And another take his office!
9 May his children be fatherless,
And his wife a widow!
10 May his children be vagabonds and beggars,
And from their ruined dwellings seek their bread!
11 May a creditor seize on all that he hath,
And a stranger plunder his substance!
12 May there be none to show him compassion,
And none to pity his fatherless children!
13 May his posterity be cut off;
In the next generation may his name be blotted out!
14 May the iniquity of his fathers be remembered by the LORD,
And may the sin of his mother never be blotted out!
15 May they be before the LORD continually;
And may he cut off their memory from the earth!
16 Because he remembered not to show pity,
But persecuted the afflicted and the poor man,
And sought the death of the broken-hearted.
17 As he loved cursing, let it come upon him;
As he delighted not in blessing, let it be far from him!
18 May he be clothed with cursing as with a garment;
May it enter like water into his bowels,
And like oil into his bones!
19 May it be to him like the robe that covereth him,
Like the girdle with which he is constantly girded!
20 May this be the wages of mine adversaries from the LORD,
And of them that speak evil against me!
21 But do thou, O LORD, my God! take part with me,
For thine own name's sake!
Because great is thy mercy, O deliver me!
22 For I am afflicted and needy,
And my heart is wounded within me.
23 I am going like a shadow;
I am driven away as the locust.
24 My knees totter from fasting,
And my flesh faileth of fatness.
25 I am a reproach to my enemies;
They gaze at me; they shake their heads.
26 Help me, O LORD, my God!
O save me, according to thy mercy!

27 That they may know that this is thy hand;
That thou, O Lord! hast done it!
28 Let them curse, but do thou bless!
When they arise, let them be put to shame;
But let thy servant rejoice!
29 May my enemies be clothed with ignominy;
May they be covered with their shame, as with a mantle!
30 I will earnestly praise the LORD with my lips;
In the midst of the multitude I will praise him.
31 For he standeth at the right hand of the poor,
To save him from those who would condemn him.

PSALM CX.

Promise to the king on Mount Zion that he should be victorious over all his enemies, and have priestly as well as regal dignity.

A psalm of David.

1 JEHOVAH said to my lord,
"Sit thou at my right hand,
Until I make thy foes thy footstool."
2 Jehovah will extend the sceptre of thy power from Zion:
Rule thou in the midst of thine enemies!
3 Thy people shall be ready, when thou musterest thy forces, in holy splendor;
Thy youth shall come forth like dew from the womb of the morning.
4 Jehovah hath sworn, and he will not repent:
"Thou art a priest for ever,
After the order of Melchisedeck!"
5 The Lord is at thy right hand,
He shall crush kings in the day of his wrath.
6 He shall execute justice among the nations;
He shall fill them with dead bodies,
He shall crush the heads of his enemies over many lands.
7 He shall drink of the brook in the way;
Therefore shall he lift up his head.

PSALM CXI.

Hymn of praise for God's goodness to his people in his works and word.

1 PRAISE ye the LORD!
I will praise the LORD with my whole heart,
In the assembly of the righteous, and in the congregation.
2 The works of the LORD are great,
Sought out by all who have pleasure in them.
3 His deeds are honorable and glorious,
And his righteousness endureth for ever.
4 He hath established a memorial of his wonders;
The LORD is gracious and full of compassion.
5 He giveth meat to them that fear him;
He is ever mindful of his covenant.
6 He showed his people the greatness of his works,
When he gave them the inheritance of the heathen.
7 The deeds of his hands are truth and justice;
All his commandments are sure;
8 They stand firm for ever and ever,
Being founded in truth and justice.
9 He sent redemption to his people;
He established his covenant for ever;
Holy, and to be had in reverence, is his name.
10 The fear of the LORD is the beginning of wisdom;
A good understanding have all they who keep his commandments;
His praise endureth for ever.

PSALM CXII.

The blessedness of the righteous man.

1 PRAISE ye the LORD!
Happy the man who feareth the LORD,
Who taketh delight in his commandments!
2 His posterity shall be mighty on the earth;
The race of the righteous shall be blessed.
3 Wealth and riches shall be in his house;
His righteousness shall endure for ever.

4 To the righteous shall arise light out of darkness;
He is gracious and full of compassion and righteousness.
5 Happy the man who hath pity and lendeth!
He shall sustain his cause in judgment;
6 Yea, he shall never be moved:
The righteous shall be in everlasting remembrance.
7 He is not afraid of evil tidings;
His heart is firm, trusting in the LORD.
8 His heart is firm; he hath no fear,
Till he see his desire upon his enemies.
9 He hath scattered blessings; he hath given to the poor;
His righteousness shall endure for ever;
His horn shall be exalted with honor.
10 The wicked shall see, and be grieved;
He shall gnash his teeth, and melt away;
The desire of the wicked shall perish.

PSALM CXIII.

Praise to God for his condescending goodness.

1 PRAISE ye the LORD!
Praise, O ye servants of the LORD!
Praise the name of the LORD!
2 Blessed be the name of the LORD
From this time forth, even for ever!
3 From the rising of the sun to its going down,
May the LORD's name be praised!
4 The LORD is high above all nations;
His glory is above the heavens.
5 Who is like the LORD, our God,
That dwelleth on high,
6 That looketh down low
Upon the heavens and the earth?
7 He raiseth the poor from the dust,
And exalteth the needy from the dunghill,
8 To set him among princes,
Even among the princes of his people.
9 He causeth the barren woman to dwell in a house,
A joyful mother of children.
Praise ye the LORD!

PSALM CXIV.

On the coming forth from Egypt, under the guidance of God.

1 WHEN Israel came forth from Egypt,
The house of Jacob from a people of strange language,
2 Judah was his sanctuary,
And Israel his dominion.
3 The sea beheld, and fled;
The Jordan turned back.
4 The mountains skipped like rams,
And the hills like lambs.
5 What aileth thee, O thou sea! that thou fleest?
Thou, Jordan, that thou turnest back?
6 Ye mountains, that ye skip like rams,
And ye hills like lambs?
7 Tremble, O earth! at the presence of the Lord,
At the presence of the God of Jacob;
8 Who turned the rock into a standing lake,
And the flint into a fountain of water!

PSALM CXV.

Prayer that Jehovah would display his glory as the true God, by giving aid to his people against the worshippers of idols.

1 NOT unto us, O LORD! not unto us,
But unto thy name, give glory,
For thy mercy and thy truth's sake!
2 Why should the nations say,
"Where is now their God?"
3 Our God is in the heavens;
He doeth whatever he pleaseth.
4 Their idols are silver and gold,
The work of men's hands:
5 They have mouths, but they speak not;
Eyes have they, but they see not;
6 They have ears, but they hear not;
Noses have they, but they smell not;

7 They have hands, but they handle not;
They have feet, but they walk not;
Nor do they speak with their throats.
8 They who make them are like unto them;
And so is every one that trusteth in them.
9 O Israel! trust thou in the LORD!
He is their help and their shield.
10 O house of Aaron! trust ye in the LORD!
He is their help and their shield.
11 Ye that fear the LORD trust in the LORD!
He is their help and their shield.
12 The LORD hath been mindful of us; he will bless us;
He will bless the house of Israel;
He will bless the house of Aaron.
13 He will bless them that fear the LORD, both small and great.
14 The LORD will increase you more and more,
You and your children.
15 Blessed are ye of the LORD,
Who made heaven and earth.
16 The heaven is the LORD's heaven;
But the earth he hath given to the sons of men.
17 The dead praise not the LORD, —
No one who goeth down into silence.
18 But we will bless the LORD,
From this time forth even for ever!
Praise ye the LORD!

PSALM CXVI.

Thanksgiving for deliverance from distress.

1 I REJOICE that the LORD hath heard the voice of my supplication,
2 That he hath inclined his ear to me and heard me;
I will call upon him as long as I live.
3 The snares of death encompassed me,
And the pains of the underworld seized upon me;
I found distress and sorrow.
4 Then called I upon the LORD:
O LORD! deliver me!

5 Gracious is the LORD, and righteous;
Yea, our God is merciful.
6 The LORD preserveth the simple;
I was brought low, and he helped me.
7 Return, O my soul! to thy rest!
For the LORD hath dealt kindly with thee.
8 For thou hast preserved me from death;
Thou hast kept mine eyes from tears,
And my feet from falling!
9 I shall walk before the LORD,
In the land of the living.
10 I had trust, although I said,
"I am grievously afflicted!"
11 I said in my distress,
"All men are liars."
12 What shall I render to the LORD
For all his benefits to me?
13 I will take the cup of salvation,
And call upon the name of the LORD;
14 I will pay my vows to the LORD,
In the presence of all his people.
15 Precious in the eyes of the LORD
Is the death of his holy ones.
16 Hear, O LORD! for I am thy servant;
I am thy servant, the son of thy handmaid!
Thou hast loosed my bonds.
17 I will offer to thee the sacrifice of thanksgiving,
And will call upon the name of the LORD.
18 I will pay my vows to the LORD
In the presence of all his people,
19 In the courts of the house of the LORD,
In the midst of thee, O Jerusalem!
Praise ye the LORD!

PSALM CXVII.

A psalm of praise.

1 PRAISE the LORD, all ye nations!
Praise him, all ye people!
2 For great toward us hath been his kindness,
And the faithfulness of the LORD endureth for ever.
Praise ye the LORD!

PSALM CXVIII.

A psalm of public thanksgiving and triumph for deliverance from danger and victory over enemies.

1 O GIVE thanks to the LORD, for he is good;
For his kindness endureth for ever!
2 Let Israel now say,
His kindness endureth for ever!
3 Let the house of Aaron now say,
His goodness endureth for ever!
4 Let all who fear the LORD say,
His kindness endureth for ever!
5 I called upon the LORD in distress;
He heard, and set me in a wide place.
6 The LORD is on my side, I will not fear:
What can man do to me?
7 The LORD is my helper;
I shall see my desire upon my enemies.
8 It is better to trust in the LORD
Than to put confidence in man;
9 It is better to trust in the LORD
Than to put confidence in princes.
10 All the nations beset me around,
But in the name of the LORD I destroyed them.
11 They beset me on every side;
But in the name of the LORD I destroyed them.
12 They beset me around like bees;
They were quenched like the fire of thorns,
For in the name of the LORD I destroyed them.

13 Thou didst assail me with violence to bring me down!
But the LORD was my support.
14 The LORD is my glory and my song;
For to him I owe my salvation.
15 The voice of joy and salvation is in the habitations of the
righteous:
"The right hand of the LORD doeth valiantly;
16 The right hand of the LORD is exalted;
The right hand of the LORD doeth valiantly."
17 I shall not die, but live,
And declare the deeds of the LORD.
18 The LORD hath sorely chastened me,
But he hath not given me over to death.
19 Open to me the gates of righteousness,
That I may go in, and praise the LORD!
20 This is the gate of the LORD,
Through which the righteous enter.
21 I praise thee that thou hast heard me,
And hast been my salvation.
22 "The stone which the builders rejected
Hath become the chief corner-stone.
23 This is the LORD's doing;
It is marvellous in our eyes!
24 This is the day which the LORD hath made;
Let us rejoice and be glad in it!
25 Hear, O LORD! and bless us!
Hear, O LORD! and send us prosperity!"
26 "Blessed be he that cometh in the name of the LORD!
We bless you from the house of the LORD."
27 "Jehovah is God, he hath shone upon us:
Bind the sacrifice with cords to the horns of the altar!"
28 Thou art my God, and I will praise thee;
Thou art my God, and I will exalt thee!
29 O give thanks to the LORD, for he is good;
For his kindness endureth for ever!

PSALM CXIX.

The excellence of the divine laws, and the happiness of those who observe them. The aim of the poet seems to have been to present these two ideas in every possible variety of expression.

1 HAPPY are they who are upright in their way,
Who walk in the law of the LORD!
2 Happy are they who observe his ordinances,
And seek him with their whole heart;
3 Who also do no iniquity,
But walk in his ways!
4 Thou hast commanded us to keep thy precepts diligently.
5 O that my ways were directed to keep thy statutes!
6 Then shall I not be put to shame,
When I have respect to all thy commandments.
7 I will praise thee in uprightness of heart,
When I shall have learned thy righteous laws.
8 I will keep thy statutes;
Do not utterly forsake me!

9 How shall a young man keep his way pure?
By taking heed to it according to thy word.
10 With my whole heart have I sought thee;
O let me not wander from thy commandments!
11 Thy word have I hid in my heart,
That I might not sin against thee.
12 Blessed be thou, O LORD!
O teach me thy statutes!
13 With my lips do I declare
All the precepts of thy mouth.
14 In the way of thine ordinances I rejoice
As much as in all riches.
15 I meditate on thy precepts,
And have respect unto thy ways.
16 I delight myself in thy statutes;
I do not forget thy word.

17 Deal kindly with thy servant, that I may live,
And have regard to thy word!

18 Open thou mine eyes,
That I may behold wondrous things out of thy law!
19 I am a stranger in the earth;
O hide not thy precepts from me!
20 My soul breaketh within me,
On account of longing for thy judgments at all times.
21 Thou rebukest the proud, the accursed,
Who wander from thy commandments.
22 Remove from me reproach and contempt,
For I have kept thine ordinances!
23 Princes sit and speak against me,
But thy servant meditateth on thy statutes.
24 Thine ordinances are my delight;
Yea, they are my counsellors.

25 My soul cleaveth to the dust;
O revive me, according to thy word!
26 I have declared my ways, and thou hast heard me;
Teach me thy statutes!
27 Make me to understand the way of thy precepts!
So will I meditate upon thy wonders.
28 My soul weepeth for trouble;
O lift me up according to thy promise!
29 Remove from me the way of falsehood,
And graciously grant me thy law!
30 I have chosen the way of truth,
And set thy statutes before me.
31 I cleave to thine ordinances;
O LORD! let me not be put to shame!
32 I will run in the way of thy commandments,
When thou shalt enlarge my heart.

33 Teach me, O LORD! the way of thy statutes,
That I may keep it to the end!
34 Give me understanding, that I may keep thy law;
That I may observe it with my whole heart!
35 Cause me to tread in the path of thy commandments,
For in it I have my delight.
36 Incline my heart to thine ordinances,
And not to the love of gain!

37 Turn away mine eyes from beholding vanity,
And quicken me in thy law!
38 Fulfil to thy servant thy promise,
Which thou hast made to him who feareth thee!
39 Turn away the reproach which I fear;
For thy judgments are good.
40 Behold, I have longed for thy precepts;
O quicken thou me in thy righteousness!

41 Let thy mercies come to me, O LORD!
And thy help according to thy promise!
42 So shall I be able to answer him that reproacheth me;
For I trust in thy promise.
43 O take not the word of truth utterly out of my mouth!
For I trust in thy judgments.
44 So shall I keep thy law continually,
For ever and ever.
45 I shall walk in a wide path;
For I seek thy precepts.
46 I will speak of thine ordinances before kings,
And will not be ashamed.
47 I will delight myself in thy commandments, which I love;
48 I will lift up my hands to thy precepts, which I love;
I will meditate on thy statutes.

49 Remember thy promise to thy servant,
Because thou hast caused me to hope!
50 This is my comfort in my affliction;
For thy promise reviveth me.
51 The proud have had me greatly in derision;
Yet have I not swerved from thy law.
52 I remember thy judgments of old, O LORD!
And I comfort myself.
53 Indignation burneth within me,
On account of the wicked who forsake thy law.
54 Thy statutes have been my song
In the house of my pilgrimage.
55 In the night, O LORD! I think of thy name,
And keep thy law!
56 This have I as my own,
That I keep thy precepts.

57 Thou art my portion, O LORD!
I have resolved that I will keep thy precepts.
58 I have sought thy favor with my whole heart;
Be gracious unto me according to thy promise!
59 I think on my ways,
And turn my feet to thy statutes;
60 I make haste, and delay not,
To keep thy commandments.
61 The snares of the wicked surround me;
Yet do I not forget thy law.
62 At midnight I rise to give thanks to thee
On account of thy righteous judgments.
63 I am the companion of all who fear thee,
And who obey thy precepts.
64 The earth, O LORD! is full of thy goodness;
O teach me thy statutes!

65 Thou dost bless thy servant, O LORD!
According to thy promise!
66 Teach me sound judgment and knowledge!
For I have faith in thy commandments.
67 Before I was afflicted, I went astray;
But now I keep thy word.
68 Thou art good and doest good;
O teach me thy statutes!
69 The proud forge lies against me,
But I keep thy precepts with my whole heart.
70 Their heart is senseless like fat;
But I delight in thy law.
71 It is good for me that I have been afflicted,
That I might learn thy statutes.
72 The law of thy mouth is better to me
Than thousands of gold and silver.

73 Thy hands have made and fashioned me;
Give me understanding, that I may learn thy commandments!
74 They who fear thee shall see me and rejoice,
Because I trust in thy word.
75 I know, O LORD! that thy judgments are right,
And that in faithfulness thou hast afflicted me.

76 O let thy loving-kindness be my comfort,
According to thy promise to thy servant!
77 Let thy tender mercies come to me, that I may live!
For thy law is my delight.
78 May the proud be put to shame, who wrong me without
cause!
But I will meditate on thy precepts.
79 Let those who fear thee turn unto me,
And they that know thine ordinances!
80 May my heart be perfect in thy statutes,
That I may not be put to shame!

81 My soul fainteth for thy salvation;
In thy promise do I trust.
82 Mine eyes fail with looking for thy promise;
When, say I, wilt thou comfort me?
83 Yea, I am become like a bottle in the smoke;
Yet do I not forget thy statutes.
84 How many are the days of thy servant?
When wilt thou execute judgment upon my persecutors?
85 The proud have digged pits for me;
They who do not regard thy law.
86 All thy commandments are faithful;
They persecute me without cause; help thou me!
87 They had almost consumed me from the earth;
But I forsook not thy precepts.
88 Quicken me according to thy loving-kindness,
That I may keep the law of thy mouth!

89 Thy word, O LORD! abideth for ever,
Being established like the heavens;
90 Thy faithfulness endureth to all generations.
Thou hast established the earth, and it abideth.
91 They continue to this day according to their ordinances;
For they are all subject to thee.
92 Had not thy law been my delight,
I should have perished in my affliction.
93 I will never forget thy precepts;
For by them thou revivest me.
94 I am thine, help me!
For I seek thy precepts.

95 The wicked lie in wait to destroy me;
But I will have regard to thine ordinances.
96 I have seen an end of all perfection;
But thy law is exceeding broad.

97 O how I love thy law!
It is my daily meditation.
98 Thou hast made me wiser than my enemies by thy pre-
For they are ever before me. [cepts;
99 I have more understanding than all my teachers;
For thine ordinances are my meditation.
100 I have more wisdom than the ancients,
Because I keep thy precepts.
101 I have restrained my feet from every evil way,
That I might keep thy word.
102 I depart not from thy statutes,
For thou teachest me!
103 How sweet are thy words to my taste;
Yea, sweeter than honey to my mouth!
104 From thy precepts I learn wisdom;
Therefore do I hate every false way.

105 Thy word is a lamp to my feet,
And a light to my path.
106 I have sworn, and I will perform it,
That I will keep thy righteous statutes.
107 I am exceedingly afflicted;
Revive me, O Lord! according to thy word!
108 Accept, O Lord! the free-will offering of my mouth,
And teach me thy statutes!
109 My life is continually in my hand;
Yet do I not forget thy law.
110 The wicked lay snares for me,
Yet do I not go astray from thy precepts.
111 I have made thine ordinances my possession for ever;
For they are the joy of my heart.
112 I have inclined my heart to perform thy statutes,
Always, — even to the end.

113 I hate impious men,
And thy law I do love.

114 Thou art my hiding-place and my shield;
In thy word I put my trust!
115 Depart from me, ye evil-doers!
For I will keep the commandments of my God.
116 Uphold me according to thy promise, that I may live;
And let me not be ashamed of my hope!
117 Do thou hold me up, and I shall be safe,
And I will have respect to thy statutes continually!
118 Thou castest off all who depart from thy laws;
For their deceit is vain.
119 Thou throwest away all the wicked of the earth, like
Therefore I love thine ordinances. [dross;
120 My flesh trembleth through fear of thee,
And I am afraid of thy judgments.

121 I have done justice and equity;
O leave me not to mine oppressors
122 Be surety for thy servant for good;
Let not the proud oppress me!
123 Mine eyes fail with looking for thy help,
And for thy righteous promise.
124 Deal with thy servant according to thy mercy,
And teach me thy statutes!
125 I am thy servant; give me understanding,
That I may know thine ordinances!
126 It is time for thee, O Lord! to act;
For men have made void thy law.
127 Therefore I love thy commandments above gold;
Yea, above fine gold.
128 Therefore I esteem all thy precepts concerning all things
to be right;
I hate every false way.

129 Wonderful are thine ordinances;
Therefore do I observe them.
130 The communication of thy precepts giveth light;
It giveth understanding to the simple.
131 I open my mouth and pant;
For I long for thy commandments.
132 Look thou upon me, and be gracious to me,
As is just to those who love thy name!

133 Establish my footsteps in thy word,
And let no iniquity have dominion over me!
134 Redeem me from the oppression of men,
So will I keep thy precepts!
135 Let thy face shine on thy servant,
And teach me thy statutes!
136 Rivers of water run down mine eyes,
Because men keep not thy law.

137 Righteous art thou, O LORD!
And just are thy judgments!
138 Just are the ordinances which thou hast ordained,
And altogether righteous.
139 My zeal consumeth me,
Because my enemies forget thy word.
140 Thy word is very pure,
Therefore thy servant loveth it.
141 Of mean condition am I, and despised;
Yet do I not forget thy precepts.
142 Thy righteousness is everlasting righteousness,
And thy law is truth.
143 Trouble and anguish have taken hold of me,
But thy laws are my delight.
144 The justice of thine ordinances is everlasting;
Give me understanding, and I shall live!

145 I cry to thee with my whole heart;
Hear me, O LORD! that I may keep thy statutes.
146 I cry unto thee; save me,
And I will observe thine ordinances.
147 I come before the dawn with my prayer;
I trust in thy promise!
148 My eyes anticipate the night-watches,
That I may meditate upon thy promise.
149 Hear my voice according to thy loving-kindness;
O LORD! revive me according to thy mercy!
150 Near are they whose aim is mischief;
They are far from thy law;
151 Yet thou art near, O LORD!
And all thy commandments are truth!

152 Long have I known concerning thine ordinances,
That thou hast founded them for ever.
153 Look upon my affliction, and deliver me!
For I do not forget thy law.
154 Maintain my cause, and redeem me;
Revive me according to thy promise!
155 Salvation is far from the wicked,
Because they seek not thy statutes.
156 Great is thy compassion, O LORD!
Revive thou me according to thine equity!
157 Many are my persecutors and my enemies,
Yet do I not depart from thine ordinances.
158 I behold the transgressors, and am grieved
Because they regard not thy word.
159 Behold, how I love thy precepts!
O LORD! revive me according to thy loving-kindness!
160 The whole of thy word is truth,
And all thy righteous judgments endure for ever.

161 Princes have persecuted me without cause;
But my heart standeth in awe of thy word.
162 I rejoice in thy word,
As one that hath found great spoil.
163 I hate and abhor lying,
And thy law do I love.
164 Seven times a day do I praise thee
On account of thy righteous judgments.
165 Great peace have they who love thy law,
And no evil shall befall them.
166 O LORD! I wait for thy salvation,
And keep thy commandments!
167 My soul observeth thine ordinances,
And loveth them exceedingly.
168 I keep thy precepts and thine ordinances;
For all my ways are before thee.

169 Let my prayer come near before thee, O LORD!
According to thy promise, give me understanding!
170 Let my supplication come before thee;
O deliver me according to thy promise!

171 My lips shall pour forth praise;
For thou teachest me thy statutes.
172 My tongue shall sing of thy word;
For all thy commandments are right.
173 Let thy hand be my help;
For I have chosen thy precepts!
174 I long for thy salvation, O LORD!
And thy law is my delight!
175 Let me live, and I will praise thee;
Let thy judgments help me!
176 I wander like a lost sheep; seek thy servant,
For I do not forget thy commandments!

PSALM CXX.

Complaints concerning enemies, especially deceivers and calumniators.

A psalm of steps.

1 IN my distress I called upon the LORD,
And he answered me.
2 O LORD! deliver me from lying lips,
From the deceitful tongue!
3 What profit to thee,
Or what advantage to thee, is the false tongue?
4 It is like the sharp arrows of the mighty man;
Like coals of the juniper.
5 Alas for me, that I sojourn in Mesech,
That I dwell in the tents of Kedar!
6 Too long have I dwelt
With them that hate peace!
7 I am for peace; yet, when I speak for it,
They are for war.

PSALM CXXI.

Confidence of safety under the protection of God.

A psalm of the steps, or the goings up.

1 I LIFT up mine eyes to the hills:
Whence cometh my help?

2 My help cometh from the LORD,
Who made heaven and earth.
3 He will not suffer thy foot to stumble;
Thy guardian doth not slumber.
4 Behold, the guardian of Israel
Doth neither slumber nor sleep.
5 The LORD is thy guardian;
The LORD is thy shade at thy right hand.
6 The sun shall not smite thee by day,
Nor the moon by night.
7 The LORD will preserve thee from all evil;
He will preserve thy life.
8 The LORD will preserve thee, when thou goest out and when thou comest in,
From this time forth for ever.

PSALM CXXII.

Hymn of the Israelites on their journey to the festivals in Jerusalem.

A psalm of the steps, or the goings up. By David.

1 I WAS glad when they said to me,
Let us go up to the house of the LORD!
2 Our feet are standing
Within thy gates, O Jerusalem!
3 Jerusalem, the rebuilt city!
The city that is joined together!
4 Thither the tribes go up,
The tribes of the LORD, according to the law of Israel
To praise the name of the LORD.
5 There stand the thrones of judgment,
The thrones of the house of David.
6 Pray for the peace of Jerusalem!
May they prosper who love thee!
7 Peace be within thy walls,
And prosperity within thy palaces!
8 For my brethren and companions' sake will I say,
Peace be within thee!
9 For the sake of the house of the LORD, our God
Will I seek thy good!

PSALM CXXIII.

Prayer for the deliverance of the Jewish nation from oppression.

A song of the steps, or the goings up.

1 To thee do I lift up mine eyes,
O Thou who dwellest in the heavens!
2 Behold, as the eyes of servants look to the hand of their masters,
And as the eyes of a maiden to the hand of her mistress,
So do our eyes look to the LORD, our God,
Until he have pity upon us.
3 Have mercy upon us, O LORD! have mercy upon us,
For we are overwhelmed with contempt!
4 Our soul is filled to the full with the scorn of those who are at ease,
And with the contempt of the proud.

PSALM CXXIV.

Thanksgiving for deliverance from national calamity.

A psalm of the steps, or the goings up. By David.

1 IF the LORD had not been for us,
Now may Israel say,
2 If the LORD had not been for us,
When men rose up against us,
3 Then had they swallowed us up alive,
When their wrath burned against us;
4 Then the waters had overwhelmed us;
The stream had gone over our soul;
5 The proud waters had gone over our soul.
6 Blessed be the LORD,
Who hath not given us a prey to their teeth!
7 We have escaped like a bird from the snare of the fowler;
The snare is broken, and we have escaped.
8 Our help is in the name of the LORD,
Who made heaven and earth.

PSALM CXXV.

Trust in Jehovah, as the perpetual protector of Israel.

A psalm of the steps, or the goings up.

1 THEY who trust in the LORD shall be as Mount Zion,
Which cannot be moved, which standeth for ever.
2 As the mountains are round about Jerusalem,
So the LORD is round about his people,
Henceforth even for ever!
3 For the sceptre of the wicked shall not remain upon the portion of the righteous,
Lest the righteous put forth their hands to iniquity.
4 Do good, O LORD! to the good,
To them that are upright in heart!
5 But such as turn aside to their crooked ways, —
May the LORD destroy them with the evil-doers!
Peace be to Israel!

PSALM CXXVI.

Prayer of those who had returned from captivity for the restoration of the exiles remaining at Babylon.

A psalm of the steps, or the goings up.

1 WHEN the LORD brought back the captivity of Zion,
We were like them that dream.
2 Then was our mouth filled with laughter,
And our tongue with singing.
Then said they among the nations,
"The LORD hath done great things for them!"
3 Yea, the LORD hath done great things for us,
For which we are glad.
4 Bring back, O LORD! our captivity,
Like streams in the South!
5 They who sow in tears
Shall reap in joy.
6 Yea, he goeth forth weeping, bearing his seed;
He shall surely come back rejoicing, bearing his sheaves.

PSALM CXXVII.

Without the blessing of God, nothing prospers.

A psalm of the steps, or the goings up. By Solomon.

1 EXCEPT the LORD build the house,
The builders labor in vain;
Except the LORD guard the city,
The watchman waketh in vain.
2 In vain ye rise up early, and go to rest late,
And eat the bread of care!
The same giveth he his beloved one in sleep.
3 Behold! sons are an inheritance from the LORD,
And the fruit of the womb is his gift.
4 As arrows in the hand of the warrior,
So are the sons of young men:
5 Happy the man that hath his quiver full of them!
They shall not be put to shame,
When they speak with adversaries in the gate.

PSALM CXXVIII.

Blessings promised to the religious man.

A psalm of the steps, or the goings up.

1 HAPPY is he who feareth the LORD,
Who walketh in his ways!
2 Thou shalt eat the labor of thy hands;
Happy shalt thou be, and it shall be well with thee!
3 Thy wife shall be like a fruitful vine within thy house;
Thy children like olive-branches round about thy table.
4 Behold! thus happy is the man who feareth the LORD!
5 Jehovah shall bless thee out of Zion,
And thou shalt see the prosperity of Jerusalem all the days of thy life;
6 Yea, thou shalt see thy children's children.
Peace be to Israel!

PSALM CXXIX.

Grateful acknowledgment of past deliverances, and hopes of future aid, and of the downfall of enemies.

A psalm of the steps, or the goings up.

1 MUCH have they afflicted me from my youth,
May Israel now say;
2 Much have they afflicted me from my youth,
Yet have they not prevailed against me.
3 The ploughers ploughed up my back;
They made long their furrows;
4 But the LORD was righteous;
He cut asunder the cords of the wicked.
5 Let all be driven back with shame
Who hate Zion!
6 Let them be as grass upon the house-tops,
Which withereth before one pulleth it up;
7 With which the reaper filleth not his hand,
Nor he that bindeth sheaves his bosom!
8 And they who pass by do not say,
"The blessing of the LORD be upon you!
We bless you in the name of the LORD!"

PSALM CXXX.

Prayer for forgiveness and help for Israel.

A psalm of the steps, or the goings up.

1 OUT of the depths do I cry to thee, O LORD!
2 O Lord! listen to my voice,
Let thine ears be attentive to my supplication!
3 If thou, LORD, shouldst treasure up transgressions,
Lord, who could stand?
4 But with thee is forgiveness,
That thou mayst be feared.
5 I trust in the LORD; my soul doth trust,
And in his promise do I confide.

6 My soul waiteth for the LORD
More than they who watch for the morning;
Yea, more than they who watch for the morning!
7 O Israel! trust in the LORD!
For with the LORD is mercy,
And with him is plenteous redemption.
8 He will redeem Israel
From all his iniquities.

PSALM CXXXI.

Profession of humility, contentment, and submission.

A psalm of the steps, or the goings up. Of David.

1 O LORD! my heart is not haughty, nor my eyes lofty;
I employ not myself on great things, or things too wonderful for me!
2 Yea, I have stilled and quieted my soul
As a weaned child upon his mother;
My soul within me is like a weaned child.
3 O Israel! trust in the LORD,
Henceforth even for ever!

PSALM CXXXII.

Prayer at the dedication of the temple. With ver. 8–10, compare 2 Chron. vi. 41, 42.

A psalm of the steps, or the goings up.

1 O LORD! remember David,
And all his affliction!
2 How he sware to Jehovah,
And vowed to the Mighty One of Jacob:
3 "I will not go into my house,
Nor lie down on my bed,
4 I will not give sleep to my eyes,
Nor slumber to my eyelids,

5 Until I find a place for Jehovah,
A habitation for the Mighty One of Jacob."
6 Behold, we heard of it at Ephratah;
We found it in the fields of the forest.
7 Let us go into his habitation;
Let us worship at his footstool!
8 Arise, O LORD! into thy rest,
Thou, and the ark of thy strength!
9 Let thy priests be clothed with righteousness,
And thy holy ones shout for joy!
10 For the sake of thy servant David,
Reject not the prayer of thine anointed!
11 Jehovah hath sworn in truth unto David,
And he will not depart from it:
"Of the fruit of thy body will I place upon the throne
for thee.
12 If thy children keep my covenant,
And my statutes, which I teach them,
Their children also throughout all ages
Shall sit upon thy throne."
13 For Jehovah hath chosen Zion;
He hath desired it as his dwelling-place.

14 "This is my resting-place for ever;
Here will I dwell, for I have chosen it.
15 I will abundantly bless her provision;
I will satisfy her poor with bread.
16 I will also clothe her priests with salvation,
And her holy ones shall shout aloud for joy.
17 There will I cause to spring forth a horn for David;
I have prepared a light for mine anointed.
18 His enemies will I clothe with shame,
And the crown shall glitter upon his head."

PSALM CXXXIII.

Praise of unity among brethren.

A psalm of the steps, or the goings up. By David.

1 BEHOLD, how good and pleasant it is
For brethren to dwell together in unity!
2 It is like precious perfume upon the head,
Which ran down upon the beard,
The beard of Aaron;
Which went down to the very border of his garments;
3 Like the dew of Hermon,
Like that which descendeth upon the mountains of Zion.
For there the LORD commandeth a blessing,
Even life for evermore.

PSALM CXXXIV.

Exhortation to the servants of the temple to celebrate the praises of God.

A psalm of the steps, or the goings up.

1 O PRAISE the LORD, all ye servants of the LORD,
Who stand in the house of the LORD by night!
2 Lift up your hands to the sanctuary,
And praise the LORD!
3 May the LORD, who made heaven and earth,
Bless thee out of Zion!

PSALM CXXXV.

A national psalm of praise to Jehovah.

1 PRAISE ye the LORD!
Praise ye the name of the LORD!
Praise him, O ye servants of the LORD!
2 Ye who stand in the house of the LORD,
In the courts of the house of our God!
3 Praise ye the LORD, for the LORD is good;
Praise his name, for he is kind!

4 For the LORD chose Jacob for himself,
And Israel for his own possession.
5 I know that the LORD is great;
That our Lord is above all gods.
6 All that the LORD pleaseth, that he doeth,
In heaven and upon earth,
In the sea, and in all deeps.
7 He causeth the clouds to ascend from the ends of the earth;
He maketh lightnings for the rain;
He bringeth the wind from his store-houses.

8 He smote the first-born of Egypt,
Both of man and beast.
9 He sent signs and wonders into the midst of thee, O Egypt!
Against Pharaoh and all his servants!
10 He smote many nations,
And slew mighty kings;
11 Sihon, the king of the Amorites,
And Og, the king of Bashan,
And all the kings of Canaan;
12 And gave their land for an inheritance,
For an inheritance to Israel, his people.
13 Thy name, O LORD! endureth for ever;
Thy memorial, O LORD! to all generations!
14 For the LORD judgeth his people,
And hath compassion on his servants.
15 The idols of the nations are silver and gold,
The work of men's hands.
16 They have mouths, but they speak not;
Eyes have they, but they see not.
17 They have ears, but they hear not;
And there is no breath in their mouths.
18 They that make them are like them;
So is every one that trusteth in them.
19 Praise the LORD, O house of Israel!
Praise the LORD, O house of Aaron!
20 Praise the LORD, O house of Levi!
Ye that fear the LORD, bless the LORD!
21 Praised be the LORD out of Zion,—
He that dwelleth in Jerusalem!
Praise ye the LORD!

PSALM CXXXVI.

A psalm of thanksgiving for God's blessings to the people of Israel.

1 O GIVE thanks to the LORD! for he is kind;
For his goodness endureth for ever!
2 O give thanks to the God of gods;
For his goodness endureth for ever!
3 O give thanks to the Lord of lords;
For his goodness endureth for ever!
4 To him that alone doeth great wonders;
For his goodness endureth for ever!
5 To him that made the heavens with wisdom;
For his goodness endureth for ever!
6 To him that spread out the earth upon the waters;
For his goodness endureth for ever!
7 To him that made the great lights;
For his goodness endureth for ever!
8 The sun to rule the day;
For his goodness endureth for ever!
9 The moon and stars to rule the night;
For his goodness endureth for ever!
10 To him that smote in Egypt their first-born;
For his goodness endureth for ever!
11 And brought Israel from the midst of them;
For his goodness endureth for ever!
12 With a strong hand and an outstretched arm;
For his goodness endureth for ever!
13 To him who divided the Red sea into parts;
For his goodness endureth for ever!
14 And made Israel to pass through the midst of it;
For his goodness endureth for ever!
15 And overthrew Pharaoh and his host in the Red sea;
For his goodness endureth for ever!
16 To him who led his people through the wilderness.
For his goodness endureth for ever!
17 To him who smote great kings;
For his goodness endureth for ever!
18 And slew mighty kings;
For his goodness endureth for ever!

19 Sihon, the king of the Amorites;
For his goodness endureth for ever!
20 And Og, the king of Bashan;
For his goodness endureth for ever!
21 And gave their land for an inheritance;
For his goodness endureth for ever!
22 For an inheritance to Israel his servant;
For his goodness endureth for ever!
23 Who remembered us in our low estate;
For his goodness endureth for ever!
24 And redeemed us from our enemies;
For his goodness endureth for ever!
25 Who giveth food unto all;
For his goodness endureth for ever!
26 O give thanks to the God of heaven;
For his goodness endureth for ever!

PSALM CXXXVII.

The sadness of the captivity at Babylon.

1 By the rivers of Babylon, there we sat down, yea, we wept,
When we remembered Zion.
2 We hung our harps on the willows in the midst thereof.
3 For there they who carried us away captive required of us a song;
They who wasted us required of us mirth:
"Sing us one of the songs of Zion!"
4 How shall we sing the Lord's song
In a strange land?
5 If I forget thee, O Jerusalem,
Let my right hand forget her cunning!
6 If I do not remember thee,
Let my tongue cleave to the roof of my mouth;
If I prefer not Jerusalem above my chief joy!

7 Remember, O Lord! against the children of Edom
The day of the calamity of Jerusalem!
Who said, "Raze it,
Raze it to its foundations!"

8 O daughter of Babylon, thou destroyer!
Happy be he who requiteth thee
As thou hast dealt with us!
9 Happy be he who seizeth thy little ones
And dasheth them against the stones!

PSALM CXXXVIII.

Thanksgiving for deliverance from trouble.

A psalm of David.

1 I WILL praise thee with my whole heart;
Before the gods will I sing praise to thee;
2 I will worship toward thy holy temple,
And praise thy name for thy goodness and thy truth;
For thy promise thou hast magnified above all thy name!
3 In the day when I called, thou didst hear me;
Thou didst strengthen me, and encourage my soul.
4 All the kings of the earth shall praise thee, O LORD!
When they hear the promises of thy mouth!
5 Yea, they shall sing of the ways of the LORD;
For great is the glory of the LORD.
6 The LORD is high, yet he looketh upon the humble,
And the proud doth he know from afar.
7 Though I walk through the midst of trouble, thou wilt revive me;
Thou wilt stretch forth thy hand against the wrath of my enemies;
Thou wilt save me by thy right hand!
8 The LORD will perform all things for me;
Thy goodness, O LORD! endureth for ever:
Forsake not the works of thine hands!

PSALM CXXXIX.

The universal presence and knowledge of God.

For the leader of the music. A psalm of David.

1 O LORD! thou hast searched me and known me!
2 Thou knowest my sitting-down and my rising-up;
Thou understandest my thoughts from afar!
3 Thou seest my path and my lying-down,
And art acquainted with all my ways!
4 For before the word is upon my tongue,
Behold, O LORD! thou knowest it altogether!
5 Thou besettest me behind and before,
And layest thine hand upon me!
6 Such knowledge is too wonderful for me;
It is high, I cannot attain to it!
7 Whither shall I go from thy spirit,
And whither shall I flee from thy presence?
8 If I ascend into heaven, thou art there!
If I make my bed in the underworld, behold, thou art there!
9 If I take the wings of the morning,
And dwell in the remotest parts of the sea,
10 Even there shall thy hand lead me,
And thy right hand shall hold me!
11 If I say, "Surely the darkness shall cover me;"
Even the night shall be light about me.
12 Yea, the darkness hideth not from thee,
But the night shineth as the day;
The darkness and the light are both alike to thee!
13 For thou didst form my reins;
Thou didst weave me in my mother's womb.
14 I will praise thee; for I am fearfully and wonderfully made;
Marvellous are thy works,
And this my soul knoweth full well!
15 My frame was not hidden from thee,
When I was made in secret,
When I was curiously wrought in the lower parts of the earth.

16 Thine eyes did see my substance, while yet unformed,
And in thy book was every thing written;
My days were appointed before one of them existed.
17 How precious to me are thy thoughts, O God!
How great is the sum of them!
18 If I should count them, they would outnumber the sand:
When I awake, I am still with thee!

19 O that thou wouldst slay the wicked, O God!
Ye men of blood, depart from me!
20 For they speak against thee wickedly;
Thine enemies utter thy name for falsehood.
21 Do I not hate them that hate thee, O LORD?
Do I not abhor them that rise up against thee?
22 Yea, I hate them with perfect hatred;
I count them mine enemies.
23 Search me, O God! and know my heart;
Try me, and know my thoughts;
24 And see if the way of trouble be within me,
And lead me in the way everlasting!

PSALM CXL.

Prayer for aid against wicked enemies.

For the leader of the music. A psalm of David.

1 DELIVER me, O LORD! from the evil man,
Save me from the man of violence,
2 Who meditate mischief in their heart,
And daily stir up war!
3 They sharpen their tongues like a serpent;
The poison of the adder is under their lips. [Pause.]
4 Defend me, O LORD! from the hands of the wicked,
Preserve me from the man of violence,
Who have purposed to cause my fall! [Pause.]
5 The proud have hidden snares and cords for me;
They have spread a net by the way-side;
They have set traps for me.
6 I say to Jehovah, Thou art my God;
Hear, O Jehovah! the voice of my supplication!

7 The Lord Jehovah is my saving strength:
Thou shelterest my head in the day of battle!
8 Grant not, O Lord! the desires of the wicked;
Let not their devices prosper;
Let them not exalt themselves!
9 As for the heads of those who encompass me,
Let the mischief of their own lips cover them!
10 Let burning coals fall upon them;
May they be cast into the fire,
And into deep waters from which they shall not arise!
11 The slanderer shall not be established upon the earth;
Evil shall pursue the violent man to destruction.
12 I know that the Lord will maintain the cause of the afflicted,
And the right of the poor.
13 Yea, the righteous shall praise thy name;
The upright shall dwell in thy presence!

PSALM CXLI.

A prayer for deliverance from enemies.

For the leader of the music. A psalm of David.

1 I cry to thee, O Lord! make haste unto me!
Give ear to my voice, when I cry unto thee!
2 Let my prayer come before thee as incense,
And the lifting-up of my hands, as the evening sacrifice!
3 Set a watch, O Lord! before my mouth;
Guard the door of my lips!
4 Let not my heart incline to any evil thing;
Let me not practise wickedness with the doers of iniquity,
And let me not eat of their delicacies!
5 Let the righteous smite me, — it shall be a kindness;
Let him reprove me, and it shall be oil for my head;
Let him do it again, and my head shall not refuse it;
But now I pray against their wickedness!
6 When their judges are hurled over the side of the rock,
They shall hear how pleasant are my words.

7 So are our bones scattered at the mouth of the underworld,
As when one furroweth and ploweth up the land.
8 But to thee do my eyes look, O Lord Jehovah!
In thee is my trust;
Let not my life be poured out!
9 Preserve me from the snares which they have laid for me,
And from the nets of evil-doers!
10 Let the wicked fall together into their own traps,
Whilst I make my escape!

PSALM CXLII.

Prayer for deliverance from enemies.

A psalm of David; a prayer, when he was in the cave

1 I CRY unto the LORD with my voice;
With my voice to the LORD do I make my supplication.
2 I pour out my complaint before him;
I declare before him my distress.
3 When my spirit is overwhelmed within me,
Thou knowest my path!
In the way which I walk, they have hid a snare for me.
4 I look on my right hand, and behold,
But no man knoweth me;
Refuge faileth me;
No one careth for me.
5 I cry unto thee, O LORD!
I say, Thou art my refuge,
My portion in the land of the living.
6 Attend to my cry, for I am brought very low;
Deliver me from my persecutors,
For they prevail against me!
7 Bring me out of prison,
That I may praise thy name!
The righteous shall gather around me,
When thou shalt show me thy favor.

PSALM CXLIII.

A prayer for deliverance from enemies.

A psalm of David.

1 HEAR my prayer, O LORD! give ear to my supplications!
In thy faithfulness, and in thy righteousness, answer me!
2 Enter not into judgment with thy servant;
For before thee no man living is righteous.
3 For the enemy pursueth my life;
He hath smitten me to the ground;
He hath made me dwell in darkness,
As those that have been dead of old.
4 My spirit is overwhelmed within me;
My heart within me is desolate.
5 I remember the days of old;
I meditate on all thy works;
I muse on the deeds of thy hands.
6 I stretch forth my hands unto thee;
My soul thirsteth for thee, like a parched land.
7 Hear me speedily, O LORD!
My spirit faileth;
Hide not thy face from me,
Lest I become like those who go down to the pit!
8 Cause me to see thy loving-kindness speedily;
For in thee do I trust!
Make known to me the way which I should take;
For to thee do I lift up my soul!
9 Deliver me, O LORD! from mine enemies;
For in thee do I seek refuge!
10 Teach me to do thy will;
For thou art my God!
Let thy good spirit lead me in a plain path!
11 Revive me, O LORD! for thy name's sake!
In thy righteousness, bring me out of my distress!
12 And, in thy compassion, cut off mine enemies,
And destroy all that distress me!
For I am thy servant.

PSALM CXLIV.

Thanksgiving, prayer against enemies, and supplication for blessings upon the people.

A psalm of David.

1 BLESSED be the LORD, my rock,
Who teacheth my hands to war,
And my fingers to fight!
2 He who is my loving-kindness and my fortress;
My high tower and my deliverer,
My shield, and he in whom I trust;
Who subdueth peoples under me.
3 LORD, what is man, that thou art mindful of him,
Or the son of man, that thou makest account of him?
4 Man is like a vapor;
His day is like a shadow that passeth away.

5 Bow thy heavens, O LORD! and come down;
Touch the mountains, so that they shall smoke!
6 Cast forth lightnings, and scatter them;
Shoot forth thine arrows, and destroy them!
7 Send forth thine hand from above;
Rescue and save me from deep waters;
From the hands of aliens,
8 Whose mouth uttereth deceit,
And whose right hand is a right hand of falsehood!

9 I will sing to thee a new song, O God!
Upon a ten-stringed psaltery will I sing praise to thee;
10 To thee, who givest salvation to kings,
Who deliverest David, thy servant, from the destructive sword!
11 Rescue and deliver me from the hands of aliens,
Whose mouth uttereth deceit,
And whose right hand is a right hand of falsehood!
12 That our sons may be as plants,
Grown up in their youth;
Our daughters as corner-pillars,
Hewn like those of a palace!

13 That our garners may be full,
Affording all kinds of store;
That our sheep may bring forth thousands
And ten thousands in our streets.
14 That our cattle may be fruitful;
That there be no breaking in, or going out;
And no outcry in our streets.
15 Happy the people that is in such a state!
Yea, happy the people whose God is Jehovah!

PSALM CXLV.

Praise to God for his righteous and merciful government and his kind providence.

A song of praise. By David.

1 I WILL extol thee, my God, the King!
I will praise thy name for ever and ever!
2 Every day will I bless thee,
And praise thy name for ever and ever!
3 Great is the LORD, and greatly to be praised;
Yea, his greatness is unsearchable.
4 One generation shall praise thy works to another,
And shall declare thy mighty deeds.
5 I will speak of the glorious honor of thy majesty,
And of thy wonderful works.
6 Men shall speak of the might of thy terrible deeds,
And I will declare thy greatness;
7 They shall pour forth the praise of thy great goodness,
And sing of thy righteousness.
8 The LORD is gracious, and full of compassion,
Slow to anger, and rich in mercy.
9 The LORD is good to all,
And his tender mercies are over all his works.
10 All thy works praise thee, O LORD!
And thy holy ones bless thee!
11 They speak of the glory of thy kingdom,
And talk of thy power;
12 To make known to the sons of men his mighty deeds,
And the glorious majesty of his kingdom.

13 Thy kingdom is an everlasting kingdom,
And thy dominion endureth throughout all generations.
14 The LORD upholdeth all that fall,
And raiseth up all that are bowed down.
15 The eyes of all wait upon thee,
And thou givest them their food in due season;
16 Thou openest thine hand,
And satisfiest the desire of every living thing.
17 The LORD is righteous in all his ways,
And merciful in all his works.
18 The LORD is nigh to all that call upon him,
To all that call upon him in truth.
19 He fulfilleth the desire of them that fear him;
He heareth their cry, and saveth them.
20 The LORD preserveth all that love him;
But all the wicked he will destroy.
21 My mouth shall speak the praise of the LORD;
And let all flesh bless his holy name for ever and ever!

PSALM CXLVI.

Admonition to trust not in man, but in the justice and mercy of God.

1 PRAISE ye the LORD!
Praise the LORD, O my soul!
2 I will praise the LORD, as long as I live;
I will sing praises to my God, while I have my being.
3 Put not your trust in princes,
In the son of man, in whom is no help!
4 His breath goeth forth; he returneth to the dust;
In that very day his plans perish.
5 Happy is he that hath the God of Jacob for his help;
Whose hope is in the LORD, his God;
6 Who made heaven and earth,
The sea, and all that is therein;
Who keepeth truth for ever;
7 Who executeth judgment for the oppressed;
Who giveth food to the hungry.
The LORD setteth free the prisoners;

8 The LORD openeth the eyes of the blind;
The LORD raiseth up them that are bowed down;
The LORD loveth the righteous.
9 The LORD preserveth the strangers;
He relieveth the fatherless and the widow;
But the way of the wicked he maketh crooked.
10 The LORD shall reign for ever;
Thy God, O Zion! to all generations!
Praise ye the LORD!

PSALM CXLVII.

The power and goodness of God in nature, and in his peculiar favor to Israel.

1 PRAISE ye the LORD!
For it is good to sing praise to our God;
For it is pleasant, and praise is becoming.
2 The LORD buildeth up Jerusalem;
He gathereth together the dispersed of Israel.
3 He healeth the broken in heart,
And bindeth up their wounds.
4 He counteth the number of the stars;
He calleth them all by their names.
5 Great is our Lord, and mighty in power;
His understanding is infinite.
6 The LORD lifteth up the lowly;
He casteth the wicked down to the ground.
7 Sing to the LORD with thanksgiving;
Sing praises upon the harp to our God!
8 Who covereth the heavens with clouds,
Who prepareth rain for the earth,
Who causeth grass to grow upon the mountains.
9 He giveth to the cattle their food,
And to the young ravens, when they cry.
10 He delighteth not in the strength of the horse,
He taketh not pleasure in the legs of a man.
11 The LORD taketh pleasure in those who fear him,
In those who trust in his mercy.
12 Praise the LORD, O Jerusalem!
Praise thy God, O Zion!

13 For he hath strengthened the bars of thy gates;
He hath blessed thy children within thee.
14 He maketh peace in thy borders,
And satisfieth thee with the finest of the wheat.
15 He sendeth forth his command to the earth;
His word runneth very swiftly.
16 He giveth snow like wool,
And scattereth the hoar-frost like ashes.
17 He casteth forth his ice like morsels;
Who can stand before his cold?
18 He sendeth forth his word, and melteth them;
He causeth his wind to blow, and the waters flow.
19 He publisheth his word to Jacob,
His statutes and laws to Israel.
20 He hath dealt in this manner with no other nation;
And, as for his ordinances, they have not known them.
Praise ye the LORD!

PSALM CXLVIII.

Invocation of the heavens and the earth to praise the Lord.

1 PRAISE ye the LORD!
Praise the LORD from the heavens!
Praise him in the heights!
2 Praise him, all ye his angels!
Praise him, all ye his hosts!
3 Praise ye him, sun and moon!
Praise him, all ye stars of light!
4 Praise him, ye heavens of heavens!
Ye waters, that are above the heavens!
5 Let them praise the name of the LORD;
For he commanded, and they were created.
6 He hath also established them for ever;
He hath given them a law, and they transgress it not.

7 Praise the LORD from the earth,
Ye sea-monsters, and all deeps!
8 Fire and hail, snow and vapor;
Thou tempest, that fulfillest his word!

9 Ye mountains, and all hills!
Fruit-trees, and all cedars!
10 Ye wild beasts, and all cattle!
Ye creeping things, and winged birds!
11 Ye kings, and all peoples,
Princes, and all judges of the earth!
12 Young men and maidens,
Old men and children!
13 Let them praise the name of the LORD!
For his name alone is exalted;
His glory is above the earth and the heavens.
14 He exalteth the horn of his people,
The glory of all his godly ones,
Of the children of Israel, a people near to him.
Praise ye the LORD!

PSALM CXLIX.

Praise to God for national blessings, especially for success against foreign enemies.

1 PRAISE ye the LORD!
Sing unto the LORD a new song;
His praise in the assembly of the godly!
2 Let Israel rejoice in him that made him;
Let the sons of Zion be joyful in their king!
3 Let them praise his name in the dance;
Let them praise him with the timbrel and harp!
4 For the LORD taketh pleasure in his people;
He will beautify the distressed with salvation.
5 Let the godly rejoice in their glory;
Let them shout for joy upon their beds!
6 Let the praises of God be in their mouth,
And a two-edged sword in their hand,
7 To execute vengeance upon the nations,
And punishment upon the peoples!
8 To bind their kings with chains,
And their nobles with fetters of iron;
9 To execute upon them the sentence which is written
This honor have all his godly ones.
Praise ye the LORD!

PSALM CL.

Exhortation to praise God.

1 PRAISE ye the LORD!
Praise God in his sanctuary!
Praise him in his glorious firmament!
2 Praise him for his mighty deeds!
Praise him according to his excellent greatness!
3 Praise him with the sound of trumpets!
Praise him with the psaltery and harp!
4 Praise him with the timbrel and dance!
Praise him with stringed instruments and pipes!
5 Praise him with the clear-sounding cymbals!
Praise him with the high-sounding cymbals!
6 Let every thing that hath breath praise the LORD!
Praise ye the LORD!

THE PROVERBS.

INTRODUCTION TO THE PROVERBS.

THAT part of Hebrew literature which has come down to us under the name of the Proverbs of Solomon contains something more than the title indicates. It is not wholly composed of short, sententious maxims and enigmatical propositions, such as commonly receive the name of proverbs, but in part of several didactic discourses of considerable length, containing exhortations to prudence and virtue, warnings against vice and folly, and eulogies upon true wisdom. The first nine chapters belong to the latter species of composition. These discourses, as well as the proper proverbs, are expressed in the peculiar form and language of Hebrew poetry, and without doubt belong to the most flourishing period of Hebrew literature. On the nature and history of this kind of composition, the following just remarks have been made by Holden, in his Preliminary Dissertation to the Proverbs: —

"Short and pithy sentences have been employed from the most remote antiquity as the vehicle of ethical instruction, and particularly adapted to the simplicity of the early ages. When writings were but few, and the reasonings of systematic philosophy almost unknown, just observations on life and manners, and useful moral precepts, delivered in concise language, and often in verse, would form a body of the most valuable practical wisdom, which, by its influence on the conduct, must have contributed largely to the peace and well-being of society. An acute remark, a moral adage, an admonition conveyed in a brief and compact sentence, would arrest the attention and operate upon the hearts of a rude people with a force of which there is no example in periods of greater cultivation. Yet, in every age, they are well fitted to impress the minds of the young and the uninformed; and, as they are the most valuable guides in the affairs of life, when we are called upon, not to deliberate, but to act, not to unfold a circuitous argument, but to transact business, all must find it highly advantageous to retain in their memories the maxims of proverbial wisdom.

"This method of instruction appears to be peculiarly suited to the genius and disposition of the Asiatics, among whom it has prevailed from the earliest ages. The Gymnosophists of India delivered their philosophy in brief, enigmatical sentences;* a practice adopted and carried to a great extent by the ancient Egyptians.† The mode of conveying instruction by compendious maxims obtained among the Hebrews, from the first dawn of their literature, to its final extinction in the East through the power of the Mohammedan arms; and it was familiar to the inhabitants of Syria and Palestine, as we learn from the testimony of St. Jerome.‡ The eloquence of Arabia was mostly exhibited in detached and unconnected sentences, which, like so many loose gems, attracted attention by the fulness of the periods, the elegance of the phraseology, and the acuteness of proverbial sayings.§ Nor do the Asiatics ‖ at present differ in this respect from

---

* Diog. Laert. Prœm., p. 4, Genev. 1615.

† Jablonski, Pantheon Ægypt, Proleg., c. 3. Brucker, lib. i. c. 8.

‡ "Familiare est Syris, et maxime Palæstinis, ad omnem sermonem suum parabolas jungere." — Hieron., Comment. Matt. xviii. 23.

§ "Orationes autem eorum minime in partes suas juxta rhetoricæ apud Græcos et Latinos præcepta distributæ, nec methodice concinnatæ; adeo ut sententiarum in iis frequentium gemmæ vere dispersæ, minimeque inter se colligatæ videantur, totusque sermo arena sine calce recte dici posse videatur. In sententiarum tamen rotunditate, phrasium elegantia, ac proverbiorum acumine, invenies quod animum feriat." — Pococke, Specimen Historiæ Arabum, p. 167, ed. White, Oxon. 1806. See Sale's Prelim. Discourse to the Koran, § 1, p. 35, Lond. 1812.

‖ Hottingeri, Hist. Orient., lib. ii. cap. 5. Erpenii Prov. Arab. Cent. duæ, Leidæ, 1614. Schultens, Antholog. Senten. Arab., Lug. Bat. 1772. "Veteres Arabum sententiæ sunt innumeræ; et permulta sunt volumina, quæ Amthâl sive Sententias complectuntur." — Sir William Jones, Poeseos Asiaticæ Commentarii, p. 275, ed. Eichhorn, Lips. 1777. See D'Herbelot, Biblio-

their ancestors; as numerous *amthâl*, or moral sentences, are in circulation throughout the regions of the East, some of which have been published by Hottinger, Erpenius, the younger Schultens, and others who have distinguished themselves by the pursuit of Oriental learning. 'The moralists of the East,' says Sir William Jones, 'have in general chosen to deliver their precepts in short, sententious maxims, to illustrate them by sprightly comparisons, or to inculcate them in the very ancient forms of agreeable apologues. There are, indeed, both in Arabic and Persian, philosophical tracts on ethics, written with sound ratiocination and elegant perspicuity; but in every part of the Eastern world, from Pekin to Damascus, the popular teachers of moral wisdom have immemorially been poets, and there would be no end of enumerating their works, which are still extant in the five principal languages of Asia.'*

"The ingenious, but ever-disputing and loquacious Greeks were indebted to the same means for their earliest instruction in wisdom. The sayings of the Seven Wise Men, the Golden Verses of Pythagoras, the remains of Theognis and Phocylides, if genuine, and the Gnomai of the older poets, testify the prevalence of aphorisms in ancient Greece. Had no specimens remained of Hellenic proverbs, we might have concluded this to be the case; for the Greeks borrowed the rudiments, if not the principal part, of their knowledge from those whom they arrogantly termed barbarians;† and it is only through the medium of compendious maxims and brief sentences that traditionary knowledge can be preserved.‡ This mode of communicating moral and practical

thèque Orientale, in Amthâl; and Les Maximes des Orientaux, at the end of vol. iv. [See also Arabum Proverbia, edidit G. W. Freytag, Bonnæ ad Rhenum, 1838. This work is in four volumes, octavo.]

* Disc. on the Philos. of the Asiatics, Works, vol. i. p. 167, 4to.

† Brucker, Hist. Philos., lib. ii. cap. 1. Burnet, Archæologiæ, lib. i. cap. 9. Shuckford's Connections, Pref. to vol. i.

‡ The greatest part of Greek aphorisms have, no doubt, perished; having fallen into neglect when the dialectic art and a systematic philosophy gained ground among this acute and disputatious people. Eusebius, in his treatise against Marcellus, lib. i. cap. 3, makes mention of Greek proverbs, and collectors of them. Among the *Deperdita* are the Κύριαι Δόξαι of Epicurus.

wisdom accorded with the sedate and deliberative character of the Romans;* and, in truth, from its influence over the mind, and its fitness for popular instruction, proverbial expressions exist in all ages and in all languages." †

The whole collection seems, in the title of the book, to be ascribed to Solomon as the author; and, as in 1 Kings iv. 32, that wise monarch is said to have uttered three thousand proverbs, such has been the received opinion of the Jewish and Christian churches.

In modern times, however, this opinion has been called in question. The learned and sagacious critic, Grotius, advanced the opinion, that the Book of Proverbs was not an original composition of Solomon, but a selection made by him from the proverbs of numerous writers who lived before his time.‡ This opinion has been adopted, and maintained by a variety of arguments, by distinguished critics in modern times. The most important consideration, however, seems to be, that it is not probable, according to the analogy of the literature of other nations, that one man should be the author of so much proverbial wisdom. Such proverbs, it is said, have usually been the result of the general sense and experience of a community, and the product of a large num-

—Diog. Lært., lib. x. p. 724. Cicero, De Finibus, lib. ii. § 7; De Nat. Deor., lib. i. § 30.

* Seneca, Ep. 59. Both Suetonius (Vita Cæsaris, § 56) and Cicero (ad Divers., lib. ix. Ep. 16) speak of the Dicta Collectanea of Cæsar; namely, Apophthegms collected by him; and some aphoristic sayings of the ancients are reported by Valerius Maximus, lib. vii. cap. 2.

† Ray's Collection of English Proverbs is well known; and there is a book entitled, Adagia, sive Proverbiorum omnium quæ apud Græcos, Latinos, Hebræos, Arabes, &c., in usu fuerunt Collectio, fol., Erf. 1646. Sir William Jones mentions the precepts of Odin, written in the Runic tongue, and the work of a Persian poet, Sheikh Attâr, as instances of aphoristic composition (Comment. de Poes. Asiat., p. 274, ed. Eichhorn, Lips. 1777). Grotius, in his Proleg. to the Proverbs, speaks of the 'Εκλόγαι of the Byzantine emperors.

‡ "Videtur hic liber esse ἐχλόγη optimarum sententiarum ex plurimis qui ante Salomonem fuere scriptoribus, quales ἐκλόγας multi imperatorum Constantinopolitanorum conscribi in suos usus fecere."

ber of minds. Solomon may have composed a considerable number of proverbial maxims; and other wise men of the nation, before and after him, may have done the same. Now it is not uncommon, when one has become distinguished for wisdom or wit in a nation, that many things should be ascribed to him of which he is not the author. Thus the Greeks, it is said, ascribed most of their sententious maxims to Pythagoras; the Arabs, theirs to Lokman and a few others; the Northern nations, theirs to King Odin. In this way the Hebrews may have ascribed their proverbs to their wisest king, Solomon, because it was known of him that he had accomplished more than others in this kind of sententious poetry. Thus the opinion may have been formed, that Solomon was the author of the whole collection of the Hebrew proverbs. But that he was not in a strict sense the author of all the Proverbs has been thought probable, not only from the argument before mentioned, but also from the character of some of the maxims, which would come more naturally from persons in a situation in life different from that of a king. Chap. xxx. is expressly ascribed to another author, namely, to Agur, the son of Jakeh.*

These arguments, however, are not in the highest degree conclusive. It is very evident that the Book of Proverbs is not a mere collection of oral maxims, which were circulated among the people before they were committed to writing, like Freytag's collection of Arabic, or Ray's of English proverbs. The uniformity in the structure and expression of the proverbs shows that they were the result of elaborate composition. They are all marked by the peculiar characteristic of Hebrew poetry, the parallelism. There is also such a general similarity in the diction and style of composition in these proverbs, that it is difficult to believe, that, in their present form, they could have been the production of a great many authors. Many of the thoughts may have been in circulation among the people, expressed in a different way. But the style and the poetical form in which they are expressed seem to indicate, that very few authors could have had a hand in the composition. From these considerations, and from the historical

* Some other considerations, of little weight, are adduced in De Wette's Introduction, vol. ii. p. 543, Amer. transl.

tradition of the Jews, the more probable conclusion seems to be, that Solomon was the composer of the greater part, at least, of the proverbs ascribed to him. Of others he may have been only the collector.

The Book of Proverbs bears evident marks of being composed of several smaller collections, which were made at different times. It may accordingly be divided into five distinct parts.

I. The first part consists of the first nine chapters, and contains, not what according to the common use of language are called proverbs, but connected moral discourses in praise of wisdom, and urging to the practice of virtue, especially the virtue of chastity. The discourse or discourses in these nine chapters probably came from the same author. There seems to be no sufficient reason for rejecting the Jewish tradition, that Solomon was the author of this part of the book. De Wette* objects that its didactic and admonitory tone, and its strict injunction of chastity, indicate a teacher of youth, a prophet, or a priest, as the author, rather than a king like Solomon. This objection seems to have some weight; but whether it should be regarded as decisive against the Jewish tradition concerning the authorship of the book is very doubtful. Our knowledge of the intellectual habits and moral character of Solomon at different periods of his life is too imperfect to allow one to conclude with confidence, that he could not have been the author of this portion of the book. Bertholdt† also suggests, that a person whose harem was so crowded as that of Solomon would not be likely to speak so highly of the happiness of a man with one wife, in chap. v. 18. He suggests, also, that the warnings against adultery, in chap. vi. 24, &c., and vii. 5–23, could hardly have come from one to whom it was known that his mother became his father's wife by the commission of that sin. Some few of the sentiments also, in his opinion, indicate a private person as the author, rather than a king, such as in chap. vi. 26–31. The reader can judge how much force there is in these arguments. To me they seem to have but little weight. The experience of the effects of sin and folly may suggest wise precepts, as well as the enjoyment of the fruits of wisdom.

* Einleitung, &c., § 281. † Einleitung, &c., § 505.

II. The second part begins with chap. x., and extends to chap. xxii. 17. It is of a very different character from the nine preceding chapters. It contains proverbs properly so called; sententious maxims of morality or prudence, contained commonly in single verses, and having no connection with each other. This portion of the book has also a separate title, manifestly indicating that it once formed a collection by itself, independent of the first nine chapters.

III. At chap. xxii. 17, it seems probable that another collection begins. For it is introduced by an exhortation extending through several verses, similar to that in chap. i. 1–6. This third portion extends from chap. xxii. 17 to chap. xxv. It seems to be distinguished from the second part by a greater connection between the verses, and a more negligent use of the parallelism.

IV. The fourth part of the book begins with chap. xxv. It has a new title, or preface, setting forth that the proverbs contained in it were collected by men employed by King Hezekiah. It extends to chap. xxx.

V. The fifth portion of the book begins with chap. xxx., and extends to the end. It contains some proverbial maxims of a certain Agur, some advice addressed by his mother to a king called Lemuel, and an alphabetical poem; that is, a poem the lines of which begin with the different letters of the Hebrew alphabet in regular succession, the subject of which is the praises of a good wife.

The Book of Proverbs is, in a moral and religious point of view, one of the most valuable portions of the Old Testament. It gives a view of the Jewish religion and morality, as pervading the common life of the Jews, much more favorable than that which we receive from the accounts of the ceremonies and forms which are elsewhere enjoined.

It is true that the religion and morality of the Book of Proverbs will not bear a favorable comparison with those of Jesus Christ. Its morality is much less disinterested, being for the most part founded in prudence, rather than in love. Its motives generally are of a much less elevated kind than those which Christianity presents. The idea of the immortality of the soul does not appear to have dawned upon the mind of the author. Prudential motives, founded on a strict earthly retribution, are the principal encouragements to a life of virtue which he presents. This is well, it is true, as far as it goes; for man should ever be reminded of the laws of the Creator, and of the consequences of violating them. But higher and more disinterested and affectionate motives are necessary for the formation of a perfect character, a character which shall command our highest esteem and love.

But the religion of the Book of Proverbs, when compared with that of the heathen world, appears to the highest advantage. Jehovah is there represented as the one creator of the universe, the governor of the world, and the disposer of human destinies. He is set forth as the first cause of all things; and man's highest duty is declared to be that of acknowledging, in sentiment and practice, the power, wisdom, and goodness of God in the creation and government of mankind. He is represented as holy and just; as knowing every thing which takes place on the earth; as loving, commending, and rewarding piety and virtue; and as abhorring and punishing sin and transgression.

"For the ways of man are before the eyes of the LORD,
And he weigheth well all his paths." — Chap. v. 21.

"The eyes of the LORD are in every place;
They behold the evil and the good." — Chap. xv. 3.

"The under-world, yea, the region of death, is before the LORD;
How much more the hearts of the sons of men!" — Ib. 11.

"All the ways of a man are pure in his own eyes;
But the LORD weigheth the spirit." — Chap. xvi. 2.

The incomprehensibility of God is also set forth in this book in striking language. No human powers are capable of comprehending his nature, or understanding his works.

"I have not learned wisdom,
Nor have I the knowledge of the Most Holy.
Who hath gone up into heaven and come down?
Who hath gathered the wind in his fists?
Who hath bound up the waters in a garment?
Who hath established all the ends of the earth?
What is his name, and what his son's name, if thou knowest?"
Chap. xxx. 2-4

The providence of God is represented as ever active and universal. It is over all his works, and nothing takes place which is not in accordance with his will and ordination. It is accomplished by the almighty power of God, and no mention is made in this book of the instrumentality of angels. Not only the outward fortunes, but the minds of men, according to it, are under the complete control of God.

"Trust in the LORD with all thy heart,
And lean not on thine own understanding;
In all thy ways acknowledge him,
And he will make thy paths plain." — Chap. iii. 5, 6.

"To man belongeth the preparation of the heart;
But the answer of the tongue is from the LORD." — Chap. xvi. 1.

"Commit thy doings to the LORD,
And thy purposes shall be established." — Ib. 3.

"As streams of water,
So is the heart of the king in the hand of the LORD;
He turneth it whithersoever he will." — Chap. xxi. 1.

"It is the blessing of the LORD that maketh rich,
And he addeth no sorrow with it." — Chap. x. 22.

From this last quotation, Dr. G. L. Bauer* takes occasion to remark, that, according to this book, "blessings are granted to God's favorites, independent of any exertions on their part." A more superficial and unfounded remark, or more inconsistent with the whole tenor of the book, could not have been made. The obvious meaning of the verse is, that, while wealth, in general, may be gained with labor by the wicked as well as the righteous, only that wealth *is free from sorrow* which is gained by means which have the approbation and blessing of the Lord.

In fact, the most prevalent idea in the whole book is that of an exact temporal retribution to men for their good and bad deeds. What inconceivable rashness, then, was it in Dr. Bauer to assert the doctrine of the book to be, that blessings were granted to God's favorites, independent of any exertions on their part!

---

* See Extracts from Bauer's Theology of the Old Testament, London 1838, p. 84.

Another important religious doctrine taught in this book is, that the evils which afflict the righteous man are to be regarded by him as the chastenings inflicted by God in order to promote the moral improvement of him whom he loves.

> "My son, despise not the correction of the LORD,
> Nor be impatient under his chastisement!
> For whom the LORD loveth he chasteneth,
> Even as a father the son in whom he delighteth." — Chap. iii. 11, 12.

But the character of God, as a father seeking to reclaim the wicked by manifestations of love, is not prominent in this book. The doctrine of Christ on this subject is so far beyond what can be found in the Book of Proverbs, or in any part of the Old Testament, as to deserve the appellation of a new doctrine.

Dr. Bauer thinks that he finds in this book the doctrine, that Jehovah predestinated men to wickedness and to punishment. The passage on which he founds the remark is contained in chap. xvi. 4. In the common version it is translated, "The Lord hath made all things for himself; yea, even the wicked for the day of evil."

Against the interpretation of this passage which makes it mean, that the Lord made man wicked on purpose to inflict evil upon him, the most obvious remark is, that common sense cannot reconcile it with the strict doctrine of retribution which pervades the Book of Proverbs. The verse seems also not only to admit, but to require, a translation somewhat different. Thus, —

> "The LORD hath ordained every thing for its end;
> Even the wicked for the day of evil."

It appears to me, that, if we take into view the connection in which the verse stands, and also the general tenor of the book in regard to a righteous retribution, the meaning of the passage will appear to be nothing more than this, — that God has ordained every thing to that which answers to it, or is fit for it, and the wicked he has ordained for the day of evil, i.e. of punishment. There is not only a wise arrangement and correspondence in good things, but also in evil things; for the evil of punishment follows the evil of guilt: the evil day is appointed for the evil-doer. The idea, that the Almighty makes men wicked for the very purpose of inflicting evil on them, is too metaphysical for the writer, whose maxims are drawn from common sense and observation, and not from mystical or metaphysical musings.

The necessity of religion, which is spoken of under the name of the fear of the LORD, is inculcated in this book in strong and emphatic language, as the beginning of wisdom and the fountain of happiness. Of sacrifices and offerings very little is said. The author insists almost exclusively upon the substantial duties of morality and religion. He seems to rely upon obedience to God's laws, amendment of life, justice, purity, and mercy, as the means of securing the forgiveness and favor of God, rather than upon formal offerings for sin.

> " To do justice and equity
> Is more acceptable to the LORD than sacrifice." — Chap. xxi. 3.

Such are the views of morality and religion taught in the Book of Proverbs; views which may well command our admiration, when we consider when and where they were taught. Still, we must remember that our duty is now to be learned from Christ, rather than from Solomon. We must examine ourselves by the light of the Sermon on the Mount, rather than by that of the Book of Proverbs. A greater than Solomon is here. He is come in his kingdom, and by his laws we are to be judged.

One interesting characteristic of the Book of Proverbs is the frequent personification of wisdom, as an attribute of God, as well as the guide of men, which occurs in it. She is represented as existing prior to the creation.

> " The LORD created me, the firstling of his course,
> Before his works, of old;
> I was anointed from everlasting,
> From the beginning, even before the earth was made.
> When as yet there were no deeps, I was brought forth;
> When there were no springs abounding with water. . . .
> Then was I by him, as a master-builder;
> I was his delight day by day,

Exulting continually in his presence;
Exulting in the habitable part of his earth,
And my delight was with the sons of men."
Chap. viii. 22–24, 30, 31.

Wisdom is here represented as a female and a queen, the assistant, counsellor, and architect of the Almighty in the creation of the world out of chaos. This bold personification is perfectly agreeable to the genius of the Hebrew poets, who represent Zion as stretching out her hands, having none to comfort her; and the inanimate ways which lead to the temple of Jerusalem as mourning, because none came to the solemn festivals; and all the trees of the field as clapping their hands, in token of joy that the ransomed of Jehovah were returning to Zion.

That the representation of wisdom in the eighth chapter of this book is a personification, and not a real person, as the Church fathers and many in modern times have supposed, is perfectly manifest from the connection in which it stands, and the previous personification of wisdom as an attribute of man. It is the same attribute by which kings reign and princes decree justice, that is found by all that love her, that loves them who love her, that cries aloud to the sons of men at the corners of the streets, which is immediately afterwards represented as the counsellor and architect of the Deity. If, when he speaks of wisdom as the guide and instructor of men, he does not refer to any thing personal, we have no reason to suppose, that, when he speaks of wisdom as the counsellor and architect of the Deity, he meant any thing more than that all the works of God were created by his wisdom, and manifest its excellence.

This personification of wisdom in the Book of Proverbs is worthy of attention, as illustrating the natural origin of the doctrine of a personal Logos, or intermediate personal agent between the Deity and created things in the creation and government of the world. For how easy would be the transition from a personification of wisdom, as is contained in chap. viii., to the representation of it as a real person!

A list of the principal commentators on this book may be seen in Rosenmüller's Scholia in Vetus Testamentum. The latest

English works on the Proverbs, which I have seen, are — An Attempt towards an Improved Translation of the Proverbs, with Notes Critical and Explanatory, and a Preliminary Dissertation, by the Rev. George Holden, London, 1819, 8vo; a New Translation of the Proverbs, with Explanatory Notes, by William French, D.D., and Rev. George Skinner, M.A., London, 1831; and the translation in Boothroyd's Version of the Bible, London, 1843. The best recent works on Proverbs, which I have examined, are the Scholia of Rosenmüller, Leipzig, 1829; the German Version and Commentary of Umbreit, Heidelberg, 1826; the excellent German version of De Wette, in the fourth edition of his Translation of the Scriptures, Heidelberg, 1858; Bertheau's Sprüche Salomo's, Leipzig, 1847; and Stuart's Commentary on Proverbs, Andover, 1852.

THE PROVERBS.

I.

Introduction. Warning against evil company. — Chap. I. 1–19.

1 The proverbs of Solomon, the son of David, king of Israel:
2 That one may learn wisdom and instruction,
And receive words of understanding;
3 That one may gain the instruction of prudence,
Justice, equity, and uprightness;
4 Which will give caution to the simple,
To the young man wisdom and discretion;
5 Let the wise man hear, and he will increase his knowledge,
And the man of understanding will gain wise counsels;
6 So as to understand a proverb and a deep maxim,
The words of the wise and their dark sayings.

7 The fear of the Lord is the beginning of knowledge;
Fools despise wisdom and instruction.
8 Hear, O my son! the instruction of thy father,
And neglect not the teaching of thy mother!
9 For they shall be a graceful wreath for thy head,
And a chain around thy neck.
10 My son, if sinners entice thee,
Consent thou not!
11 If they say, "Come with us,
Let us lie in wait for blood,
Let us lurk secretly for him who is innocent in vain;
12 Let us swallow them up alive, like the underworld,
Yea, in full health, as those that go down into the pit;

13 We shall find all kinds of precious substance,
We shall fill our houses with spoil;
14 Thou shalt cast thy lot among us;
We will all have one purse;" —
15 My son, walk thou not in their way,
Refrain thy foot from their path!
16 For their feet run to evil,
And make haste to shed blood.
17 For as the net is spread in vain
Before the eyes of any bird,
18 So they lie in wait for their own blood;
They lurk secretly for their own lives.
19 Such are the ways of every one greedy of unjust gain;
It taketh away the life of the possessor thereof.

II.

The exhortation of Wisdom to the observance of her counsels, and warning against neglecting them. — CHAP. I. 20–33.

20 WISDOM crieth out in the highway;
In the market-place she uttereth her voice;
21 At the head of the noisy streets she crieth aloud;
At the entrances of the gates, throughout the city, she proclaimeth her words [saying]:
22 "How long, ye simple ones, will ye love simplicity?
How long will scoffers delight themselves in scoffing,
And fools hate knowledge?
23 Turn ye at my reproof!
Behold, I will pour out my spirit to you;
I will make known my words to you!
24 "Because I have called, and ye have refused, —
Because I have stretched out my hand, and no one hath regarded, —
25 Because ye have rejected all my counsel,
And have slighted my rebuke, —
26 I also will laugh at your calamity,
I will mock when your fear cometh;
27 When your fear cometh upon you like a storm,
And destruction overtaketh you like a whirlwind,
When distress and anguish come upon you.

28 Then will they call upon me, but I will not answer!
They will seek me early,
But they shall not find me!
29 Because they have hated knowledge,
And have not chosen the fear of the LORD, —
30 Because they would not attend to my counsel,
And have despised all my reproof, —
31 Therefore shall they eat of the fruit of their own way,
And be filled to the full with their own devices;
32 Yea, the turning away of the simple shall slay them,
And the carelessness of fools shall destroy them.
33 But whoso hearkeneth to me shall dwell securely,
And shall not be disquieted with the fear of evil."

III.

The advantages attending the pursuit of wisdom, and the evils to be avoided by such a course. — CHAP. II.

1 OH, my son, that thou wouldst receive my words,
And treasure up my precepts within thee;
2 That thou wouldst apply thine ear to wisdom,
And incline thy heart to understanding!
3 For if thou wilt call aloud to knowledge,
And lift up thy voice to understanding, —
4 If thou wilt seek her as silver,
And search for her as for hidden treasures, —
5 Then shalt thou understand the fear of the LORD,
And find the knowledge of God.
6 For the LORD giveth wisdom;
From his mouth proceed knowledge and understanding:
7 He layeth up safety for the righteous;
He is a shield to them that walk uprightly:
8 He guardeth the paths of equity,
And defendeth the way of his servants.
9 Then shalt thou understand righteousness and equity
And uprightness, yea, every good path.
10 When wisdom entereth into thy heart,
And knowledge is pleasant to thy soul,
11 Discretion will guard thee,
Understanding will preserve thee.

12 It will deliver thee from the way of the wicked,
From the men who speak perverse things;
13 Who forsake the paths of uprightness,
To walk in the ways of darkness;
14 Who rejoice in doing evil,
And delight in the perverseness of the wicked;
15 Whose paths are crooked,
And who are froward in their ways.
16 It will deliver thee from the wife of another,
From the stranger, who useth smooth words;
17 Who forsaketh the friend of her youth,
And forgetteth the covenant of her God.
18 For her house sinketh down to Death,
And her paths to the shades of the dead:
19 None that go to her return again;
They will not attain the paths of life.
20 Therefore walk thou in the way of good men,
And keep the paths of the righteous:
21 For the upright shall dwell in the land,
And the righteous shall remain in it;
22 But the wicked shall be cut off from the land,
And transgressors shall be rooted out of it.

IV.

Exhortation to obedience, to reliance upon God, to the due payment of offerings prescribed by the law, and to patience under the divine chastisements The inestimable value of wisdom set forth. — CHAP. III. 1-26.

1 MY son, forget not my teaching,
And let thy heart observe my precepts!
2 For length of days, and years of life,
And peace shall they multiply to thee.
3 Let not kindness and truth forsake thee;
Bind them around thy neck,
Write them upon the tablet of thy heart:
4 Then shalt thou find favor and good success
In the sight of God and man.
5 Trust in the LORD with all thy heart,
And lean not on thine own understanding;
6 In all thy ways acknowledge him,
And he will make thy paths plain.

7 Be not wise in thine own eyes;
Fear the LORD, and depart from evil.
8 It shall be health to thy muscles,
And moisture to thy bones.
9 Honor the LORD with thy substance,
And with the first-fruits of all thy increase;
10 So shall thy barns be filled with plenty,
And thy vats overflow with new wine.
11 My son, despise not the correction of the LORD,
Nor be impatient under his chastisement!
12 For whom the LORD loveth he chasteneth,
Even as a father the son in whom he delighteth.
13 Happy the man who findeth wisdom;
Yea, the man who getteth understanding!
14 For the profit thereof is greater than that of silver,
And the gain thereof than that of fine gold.
15 More precious is she than pearls,
And none of thy jewels is to be compared with her.
16 Length of days is in her right hand;
In her left hand are riches and honor.
17 Her ways are ways of pleasantness,
And all her paths are peace.
18 She is a tree of life to them that lay hold of her,
And happy is every one who hath her in his grasp.
19 The LORD by wisdom founded the earth;
By understanding he framed the heavens.
20 By his knowledge the deep waters were cleft,
And the clouds drop down the dew.
21 My son, let them not depart from thine eyes;
Keep sound wisdom and discretion!
22 For they shall be life to thy soul,
And grace to thy neck.
23 Then shalt thou go on thy way securely,
And thy foot shall not stumble;
24 When thou liest down, thou shalt not be afraid,
Yea, thou shalt lie down, and thy sleep shall be sweet.
25 Be not thou afraid of sudden alarm,
Nor of the storm that is for the wicked, when it cometh;
26 For the LORD shall be thy confidence;
Yea, he will keep thy foot from being taken.

V.

Various precepts. — CHAP. III. 27–35.

27 WITHHOLD not kindness from those who need it,
When it is in the power of thy hand to do it.
28 Say not to thy neighbor, "Go, and come again,
And to-morrow I will give to thee," when thou hast it by thee.
29 Devise not evil against thy neighbor,
While he dwelleth securely by thee.
30 Contend not with a man without cause,
When he hath done thee no harm.
31 Envy not the oppressor,
And choose none of his ways.
32 For the perverse man is the abomination of the LORD,
But he is in friendship with the upright.
33 The curse of the LORD is upon the house of the wicked,
But he blesseth the dwelling of the righteous.
34 Surely the scorners he treateth scornfully,
But giveth favor to the lowly.
35 The wise shall obtain honor,
But fools shall bear off shame.

VI.

Exhortation to wisdom and virtue. — CHAP. IV.

1 HEAR, ye children, the instruction of a father,
And attend, that ye may learn understanding!
2 For I give you good instruction;
Forsake ye not my commandments.
3 For I was my father's son,
A tender and only child in the sight of my mother.
4 He taught me, and said to me,
Let thy heart hold fast my words;
Keep my commandments, and live.
5 Get wisdom, get understanding;
Forget not, and depart not from, the words of my mouth.
6 Forsake her not, and she will guard thee;
Love her, and she will preserve thee.

7 Wisdom is the principal thing; therefore gain wisdom,
And with all thy gain, gain understanding.
8 Exalt her, and she will promote thee;
She will bring thee to honor, when thou dost embrace her;
9 She will give to thy head a graceful wreath,
A beautiful crown will she bestow upon thee.
10 Hear, O my son! and receive my sayings!
So shall the years of thy life be many.
11 I have taught thee the way of wisdom,
I have guided thee in the right path.
12 When thou goest, thy steps shall not be confined;
And, when thou runnest, thou shalt not stumble.
13 Take fast hold of instruction; let her not go;
Keep her, for she is thy life.
14 Enter not into the path of the wicked,
And go not in the way of evil men;
15 Avoid it, pass not upon it,
Turn from it, and go away.
16 For they sleep not, unless they have done mischief;
Yea, their sleep is taken away, unless they have caused some to fall.
17 For they eat the bread of wickedness,
And drink the wine of violence.
18 But the path of the righteous is as the light of dawn,
Which groweth brighter and brighter unto the perfect day.
19 The way of the wicked is as thick darkness;
They know not at what they stumble.
20 My son, attend to my words;
Incline thine ear to my sayings;
21 Let them not depart from thine eyes;
Keep them in the midst of thy heart!
22 For they are life to those who find them,
And health to all their flesh.
23 More than any thing which thou watchest, watch thy heart;
For from it goeth forth life.
24 Put away from thee a deceitful mouth,
And remove far from thee perverse lips.
25 Let thine eyes look straight forward,
And thine eyelids be directed before thee.

26 Give heed to the path of thy foot,
And let all thy ways be steadfast.
27 Turn not to the right hand or to the left;
Remove thy foot from evil.

VII.

Warning against unchastity.—CHAP. V.

1 My son, attend to my wisdom,
And bow thine ear to my understanding;
2 That thou mayst keep discretion,
And that thy lips may preserve knowledge!
3 Truly, the lips of a strange woman drop honey,
And her mouth is smoother than oil;
4 But her end is bitter as wormwood,
Sharp as a two-edged sword.
5 Her feet go down to death;
Her steps lay hold of the under-world.
6 That she may not ponder the way of life,
Her paths waver when she heedeth it not.
7 Hear me now, therefore, O children!
And turn not away from the words of my mouth!
8 Remove thy way far from her,
And come not nigh the door of her house:
9 Lest thou give thy bloom to others,
And thy years to a cruel one;
10 Lest strangers be filled with thy wealth,
And thine earnings be in the house of an alien;
11 And lest thou mourn in thy latter end,
When thy flesh and thy body are consumed,
12 And say, "How have I hated instruction!
And how hath my heart despised reproof!
13 I have not obeyed the voice of my teachers,
Nor inclined mine ear to my instructors;
14 I have well-nigh fallen into utter misery,
In the midst of the congregation and the assembly."

15 Drink water out of thine own cistern,
And running water out of thine own well:

16 So shall thy fountains overflow in the streets,
In the wide streets, as streams of water;
17 They shall belong to thee alone,
And not to strangers with thee;
18 And thy fountain shall be blessed,
Yea, thou shalt have joy in the wife of thy youth.
19 A lovely hind, a graceful doe,
Her breasts shall satisfy thee at all times,
And thou shalt be always ravished with her love.
20 Why, then, my son, wilt thou be ravished with a wanton,
And embrace the bosom of a stranger?
21 For the ways of man are before the eyes of the LORD,
And he weigheth well all his paths.
22 His own iniquities shall ensnare the wicked;
Yea, he shall be held fast by the cords of his own sins.
23 He shall die for want of instruction;
Yea, through the greatness of his folly he shall stagger.

VIII.

Warning against suretyship, indolence, falsehood, and other vices.
CHAP. VI. 1–19.

1 MY son, if thou hast become surety for another,
If thou hast stricken hands for another,
2 If thou hast become ensnared by the words of thy mouth,
If thou hast been caught by the words of thy mouth,
3 Do this now, my son, and rescue thyself, —
Since thou hast fallen into the hands of thy neighbor, —
Go, prostrate thyself, and be urgent with thy neighbor!
4 Give not sleep to thine eyes, nor slumber to thine eyelids;
5 Rescue thyself, as a roe from the hand,
And as a bird from the hand of the fowler.

6 Go to the ant, O sluggard!
Consider her ways, and be wise!
7 She hath no governor,
Nor overseer, nor ruler;
8 Yet she prepareth in the summer her food,
She gathereth in the harvest her meat.

9 How long wilt thou lie in bed, O sluggard?
When wilt thou arise from thy sleep?
10 "A little sleep, — a little slumber, —
A little folding of the hands to rest:"
11 So shall thy poverty come upon thee like a robber,
Yea, thy want, as an armed man!

12 A worthless wretch is the unrighteous man,
Who walketh with a deceitful mouth;
13 Who winketh with his eyes,
Speaketh with his feet,
And teacheth with his fingers.
14 Fraud is in his heart;
He deviseth mischief continually;
He scattereth contentions.
15 Therefore shall calamity come upon him suddenly;
In a moment shall he be destroyed, and that without remedy.

16 These six things doth the LORD hate;
Yea, seven are an abomination to him:
17 Lofty eyes, a false tongue,
And hands which shed innocent blood;
18 A heart that contriveth wicked devices,
Feet that are swift in running to mischief,
19 A false witness, that uttereth lies,
And him that soweth discord among brethren.

IX.

Exhortation of obedience to parents, and warning against unchastity.
CHAP. VI. 20–VII.

20 KEEP, O my son! the commandment of thy father,
And forsake not the precepts of thy mother!
21 Bind them continually to thy heart,
Tie them around thy neck!
22 When thou goest forth, they shall guide thee;
When thou sleepest, they shall watch over thee;
And, when thou awakest, they shall talk with thee.

23 For the commandment is a lamp, and instruction a light;
Yea, the rebukes of correction lead to life.
24 They shall guard thee from the evil woman,
From the smooth tongue of the unchaste woman.
25 Desire not her beauty in thy heart,
Nor let her catch thee with her eyelids;
26 For by a harlot a man is brought to a morsel of bread,
And the adulteress layeth snares for the precious life.
27 Can a man take fire into his bosom,
And his clothes not be burned?
28 Can one walk upon burning coals,
And his feet not be scorched?
29 So is it with him who goeth in to his neighbor's wife;
Whoever toucheth her shall not go unpunished.
30 Men do not overlook a thief,
Though he steal to satisfy his appetite, when he is hungry;
31 If found, he must repay sevenfold,
And give up all the substance of his house.
32 Whoso committeth adultery with a woman lacketh understanding;
He that doeth it destroyeth himself;
33 Blows and dishonor shall he get,
And his reproach shall not be wiped away.
34 For jealousy is the fury of a man;
He will not spare in the day of vengeance;
35 And he will not pay regard to any ransom,
Nor be content, though thou offer many gifts.

1 My son, keep my words,
And treasure up my commandments with thee!
2 Keep my commandments and live!
Yea, my teaching, as the apple of thine eye!
3 Bind them upon thy fingers,
Write them upon the tablet of thy heart!
4 Say unto wisdom, "Thou art my sister!"
And call understanding thy near acquaintance;
5 That they may keep thee from the wife of another,
From the stranger, that useth smooth words.
6 For through the window of my house,
Through the lattice I was looking forth,

7 And I saw among the simple ones,
I discerned among the youths,
A young man void of understanding.
8 He was passing through the street near her corner,
And was going the way to her house,
9 At twilight, in the evening,
At midnight, yea, in the thick darkness.
10 And, behold, a woman met him,
In the attire of a harlot, and subtle of heart, —
11 One noisy and unruly,
Whose feet abide not in her house;
12 Who is now in the streets, now in the broad places,
And lurketh near every corner.
13 She caught hold of him and kissed him,
And with a shameless face said to him,
14 "Thank-offerings have been upon me,
And this day have I performed my vows;
15 Therefore came I forth to meet thee, —
Diligently to seek thy face, and I have found thee!
16 I have spread my bed with coverlets,
With tapestry of the thread of Egypt.
17 I have sprinkled my bed
With myrrh, aloes, and cinnamon.
18 Come, let us take our fill of love until the morning;
Let us solace ourselves with caresses.
19 For the good-man is not at home;
He is gone a long journey;
20 He hath taken a purse of money with him;
At the day of the full moon he will return."
21 By her much fair speech she seduced him;
By the smoothness of her lips she drew him away.
22 He goeth after her straightway,
As an ox goeth to the slaughter,
Or as one in fetters to the chastisement of the fool,
23 Till an arrow strike through his liver; —
As a bird hasteneth into the snare,
And knoweth not that it is laid for its life.
24 Now, therefore, ye children, hearken to me,
And attend to the words of my mouth!
25 Let not thy heart turn aside to her ways;
Go not astray in her paths!

26 For many are the wounded which she hath cast down;
Yea, countless is the number of those slain by her.
27 Her house is the way to the under-world,
Leading down to the chambers of death.

X.

The excellence of wisdom. — CHAP. VIII.

1 DOTH not wisdom cry aloud,
And understanding put forth her voice?
2 Upon the top of the high places,
By the wayside,
In the cross-ways,
She taketh her station.
3 By the side of the gates,
In the entrance of the city,
In the approaches to the doors, she crieth aloud.
4 "To you, O men! do I call,
And my voice is to the sons of men!
5 O ye simple ones! learn wisdom,
And ye fools, be ye of an understanding heart!
6 Hear, for I speak excellent things,
And my lips utter that which is right.
7 For my mouth speaketh truth,
And wickedness is an abomination to my lips.
8 All the words of my mouth are in uprightness;
There is nothing crooked or deceitful in them;
9 They are all plain to the man of understanding,
And right to those who find knowledge.
10 Receive my instruction, and not silver,
And knowledge rather than choice gold!
11 For wisdom is better than pearls,
And no precious things are to be compared with her.

12 "I, wisdom, dwell with prudence,
And find out the knowledge of sagacious counsels.
13 The fear of the LORD is to hate evil;
Pride, and arrogance, and the evil way,
And the deceitful mouth, do I hate.

14 Counsel is mine, and sound reason;
I am understanding; I have strength.
15 By me kings reign,
And princes decree justice.
16 By me princes rule,
And nobles, even all the judges of the earth.
17 I love them that love me,
And they who seek me early shall find me.
18 Riches and honor are with me;
Yea, durable riches and prosperity.
19 My fruit is better than gold, yea, than fine gold,
And my revenue than choice silver.
20 I walk in the way of righteousness,
In the midst of the paths of equity.
21 I cause those who love me to possess substance;
Yea, I fill their treasuries.
22 "The LORD created me, the firstling of his course,
Before his works, of old;
23 I was anointed from everlasting,
From the beginning, even before the earth was made.
24 When as yet there were no deeps, I was brought forth;
When there were no springs, abounding with water.
25 Before the mountains were settled,
Yea, before the hills, I was brought forth;
26 Ere yet he had made the land and the wastes,
And the first of the clods of the earth.
27 When he framed the heavens, I was there;
When he drew a circle upon the face of the deep;
28 When he made firm the sky above,
And the fountains of the deep rushed forth;
29 When he gave to the sea its bounds,
That the waters should not pass their border;
When he marked out the foundations of the earth,—
30 Then was I by him as a master-builder;
I was his delight day by day,
Exulting before him at all times;
31 Exulting in the habitable part of his earth,
And my delight was with the sons of men.
32 "Now, therefore, ye children, hearken to me!
For happy are they who keep my ways!
33 Hear instruction, and be wise!
Yea, reject it not!

34 Happy the man who hearkeneth to me,
Who watcheth day by day at my gates,
Who waiteth at the posts of my doors;
35 For he that findeth me findeth life,
And obtaineth favor from the LORD;
36 But he who misseth me doeth violence to himself;
All they who hate me love death."

XI.

Wisdom represented as inviting to a sumptuous feast all who need her bounty. The different reception given to admonition by a wise man and a scoffer. The foundation of true wisdom. Warning against the delusions of folly. — CHAP. IX.

1 WISDOM hath builded her house;
She hath hewn out her seven pillars.
2 She hath killed her fatlings;
She hath mingled her wine;
Yea, she hath furnished her table.
3 She hath sent forth her maidens;
She crieth aloud upon the highest places of the city:
4 "Whoever is simple, let him turn in hither!"
To him that is void of understanding she saith,
5 "Come, eat of my bread,
And drink of the wine which I have mingled!
6 Forsake folly, and live!
And go forward in the way of understanding!

7 "He who correcteth a scoffer
Bringeth shame upon himself;
And he who rebuketh the wicked
Bringeth upon himself a stain.
8 Rebuke not a scoffer, lest he hate thee;
Rebuke a wise man, and he will love thee.
9 Give instruction to a wise man, and he will be yet wiser;
Teach a righteous man, and he will increase his learning.
10 The fear of the LORD is the beginning of wisdom,
And the knowledge of the Most Holy is understanding.
11 Yea, through me thy days shall be multiplied,
And the years of thy life shall be increased.

12 If thou art wise, thou art wise for thyself;
And if thou art a scoffer, thou alone must bear it."

13 The foolish woman is clamorous;
She is very simple, and careth for nothing.
14 She sitteth at the door of her house,
Upon a seat in the high places of the city,
15 To call aloud to those that pass by,
Who go straight forward in their ways,
16 "Whoever is simple, let him turn in hither!"
And to him that is void of understanding she saith,
17 "Stolen water is sweet,
And bread eaten in secret is pleasant."
18 But he considereth not that the dead are there,
That in the vales of the under-world are her guests.

XII.

Various unconnected Proverbs.—CHAP. X.–XXII. 16.

1 THE Proverbs of Solomon.

A wise son maketh a glad father,
But a foolish son is the grief of his mother.
2 Treasures of wickedness do not profit;
But righteousness delivereth from death.
3 The LORD will not suffer the righteous to famish;
But he disappointeth the craving of the wicked.
4 He that worketh with a slack hand becometh poor;
But the hand of the diligent maketh rich.
5 He that gathereth in summer is a wise son;
But he that sleepeth in harvest is a son causing shame.
6 Blessings are upon the head of the just;
But the mouth of the wicked concealeth violence.
7 The memory of the righteous man shall be blessed;
But the name of the wicked shall rot.
8 He who is wise in heart receiveth precepts;
But the foolish talker falleth headlong.
9 He that walketh uprightly walketh securely;
But he that perverteth his ways shall be punished.

10 He that winketh with the eye causeth sorrow;
And a foolish talker falleth headlong.
11 The mouth of the righteous is a fountain of life;
But the mouth of the wicked concealeth violence.
12 Hatred stirreth up strife;
But love covereth all offences.
13 Upon the lips of a man of understanding wisdom is found;
But a rod is for the back of him that lacketh understanding.
14 Wise men treasure up knowledge;
But the mouth of the foolish is destruction close at hand.
15 The rich man's wealth is his strong city;
The destruction of the poor is their poverty.
16 The earnings of the righteous minister to life;
The revenues of the wicked, to sin.
17 He that keepeth instruction is in the path of life;
But he that refuseth reproof goeth astray.
18 He that hideth hatred hath lying lips;
And he that uttereth slander is a fool.
19 In the multitude of words there wanteth not offence;
But he who restraineth his lips is wise.
20 The tongue of the righteous is as choice silver;
The understanding of the wicked is of little worth.
21 The lips of the righteous feed many;
But fools die through want of wisdom.
22 It is the blessing of the LORD that maketh rich,
And he addeth no sorrow with it.
23 It is as sport to a fool to do mischief;
But a man of understanding hath wisdom.
24 The fear of the wicked shall come upon him;
But the desire of the righteous shall be granted.
25 When the whirlwind passeth by, the wicked is no more;
But the righteous is an everlasting foundation.
26 As vinegar to the teeth, and as smoke to the eyes,
So is the sluggard to them that send him.
27 The fear of the LORD prolongeth life;
But the years of the wicked shall be shortened.
28 The hope of the righteous shall be gladness,
But the expectation of the wicked shall come to nothing.
29 The way of the LORD is a stronghold for the upright,
But destruction for those who do iniquity.

30 The righteous shall never be moved;
But the wicked shall not dwell in the land.
31 The mouth of the righteous man yieldeth wisdom;
But the perverse tongue shall be cut off.
32 The lips of the righteous know what is acceptable;
But the mouth of the wicked what is perverse.
1 False scales are an abomination to the LORD;
But a perfect weight is his delight.
2 When pride cometh, then cometh disgrace;
But with the humble is wisdom.
3 The integrity of the upright shall guide them;
But the perverseness of transgressors shall destroy them.
4 Riches do not profit in the day of wrath;
But righteousness delivereth from death.
5 The righteousness of the good man maketh his way plain;
But the wicked falleth through his wickedness.
6 The righteousness of the upright delivereth them;
But transgressors are ensnared in their own mischief.
7 When the wicked man dieth, his hope cometh to an end;
Yea, the expectation of the unjust cometh to an end.
8 The righteous man is delivered from trouble,
And the wicked cometh into it in his stead.
9 By his mouth the vile man destroyeth his neighbor;
But by the knowledge of the righteous are men delivered.
10 When it goeth well with the righteous, the city rejoiceth;
And when the wicked perish, there is shouting.
11 By the blessing of the upright the city is exalted;
But it is overthrown by the mouth of the wicked.
12 He who despiseth his neighbor is void of understanding;
A man of discernment holdeth his peace.
13 He who goeth about as a tale-bearer revealeth secrets;
But he who is of a faithful spirit concealeth a matter.
14 Where there is no counsel, the people fall;
But in a multitude of counsellors there is safety.
15 He that is surety for another shall smart for it;
But he that hateth suretyship is sure.
16 A graceful woman obtaineth honor,
Even as strong men obtain riches.
17 He that doeth good to himself is a man of kindness;
But he that tormenteth his own flesh is cruel.

18 The wicked toileth for deceitful wages;
But he who soweth righteousness shall have a sure reward.
19 As righteousness tendeth to life,
So he who pursueth evil pursueth it to his death.
20 The perverse in heart are the abomination of the LORD;
But the upright in their way are his delight.
21 From generation to generation the wicked shall not go unpunished;
But the posterity of the righteous shall be delivered.
22 As a jewel of gold in a swine's snout,
So is a beautiful woman who is without discretion.
23 The desire of the righteous is only good;
But the expectation of the wicked is wrath.
24 There is that scattereth, and yet increaseth;
And there is that withholdeth more than is right, yet he cometh to want.
25 The bountiful man shall be enriched,
And he that watereth shall himself be watered.
26 Him that keepeth back corn the people curse;
But blessing shall be upon the head of him that selleth it.
27 He, who earnestly seeketh good, seeketh favor;
But he that seeketh mischief, it shall come upon him.
28 He who trusteth in his riches shall fall;
But the righteous shall flourish as a leaf.
29 He that harasseth his household shall inherit wind;
And the fool shall be the servant of the wise.
30 The fruit of a righteous man is a tree of life;
And the wise man winneth souls.
31 Behold, the righteous man is requited on the earth;
Much more the wicked man and the sinner!
1 He who loveth correction loveth knowledge;
But he who hateth rebuke remaineth stupid.
2 The good man obtaineth favor from the LORD;
But the man of wicked devices he condemneth.
3 A man shall not be established by wickedness;
But the root of the righteous shall not be moved.
4 A virtuous woman is a crown to her husband;
But she who causeth shame is as rottenness in his bones.
5 The purposes of the righteous are just;
The designs of the wicked are deceitful.

6 The words of the wicked lie in wait for men's blood;
But the mouth of the upright delivereth them.
7 The wicked are overthrown, and are no more;
But the house of the righteous shall stand.
8 A man will be commended according to his wisdom;
But he that is of a perverse heart shall be despised.
9 Better is he that demeaneth himself, and hath a servant,
Than he that exalteth himself, and hath no bread.
10 The righteous man careth for the life of his beast;
But the tender mercies of the wicked are cruel.
11 He who tilleth his own land shall be satisfied with bread;
But he who followeth worthless persons is void of understanding.
12 The wicked man longeth after the prey of evil-doers;
But the root of the righteous yieldeth fruit.
13 In the transgression of the lips is a dangerous snare;
But the righteous man shall escape from trouble.
14 By the fruit of a man's mouth he shall be filled with good,
And the recompense of a man's hands shall be rendered unto him.
15 The way of a fool is right in his own eyes;
But he that hearkeneth to counsel is wise.
16 A fool's wrath is instantly known;
But he that hideth insult is wise.
17 He that speaketh truth testifieth what is right;
But a false witness, deceit.
18 There is who babbleth like the piercing of a sword;
But the tongue of the wise is health.
19 The lip of truth shall be established for ever;
But the tongue of falsehood, but for a moment.
20 Deceit is in the heart of those who contrive evil;
But to the counsellors of peace shall be joy.
21 No evil shall happen to the righteous;
But the wicked shall be filled with calamity.
22 False lips are the abomination of the Lord;
But they who deal truly are his delight.
23 A prudent man concealeth his knowledge;
But the heart of fools proclaimeth their foolishness

24 The hand of the diligent shall bear rule;
But the slothful shall be under tribute.
25 Anxiety in the heart of a man boweth it down;
But a kind word maketh it glad.
26 The righteous showeth the way to his neighbor;
But the way of the wicked leadeth them astray.
27 The slothful man shall not roast his game;
But a precious treasure to any man is he that is diligent.
28 In the path of righteousness is life,
And in her pathway there is no death.
1 A wise son listeneth to the instruction of his father;
But a scoffer listeneth not to rebuke.
2 By the fruit of a man's mouth he shall eat good;
But the appetite of transgressors shall be sated with violence.
3 He who keepeth his mouth keepeth his life;
But destruction shall be to him who openeth wide his lips.
4 The appetite of the sluggard longeth, and hath nothing;
But the appetite of the diligent is fully satisfied.
5 A righteous man hateth words of falsehood;
But a wicked man causeth disgrace and shame.
6 Righteousness preserveth him who is upright in his way;
But wickedness overthroweth the sinner.
7 There is who maketh himself rich, yet hath nothing,—
Who maketh himself poor, yet hath great riches.
8 A man's wealth is the ransom of his life;
But the poor man heareth no threatenings.
9 The light of the righteous shall rejoice;
But the lamp of the wicked shall be put out.
10 By pride cometh only contention;
But with the well-advised is wisdom.
11 Wealth gotten by vanity will become small;
But he who gathereth it into the hand increaseth it.
12 Hope deferred maketh the heart sick;
But the desire accomplished is a tree of life.
13 He that despiseth the word shall be destroyed;
But he who revereth the commandment shall be rewarded
14 The instruction of the wise is a fountain of life;
By it men escape from the snares of death.
15 A good understanding winneth favor;
But the way of transgressors is hard.

16 Every prudent man acteth with knowledge;
But a fool spreadeth abroad his folly.
17 A wicked messenger falleth into trouble;
But a faithful ambassador is health.
18 Poverty and shame are for him who rejecteth instruction;
But he that regardeth reproof shall come to honor.
19 The desire accomplished is sweet to the soul;
But it is an abomination to fools to depart from evil.
20 He who walketh with wise men shall be wise;
But the companion of fools shall be destroyed.
21 Calamity pursueth the wicked;
But the righteous is rewarded with good.
22 The good man leaveth his substance to his children's children;
But the wealth of the sinner is laid up for the just.
23 There is much food from the fallow-ground of the poor;
But there is who is brought low for want of uprightness.
24 He that spareth the rod hateth his son;
But he who loveth him chasteneth him early.
25 The righteous man eateth to the satisfying of his desire;
But the stomach of the wicked suffereth want.
1 The wise woman buildeth her house;
But the foolish teareth it down with her hands.
2 He who walketh in uprightness feareth the LORD;
But he who is perverse in his ways despiseth him.
3 In the mouth of the foolish pride is a scourge;
But the lips of the wise preserve them.
4 Where there are no oxen, the crib is clean;
But there is great increase by the strength of the ox.
5 A faithful witness doth not lie;
But a false witness poureth forth lies.
6 The scoffer seeketh wisdom, and findeth it not;
But knowledge is easy to the man of understanding.
7 Go from the presence of a foolish man;
For thou hast not perceived in him the lips of knowledge.
8 The wisdom of the prudent is in giving heed to his way;
But the folly of fools is deceit.

9 Fools make a mock at sin;
But with the upright is favor.
10 The heart knoweth its own bitterness,
And a stranger cannot intermeddle with its joy.
11 The house of the wicked shall be destroyed;
But the tent of the upright shall flourish.
12 There is a way which seemeth right to a man,
But its end is the way to death.
13 Even in laughter the heart is sorrowful,
And the end of joy is grief.
14 The perverse in heart shall be filled with his own ways;
And from himself shall the good man be satisfied.
15 The simple man believeth every word;
But the prudent looketh well to his steps.
16 The wise man feareth, and departeth from evil;
But the fool is haughty and confident.
17 He who is hasty in his anger will commit folly;
And the man of wicked devices will be hated.
18 The simple inherit folly;
But the prudent are crowned with knowledge.
19 The evil bow before the good;
Yea, the wicked at the gates of the righteous.
20 The poor is hated even by his own neighbor;
But the rich hath many friends.
21 He who despiseth his neighbor sinneth;
But happy is he who hath mercy on the poor.
22 Do not they who devise evil fail of their end?
But they who devise good meet with kindness and truth.
23 In all labor there is profit;
But the talk of the lips tendeth only to penury.
24 Riches are a crown to the wise;
But the promotion of fools is folly.
25 A true witness saveth lives;
But a deceitful witness poureth forth lies.
26 In the fear of the LORD is strong confidence;
Yea, to his children he will be a refuge.
27 The fear of the LORD is a fountain of life;
By it men escape from the snares of death.
28 In a numerous people is the glory of a king;
But the want of people is the destruction of a prince.

29 He who is slow to anger is of great understanding;
But he who is of a hasty spirit setteth folly on high.
30 A quiet heart is the life of the flesh;
But the ferment of passion is rottenness to the bones.
31 He who oppresseth the poor reproacheth his Maker;
But he who hath mercy on the poor honoreth him.
32 By his wickedness the wicked is thrust down;
But the righteous hath hope even in death.
33 Wisdom resteth quietly in the heart of the wise;
But in the breast of fools it will be made known.
34 Righteousness exalteth a people;
But the reproach of nations is sin.
35 The king's favor is toward a wise servant;
But his wrath is against him that causeth shame.
1 A soft answer turneth away wrath;
But harsh words stir up anger.
2 The tongue of the wise maketh knowledge pleasing;
But the mouth of fools poureth forth folly.
3 The eyes of the LORD are in every place;
They behold the evil and the good.
4 A mild tongue is a tree of life;
But perverseness therein is a wound in the spirit.
5 The fool despiseth the correction of his father;
But he that regardeth reproof is prudent.
6 In the house of the righteous is much wealth;
But in the revenues of the wicked there is trouble.
7 The lips of the wise spread abroad knowledge;
But the heart of the foolish is not sound.
8 The sacrifice of the wicked is an abomination to the LORD;
But the prayer of the righteous is his delight.
9 The way of the wicked is an abomination to the LORD;
But him who followeth after righteousness he loveth.
10 Sore chastisement shall be to him that forsaketh the way;
He that hateth reproof shall die.
11 The underworld, yea, the region of death, is before the LORD;
How much more the hearts of the sons of men!
12 The scoffer loveth not his reprover;
He will not resort to the wise.

13 A joyous heart maketh a bright countenance;
But by sorrow of the heart the spirit is broken.
14 The heart of the man of understanding seeketh knowledge;
But the mouth of fools feedeth on folly.
15 The days of the afflicted are all evil;
But he that hath a cheerful heart hath a continual feast.
16 Better is a little, with the fear of the LORD,
Than much treasure, and trouble therewith.
17 Better is a dinner of herbs, where there is love,
Than a fatted ox, and hatred therewith.
18 The passionate man stirreth up strife;
But he who is slow to anger appeaseth strife.
19 The way of the slothful is as a hedge of thorns;
But the way of the righteous is a highway.
20 A wise son maketh a glad father;
But a foolish man despiseth his mother.
21 Folly is joy to him who lacketh wisdom;
But the man of understanding walketh uprightly.
22 Without counsel, plans come to nought;
But with a multitude of counsellors they are established.
23 A man hath joy by the answer of his mouth;
And a word in due season, how good it is!
24 The path of life is upward for the wise,
So that he turneth away from the underworld beneath.
25 The LORD destroyeth the house of the proud;
But he will establish the border of the widow.
26 Evil devices are an abomination to the LORD;
But pleasant words are pure.
27 He who is greedy of gain troubleth his own house;
But he who hateth bribes shall live.
28 The heart of the righteous meditateth on his answer;
But the mouth of the wicked poureth out evil things.
29 The LORD is far from the wicked;
But he heareth the prayer of the righteous.
30 The light of the eyes rejoiceth the heart,
And good tidings make the bones fat.
31 The ear that hearkeneth to the reproof of life
Shall dwell among the wise.
32 He that refuseth instruction despiseth his own life;
But he that hearkeneth to rebuke getteth understanding.

33 The fear of the LORD guideth to wisdom,
And before honor is humility.
1 To man belongeth the preparation of the heart;
But the answer of the tongue is from the LORD.
2 All the ways of a man are pure in his own eyes;
But the LORD weigheth the spirit.
3 Commit thy doings to the LORD,
And thy purposes shall be established.
4 The LORD hath ordained every thing for its end;
Yea, even the wicked for the day of evil.
5 Every one that is proud in heart is an abomination to the LORD;
From generation to generation he shall not be unpunished.
6 Through kindness and truth, iniquity is expiated;
And, through the fear of the LORD, men depart from evil.
7 When a man's ways please the LORD,
He maketh even his enemies to be at peace with him.
8 Better is a little with righteousness,
Than great revenues without right.
9 The heart of man deviseth his way,
But the LORD establisheth his steps.
10 A divine sentence is upon the lips of a king;
His mouth transgresseth not in judgment.
11 A just balance and scales are the appointment of the LORD;
All the weights of the bag are his work.
12 The doing of wickedness is an abomination to kings;
For by righteousness is the throne established.
13 Righteous lips are the delight of kings,
And they love him who speaketh right things.
14 The wrath of a king is messengers of death;
But a wise man will pacify it.
15 In the light of the king's countenance is life,
And his favor is a like a cloud bringing the latter rain.
16 How much better is it to get wisdom than gold!
Yea, to get understanding is rather to be chosen than silver.
17 It is the highway of the upright to depart from evil;
He that taketh heed to his way preserveth his life.
18 Pride goeth before destruction,
And a haughty spirit before a fall.

19 Better is it to be of a humble spirit with the lowly,
Than to share the spoil with the proud.
20 He who giveth heed to the word shall find good;
And he who trusteth in the LORD, happy is he!
21 The wise in heart shall be called intelligent,
And sweetness of the lips increaseth learning.
22 Understanding is a wellspring of life to him that hath it.
And the chastisement of fools is their folly.
23 The heart of the wise man instructeth his mouth,
And addeth learning to his lips.
24 Pleasant words are like a honeycomb, —
Sweet to the taste, and health to the bones.
25 There is a way that seemeth right to a man,
But the end thereof is the way to death.
26 The hunger of the laborer laboreth for him;
For his mouth urgeth him on.
27 A worthless man diggeth mischief,
And on his lips there is, as it were, a burning fire.
28 A deceitful man stirreth up strife,
And a whisperer separateth friends.
29 A man of violence enticeth his neighbor,
And leadeth him into a way which is not good.
30 He who shutteth his eyes to devise fraud, —
He who compresseth his lips, hath accomplished mischief!
31 The hoary head is a crown of glory,
If it be found in the way of righteousness.
32 He who is slow to anger is better than the mighty;
And he who ruleth his spirit, than he that taketh a city.
33 The lot is cast into the lap;
But the whole decision thereof is from the LORD.
1 Better is a dry morsel, and quietness therewith,
Than a house full of flesh-banquets with strife.
2 A prudent servant shall rule over a son who causeth shame;
Yea, with brothers he shall share the inheritance.
3 The refining-pot is for silver, and the furnace for gold;
But the LORD trieth hearts.
4 An evil doer listeneth to mischievous lips;
And a lier giveth ear to a destructive tongue.

5 Whoso mocketh the poor reproacheth his Maker;
He that is glad at calamities shall not go unpunished.
6 Children's children are the crown of the aged,
And their fathers the glory of sons.
7 Excellent speech becometh not the base;
How much less lying lips the noble!
8 A gift is a precious stone in the eyes of him who taketh it;
Whithersoever it turneth, it hath success.
9 He who covereth an offence seeketh love;
But he who recurreth to a matter removeth a friend.
10 A reproof will penetrate deeper into a wise man
Than a hundred stripes into a fool.
11 An evil man seeketh only rebellion;
Therefore shall a cruel messenger be sent against him.
12 Let a man meet a bear robbed of her whelps,
Rather than a fool in his folly.
13 Whoso returneth evil for good,
Evil shall not depart from his house.
14 The beginning of strife is as when one letteth out water
Therefore leave off contention before it rolleth onward.
15 He that justifieth the wicked,
And he that condemneth the just,
Both alike are an abomination to the LORD.
16 Why should a price be in the hand of a fool
To get wisdom, seeing he hath no sense?
17 A friend loveth at all times;
But in adversity he is born a brother.
18 A man who lacketh understanding striketh hands,
And becometh surety in the presence of his friend.
19 He who loveth strife loveth transgression;
He who raiseth high his gate seeketh ruin.
20 He that is of a deceitful heart shall find no good;
And he that turneth about with his tongue shall fall into mischief.
21 Whoso begetteth a fool doeth it to his sorrow;
Yea, the father of the fool hath no joy.
22 A merry heart doeth good to the body;
But a broken spirit drieth up the bones.
23 The wicked man taketh a gift out of the bosom,
To pervert the ways of judgment.

24 Wisdom is before the face of him that hath understanding;
But the eyes of a fool are in the ends of the earth.
25 A foolish son is a grief to his father,
And bitterness to her that bore him.
26 Moreover, to punish the righteous is not good,
Nor to smite the noble for their equity.
27 He that spareth his words is imbued with knowledge;
And he that is of a cool spirit is a man of understanding.
28 Even a fool, when he is silent, is accounted wise;
He that shutteth his lips is a man of understanding.
1 He who separateth himself seeketh his own desire;
Against all sound discretion he rusheth on.
2 The fool hath no delight in understanding,
But rather in revealing his own mind.
3 When the wicked cometh, then cometh also contempt;
And with baseness, shame.
4 The words of a man's mouth are deep waters,
And the wellspring of wisdom is an overflowing brook.
5 It is not good to be partial to the wicked,
So as to overthrow the righteous in judgment.
6 The lips of a fool enter into strife,
And his mouth calleth for blows.
7 A fool's mouth is his destruction,
And his lips are a snare for his life.
8 The words of a talebearer are like sweet morsels;
For they go down to the innermost parts of the body.
9 Moreover, he that is slothful in his work
Is brother to him that is a great waster.
10 The name of the LORD is a strong tower;
The righteous runneth to it, and is safe.
11 The rich man's wealth is his strong city,
And as a high wall, in his own conceit.
12 Before destruction the heart of a man is haughty,
And before honor is humility.
13 He who answereth a matter before he hath heard it,
It is folly and shame to him.
14 The spirit of a man will sustain his infirmity;
But a wounded spirit who can bear?
15 The heart of the intelligent will acquire knowledge,
And the ear of the wise will seek knowledge.

16 A gift maketh room for a man,
And bringeth him into the presence of the great.
17 He that first pleadeth his cause appeareth just;
But his opponent cometh, and searcheth him through.
18 The lot causeth contentions to cease,
And parteth asunder the mighty.
19 A brother offended is harder to be won than a strong city;
Yea, their contentions are like the bars of a castle.
20 With the fruit of a man's mouth shall his stomach be filled;
He shall be filled with the produce of his lips.
21 Death and life are in the power of the tongue;
They that love it shall eat its fruit.
22 He that findeth a wife findeth a blessing,
And obtaineth favor from the LORD.
23 The poor useth entreaties;
But the rich answereth roughly.
24 A man of many friends will show himself false;
Yet there is a friend who sticketh closer than a brother.
1 Better is the poor man who walketh in his integrity,
Than he who is of false lips and a fool.
2 Moreover, that the soul be without knowledge is not good,
And he that hasteth with his feet stumbleth.
3 The folly of man destroyeth his way,
And then his heart fretteth against the LORD.
4 Wealth maketh many friends;
But the poor is separated from his neighbor
5 A false witness shall not be unpunished,
And he that speaketh lies shall not escape.
6 Many are they who caress the noble,
And every one is the friend of him who giveth gifts.
7 All the brethren of the poor man hate him;
How much more do his friends go far from him!
He runneth after their words, — they are gone!
8 He that getteth wisdom loveth himself;
He that keepeth understanding shall find good.
9 A false witness shall not be unpunished,
And he that speaketh lies shall perish.
10 Luxury is not seemly for a fool;
Much less should a servant have rule over princes.

11 A man of understanding is slow to anger;
Yea, it is his glory to pass over an offence.
12 The wrath of a king is like the roaring of a lion;
But his favor, like dew upon the grass.
13 A foolish son is a calamity to his father,
And the contentions of a wife are a continual dropping.
14 Houses and riches are an inheritance from fathers;
But a prudent wife is from the LORD.
15 Slothfulness casteth into a deep sleep,
And the idle person shall suffer hunger.
16 He that keepeth the commandment keepeth his life;
But he that neglecteth his ways shall die.
17 He who hath pity on the poor lendeth to the LORD,
And that which he giveth will he repay him.
18 Chasten thy son because there is hope,
But let not thy soul desire to slay him.
19 A man of great wrath will suffer punishment;
For if thou deliver him, yet must thou do it again.
20 Listen to counsel and receive instruction,
That thou mayst be wise in thy latter years.
21 Many are the devices in the heart of a man;
But the purpose of the LORD, that shall stand.
22 The charm of a man is his kindness;
And better is a poor man than a liar.
23 The fear of the LORD tendeth to life,
And he that hath it shall abide satisfied;
He shall not be visited with evil.
24 The slothful man dippeth his hand into the dish:
He doth not bring it back even to his mouth.
25 Strike the scoffer, and the simple will become prudent;
Reprove a man of understanding, and he will discern knowledge.
26 The son that causeth shame and disgrace doeth violence to his father,
And chaseth away his mother.
27 Cease, my son, to listen to the instruction
That causeth thee to wander from the words of knowledge!
28 A worthless witness scoffeth at justice,
And the mouth of the wicked swalloweth down iniquity.
29 Punishments are prepared for scoffers,
And stripes for the back of fools.

1 Wine is a mocker, strong drink a brawler,
And he that reeleth with it is not wise.
2 The terror of a king is like the roaring of a lion;
He who provoketh him sinneth against himself.
3 It is an honor to a man to cease from strife;
But every fool rusheth into it.
4 The sluggard will not plough by reason of the cold;
Therefore shall he beg in harvest, and have nothing.
5 A design in the heart of a man is like deep waters;
But a man of understanding draweth it out.
6 Many will proclaim their own kindness;
But a faithful man who can find?
7 He who walketh in his integrity is a righteous man;
Happy will be his children after him!
8 The king, sitting upon the throne of judgment,
Scattereth with his eyes all the wicked like chaff.
9 Who can say, "I have kept my heart clean;
I am free from my sin?"
10 Divers weights and divers measures, —
Both of them are an abomination to the LORD.
11 Even in childhood one maketh himself known by his doings,
Whether his actions will be pure and right.
12 The ear that heareth, and the eye that seeth, —
The LORD made them both.
13 Love not sleep, lest thou come to poverty;
Open thine eyes, and thou shalt be satisfied with bread.
14 "Bad! bad!" saith the buyer;
But when he hath gone his way, then he boasteth.
15 There is gold and abundance of pearls;
But the lips of knowledge are a precious vase.
16 Take his garment who is surety for another;
Yea, take a pledge of him who is bound for a stranger.
17 The bread of falsehood is sweet to a man;
But afterwards his mouth is filled with gravel.
18 Purposes are established by counsel;
Therefore with good advice make war.
19 He who goeth about as a tale-bearer revealeth secrets;
Therefore associate not with him who keepeth open his lips.
20 Whoso curseth his father or his mother,
His lamp shall be put out in midnight darkness.

21 A possession may be gotten hastily in the beginning,
But in the end it will not be blessed.
22 Say not thou, "I will repay evil;"
Wait on the LORD, and he will help thee.
23 Divers weights are an abomination to the LORD,
And a false balance is not good.
24 A man's steps are from the LORD;
How, then, can a man understand his way?
25 It is a snare to a man to utter a vow rashly,
And after vows to consider.
26 A wise king scattereth the wicked like chaff,
And bringeth over them the wheel.
27 The spirit of a man is the lamp of the LORD,
Which searcheth all the inner chambers of his body.
28 Mercy and truth preserve the king;
Yea, his throne is upholden by mercy.
29 The glory of young men is their strength,
And the beauty of old men is the gray head.
30 Wounding stripes are the remedy for a bad man;
Yea, stripes which reach to the inner chambers of the body.
1 As streams of water,
So is the heart of the king in the hand of the LORD;
He turneth it whithersoever he will.
2 All the ways of a man are right in his own eyes;
But the LORD weigheth the heart.
3 To do justice and equity
Is more acceptable to the LORD than sacrifice.
4 The lofty look, the proud heart,
The lamp of the wicked, is ruin.
5 The plans of the diligent tend only to plenty;
But the hasty hasteneth only to want.
6 The getting of treasures by a false tongue
Is the fleeting breath of them that seek death.
7 The rapine of the wicked shall snatch them away,
Because they refuse to do justice.
8 The way of the guilty man is crooked;
But he that is pure, his doings are right.
9 Better is it to dwell in a corner of the housetop
Than with a brawling woman in a large house.
10 The soul of the wicked longeth to do evil;
His neighbor findeth no compassion in his eyes.

11 When the scoffer is punished, the simple is made wise;
When the wise man is taught, he receiveth knowledge.
12 The righteous man hath regard to the house of the wicked;
He casteth the wicked headlong into ruin.
13 Whoso stoppeth his ears at the cry of the poor,
He also shall cry aloud, but shall not be heard.
14 A gift in secret pacifieth anger;
And a present in the bosom, strong wrath.
15 To do justice shall be joy to the righteous;
But destruction is for them that do iniquity.
16 A man who wandereth from the way of discretion
Shall rest in the assembly of the dead.
17 He that loveth pleasure will be a poor man;
He that loveth wine and oil will not be rich.
18 The wicked shall be a ransom for the righteous;
And in the room of the upright shall be the transgressor.
19 It is better to dwell in a desert land
Than with a contentious and fretful woman.
20 Precious treasure and oil are in the dwelling of the wise;
But the foolish man swalloweth them up.
21 He who followeth after righteousness and mercy
Shall find life, prosperity, and honor.
22 A wise man scaleth the city of the mighty,
And bringeth down the strength in which it trusted.
23 Whoso keepeth his mouth and his tongue
Keepeth his soul from trouble.
24 The proud and haughty,—scoffer is his name;
He acteth with haughty arrogance.
25 The desire of the sluggard will destroy him;
For his hands refuse to labor.
26 The covetous man coveteth all the day long;
But the righteous man giveth, and doth not withhold.
27 The sacrifice of the wicked is an abomination;
How much more when he bringeth it with an evil design!
28 A false witness shall perish;
But a man that hearkeneth shall speak forever.
29 The wicked man hardeneth his face;
But the upright directeth his way.
30 Wisdom is nothing, and understanding is nothing,
And devices are nothing, against the LORD.

31 The horse is prepared for the day of battle;
But victory is from the LORD.
1 A good name is rather to be chosen than great riches;
And better is good-will than silver and gold.
2 The rich and the poor meet together;
The LORD is the Maker of them all.
3 The prudent man seeth the evil, and hideth himself;
But the simple rush on, and are punished.
4 By humility and the fear of the LORD
Are riches and honor and life.
5 Thorns and snares are in the way of the deceitful;
He that will preserve his life will be far from them.
6 Train up a child in accordance with his way,
And when he is old he will not depart from it.
7 The rich ruleth over the poor,
And the borrower is servant to the lender.
8 He who soweth iniquity shall reap calamity,
And the rod of his punishment is prepared.
9 He who hath a bountiful eye shall be blessed,
Because he giveth of his bread to the poor.
10 Cast out the scoffer, and contention will go out;
Yea, strife and reproach will cease.
11 He who loveth purity of heart,
Grace is upon his lips, and the king will be his friend.
12 The eyes of the LORD watch over knowledge;
But he overthroweth the words of the treacherous.
13 The slothful man saith, "There is a lion without;
I shall be slain in the streets."
14 The mouth of strange women is a deep pit;
He with whom the LORD is angry shall fall therein.
15 Folly is bound to the heart of a child;
But the rod of correction will drive it far from him.
16 He that oppresseth the poor to increase his wealth,
And he that giveth to the rich, shall surely come to want.

XIII.

Other Proverbs. — Chap. XXII. 17–XXIV. 22.

17 Incline thine ear, and hear the words of the wise,
And give heed to my instruction!
18 For it will be a pleasant thing, if thou keep them in thy bosom,
When they are altogether established upon thy lips.
19 That thy trust may be in the Lord,
I have this day given to thee instruction, yea, to thee.
20 Behold, I have written to thee excellent things
Concerning counsel and knowledge;
21 That I may make thee know rectitude, and words of truth·
That thou mayst bring back words of truth to them that send thee.

22 Rob not the poor man, because he is poor,
Nor crush thou the destitute at the gate;
23 For the Lord will maintain their cause,
And despoil their spoilers of life.
24 Make no friendship with a passionate man,
Nor be the companion of a man prone to wrath;
25 Lest thou learn his ways,
And take to thyself a snare.
26 Be not thou one of those who strike hands, —
Of those who are sureties for debts.
27 When thou hast nothing to pay,
Why should thy bed be taken from under thee?
28 Remove not the ancient landmark,
Which thy fathers have made.
29 Seest thou a man diligent in his business?
He shall be the minister of kings;
He shall not serve obscure men.
1 When thou sittest to eat with a ruler,
Consider well what is before thee;
2 For thou wilt put a knife to thy throat,
If thou art a man given to appetite!
3 Long not for his dainties,
For they are deceitful meat.

4 Toil not to become rich;
Cease from this, thy wisdom.
5 Wilt thou let thine eyes fly toward them? They are gone!
For riches truly make to themselves wings;
They fly away like the eagle toward heaven.
6 Eat not the bread of him that hath an evil eye,
And long not for his dainties;
7 For as he thinketh in his heart, so is he.
"Eat and drink!" saith he to thee;
But his heart is not with thee.
8 The morsel, which thou hast eaten, thou shalt vomit up;
And thou wilt have thrown away thy sweet words.
9 Speak not in the ears of a fool;
For he will despise the wisdom of thy words.
10 Remove not the ancient landmark,
And enter not into the fields of the fatherless!
11 For their avenger is mighty;
He will maintain their cause against thee.
12 Apply thy heart to instruction,
And thine ears to the words of knowledge.
13 Withhold not correction from a child;
If thou beat him with the rod, he will not die.
14 Beat him thyself with the rod,
And thou shalt rescue him from the underworld.
15 My son, if thy heart be wise,
My heart shall rejoice, even mine;
16 Yea, my reins shall exult,
When thy lips speak right things.
17 Let not thy heart envy sinners,
But continue thou in the fear of the LORD all the day long;
18 For surely there shall be a reward,
And thine expectation shall not be cut off.
19 Hear thou, my son, and be wise;
And let thy heart go forward in the way!
20 Be not thou among winebibbers,
And riotous eaters of flesh;
21 For the drunkard and the glutton shall come to poverty,
And drowsiness will clothe a man with rags.
22 Hearken to thy father, who begat thee,
And despise not thy mother when she is old.

23 Buy the truth, and sell it not;
Buy wisdom and instruction and understanding.
24 The father of a righteous man shall greatly rejoice;
Yea, he who begetteth a wise child shall have joy in him.
25 Let thy father and thy mother have joy;
Yea, let her that bore thee rejoice!
26 My son, give me thy heart,
And let thine eyes observe my ways!
27 For a harlot is a deep ditch;
Yea, a strange woman is a narrow pit.
28 Like a robber she lieth in wait,
And increaseth the treacherous among men.
29 Who hath woe? Who hath sorrow?
Who contentions? Who anxiety?
Who wounds without cause? Who dimness of eyes?
30 They that tarry long at the wine;
They that go in to seek mixed wine.
31 Look not thou upon the wine when it is red,
When it sparkleth in the cup,
When it goeth down smoothly.
32 At the last it biteth like a serpent,
And stingeth like an adder.
33 Thine eyes will look upon strange women,
And thy heart will utter perverse things.
34 Yea, thou shalt be as one that lieth down in the midst of the sea,
And as one that lieth down upon the top of a mast.
35 They have stricken me [shalt thou say], — I suffered no pain!
They have beaten me, — I felt it not!
When shall I awake? I will seek it yet again.

1 Be not thou envious of wicked men,
And desire not to be with them!
2 For their heart studieth destruction,
And their lips speak mischief.
3 Through wisdom is a house builded,
And by understanding is it established;
4 Yea, by knowledge are the chambers filled
With all precious and goodly substance.

5 The wise man is strong;
Yea, the man of understanding establisheth his strength.
6 For by wise counsel shalt thou make war,
And by the multitude of counsellors cometh success.
7 Wisdom is too high for the fool;
He openeth not his mouth at the gate.
8 He that deviseth to do evil
Shall be called mischief-master.
9 The purpose of folly is sin;
And a scoffer is an abomination to men.
10 If thy spirit faint in the day of adversity,
Faint will be thy strength.

11 Deliver thou those who are dragged to death,
And those who totter to the slaughter, — O keep them back!
12 If thou sayst, "Behold, we knew it not!"
Doth not he that weigheth the heart observe it?
Yea, he that keepeth thy soul knoweth it,
And he will render to every man according to his works.

13 Eat honey, my son, for it is good,
And the honeycomb, which is sweet to thy taste;
14 So learn thou wisdom for thy soul!
When thou hast found it, there shall be a reward,
And thy expectation shall not be cut off.
15 Plot not, O wicked man! against the habitation of the righteous;
Spoil not his resting-place!
16 For though the righteous fall seven times, yet shall he rise up again;
But the wicked shall fall into mischief.
17 Rejoice not when thine enemy falleth,
And let not thy heart be glad when he stumbleth;
18 Lest the LORD see, and it displease him,
And he turn away his anger from him.
19 Fret not thyself on account of evil men,
Neither be thou envious of the wicked;
20 For there shall be no posterity to the evil man;
The lamp of the wicked shall be put out.

21 My son, fear thou the LORD and the king;
And mingle not with them that are given to change!
22 For their calamity shall rise up suddenly,
And their ruin, coming from them both, in a moment.

XIV.

Other Proverbs. — CHAP. XXIV. 23-34.

23 THESE also are words of the wise.
It is not good to have respect of persons in judgment.
24 He that saith to the wicked, "Thou art righteous,"
Him shall the people curse;
Nations shall abhor him.
25 But it shall be well with them that punish him,
And the blessing of prosperity shall come upon them.
26 He that giveth a right answer
Kisseth the lips.
27 Arrange thy work without,
And prepare it in thy field:
Afterwards thou mayst build thy house.
28 Be not a witness without cause against thy neighbor,
And deceive not with thy lips.
29 Say not, "As he hath done to me,
So will I do to him;
I will render to the man according to his doings."
30 I passed by the field of the slothful,
And by the vineyard of the man void of understanding,
31 And, lo! it was all overgrown with thorns,
And the face thereof was covered with nettles,
And the stone wall thereof was broken down.
32 Then I saw, and considered it well;
I looked upon it, and received instruction.
33 "A little sleep, a little slumber!
A little folding of the hands to rest!"
34 So shall poverty come upon thee like a highwayman;
Yea, want like an armed man.

XV.

Other Proverbs.—CHAP. XXV.–XXIX.

1 THESE also are proverbs of Solomon, which the men
of Hezekiah, king of Judah, collected.
2 It is the glory of God to conceal a thing;
But it is the glory of kings to search out a matter.
3 As the heavens for their height,
And as the earth for its depth,
So is the heart of kings unsearchable!
4 Take away the dross from the silver,
And there will come forth a vessel for the founder;
5 Take away the wicked man from the presence of the
king,
And his throne will be established by righteousness.
6 Put not thyself forth in the presence of the king,
Nor set thyself in the place of the great;
7 For better is it that one should say to thee,
"Come up hither!"
Than that he should put thee in a lower place,
In the presence of the prince whom thine eyes behold.
8 Go not forth hastily to engage in a suit,
Lest thou know not what to do in the end of it,
When thine adversary hath put thee to shame.
9 Maintain thy cause with thine adversary,
But reveal not another's secret;
10 Lest he that heareth it put thee to shame,
And thy infamy depart not from thee.
11 A word spoken in season
Is like apples of gold in figured-work of silver.
12 As a ring of gold, and an ornament of fine gold,
So is a wise reprover to an attentive ear.
13 As the cold of snow in the time of harvest,
So is a faithful messenger to them that send him;
For he refresheth the spirit of his masters.
14 As clouds and wind without rain,
So is the man that boasteth falsely of giving.
15 By long forbearing is a prince appeased;
And a soft tongue breaketh bones.

16 Hast thou found honey? eat what is sufficient for thee,
Lest thou be surfeited with it, and vomit it up.
17 Let thy foot be seldom in the house of thy friend,
Lest he be surfeited with thee and hate thee.
18 A battle-hammer, and a sword, and a sharp arrow,
Is the man who beareth false witness against his neighbor.
19 As a broken tooth, and a wavering foot,
So is trust in an unfaithful man in time of trouble.
20 As he that taketh off a garment on a cold day,
As vinegar upon nitre,
So is he that singeth songs to a heavy heart.
21 If thine enemy be hungry, give him bread to eat;
And if he be thirsty, give him water to drink;
22 For thou wilt heap coals of fire upon his head,
And the LORD will reward thee.
23 As the north wind bringeth forth rain,
So a backbiting tongue maketh an angry countenance.
24 Better is it to dwell in a corner of the housetop,
Than with a quarrelsome woman in a large house.
25 As cold water to the thirsty,
So is good news from a far country.
26 As a troubled fountain, and as a corrupted spring,
So is a righteous man falling before the wicked.
27 To eat much honey is not good;
So the search of high things is weariness.
28 As a city broken through and without a wall,
So is he that hath no rule over his spirit.
1 As snow in summer, and as rain in harvest,
So honor is not becoming to a fool.
2 As the sparrow wandereth, and the swallow flieth away,
So the curse without cause shall not come.
3 A whip for the horse, a bridle for the ass,
And a rod for the back of the fool.
4 Answer not a fool according to his folly,
Let thou also become like to him.
5 Answer a fool according to his folly,
Lest he be wise in his own conceit.
6 He cutteth off the feet, and drinketh damage,
Who sendeth a message by the hand of a fool.

7 The legs of a lame man hang loose;
So is it with a proverb in the mouth of fools.
8 As he who bindeth a stone in a sling,
So is he that giveth honor to a fool.
9 As a thorn lifted up by the hand of a drunkard,
So is a proverb in the mouth of fools.
10 As an archer who woundeth every one,
So is he who hireth fools and hireth wayfarers.
11 As a dog returneth to that which he hath vomited,
So a fool repeateth his folly.
12 Seest thou a man wise in his own conceit?
There is more hope of a fool than of him.
13 The slothful man saith, "There is a lion in the way,
There is a lion in the streets."
14 As a door turneth upon its hinges,
So doth the sluggard upon his bed.
15 The sluggard dippeth his hand into the dish;
It grieveth him to bring it again to his mouth.
16 The sluggard is wiser in his own conceit
Than seven men who can render a reason.
17 As one that taketh a dog by the ears,
So is he who, passing by, is enraged on account of the quarrel of another.
18 As a madman
That casteth about darts, arrows, and death,
19 So is the man who deceiveth his neighbor,
And saith, "Was I not in sport?"
20 Where there is no wood, the fire goeth out;
So, where there is no talebearer, contention ceaseth.
21 As coal is for heat, and as wood for fire,
So is a contentious man for kindling strife.
22 The words of a talebearer are like dainties;
For they go down to the innermost parts of the body.
23 As drossy silver spread over an earthen vessel,
So are warm lips and an evil heart.
24 The hater dissembleth with his lips,
And layeth up deceit within him.
25 When he speaketh fair, believe him not!
For there are seven abominations in his heart.
26 His hatred is covered by deceit;
His wickedness shall be revealed in the great assembly.

27 He that diggeth a pit shall fall therein;
And he that rolleth a stone, it shall return upon him.
28 A lying tongue hateth those whom it woundeth,
And a flattering mouth worketh ruin.
1 Boast not thyself of to-morrow;
For thou knowest not what a day may bring forth!
2 Let another man praise thee, and not thine own mouth;
A stranger, and not thine own lips.
3 A stone is heavy and sand is weighty;
But a fool's wrath is heavier than both.
4 Wrath is cruel, and anger overwhelming;
But who is able to stand before jealousy?
5 Better is open rebuke
Than love kept concealed.
6 Faithful are the wounds of a friend;
But the kisses of an enemy are deceitful.
7 He who is fed to the full loatheth the honeycomb;
But to the hungry any bitter thing is sweet.
8 As a bird that wandereth from its nest,
So is a man who wandereth from his place.
9 Oil and perfume gladden the heart;
Sweet also is one's friend by hearty counsel.
10 Thine own friend and thy father's friend forsake not;
And go not into thy brother's house in the day of thy calamity.
Better is a neighbor that is near, than a brother far off.
11 Be wise, my son, and make my heart glad,
That I may give an answer to him that reproacheth me.
12 A prudent man foreseeth the evil, and hideth himself;
The simple pass on, and are punished.
13 Take his garment who is surety for another;
Yea, take a pledge of him who is bound for a stranger.
14 He who blesseth his neighbor with a loud voice, rising early for it,
It shall be accounted to him as a curse.
15 A continual dropping in a very rainy day
And a quarrelsome wife are alike.
16 He who restraineth her restraineth the wind;
And his right hand layeth hold of oil.

17 Iron sharpeneth iron;
So one man sharpeneth the face of another.
18 He that watcheth the fig-tree shall eat its fruit;
So he that is careful for his master shall come to honor.
19 As in water face answereth to face,
So doth the heart of man to man.
20 The realms of the dead are never full;
So the eyes of man are never satisfied.
21 The refining-pot is for silver, and the furnace for gold;
So let a man be to the mouth that giveth him praise.
22 Though thou shouldst beat a fool in a mortar,
Among bruised wheat, with a pestle,
Yet will not his folly depart from him.
23 Be thou diligent to know the state of thy flocks,
And look well to thy herds!
24 For riches last not for ever;
Not even a crown endureth from generation to generation.
25 The hay disappeareth, and the tender grass showeth itself,
And the herbage of the mountains is gathered in.
26 The lambs are thy clothing,
And the goats the price of thy field.
27 There is goat's milk enough for thy food,
For the food of thy household,
And for the sustenance of thy maidens.
1 The wicked flee when no one pursueth;
But the righteous is as bold as a lion.
2 Through the transgression of a land many are its rulers;
But through men of prudence and understanding the prince shall live long.
3 A poor man who oppresseth the needy
Is a sweeping rain which leaveth no food.
4 They who forsake the law praise the wicked;
But they who keep the law contend with them.
5 Wicked men understand not equity;
But they who seek the LORD understand all things.
6 Better is a poor man who walketh in uprightness,
Than he who is perverse in his ways, though he be rich.
7 He that keepeth the law is a wise son;
But he that is the companion of prodigals bringeth shame on his father.

8 He that increaseth his substance by usurious gain
Gathereth it for him who will pity the poor.
9 He that turneth away his ear from hearing the law,
Even his prayer shall be an abomination.
10 He that causeth the righteous to go astray in an evil way
Shall himself fall into his own pit;
But the upright shall have good things in possession.
11 The rich man is wise in his own conceit;
But the poor man, who hath understanding, will search him through.
12 When the righteous rejoice, there is great glorying;
But, when the wicked are exalted, men hide themselves.
13 He that covereth his sins shall not prosper;
But he that confesseth and forsaketh them shall have mercy.
14 Happy the man who feareth always!
But he who hardeneth his heart shall fall into mischief.
15 As a roaring lion and a hungry bear,
So is a wicked ruler over a needy people.
16 The prince who is weak in understanding is great in oppression;
But he who hateth unjust gain shall prolong his days.
17 A man who is burdened with life-blood —
Let him flee to the pit! let no man stay him!
18 He who walketh uprightly shall be safe;
But he who is perverse in his ways shall fall at once.
19 He who tilleth his land shall have bread enough;
And he that followeth after worthless persons shall have poverty enough.
20 A faithful man shall abound with blessings;
But he that maketh haste to be rich shall not go unpunished.
21 To have respect to persons is not good;
Since for a piece of bread that man will transgress.
22 He who hath an evil eye hasteth after wealth,
And considereth not that poverty will come upon him.
23 He who rebuketh a man shall afterwards find favor
More than he who flattereth with his tongue.
24 Whoso stealeth from his father or his mother,
And saith, "It is no transgression,"
The same is the companion of a robber.

25 He who is of a proud heart stirreth up strife;
But he that trusteth in the LORD shall be rich.
26 He who trusteth in his own understanding is a fool;
But he who walketh wisely shall be delivered.
27 He who giveth to the poor shall not want;
But he that hideth his eyes shall have many a curse.
28 When the wicked are exalted, men hide themselves;
But, when they perish, the righteous increase.
1 He who, being often reproved, hardeneth his neck,
Shall suddenly be destroyed, and that without remedy.
2 When the righteous are powerful, the people rejoice;
But when the wicked beareth rule, the people mourn.
3 He who loveth wisdom rejoiceth his father;
But he who is a companion of harlots destroyeth his substance.
4 A king by equity establisheth a land;
But he who receiveth gifts overthroweth it.
5 A man who flattereth his neighbor
Spreadeth a net for his feet.
6 In the transgression of a wicked man there is a snare;
But the righteous shall sing and rejoice.
7 A righteous man careth for the cause of the poor;
A wicked man discerneth not knowledge.
8 Scoffers kindle a city into a flame;
But wise men pacify wrath.
9 If a wise man contend in a cause with a fool,
Whether he rage or laugh, there will be no rest.
10 The bloodthirsty man hateth the upright;
But the righteous seek to preserve his life.
11 A fool letteth all his anger come out;
But a wise man keepeth it back.
12 If a ruler listen to words of falsehood,
All his servants become wicked.
13 The poor man and the oppressor meet together:
The LORD giveth light to the eyes of them both.
14 The king that judgeth the poor with uprightness,
His throne shall be established for ever.
15 The rod and reproof give wisdom;
But a child left to himself bringeth shame to his mother.
16 When the wicked are powerful, transgression increaseth;
But the righteous shall see their fall.

17 Chastise thy son, and he will give thee rest;
Yea, he will give delight to thy soul.
18 Where there is no vision, the people become unruly;
But he that keepeth the law, happy is he.
19 A servant will not be corrected by words;
For, though he understand, he will not obey.
20 Seest thou a man hasty in his words?
There is more hope of a fool than of him.
21 He that bringeth up his servant delicately from childhood
Shall have him become a son at the last.
22 An angry man stirreth up strife,
And a passionate man aboundeth in transgression.
23 A man's pride will bring him low;
But he that is of a humble spirit shall obtain honor.
24 He who shareth with a thief hateth himself:
He heareth the curse, but maketh no discovery.
25 The fear of man bringeth a snare;
But whoso putteth his trust in the LORD shall be safe.
26 Many are they who seek the ruler's favor;
But every man's judgment cometh from the LORD.
27 As the unjust man is an abomination to the righteous,
So the upright in his way is an abomination to the wicked.

XVI.

The words of Agur. — CHAP. XXX.

1 THE words of Agur, the son of Jakeh, even his prophecy; the inspired utterance of the man to Ithiel, even to Ithiel and Ucal.
2 Truly I am more stupid than any man;
There is not in me the understanding of a man.
3 I have not learned wisdom,
Nor have I gained the knowledge of the Most Holy.
4 Who hath gone up into heaven and come down?
Who hath gathered the wind in his fists?
Who hath bound up the waters in a garment?
Who hath established all the ends of the earth?
What is his name, and what his son's name, if thou knowest?

5 Every word of God is pure;
A shield is he to them that put their trust in him.
6 Add not to his words,
Lest he rebuke thee, and thou be found a liar.
7 Two things do I ask of thee;
Withhold them not from me, before I die!
8 Remove far from me falsehood and lies;
Give me neither poverty nor riches;
Feed me with the food which is needful for me;
9 Lest I be full, and deny thee,
And say, "Who is the LORD?"
Or lest I be poor, and steal,
And violate the name of my God.

10 Talk not against a servant to his master,
Lest he curse thee, and thou suffer for it.

11 There is a class of men that curse their fathers,
And do not bless their mothers.
12 There is a class who are pure in their own eyes,
And yet are not washed from their filthiness.
13 There is a class, — O how lofty are their eyes,
And how are their eyelids lifted up!
14 There is a class, whose teeth are swords,
And their jaw-teeth knives,
To devour the poor from off the earth,
And the needy from among men.
15 The vampire hath two daughters;
"Give! give!" [is their cry.]
There are three things which are never satisfied;
Yea, four which say not, "Enough!"
16 The underworld, and the barren womb;
The earth, which is not satiated with water,
And fire, which never saith, "It is enough!"

17 The eye that mocketh at a father,
And scorneth to obey a mother,
The ravens of the valley shall pick it out,
And the young eagles shall eat it.

18 These three things are too wonderful for me;
Yea, there are four which I understand not:

19 The track of an eagle in the air,
The track of a serpent upon a rock,
The track of a ship in the midst of the sea,
And the track of a man with a maid.
20 Such is the way of an adulterous woman;
She eateth, and wipeth her mouth,
And saith, "I have done nothing wrong."
21 Under three things is the earth disquieted;
Yea, under four it cannot bear up:
22 Under a servant when he becometh a king,
And a fool when he is filled with bread;
23 Under an odious woman when she becometh a wife,
And a handmaid when she becometh heir to her mistress.

24 There are four things which are small upon the earth,
Yet are they wise, instructed in wisdom.
25 The ants are a people not strong,
Yet they prepare in the summer their food.
26 The conies are a feeble people,
Yet do they make their houses in the rocks.
27 The locusts have no king,
Yet do they all go forth in bands.
28 The lizard seizeth with its hands,
And is in king's palaces.

29 These three have a graceful step;
Yea, four are graceful in their walk:
30 The lion, the hero among beasts,
Which turneth not back for any;
31 The loin-girded war-horse, the he-goat,
And a king who cannot be withstood.

32 If thou hast been foolish in lifting thyself up,
And hast meditated evil,
Put thy hand on thy mouth!
33 For, as the pressing of milk bringeth forth cheese,
And as the pressing of the nose bringeth forth blood,
So the pressing of anger bringeth forth strife.

XVII.

Advice given to a king. — CHAP. XXXI. 1–9.

1 THE words given to King Lemuel; the prophecy which
his mother taught him.
2 What, O my son! and what, O son of my womb!
Yea, what, O son of my vows! [shall I say to thee?]
3 Give not thy strength to women,
Nor thy ways to that which destroyeth kings!
4 It is not for kings, O Lemuel! —
It is not for kings to drink wine,
Nor for princes to desire strong drink;
5 Lest they drink, and forget the law,
And pervert the rights of any of the afflicted.
6 Give strong drink to him who is ready to perish,
And wine to him that hath a heavy heart;
7 Let him drink and forget his poverty,
And remember his misery no more!
8 Open thy mouth for the dumb,
In the cause of every orphan!
9 Open thy mouth, judge righteously,
And maintain the cause of the poor and needy!

XVIII.

Character of a good wife. — CHAP. XXXI. 10–31.

10 WHO can find a capable woman?
Her worth is far above pearls.
11 The heart of her husband trusteth in her,
And he is in no want of gain.
12 She doeth him good, and not evil,
All the days of her life.
13 She seeketh wool and flax,
And worketh willingly with her hands.
14 She is like the merchants' ships;
She bringeth her food from afar.
15 She riseth while it is yet night,
And giveth food to her family,
And a task to her maidens.

16 She layeth a plan for a field, and buyeth it;
With the fruit of her hands she planteth a vineyard.
17 She girdeth her loins with strength,
And maketh strong her arms.
18 She perceiveth how pleasant is her gain,
And her lamp is not extinguished in the night.
19 She putteth forth her hands to the distaff,
And her hands take hold of the spindle.
20 She spreadeth out her hand to the poor,
Yea, she reacheth forth her hands to the needy.
21 She hath no fear for her household on account of the snow,
For all her household are clothed with crimson.
22 She maketh for herself coverlets;
Her clothing is of fine linen and purple.
23 Her husband is known in the gates,
When he sitteth with the elders of the land.
24 She maketh linen garments and selleth them,
And delivereth girdles to the merchant.
25 Strength and honor are her clothing;
And she laugheth at the days to come.
26 She openeth her mouth with wisdom,
And kind instruction is upon her tongue.
27 She looketh well to the ways of her household,
And eateth not the bread of idleness.
28 Her children rise up, and extol her;
Her husband, and praiseth her, [saying,]
29 "Many daughters have done virtuously,
But thou excellest them all."
30 Grace is deceitful, and beauty vain;
But the woman that feareth the LORD, she shall be praised.
31 Give ye her of the fruit of her hands,
And let her works praise her in the gates.

NOTES TO THE PSALMS.

Ps. I.

This psalm sets forth, in vivid and picturesque description, the happiness of the righteous and the misery of the wicked. It is quite a probable supposition, that it was prefixed by one of the compilers of the Psalms (see p. 31, &c.), as an introduction to his collection. This may be the reason, that in some manuscripts it seems not to have been numbered with the other psalms, and in others to have been united with the second psalm.

The promises of the Jewish religion, limited as they are to the present world, are to be regarded as statements of what is generally true, or of what is the tendency of piety and virtue, other things being equal. Our Saviour, in his instructions, makes much less account of outward good than the Jewish writers. He had meat to give, as well as to eat, which the world knew not of. He promises his followers something better than length of days, or riches and honors, — a treasure which the world can neither give nor take away; namely, riches of the soul, a heart at peace with itself and with God, a consciousness of the divine favor, and a hope extending into eternity: in a word, spiritual and everlasting life.

1. — *counsel;* i.e., his purposes, plan of life.

3. — *like a tree.* In a country where water was scarce, and the trees and herbs were often parched with heat, this image was more striking than it can appear to us, who live in a climate where the trees are usually green, wherever they stand. (See Bush's Illustrations, ad loc.)

5. — *shall not stand.* This may be understood in a general sense, that the wicked shall fall into ruin; or, in a legal sense, that they shall fail in their cause. — *in judgment;* i.e., when they are judged by the Almighty. The allusion is to those signal seasons of retribution with which Divine Providence visits evil-doers in this world. (Comp. Isa. iii. 14; Mal. iii. 5; Job xix. 29.) — *in the assembly of the just;* i.e., in the assembly of the righteous Israelites, who are preserved and blessed by the Almighty, the wicked shall not be found, having been separated therefrom by the just judgments of God. (Comp. Isa. i. 24–28; iv. 2–6.)

6. — *knoweth;* i.e., he is well acquainted with the righteous, and cares for them.

Ps. II.

This psalm purports to have been composed by a king, soon after his inauguration to his office. He is full of pious confidence in God, as having appointed him to his high destiny. He feels himself to be the earthly representative of Jehovah, and regards the attempts of subject nations to throw off his yoke as offences against his God. The sentiments which he expresses are not very different from those which have been entertained by modern kings and their supporters, though the language is peculiar to a king of Israel, an Eastern monarch of a peculiar religious faith. The young king feels sure, that the attempts of his enemies — being offences against Jehovah as well as himself, the anointed vicegerent of Jehovah — will be frustrated, and that he shall be signally victorious over them all. He earnestly admonishes the insurgents to desist from their rebellious attempts, and put themselves under the protection of Jehovah by paying homage to his earthly representative, before they should feel the effects of his anger.

The language of the psalm in ver. 7 evidently implies, that the writer of the psalm is the king who is the subject of it, whether it be David or some other Jewish king. The rebellion described in it is also represented as existing in the time of the writer. It is only in a typical sense, therefore, that Christ and his kingdom can be regarded as the subject of the psalm. This has been the general opinion of the Christian Church. Thus, the version of the Scriptures published by Barker in 1606, before the common version, has for the caption of this psalm, "The prophet David rejoiceth, that, notwithstanding his enemies' rage, yet God will continue his kingdom for ever, and advance it even to the end of the world; and therefore exhorteth kings and rulers, that they would humbly submit themselves under God's yoke, because it is in vain to resist God. *Herein is figured Christ's kingdom.*" But there is no reason for supposing that the writer had in view any kingdom but his own. (See Introduction, p. 9, &c.)

2. — *Against Jehovah.* The government of the Israelites was theocratic. Jehovah was regarded as king of the Jewish state, so that the nations which combined against it are represented as combining against Jehovah. Thus, in 1 Chron. xxix. 23, Solomon is said to have sat upon the throne of Jehovah; that is, the throne of Israel. — *his anointed king.* This epithet was appropriate to every king of Israel, as receiving from Jehovah the power and authority, of which consecration by pouring oil upon the head was the outward symbol.

4. — *will laugh.* This expression is designed to represent in a lively manner the futility of exertions made in opposition to the will of Jehovah.

7. This verse expresses the confidence of the writer, who was king of Israel, that he was the special care of Jehovah as king. — *Thou art my son;* i.e., Thou art my favored king, dear to me as a son. The term *son of God* is used in the Scriptures in different senses, — sometimes denoting that one is the object of special love to God, as a son is to a father (see Exod. iv. 22); sometimes denoting a moral resemblance to the Deity, as a son resembles his father: thus Christians are

called sons of God. And sometimes the expression denotes resemblance to God in power and dominion: thus the term is applied to kings. Sometimes two of these senses are united. In this verse, the expression seems to be one both of endearment and of office. — *begotten thee;* i.e., made thee my favored king. (Comp. Ps. lxxxix. 26, 27; 2 Sam. vii. 14.)

8. — *ends of the earth.* A hyperbolical expression, denoting the most distant lands.

11. *Be subject to Jehovah;* i.e., in a political sense, by submitting to the king of Israel, his vicegerent. (See the note on ver. 2.)

12. *Kiss the son.* Give the sign of political subjection and homage to the king of Israel. This must be admitted to be a very doubtful rendering. When the Hebrew word בֵּן has been used to denote *son* in ver. 7, it is very strange that the Chaldee בַּר should be used here in the same sense, and that, too, without the article. But I cannot persuade myself, that either of the renderings which have been proposed in its place — whether *Lay hold of instruction,* according to the ancient versions; or *Lay hold of obedience* or *duty,* according to Hitzig; or *Lay hold of purity,* or *Worship purely,* according to other critics — has any better support from the usage of words, or other philological considerations. I prefer, therefore, to retain the rendering of the common version, which is that of De Wette, Gesenius, Hengstenberg, and others. (See 1 Sam. x. 1.) — *lest He be angry;* i.e., lest Jehovah be angry; the pronoun here referring to the more distant antecedent.

Ps. III.

The subject of this psalm is a pious man in eminent station, probably King David, surrounded by enemies who regarded his downfall as certain. But he has confidence in the protection of Jehovah, and prays to him as one who can and will deliver him. The superscription of this psalm assigns it to David, and mentions the occasion on which it was composed; namely, his flight from his rebellious son, Absalom. If this be correct, it is singular that there should be in the psalm no allusion to the feelings which must have agitated the royal parent's heart on being compelled to flee for his life from his own son.

2. — *no help,* &c.; i.e., it is all over with him: God will not interfere to save him.

3. — *My glory;* the cause or vindicator of my glory and greatness. — *lifter-up of my head.* The image may be drawn from a person sinking in deep waters; or from one whose head is bowed down, and his eyes fixed on the ground in affliction.

4. — *with my voice;* i.e., probably, with my whole voice, earnestly or aloud.

7. — *smitest the cheek,* &c. Images drawn from the slaying of a wild beast.

Ps. IV.

The occasion of this psalm was similar to that of the last. On account of ver. 8, some suppose it to have been composed on the evening of the day when the preceding psalm was sung.

For the leader of the music; i.e., to be used by him in public worship. (See Introduction, p. 27.)

1. — *O God of my righteousness;* i.e., vindicator of my righteous cause.

2. — *dishonor my dignity;* i.e., my royal dignity, by your conspiracy and rebellion. — *seek disappointment;* i.e., How long will ye seek ends which will prove vain, and be sure to disappoint you? (Comp. Ps. vii. 14.)

4. — *upon your beds;* i.e., in the season and place for independent reflection. — *desist;* i.e., from your unrighteous or rebellious undertakings.

5. *Offer sacrifices of righteousness;* i.e., think not to please God by sacrifices offered without pure and pious intentions. Or, Offer sacrifices which are due.

6. — *Who will show,* &c.; i.e., even many of my friends are discouraged, and long for the least bright interval of success.

7. — *corn and wine,* &c. Isa. ix. 3: "They rejoice before thee with the joy of harvest."

Ps. V.

3. *In the morning,* &c. These words, being repeated in the parallel line, are probably to be understood as referring, not to a customary time of prayer, but to the earnestness with which the writer called upon the Deity, and the speedy aid which he hoped to obtain. (See Ps. lxxxviii. 13.)

4. — *dwelleth not,* &c.; i.e., as a guest or friend; i.e., he enjoys not thy favor and protection. (Comp. Ps. xv. 1; lxi. 4.)

5. — *stand in thy sight;* i.e., they find no favor with thee; as explained by the parallel line, and by the preceding verse.

8. — *thy righteousness;* i.e., that which thou requirest, which is pleasing to thee. — *because of mine enemies;* i.e., because my enemies study to ensnare me. (Comp. Jer. xx. 10.)

9. — *Their heart;* literally, *inward part:* used to denote the seat of the feelings, intentions, &c. (Ps. xlix. 11; lxiv. 6.) — *an open sepulchre;* an image of destruction, because, when a sepulchre is open, it is for the purpose of receiving a person into it. Possibly, the danger of falling into an opened sepulchre may be referred to.

10. — *Cast them out;* i.e., destroy them from the congregation of thy people, who are favored and blessed by thee. (Comp. Ps. i. 5.) — *For against thee,* &c.; i.e., by rebelling against the king of thine appointment.

Ps. VI.

This psalm seems to contain nothing which indicates the occasion on which it was composed. If it be a composition of David, it may be referred to his situation in his flight from his son Absalom as well as to any which the Jewish history records.

1. — *not in thine anger;* i.e., in measure, with kindness and moderation.

3. — *how long* —; i.e., wilt thou be angry? or, How long wilt thou delay to help me? The incompleteness of the sentence was designed to be expressive of emotion.

5. *For in death,* &c. The poet mentions as a reason why his life should be spared, that, in the regions of the dead, he should have no opportunity or ability to praise God. The ancient Hebrews do not appear to have attained to faith in a desirable immortality after death. They supposed that the disembodied spirits of the righteous and wicked alike went to a dark place under ground, called Sheol, where they existed in a half-conscious, thoughtless, inactive condition. (See, in the New Translation of Job, the remarks prefixed to chap. xii.)

6. — *to swim;* i.e., with tears. A hyperbolical expression to denote the depth of his grief.

8. *Depart,* &c. Having made his supplication to the Deity, the poet, after a pause, breaks forth into the language of hope and triumph.

Ps. VII.

This psalm contains the prayer of a persecuted person against his enemies, especially against one enemy who had uttered gross calumny against him. The inscription of the psalm sets forth, that it was occasioned by the calumnies of a certain Cush, a Benjamite. There is no mention in the Scripture history of such a person; but it is probable that he was one of the courtiers of Saul, who, knowing the hatred of his master towards David, had pretended to be David's friend in order the more effectually to secure his ruin by his calumnies.

This psalm is called *a Shiggaion* of David. That the term denotes a particular species of psalm is evident. But what it is, is altogether uncertain. (See p. 29.)

3. — *If I have done this;* i.e., which my enemy or the courtiers of Saul lay to my charge. (See 1 Sam. xxiv. 10; xxvi. 9–11.)

7. — *The nations.* The tribes of Israel seem to be denoted; possibly, all the nations of the world. — *the height.* The lofty judgment-seat of Jehovah upon Mount Zion seems to be denoted. The judgment which God administers is scenically represented in images borrowed from the circumstances of Eastern tribunals, which were usually held in the midst of large assemblies.

10. *My shield,* &c.; i.e., God is, as it were, the shield-bearer of the righteous; he defends them.

11. — *angry every day,* &c.; i.e., though he may seem to overlook wickedness, yet in fact he is constantly punishing it.

12. *If he do not desist;* i.e., if the wicked man do not desist from his purpose. — *He sharpeneth;* i.e., God sharpeneth.
13. — *burning arrows;* i.e., lightning.
14. — *disappointment;* or delusion, that which is false to one's expectations.

Ps. VIII.

It is a very plausible supposition, that this psalm was composed by David while in the employment of a shepherd, before he came into the sphere of human passions and regal cares. The images which it contains are drawn from the starry heavens, which in his nightly watches he had so often contemplated, and from the herds and flocks which were his daily care.

The author of the Epistle to the Hebrews appears to apply this psalm to the Messiah; but he could do it only in the mystical or allegorical sense. David is evidently speaking, not of any particular man, but of mankind in general, in distinction from the glorious works of God above them and the inferior animals below them.

1. — *Thou hast set,* &c. Otherwise, *Set thou,* &c. Otherwise, *Which glory of thine extendeth to the heavens.*

2. — *babes and sucklings.* This phrase is supposed by most modern critics to refer to literal babes and sucklings; the glory of God being illustrated by the manner in which infants draw their nourishment from the breast; or by their childish prattle, and the curious questions which they sometimes propose. It appears to me, that the words, being used in connection with *enemy* and *avenger,* are rather used in a figurative sense, as when our Saviour says, "Having hidden these things from the wise and prudent, thou hast revealed them to babes" (Matt. xi. 25). They are terms of humility or disparagement in reference to man; perhaps such men as the author of the psalm, who were so highly blessed as to have reason to praise God, or who were gifted with poetic inspiration so as to be able to celebrate worthily his high praises.

5. — *than God.* This is the usual meaning of the term, and is best suited to the connection. It is so rendered in some of the English versions previous to the common version. The expression, *a little lower than God,* probably refers particularly to man's sovereignty over the animal creation.

6. — *all things under his feet.* The connection evidently limits this expression to the lower animals, enumerated in the following lines. Roberts observes that the expression is a common one in Hindostan. Thus they say, "Ah! a mighty king was he: all things were under his feet."

Ps. IX.

This psalm appears to be an ode of triumph and thanksgiving on account of a victory, with prayers for continued aid. It evidently has reference to foreign enemies of the whole Jewish nation. It may have been composed after the wars mentioned in 2 Sam. viii., or it may have had an occasion not recorded in the Jewish annals.

To the Benites, or *To Ben*. The name of an individual *singer*. Otherwise, *On the death of Ben*, or *Labben*. Otherwise, *To* the tune, "*Die for the son!*"

1. — *marvellous works;* namely, such as are mentioned in ver. 3 and 4.

3. — *at thy presence;* i.e., because thou wert present, aiding me and destroying them.

4. — *upon the throne;* i.e., the seat of judgment.

6. — *Their memory*, &c. This is a hyperbolical expression, denoting the completeness of the downfall of David's enemies.

12. — *avenger of blood;* i.e., of the blood of his servants and worshippers, shed by their enemies.

13. — *gates of death;* i.e., of Sheol, conceived of as a strong palace under ground, with gates and bars; a conception founded on the idea that no return from the habitation of the dead is possible. (Comp. Job xxxviii. 17; Isa. xxxviii. 10.)

14. — *in the gates of the daughter of Zion*. In the gates of cities the great multitude used to assemble. By a peculiar idiom of the Hebrew and Syriac languages, the *daughter* of a city means its inhabitants. Thus, *daughter of Tyre* denotes the Tyrians (Ps. xlv. 12); *daughter of Jerusalem*, the inhabitants of Jerusalem (Isa. xxxvii. 22); *daughter of my people*, my countrymen (Isa. xxii. 4; Jer. iv. 11, ix. 7). The city itself, in reference to the inhabitants personified as a virgin, is the mother city. (See 2 Sam. xx. 19; Gal. iv. 26. See Gesen. Heb. Lex. on בת.)

15. The answer to his prayer is now described in the ruin of his enemies.

16. At the end of this verse occur the words, *Higgaion! Selah!* — the meaning of which probably is, Instrumental music! Pause! i.e., Let the singers pause, and the instrumental music strike up.

17. — *into the underworld;* i.e., they shall turn back and flee from their enemies, the Jews (comp. ver. 13), till they are destroyed, or go down into Sheol, the receptacle of all the dead.

Ps. X.

In the Septuagint, and some other ancient versions, this psalm forms the concluding part of the last. But the subject of it seems to be different. Ps. ix. is a song of triumph; Ps. x., one of complaint and distress. It seems to have been occasioned by the incursions of foreign enemies into the land of Israel. (See ver. 16 and 18.)

1. — *afar off*. God is said *to stand afar off*, and *to hide himself*, when he does not give his aid. On the other hand, he is said *to be with* a person or a people, when he aids or delivers them.

3. — *boasteth of his heart's desire*. The meaning may be, that he succeeds in obtaining all that he desires, or that he boasts of the success of his evil plans.

4. — *He careth not;* i.e., God careth not.

5. — *far from him;* i.e., he thinks not of them.

10. — *into his paws;* otherwise, *by his strong ones.*

13. *Wherefore doth the wicked,* &c.; i.e., why dost thou, by suffering the wicked to go unpunished, give him occasion to contemn thee?

14. — *markest it upon thy hand;* i.e., for the purpose of remembering it. Thus, Isa. xlix. 16, "Behold, I have graven thee on the palms of my hands: thy walls are ever before my eyes." (See also Maundrell's Travels, p. 126, Amer. edit.)

15. — *Seek out,* &c. The Hebrews expressed the destruction of a thing by the expression, *to seek and not find it* (Job vii. 21; Isa. xli. 12).

Ps. XI.

Of the occasions recorded in the Scriptures on which David might have composed this psalm, the most probable seems to be his persecution by Saul. But, as the psalm is not very appropriate to that occasion, it may have been written by David or some other poet, on some occasion which is not recorded.

In opposition to the timid counsels of dejected friends, who represented his affairs as desperate, the poet expresses a sublime confidence in the aid which God would afford to the righteous cause, as the omniscient governor of men, the defender of the righteous, and the punisher of the wicked.

The abruptness with which the third verse commences has a fine effect, and places in a strong light the thought, that in the most discouraging circumstances man should not despair, seeing there is a righteous government in the heavens.

2. — *bend their bow,* &c. Observe the continuance of the figure drawn from the bird flying away before the archer, ver. 1.

3. *If the pillars be broken down;* i.e., the distinguished supporters of what is right in a state,—firm and true patriots. Comp. Isa. xix. 10:

"The pillars of the land are cast down,
And all who labor for hire are grieved in heart."

— *can the righteous do;* i.e., what else can he do but to endeavor to escape?

6. — *burning wind;* referring to the wind *Samûm,* on which see the note on Job iii. 5; or Robinson's Calmet, art. *Wind.* — *portion of their cup.* It is a favorite mode of representing punishment among the Hebrews, that the wicked shall be made *to drink* it. (See Job xx. 23; Ps. lxxv. 8.)

7. — *see his face;* i.e., enjoy his favor. When God withholds his favor, he is said *to hide his face.* (Comp. Ps. xvii. 15.)

Ps. XII.

This psalm is one of complaint on account of the degeneracy of the times, especially of the efforts made to weaken just authority by calumny and treachery. If the psalm be a production of David, it may be referred to the time of the rebellion of Absalom. Others refer it to the persecution of David by Saul and his courtiers.

4. — *With our tongues,* &c.; i.e., by uttering calumnies against the rulers, and deceiving the people.

6. *The words of the Lord,* &c. This refers to the promises of Jehovah, such as that in the preceding verse.

8. — *the vilest of men;* otherwise, *they who are a terror to men;* otherwise, *like exaltation is disgrace to men.*

Ps. XIII.

The poet complains of being forgotten by Jehovah; looks to him for aid; and, by the exercise of devotion, attains to peace and confidence. The psalm may be referred to the time of David's persecution by Saul. Some of the Jewish commentators suppose the subject of the psalm to be the whole exiled Jewish people personified.

3. *Enlighten my eyes.* When a person is in a faint and dying condition, the sight seems to go from his eyes. Hence the phrase, *Enlighten my eyes,* means, Restore me from my faint and languishing condition. So in 1 Sam. xiv. 27, "He put forth the end of the rod that was in his hand, and dipped it in an honeycomb, and put his hand to his mouth; and *his eyes were enlightened.*" (Comp. Ezra ix. 8; Ps. xix. 8.) —*forget me for ever?* Understood strictly to the letter, this line might seem to contain a contradiction; but, regarded as a poetic expression of feeling, the meaning is, How long wilt thou deal with me as if it was thy design to abandon me for ever, and thus deprive me of all hope? (Comp. lxxix. 5; lxxxix. 46; lxxiv. 10.)

Ps. XIV.

In this psalm, a Hebrew poet, living in exile with his countrymen, who experienced harsh treatment from their enemies, brings his complaint to God respecting the wickedness of men. In his melancholy state of feeling, all appears to him to be disorder and corruption. He represents God himself as surveying from his heavenly throne the sons of men and their proceedings on the earth, like a watchman on the top of some lofty tower. He is said to search diligently to find a man of true wisdom and piety, but without success. The poet expresses the confident expectation that these evil-doers will meet with a righteous retribution, and sighs for the deliverance of his countrymen from captivity.

It is probable that ver. 7 relates to the captivity at Babylon, rather than to the temporary expulsion of David and his followers by Absalom. Of course, David could not have been the author of it.

This psalm we find repeated, with some alterations, in Ps. liii. The Book of Psalms being made up of at least five smaller collections, the compiler of the second collection inserted in it Ps. liii., either from inadvertence, or on account of the variations in his copy of it.

1. *The fool;* i.e., unwise in a moral and religious point of view. The ideas of impiety and folly were closely associated in the mind of a Hebrew.

3. — *no, not one.* This is a poetical, hyperbolical way of describing general depravity. It is the language of indignation, inspired by the oppression of the Jewish people by their enemies. (See ver. 4.)

7. — *out of Zion;* i.e., from God, the supreme king of Israel, whose earthly dwelling-place was said to be on Mount Zion.

Ps. XV.

It has been commonly supposed, that this psalm was composed by David on the occasion of the removal of the ark of the covenant to Mount Zion, and the consecration of the new tabernacle, as recorded in 2 Sam. vi. 12, &c. But it is also appropriate to religious worship on any occasion.

1. —*abide,* — *dwell.* These terms probably have reference to the circumstance, that a Jewish worshipper, coming from a distant part of Palestine, would tarry some time in Jerusalem, for the purpose of worship.

3. — *his neighbor;* i.e., any one, according to Hebrew usage.

4. — *to his own hurt;* literally, *to do hurt* or *injury;* i.e., to do that which may in its consequences be hurtful to himself. The object of the injury, in this case, is so self-evident, that the writer did not think it necessary to express it. Otherwise, *sweareth to his neighbor,* &c. So the Sept.

5. — *be moved;* i.e., he shall stand firm, safe, secure from all misfortune.

Ps. XVI.

In this psalm, David, being in circumstances of danger, looks to God for help. He acknowledges that all his happiness is in God; expresses his feeling of dependence upon him, his hatred of idolatry, and his determination not to adopt any heathenish customs; avows his satisfaction with the outward condition assigned him, his confidence in Divine aid to deliver him from the danger of death, and his hopes of future protection and favor.

Nothing can be more evident than that David is the subject of the psalm throughout. For the writer constantly uses the first person, and gives no notice that he writes in the name of any other person. But on account of the use which is made of the psalm by the apostles Peter and Paul, in Acts ii. 25 and xiii. 34, it has commonly been supposed to refer in the literal sense to David, and in the mystical or typical sense to Christ. They who have no belief in a mystical sense of Scripture must suppose an error of interpretation on the part of the apostles. The view of Hengstenberg, however, may be true, that David composed the psalm to express the sentiments of others as well as himself. "The psalmist has presented here a mirror in which all pious men may recognize themselves, a pattern after which they might conform themselves; not as if for that purpose he transported himself into a situation and frame of mind quite foreign to himself, but only that he, drawing from the source of his natural experience, just extended his consciousness so as to embrace that of the pious at large. This supposition is raised into certainty, when we ascertain the correct reading in ver. 10 to be "thy holy ones." — Comment. ad loc.

2. — *beyond thee;* i.e., thou art the only source of my happiness. No other gods, and no practices disapproved by thee, can confer happiness.

4. —*drink-offerings of blood.* It is uncertain whether this expression is to be understood as signifying blood which the heathen actually mixed in their libations when they bound themselves to the commission of some dreadful deed; or whether their libations are figuratively called offerings of blood, to denote the horror with which the writer regarded them. —*take their names;* i.e., of worshippers of idols. I will have no intercourse with them.

5. —*my portion and my cup.* An image drawn from a festive entertainment. The meaning is, I am indebted to Jehovah for all that I have. He is my patron and benefactor.

7. —*admonisheth me.* In the stillness of the night, the season of reflection as well as of repose, my heart admonishes me to remember and praise God.

8. —*I shall not fall;* i.e., into ruin; or, I shall not waver, or lose my confidence.

9. —*my heart,* —*my spirit,* —*my flesh.* These three terms are only an emphatic way of denoting the whole person. Thus Ps. lxxxiv. 2:—

> "My soul longeth, yea, fainteth, for the courts of the Lord;
> My heart and my flesh cry aloud for the living God."

So in lxiii. 1:—

> "O God! thou art my God: earnestly do I seek thee!
> My soul thirsteth, my flesh longeth for thee."

The expression, *My flesh dwelleth in security,* therefore means, I dwell in security. The Hebrew expression, rendered *dwell in security,* is the same which is used in Deut. xxxiii. 12, translated in the common version, "The beloved of the Lord shall *dwell in safety* by him." So in Judg. xviii. 7, "How they *dwelt careless,* after the manner of the Zidonians." In Jer. xxiii. 6 and xxxiii. 16, "Israel shall *dwell safely.*" See also Deut. xxxiii. 28; Judg. viii. 11. *To dwell in security,* then, means *to be safe from calamity,* or *to be fearless of calamity.* It cannot mean *to hope for an escape* from one which has already overtaken a person.

10. —*give me up to the underworld,* לִשְׁאוֹל, *to* Sheol, not *in* Sheol. To express the latter meaning, the preposition ב would have been used. (Comp. in the original Ps. xlix. 10; Job xxxix. 14.) The expression, *Thou wilt not give me up,* or *leave me,* to *the underworld,* means, Thou wilt not suffer me to be brought to the grave, or to a premature death, by the enemies which threaten me. —*thy holy one.* The received text of the Hebrew reads, *thy holy ones.* Many critics prefer the latter reading as the more difficult one; i.e., the least likely to have been designedly put into the text by transcribers. On account of the parallelism and the reading of the ancient versions, I prefer the singular, *thy holy one,* referring to the writer of the psalm. —*to see the pit;* i.e., to die. That this is the proper translation and sense of the phrase is obvious from the following passages, where the same term, שָׁחַת, is used. Ps. xlix. 9:—

> "That he should live to eternity,
> And not see *the pit.*"

Ps. vii. 15; Job xxxiii. 24, 28, 30; Prov. xxvi. 27; Ezek. xix. 4, 8. See also Gesen. Lex. on the word שַׁחַת. There can, in view of Hebrew usage and of the connection, be no reasonable doubt that I have translated the verse correctly, and that the meaning is, Thou wilt not suffer me to come to a premature grave by the hands of my enemies. (Comp. xlix. 16.) As Jehovah by the voice of religion had guided the poet in early life, he is confident, that, being delivered from his present dangers, he shall experience the same guidance in the time to come.

11. — *path of life,* &c.; i.e., Thou wilt show me the means of preserving my life, or of obtaining deliverance and happiness; thou hast in thy gift fulness of joy and perpetual pleasures. "Life stands immediately opposed to the death from which the psalmist hopes, in ver. 10, to be preserved; and improperly would several here give to *life* exactly the signification of salvation." — Hengstenberg.

It may be remarked, that the most distinguished scholars, such as Hammond, Grotius, Le Clerc, Calvin, and others, suppose that David is the subject of the psalm throughout. So the authors of the common version, as appears from its caption to this psalm. It was only in a mystical sense that they applied it to Christ. For a more critical examination of this psalm, see Christian Examiner for July, 1834, p. 347, &c.

Ps. XVII.

The subject of this psalm is very similar to that of the last. A pious man, in circumstances of distress, looks to God for help, and makes solemn protestations of his innocence to the Searcher of hearts. He urges his requests with earnestness, on account of the general wickedness of his adversaries, as well as their deadly enmity towards himself. He sets forth the prosperous outward condition of his enemies, but congratulates himself on having a superior happiness in communion with God, and hopes of his favor.

1. — *lips without deceit.* This probably refers rather to the general sincerity of his language than to the sincerity of this particular prayer.

2. — *my sentence;* i.e., of acquittal; my justification. — *behold uprightness;* i.e., have regard to my uprightness in relation to that with which I am charged by my enemies.

3. — *in the night;* i.e., when secret plans are usually adopted by those who wish to escape detection. — *find nothing;* i.e., nothing of evil; no dross. Literally, *Provest thou my heart, visitest thou me in the night, triest thou me like gold, thou wilt find nothing.*

5. — *in thy paths;* i.e., in obedience to thy precepts.

8. — *shadow of thy wings;* i.e., as the bird gathers her brood under her wings. (Comp. Matt. xxiii. 37.)

10. — *their hard heart;* literally, *their fat.* Fat, according to Hebrew usage, denotes that which is inert, unfeeling.

14. — *men of the world;* i.e., who love the world, in distinction from the religious, the spiritually-minded. — *Whose portion is in life;*

i.e., whose most valued good is in life. Whether the term *in life* is spoken of in contrast with the life after death, or whether a mere worldly life is spoken of in contrast with a life of religion and communion with God, is doubtful. Hengstenberg says, "That חַיִּים by itself can denote the earthly life as opposed to the eternal, is destitute of all proof." If the doctrine of immortality is alluded to, the psalm could hardly have been written by David. (See Ps. vi. 5.) In Ps. xvi. 2, occurs the sentiment, "I have no happiness beyond thee;" and in xvi. 5, "Jehovah is my portion and my cup." Perhaps it is most probable, that it is with such a portion that a "portion in life" is contrasted. (See the note on Ps. xlix. 15.)

15. — *shall see thy face;* i.e., enjoy thy favor; hold intimate communion with thee. (Comp. Isa. xxxviii. 11.) — *with the revival of thy countenance;* literally, *with the awaking of thine image.* The word תְּמוּנָה, *image, similitude,* or *manifestation,* is used in Numb. xii. 8, where it is said, "And *the similitude* of the Lord shall he behold." In this verse it is parallel with פָּנֶיךָ, *thy face,* and seems to be synonymous with it. The Septuagint, Syriac, Arabic, Ethiopic, and Vulgate versions construe the line substantially as I have done. So Drs. Hammond and Geddes. Otherwise, *I shall be satisfied, when I awake, with thy countenance.* But this is not a natural construction. If it be admissible, the meaning of *when I awake* may be, when I awake in the morning, after the composition of the psalm, or every morning; or, when I awake from my present state of adversity; or, when I awake from the sleep of death. I consider the last as the least probable.

Ps. XVIII.

The subject and design of this psalm are sufficiently evident from its inscription; and from 2 Sam. xxii. 1, &c. It was probably written by David, near the close of his reign, in view of the experience of his whole life.

2. — *my strong defence;* literally, *my horn of defence,* or *safety.* The horn is often used by the Hebrews as a symbol of strength or power, the image being drawn from animals which use their horns for defence or assault.

4. — *snares of death,* — *floods of destruction.* We are not to suppose that death was conceived of as a mighty hunter, or of "the floods of destruction" as corresponding to the Acheron of the Greek poets. These conceptions cannot be shown to have prevailed among the Hebrews. Snares and floods are often used as images of danger and overwhelming calamity.

6. — *his palace;* i.e., from heaven. (See xi. 4.)

7, &c. This magnificent theophany is to be regarded as a poetic fiction in the Oriental hyperbolic style. It is doubtful, whether, in the description from ver. 7 to 15, any thing of an historical nature is intimated, except that God gave remarkable success to the means which David employed for his deliverance. It is possible that the idea is conveyed, that God helped David in battle by means of a thunder-storm. But it is more probable, that the storm is introduced only to heighten the grandeur and impressiveness of the theophany. (Comp. Ps. cxliv. 5, 6; Hab. iii. 4, 5, 6.)

8. *A smoke went up,* &c. An image of anger, borrowed from the circumstance, that animals, when enraged, breathe hard, so that in cold weather their breath ascends like smoke. (Comp. Job iv. 9.) — *Burning coals;* i.e., lightning.

9. — *bowed the heavens,* &c. In a storm, the sky seems to come down lower. The thick and dark clouds are in fact near us.

10. — *rode upon a cherub.* Jehovah is elsewhere represented as on a throne borne upon cherubs; i.e., beings of a celestial nature, having a form composed of the figures of a man, an ox, a lion, and an eagle, — symbols of strength and wisdom. In this passage, however, the cherubs seem to be a personification of the thunder-clouds and the wind.

15. — *foundations of the earth.* The expression seems to be equivalent to *the channels of the deep;* i.e., the bottom of the sea, in the parallel line.

19. — *a large place;* i.e., freedom from the danger and distress, — the opposite of *straits.*

26. — *thou showest thyself perverse.* See the note on Prov. iii. 34.

28. — *my lamp to shine.* See the notes on Job xviii. 6; xxix. 3.

30. — *His word is pure,* &c.; i.e., His promise, when tried, will stand the test.

33. — *like the hind's;* i.e., in swiftness. Swiftness of foot was a great qualification of an ancient warrior. (Comp. 1 Chron. xii. 8; 2 Sam. i. 23.) So an epithet of Achilles in Homer is *πόδας ὠκύς, the swift-footed.*

34. — *bow of brass.* It is probable that the bow was actually of brass or bronze; i.e., of copper tempered with another metal, which came into use before iron or steel. (See Hesiod, Ἔργαι καὶ Ἡμέραι, v. 149, &c.; Lucret. De Rer. Nat., lib. v., v. 1282; Herod., i. 25.)

Ps. XIX.

The theory which is adopted by Davidson, that this psalm consists of two, arbitrarily put together by the collector, does not recommend itself to my judgment or taste.

2. *Day uttereth instruction,* &c.; i.e., every day hands down to the following day, and every night to the following night, the knowledge of God's glory.

3. *They have no speech,* &c.; i.e., their speech is not that of the human voice; they utter no articulate sounds. Their language is a silent but real language. Mr. Addison has adopted this meaning in his versification of the psalm: —

"What though in solemn silence all
Move round this dark terrestrial ball?
What though no real voice nor sound
Amid their radiant orbs be found?
In reason's ear, they all rejoice,
And utter forth a glorious voice;
For ever singing, as they shine,
'The hand that made us is divine.'"

There is another mode of rendering, which seems to be that of the Septuagint and Vulgate; and which is admissible, though less probable.

"It is no speech nor language,
Of which the voice is not heard;
Their sound goeth forth to all the earth,
And their words to the end of the world."

4. *In them*, referring to the heavens, may allude to that part of them, near the horizon, where the sun was supposed to have his tabernacle or pavilion, into which he retired after his journey through the heavens in the day, and from which he came forth fresh and vigorous in the morning.

5. — *like a bridegroom*. The allusion is to the joyous, youthful freshness of the bridegroom. Some, however, suppose it to be to the freshness of his dress. — *a strong man;* or hero. It is to be recollected that swiftness of foot was one of the greatest recommendations of a hero of antiquity. (See the note on xviii. 33.)

7. — *reviving the soul;* literally, *bringing back the soul* or *spirit*, when it is drooping, and, as it were, leaving the body. (See Lam. i. 16; Ruth iv. 15.)

8. — *are pure;* i.e., free from error and imperfection. — *enlightening the eyes*. This expression is nearly equivalent to *rejoicing the heart*, in the parallel line. (See the note on xiii. 3.)

9. *The fear of the Lord;* i.e., the precepts inculcating fear or reverence.

12. *Who knoweth*, &c.; i.e., who can estimate the number and magnitude of his own sins? — *secret faults;* i.e., those of which I am unconscious; those which escape the detection of conscience, blinded, as it often is, by error, passion, and sin.

13. — *presumptuous sins;* i.e., those committed knowingly, deliberately, and with a high hand. As the word *sins* is supplied, some translate *from the presumptuous;* i.e., the proud.

Ps. XX.

6. *Now I know*, &c. This is evidently sung by a different choir from that which sung ver. 1–5 and ver. 9. Some suppose that David himself is the speaker; others, another choir representing another portion of the people.

Ps. XXI.

This is a psalm of thanksgiving, which some suppose to be on account of the victory prayed for in the preceding psalm. Others think it may have been written after the victory over the united hosts of the Syrians and Ammonites. (See 2 Sam. chap. xii.) The psalm evidently appears, from ver. 1–6, to relate to a king then living; and the opinion that it relates to the Messiah is without the slightest foundation.

4. — *enduring for ever*. A hyperbolical expression for *very long*. (Comp. ver. 6; Dan. ii. 4, iii. 9; 2 Sam. vii. 13.)

8. Here the king is addressed by another choir.

Ps. XXII.

In this psalm, a pious Israelite makes his supplication to God in the midst of great distress, on the borders of despair. God had heard his ancestors when they cried for help, but himself he allowed to be reduced to the utmost contempt on account of his religion (1–9). Yet he retains his confidence in God, and prays for help, enumerating the dangerous and fierce enemies which encompassed him (12–18), repeating his supplications (19–21). And now, as in several of the psalms which begin with lamentation, the poet rises to the confidence, that he and his companions in religious fidelity, though at present afflicted and depressed, will one day greatly prosper; and that the true religion will have an extensive triumph.

The psalm is ascribed to David; and, if this ascription be correct, the occasion of its composition was probably the same with that of Ps. v., vi., xii., and similar psalms. But the psalm is not very descriptive of any circumstances in the life of David which are recorded in the Jewish history. It may be said, however, that the Jewish history is very brief, and that many seasons of distress may have occurred to David which have not been recorded.

One reason for doubting whether the psalm relates to the circumstances of David is, that the persecutions which the writer suffers seem to have been occasioned by his religion; and that, in the latter part of the psalm, the relief which the writer and his brothers in affliction are to experience is connected with the flourishing state of the true religion. But the difficulties of David with Saul and with his son Absalom do not appear to have arisen from his religion. It is not improbable, therefore, that the psalm was written by some Jewish prophet, who, with his followers, was exposed to contempt on account of his adherence to Jehovah and his religion, in the midst of idolatry and vice. In the case of Jeremiah (i. 17–19; ix. 1–6; xi. 18–23; xv. 15–21), we have an instance of a prophet in circumstances very similar to those described in this psalm, and using similar language.

The psalm has been supposed by many interpreters to refer to the sufferings of Jesus and his subsequent exaltation. A decisive objection to this opinion is, that the writer is introduced praying in the first person, and describing his past and present condition. If the writer had intended his language to refer to a person who was to live many hundred years after the composition of the psalm, he was bound to inform us of it in some way. In the absence of such information, we are bound to believe that the writer of the psalm is the subject of it. Besides, it appears to me that the spirit of the psalm bears no great resemblance to the spirit of Jesus. There is no spirit of martyrdom in it. He speaks of impending death in a very different manner from that in which Jesus spake of his. As to the expressions which are cited in the Gospel of John (chap. xix. 24), "They divide my garments among them, and for my vesture they cast lots," these are evidently statements of matters of fact, — of what had happened to the writer of the psalm, and not predictions of the future. There is nothing in the New-Testament application of them inconsistent with this view. As to the typical or mystical sense which has been assigned to this and other psalms, it seems to be beyond the province of the interpreter. There are no human means by which to ascertain it. None but the Divine Spirit can be sure what it is. As has been well observed by Ernesti, in his Principles of Biblical Interpretation,* "Nor, in searching for this typical sense, is there need of the care and talents of an interpreter. For it is revealed by the information and testimony of the Holy Spirit, beyond whose showing we should not in this matter attempt to advance."

The view of Hengstenberg, in his Commentary on the Psalms, appears to me deserving of consideration. I quote him the more readily, because he stands at the head of the Orthodox school in Germany. He maintains, that, though David wrote the psalm, he did not, in all its circumstances, intend to describe his own personal experience, but that of an ideal righteous man, in the manner of many of our modern hymns. "In this interpretation," says he, "justice is done to the truth which lies at the foundation of every one of the existing views; while, at the same time, the difficulties which stand in the way of every one of them are avoided. David composed the poem for the use of the church, on the groundwork of his own experience. How the righteous man in this world of sin must suffer much; and how the Lord, when it comes to the last extremity, gloriously delivers him; and how his sufferings, through the manifestation of the Divine glory in his deliverance, and in his victory over an ungodly world, subserve the honor of God and the sanctifying of his name, and accelerate the approach of his kingdom, — this is the theme. *Every particular righteous man* might appropriate to himself the consolation of this psalm, might expect in his own experience the realization of the hopes expressed in it, in so far as the reality in him corresponded to the idea, in so far as he imbodied in his own person the ideal righteous man. That, according to this view, justice is done to all the references which occur in the New Testament to our psalm is clear as day, and becomes particularly obvious when we direct our attention to the other quotations from the psalms in the history of our Saviour's sufferings. Not one of them refers to a psalm which directly and exclusively is of a Messianic import." — "The psalm would have been fulfilled in Christ, even though the passers-by had not shaken the head, or the mockers quoted its very words; even though there had been no dividing of his garments or casting lots upon his vestures." (Comment. ad loc.)

The hind of the morning. This was probably the name of some other poem or song, to the measure of which this psalm was sung or chanted. Compare the expression, the song of "the bow," in 2 Sam. i. 18. The phrase probably denotes the morning sun scattering his first rays upon the earth; as the Arabian poets call the rising sun the gazelle, comparing his rays with the horns of that animal. Quotations to this effect may be seen in Rosenmüller ad loc.

1. — *forsaken me.* The meaning is explained by the parallel line, *Why so far from mine aid*, &c., and by Ps. x. 1. It is equivalent to the

---

* Vol. i. p. 25, Engl. translation.

question, Why am I left without any visible means of escaping with my life?

2. — *have no rest;* i.e., from my fears, anxieties, and persecutions.

3. — *art holy;* i.e., not approving the wickedness of my enemies. (Comp. Jer. xii. 1.) Otherwise, *And yet thou art the Holy One;* i.e., the peculiar God of the Jewish nation.

6. — *a worm;* i.e., weak, despised, trampled on, as a worm.

12. — *bulls, — bulls of Bashan,* &c. These are images of mighty and fierce enemies.

14. — *poured out like water.* To melt, or be dissolved, was an image of fear and consternation with the Hebrews. (Comp. Josh. vii. 5.)

15. *My strength,* &c. Sadness and sorrow have quite dried up my vital moisture; I have scarce strength enough left to complain, but am just on the point to expire, and to be laid in my grave.

16. — *dogs;* i.e., my enemies, greedy and fierce as dogs. — *my hands and my feet.* I am now satisfied that the rendering, *bound*, which in the former edition I adopted from De Wette and Ewald, is not supported by the Arabic word to which they refer. But whether the term כָּאֲרִי should be rendered, with the Vulgate, *Like a lion,* or *lions, my hands and my feet,* as Gesenius decides, or, *They have pierced,* &c., according to the common version, admits of considerable doubt. That the enemies should *surround* his *hands* and his *feet,* like a lion, is not a very natural expression. But it may mean that they followed him, with special reference to those parts of his body which might help him to escape. On the whole, the reading כָּרוּ and כָּאֲרוּ seem to have no sufficient support; and כָּאָרֵי is inadmissible.

17. — *my bones;* i.e., on account of my emaciation.

18. *They divide my garments,* &c. The sense may be, My enemies are so sure of my death, that they proceed to divide my garments, as if I were dead; or, My enemies look on me as their prey, and divide my possessions, even my garments, among themselves.

20. — *the sword;* i.e., the danger of death. — *My blood;* literally, *my darling;* a poetic name, to denote *the life.*

22. — *my brethren;* i.e., in country and religion.

26. *The afflicted shall eat,* &c.; i.e., the oppressed countrymen of the poet, who had shared his dangers and sufferings, shall partake of the festal sacrifices, and share his joy and gladness.

27. — *the ends of the earth;* i.e., the inhabitants of the most distant lands.

29. — *the rich,* &c. These, with the poor in the next line, are mentioned as composing the whole of mankind. (Comp. Ps. xlix. 2.) — *eat and worship;* i.e., keep the festivals and worship. — *going down to the dust;* i.e., ready to sink into the grave on account of extreme want and misery.

31. — *his righteousness;* i.e., in granting protection and deliverance to the writer of the psalm. (See ver. 24.)

Ps. XXIII.

This psalm, which needs no analysis, was not probably written during the royal poet's pastoral life, but after he had become acquainted with adversity, and had been surrounded by enemies, whom, however, he had probably subdued. (See ver. 5.)

3. — *reviveth my soul;* i.e., refreshes me when drooping and fainting with fatigue, distress, &c. — *in paths of safety*, &c. The allusion is still kept up to the sheep or flock, who are led, not over mountains, or through bushes and stony places, but in plain and safe paths.

4. — *a valley of deathlike shade*, &c. The allusion is still to the flock; and the meaning is, that, if, like the flock, the poet should stray into some gloomy valley as dark as death, he should fear no evil, being under the care of the heavenly Shepherd.

5. Here the image is changed. The blessings received by the poet are so great as to be compared to a feast. — *anointest*, &c. To the abundance and luxury of a feast it belongs, according to the customs of the East in ancient and modern times, to pour fragrant oil on the guests. (Comp. Matt. xxvi. 7; Amos vi. 7.)

6. — *I shall dwell*, &c.; i.e., released from the dangers and toils of war, I shall have abundant opportunity to worship thee in the sanctuary; or perhaps, in a figurative sense, I shall enjoy the most intimate communion with thee. (See xvi. 8, &c.)

Ps. XXIV.

In this psalm, it is set forth that Jehovah, the maker of heaven and earth, has yet a chosen dwelling-place upon the earth, where he is to be worshipped by the pure and righteous. This glorious heavenly king of the Jewish nation is represented as entering the sanctuary, which is personified and exhorted to receive him worthily.

It is commonly supposed that the occasion of it was the transfer of the ark of the covenant to the tabernacle on Mount Zion, as related in 2 Sam. vi. 1, &c. But it seems more probable to me, that the psalm was written after the time of David, and that the gates which are so strikingly personified in the seventh verse are the gates of the temple. In this case, we may suppose the psalm to have been sung at the consecration of the temple, and the removal of the ark to it. There can be no doubt that this is one of the psalms which were sung responsively by several choirs of singers.

5. — *And favor.* There can be no doubt that צְדָקָה is often used in the sense of favor or kindness, considered as the consequence or reward of righteousness. (See Gesenius and Fürst ad verb.) This rendering is also supported by the Septuagint and Vulgate, and the parallelism.

6. *They that seek thy face are Jacob;* i.e., the true Jacob, or Israel of God. (Comp. Isa. xlix. 3; and Introduction to Prophets, p. lvi.)

7. *Lift up your heads*, &c. Here, by a highly poetical conception, the gates even of the splendid temple of Solomon are represented as being

too low for the entrance of the symbol of the King of kings. They are commanded to elevate and expand themselves for his admission, or to assume an attitude suited to the grandeur of the occasion.

Ps. XXV.

This is the first of the alphabetic psalms, each verse beginning with a letter in the order of the Hebrew alphabet.

4. — *thy ways;* i.e., those which are acceptable to thee.

5. — *thy truth;* i.e., the true righteousness or piety which thou requirest.

7. — *of my youth;* i.e., when, through want of knowledge and consideration, or strength of appetite and passion, one is most prone to go astray.

10. — *his covenant;* i.e., his laws, to the observers of which he has covenanted peculiar protection and favor.

11. — *thy name's sake;* i.e., in order to manifest thy goodness and mercy, as in ver. 7.

14. *The friendship;* i.e., intimate converse, confidential intercourse. (Comp. Job xv. 8; Jer. xxiii. 18, lxxix. 4.)

Ps. XXVI.

3. — *before my eyes;* i.e., in my thoughts continually.

6. — *wash my hands in innocence;* not "I perform the ceremony of washing my hands in testimony of my innocence," but "I keep myself innocent." (Comp. lxxiii. 13.) — *go around thine altar;* i.e., bring offerings, and frequently appear around thine altar for the purpose of thanksgiving.

8. — *thine honor dwelleth.* This may mean, "where thy glorious presence is found;" or "where thy wisdom, goodness, and mercy are manifested in hearing prayer, accepting worship," &c.

Ps. XXVII.

4. — *the grace* or *favor of the Lord.* See xc. 17; Zech. xi. 7.

5. — *in his pavilion,* — *secret place of his tabernacle.* These are metaphorical expressions, denoting simply the sure protection and safety which would be afforded by God.

10. — *my father,* &c. Figurative expressions to denote extreme desertion. — *take me up;* i.e., under his protection, and be my patron.

Ps. XXVIII.

2. — *most holy sanctuary;* namely, that part of the tabernacle or temple called the holy of holies.

5. — *doings of the Lord;* i.e., in his moral government of the world, such as the punishments which he often inflicts on evil-doers.

Ps. XXIX.

1. — *sons of God;* angels, or the inhabitants of heaven, seem to be denoted. (See Ps. lxxxix. 6.)
2. — *holy attire;* in allusion to the garments worn by priests. (See Exod. xxxix. 1.)
3. *The voice of Jehovah;* i.e., the thunder. A personification. — *the great waters;* i.e., the waters above the firmament. (Comp. ver. 10, civ. 3; Gen. i. 7.)
6. — *Sirion;* another name of Hermon. See Deut. iii. 9.
9. — *the hinds,* &c.; i.e., through terror. (Comp. 1 Sam. iv. 19.) — *in his palace;* i.e., in heaven.

Ps. XXX.

7. — *made my mountain strong.* This may be a metaphorical expression, meaning, thou hast placed me in safety. (Comp. xxvii. 1.) Or, less probably, *my mountain* may mean my power, my greatness.
9. — *dust;* i.e., my body, turned to dust.
11. — *sackcloth;* the garment of mourning. (Comp. 2 Sam. iii. 31; 1 Kings xx. 32.)

Ps. XXXI.

The occasion of this psalm seems to be altogether uncertain. "It is a mixture of prayers and praises, and professions of confidence in God, all which do well together and are helpful to one another. Faith and prayer must go together. He that believes, let him pray; and he that prays, let him believe; for the prayer of faith is the prevailing prayer."
6. — *lying vanities;* i.e., idols. (Deut. xxxii. 21; Jer. ii. 5, x. 15.)
12. — *like a broken vessel;* i.e., neglected and despised as worthless.
15. — *destiny;* literally, *times;* i.e., what takes place in times; namely, events, fortunes, destinies. So we speak of good times, bad times, &c.
20. — *secret place,* &c. (See the note on xxvii. 5.)
21. — *As in a fortified city;* i.e., I have been protected by him as effectually as I could have been by a fortified city.

Ps. XXXII.

2. — *no guile;* i.e., He does not dissemble with God in his acknowledgment of sin and profession of penitence.
3. — *kept silence;* i.e., did not acknowledge my sins to God. — *my bones.* Comp. Prov. xvii. 22.
4. — *My moisture;* i.e., vital moisture, life-blood.
6. — *floods of great waters.* An image denoting overwhelming calamities.

9. — *Because they will not come near thee.* The meaning is, Be ye not distrustful of God, and unwilling to approach him in confidence and obedience, like the horse and the mule, who will not come near the owner to observe his directions, unless they are forced by the bridle and curb.

Ps. XXXIII.

2. — *harp,* — *psaltery.* Both these instruments seem to have been harps of different species. It is not known in what respects they differed.

17. *The horse,* &c. Comp. Prov. xxi. 31.

Ps. XXXIV.

This is the second alphabetical psalm. (See the Introduction.) The Hebrew inscription assigns an occasion for the composition of the psalm. But it is not very consistent with this inscription, that the psalm should contain no definite allusions to the circumstances of David, and that it should contain so much of a merely didactic nature, drawn from the general experience of human life. It is also doubtful whether any of the alphabetical psalms belong to so early a period as that of David.

5. — *shall have light;* i.e., your countenances shall be brightened with joy. (See the note on xiii. 3.) — *be ashamed;* i.e., through disappointment, or failure of your expectations.

6. *This afflicted man.* The poet points to himself, as an instance of one delivered from trouble.

7. — *angels of the Lord.* Comp. Gen. xxxii. 1, 2; 2 Kings vi. 17.

10. *Young lions.* It is doubtful whether this is to be understood in a literal or a figurative sense. According to the former, the meaning will be, that even young lions, with all their strength, cannot always procure food for themselves; according to the latter, young lions will mean powerful and rapacious men, who are often reduced to want. Perhaps the last is preferable, though the first is adopted by several critics. (Comp. xxxv. 17, lviii. 6; Jer. ii. 15.)

20. — *all his bones;* an emphatic expression to denote the whole man. (Comp. xxxv. 10.)

21. — *destroyeth;* because he has none to deliver him, like the righteous.

Ps. XXXV.

One opinion in regard to the occasion of this psalm is mentioned in the text. Another is, that it relates to the enemies of David who sided with Absalom. Perhaps the most probable supposition is, that the occasion of the psalm is unknown.

5. — *May the angel of the Lord drive them;* i.e., so that they shall stumble and fall. Probably the writer conceived of the angel as a person employing the elements, or human means, to inflict punishment on his enemies.

12. — *bereavement;* i.e., They cause me to feel myself deprived of all which can support or delight my soul; as a mother who is deprived of children.

13. — *turned to my bosom;* i.e., I prayed with my head bent towards my bosom. This was a posture in prayer said to be common among the Orientals. (Comp. 1 Kings xviii. 42.) In Lane's Modern Egyptians (vol. i. p. 109), a Mahometan posture in prayer somewhat similar is represented.

19. — *wink with the eye.* The parallelism seems to show that this was a token of triumph.

20. — *not peace;* i.e., what is injurious and destructive.

21. — *seeth it;* i.e., what we have long wished for concerning our enemy.

22. — *be not silent;* i.e., do not refuse to answer my prayer.

Ps. XXXVI.

It seems to me to be idle to think of finding in the history of David an occasion for a psalm having so general a subject as this.

1. *To speak,* &c. The translation of this difficult passage which I have adopted, is substantially that of Luther, Le Clerc, Gesenius, and De Wette. Somewhat similar commencements of poetical compositions may be seen in xlv. 1, ci. 1; Isa. xlv. 1. If we might adopt a various reading, which is found in most of the ancient versions, the rendering might be, *The wicked hath an oracle* or *inspiration of ungodliness in his heart.* On the whole, it seems best to adhere to the Hebrew text.

2. — *in his own eyes;* i.e., the wicked flatters and beguiles his own conscience. — *found out and hated.* Literally, *to the finding out of his iniquity, the hating.* To find out iniquity, seems, according to Scripture usage, to carry with it the idea of retribution. (See Gen. xliv. 16.) As there are nearly as many expositions of ver. 1 and 2 as there are commentators, of course their meaning must be considered doubtful.

6. — *a great deep.* This expression seems here to refer to the extent and all-pervading character of the Divine judgments, rather than to their unsearchableness or mysteriousness.

8. — *abundance of thy house.* The world full of the riches of God's bounty seems here to be figuratively represented as a father's house filled with wealth.

9. — *of life;* i.e., of happiness. — *Through thy light,* &c.; i.e., through thy favor we enjoy happiness or prosperity. (Comp. iv. 6; Esth. viii. 16; Isa. lix. 9.)

11. — *remove me;* i.e., compel me to wander from my house, city, country, &c.

Ps. XXXVII.

This is the third of the alphabetical psalms. (See pp. 47, 48.)

3. — *Abide in the land,* &c.; i.e., do not forsake the land in despair,

on account of the oppression which you are obliged to endure (Comp. x. 18.) — *delight in*, or *feed on*. Comp. Prov. xv. 14.

9. — *inherit the land*. This expression seems here, and in ver. 11, to denote a quiet, undisturbed possession of the country, unmolested by oppressors. In other passages it may have a figurative sense.

13. — *his day*; i.e., of punishment. (Comp. ver. 36; Job xviii. 20.)

18. — *their inheritance shall endure for ever*; i.e., in the land of Canaan, as in ver. 11, 27, 29. They shall never be driven from the land. If the phrase be used in a figurative sense, it is plain, from the connection, that it must denote temporal blessings.

21. *The wicked borroweth*, &c. It is probable, from the connection, that the meaning of this verse is that the wicked is continually borrowing, without having the means to repay, while the righteous has the ability to be generous. (Comp. Deut. xxviii. 12.)

37, 38. Comp. Prov. xxiii. 18; xxiv. 14, 20; v. 4; Job xlii. 12. *Posterity*. This meaning seems to be favored by the following verse, where the term אַחֲרִית, again occurs. To say that *the end* of the wicked *shall be cut off* seems incongruous. The term certainly has the meaning "posterity" in Amos iv. 2, ix. 1; Dan. xi. 4. The Septuagint version, *a remnant*, *ἐγκατάλειμμα*, *is to the peaceful man*, also supports it. Some translate the line, *That a future*, or *hereafter*, i.e., a happy one, *is to the man of peace*. But this does not so well suit ver. 38. The principal objection to the translation of the common version is, that neither Hebrew grammar, nor usage, will allow לְאִישׁ to be rendered, *of that man*, in such a connection.

Ps. XXXVIII.

The opinion of some commentators, that this and other psalms represent the condition of the whole Jewish nation, under the image of a single man in distress, seems to me to carry very little probability with it.

3. — *no soundness in my flesh*. A condition of distress is probably represented figuratively by disease.

4. — *gone over my head*, &c.; i.e., the consequences of my sins have overwhelmed me like a flood of waters.

14. — *is no reply*; i.e., who is able to give no answer, or reproof, to those who upbraid him.

18. *For I confess*, &c. He gives a reason why he hopes to be heard; namely, that he has experienced great sorrow and pain on account of his sins.

Ps. XXXIX.

2. — *even what was good*; i.e., lest I should say something wrong, I resolved to say nothing either good or bad.

3. — *the fire burst forth*. The fire of discontent and complaint seems to be intended. Dr. Henry thus correctly comments upon it:

"Binding the distempered part did but draw the humor to it. He could bridle his tongue, but could not keep his passion under."

6. — *in a vain show;* literally, *in an image;* i.e., as Dr. Hammond remarks, "Our life is but a picture or image, shadow or dream of life; it vanisheth in a trice."

8. — *all my transgressions;* i.e., from my distresses, the consequences of my transgressions.

Ps. XL.

In this psalm the writer gives fervent thanks to God for some great deliverance which he had experienced, and for many general mercies. He expresses also the feeling, that the best acknowledgment which he can make to God is, not by sacrifices, but by obedience to his law. The latter part of the psalm contains a prayer for deliverance from evils and dangers which still encompassed the writer.

It is so plain that the writer of the psalm who begins in the first person, "I trusted steadfastly," &c., is the subject of it throughout, that it is surprising that any one, who rejects the typical or allegorical mode of interpretation as unfounded, can suppose the psalm to relate to any other person except the writer of it. The psalm contains no prophecy of any kind, but only thanksgiving for the past, a description of the present, and prayer for the future. The author of the Epistle to the Hebrews, adopting an erroneous translation of the Septuagint version, namely, "A body thou hast prepared for me," instead of, "Mine ears thou hast opened," applies ver. 6–8 to the Messiah. But he does this according to the typical or allegorical mode of interpretation which he employs elsewhere in the Epistle, and which was regarded as valid by his contemporaries. It is only in this typical sense, that the great mass of Christian interpreters have supposed the psalm to relate to the Messiah. In its primary sense, they have supposed David to be the subject of it throughout. Hengstenberg observes (Comment. on Psalms, p. 65), "The direct Messianic exposition, which was very wide-spread in former times, has but a weak foundation in the quotation of ver. 6–8 in Hebrews, chap. x. And affirmations such as that put forth by the author himself (i.e., Hengstenberg), at the beginning of his career,— 'There can be no doubt, that he who acknowledges the Divine authority of the Epistle to the Hebrews must decide for the Messianic exposition,'—lose all meaning when a deeper insight has been obtained into the way and manner in which the New Testament, and especially the Epistle to the Hebrews, handles the declarations of the Old Testament."

The last five verses are found repeated as the seventieth psalm, which was probably an extract from this for purposes of religious worship.

6. — *Mine ears thou hast opened.* This may mean, Thou hast revealed to me the truth, that sacrifices and oblations are not acceptable to thee, except as they are expressive of inward feeling, of an obedient will, and the devotion of myself to God; or, Thou hast

inclined me to obey thy commands. As one's ears are opened, or attentive, either to receive information, or to listen to commands as a servant. In 1 Sam. ix. 15; xx. 2, 12, 13; xxii. 8, 17, the expressions, "he had told in his ear," "will show it me," are, in the Hebrew, גָּלָה אֶת־אָזְנִי or יִגְלֶה, "he had uncovered," or "will uncover his, or my ear." (Comp. Isa. l. 4, 5.) In Ruth iv. 4, "I thought to advertise thee," is, in the original, "I thought to uncover thine ear." (Comp. Job xxxiii 16; xxxvi. 10.) On the whole, the first meaning seems best supported by analogous phrases and by the connection.

7. *Therefore I said*; i.e, since thou dost not desire offerings, but obedience, I said to myself, or purposed. A very common Hebrew idiom. — *Lo, I come*; i.e., instead of bringing sacrifices and offerings, I come and personally devote myself to thy service; I stand ready to do thy will. So Le Clerc, "Venio, ut tibi parerem." Some critics find a difficulty in making the phrase "I come" mean so much as I come *in the way of obedience*. It is true, there is no instance of phraseology precisely similar. But the connection is very much in favor of this meaning, and it is difficult to conceive what other meaning David could have had, when he said, "I come." We may even suppose ver. 8 to be the completion of the thought, which he may not have fully expressed in the words "I come." That is, supposing that he intended to say, *I come to do thy will*, the parenthesis "In the scroll of the book it is prescribed to me" being introduced, instead of closing the sentence in form, he closes it virtually by the exclamation, "O my God! to do thy will is my delight," &c. Lengerke says, "*I come;*" i.e., to thy house (ver. 7). I appear in thy presence, (xlii. 4); or, to the altar of God (xliii. 4), not with offerings, but prepared to do thy will. — *In the scroll of the book*; i.e., the book of the law, of the well-known Oriental form. Some understand the phrase to denote the book of the divine purposes. But it does not seem agreeable to the phraseology of the Scriptures that any one should say of himself, that it was written in the Divine mind that he should be obedient to the will of God. The connection in this passage rather points us to the book-roll of the divine law. — *it is prescribed to me*. The same Hebrew expression is used in 2 Kings xxii. 13, translated in the common version, "Our fathers have not hearkened unto the words of this book, to do according unto all that which is written concerning us," where the meaning evidently is, "prescribed to us." Hengstenberg observes (p. 72), "The parallel passages, as also the connection, decide against the expositions of the Messianic interpreters, '*It is written of me.*'" (Comp. Esth. ix. 23; Prov. xxii. 20; Hos. viii. 12.) Another translation of ver. 7 is given by Gesenius and Ewald, as follows: —

"Then I said, Lo, I come
With the scroll of the book which is prescribed to me."

That of De Wette is, "Lo, I come with the scroll of the book written in my heart;" a free rendering for "written upon me." But if, by "coming with the scroll of the book," we understand, with Ewald, that the poet came into the temple before God with the book of the law in his hands, this would be a mere symbol, as much as the offering of sacrifices, and might be performed without true obedience. The translation, or rather paraphrase, of De Wette strikes me as quite forced.

12. — *My iniquities have overtaken me.* Some who apply the whole psalm exclusively to the Messiah, being pressed with the difficulty which this line presents, translate, "My *distresses* have overtaken me." But there is no clear case in the Scriptures, in which עָוֹן, though a word of very common occurrence, denotes *distress* or *calamity*, except in passages where, by synecdoche of the effect for the cause, it denotes that distress which is the consequence of sin. If, therefore, we do not translate the line, *My iniquities*, &c., we must translate *My punishments*, or *My distresses, the consequences of my sins.* 2 Sam. xvi. 12 may seem to be an exception. But why may not David have regarded the rebellion of Absalom as a punishment for his sins? The new translation, therefore, which Professor Stuart* proposes, does not remove the difficulty.

Ps. XLI.

This psalm is commonly supposed to have been composed by David during the rebellion of Absalom. A dangerous sickness, as well as the reproaches and persecution of domestic enemies, seems to have been the occasion of it.

1. — *the poor.* The poet is led to make this commendation of kindness to the afflicted, in consequence of having felt the want of it.

3. — *all his bed,* &c.; i.e., thou wilt change his bed of sickness into a bed of health.

4. — *sinned against thee;* i.e., I am suffering on account of my sins against thee.

8. — *cleaveth,* &c.; i.e., in its consequences; in the miseries which are upon him.

9. — *who did eat of my bread.* If the same sentiment prevailed among the Hebrews, which prevails at the present day among the Bedouin Arabs, of sacred regard to the person and property of one with whom they have eaten bread and salt, the language is very forcible. — *lifted up his heel;* a metaphor drawn from the horse, which attacks with its heels. This language may well have been used by our Saviour, in John xiii. 18, in the way of rhetorical illustration or emphasis.

13. This doxology was, in all probability, placed here by the collector of this first book of forty-one psalms. (See p. 31, &c.)

Ps. XLII., XLIII.

These two psalms undoubtedly form but one composition. They have one subject, and are written in the same style. The concluding verse or refrain is the same that occurs in Ps. xlii., and which is re-

* Excursus to Hebrews, p. 594.

peated after every five verses. In forty-six Hebrew manuscripts, there is no separation between the two psalms. For beauty of imagery, depth, and naturalness of religious feeling, and the very striking manner in which the voice of religion in the poet's inmost soul is heard in the refrains, stilling the tempest of anxiety and grief caused by his situation, this psalm is so admirable that it probably has no superior in any language. It seems to have been written in exile, among enemies of the Jewish nation and religion.

1. *As the hart*, &c. "In the East, where streams are not common, and where the deer are so often chased by their savage cotenants of the forest and the glade, no wonder that they are often driven from their favorite haunts to the parched grounds. After this, their thirst becomes excessive; but they dare not return to the water, lest they should again meet the enemy. When the good Ramar and his people went through the thirsty wilderness, it is written, 'As the deer cried for water, so did they.' In going through the desert yesterday, my thirst was so great, I cried out like the deer for water." — Roberts's Illustrations.

2. — *the living God;* in contradistinction from the idol gods, by the worshippers of which the poet was surrounded. — *appear before God;* i.e., in his house of worship. The Hebrews attached an importance to the *place* of worship almost beyond the conception of Christians at the present day.

5. — *I shall yet praise him*, &c.; i.e., I shall yet be delivered or restored, and thus have cause to praise him.

6. — *of Jordan.* This may mean the land beyond the Jordan, or the land lying near the sources of the Jordan.

7. *Deep calleth*, &c.; i.e., one billow calleth for another to follow close upon it; i.e., one trouble comes upon me after another in quick succession. — *waterfalls*, &c. The irresistible and overwhelming calamities which came upon the poet are denoted.

8. — *his praise was with me;* i.e., on account of the happy condition in which I found myself. — *God of my life;* i.e., the Preserver of my life.

XLIII. 3. — *thy light and thy truth;* i.e., thy favor and thy faithfulness. (See xxxvi. 9 and the note.)

Ps. XLIV.

This psalm is supposed by Calvin and many modern interpreters to have been composed in the time of the Maccabees (see 1 Macc. chap. i.; 2 Macc. chap. v.), a supposition to which there seems to be no valid objection, and which is as well suited to the contents of the psalm as any which has been made.

12. — *sellest*, &c. This language is probably figurative, denoting, Thou deliverest thy people into the hands of their enemies, without promoting thine own interest or honor.

22. — *for thy sake;* i.e., for no other reason than our attachment to thy service and worship. (Comp. 1 Macc. chap. i.)

25. — *bowed down*, — *cleaveth*, &c. These are images denoting extreme depression and sorrow. (Comp. cxiii. 7; Lam. ii. 10; Job ii. 8.)

Ps. XLV.

This ode appears to have been composed by some courtly bard on the occasion of the king's taking to himself a queen. There seems to be no objection to the prevalent opinion, that it was composed on the marriage of Solomon with a daughter of the king of Egypt, as recorded in 1 Kings iii. 1. It has been objected, that the ascription of warlike qualities to the king is inconsistent with this supposition. But has it been the custom of poet laureates, or even of writers of dedicatory epistles to kings, to confine themselves to strict history, in setting forth the praises of their patrons? We must also recollect that Oriental usage allows a much higher degree of exaggeration than that of the Western world. The application of the ode to Solomon as its subject is, however, matter of conjecture, favored by the fact that Solomon is known to have married a foreign princess. But it may have been composed in honor of several of the Jewish kings.

The ode begins with a sort of prœmium, having some resemblance to a poet's address to his Muse (ver. 1). The king is then praised for his personal beauty and graceful speech (ver. 2); for his military qualifications (ver. 3–5), and the stability and rectitude of his government (ver. 6, 7); for the splendor of his dress, and the magnificence of his establishment, especially for the beauty and high birth of the members of his harem, among whom the queen is pre-eminent (ver. 8, 9). Then follows an appropriate apostrophe to the queen (ver. 10–12), and a description of her splendid dress and retinue (ver. 13–15), and of her future happiness as the mother of a long line of kings and princes (ver. 16). Finally, the poet expresses his conviction, that he, by his poem, shall preserve her name and fame to all coming generations.

In this general account of the ode, most Christian interpreters agree. But it has been maintained, that there is a sense in which the language is applicable to Jesus Christ. Thus, the English version most in use before King James's has the following caption to the psalm: "The majesty of Solomon, his honor, strength, beauty, riches, and power are praised; and also his marriage with the Egyptian, being an heathen woman, is blessed, if that she can renounce her people and the love of her country, and give herself wholly to her husband. Under the which figure, the wonderful majesty and increase of the kingdom of Christ, and the Church, his spouse, now taken of the Gentiles, is described."

The arguments by which the application of the psalm to our Saviour has been defended are the same as those which have been used in relation to the Canticles, and may be answered in the same way. (See the Introduction to Canticles.)

The unknown author of the Epistle to the Hebrews, who delights in mystical or allegorical interpretations, has applied two verses of this psalm to Jesus Christ. But it by no means follows that he would have applied the whole of it to him. The allegorical interpretation knows no laws. All the acknowledged laws by which the meaning of language is obtained, lead to its absolute and entire rejection. With respect to the application of ver. 6 and 7 by the author of the Epistle to the Hebrews, it was made according to a mode of interpretation which was regarded by his contemporaries as valid, but which can have no force with a logical interpreter of the present day. It seems that the Jews do not regard the province of inspiration as extending to matters of interpretation. Thus, Maimonides,* giving the sentiments of the Jewish doctors or wise men, says, "In disquisition and reasoning, and judgment in the law, prophets are on a level with other wise men of equal abilities who are not endued with the spirit of prophecy. If a thousand prophets, all equal to Elijah and Elisha, should offer an interpretation of any precept, and a thousand and one wise men should give a contrary interpretation of it, we are bound to abide by the opinion of the thousand and one wise men, and to reject the opinion of the thousand illustrious prophets." It appears to me that this distinction is just. Infallible inspiration will assert, not argue. When one undertakes to argue, he refers the matter, by the very nature of the process, to the reason and judgment of him whom he addresses.

Shoshannim. Musical instruments, probably so called from their resemblance in form to lilies. — *lovely song;* otherwise, *love-song, epithalamium.*

1. — *is overflowing;* literally, bubbles up or boils over with a good matter; more strictly, good discourse. But this word is not applicable to a poem. Literally, *my work,* like the Greek *ποίημα, poem* or *song.* Otherwise, *I will say, My work is for the king.* — *like the pen of a ready writer;* i.e., I compose as fast, perhaps as finely, as an expert penman can take down words with his pen or reed.

2. Personal beauty was regarded by the ancients as an important accomplishment in a hero. Thus, David, in 1 Sam. xvi. 12, is praised for his beauty. So in Homer, Agamemnon, Achilles, Hector, &c.

3, 4, 5. Instead of promising to the king in general terms prosperity and victory, the poet, in a vivid and picturesque way, represents him as arming for the conflict, and going forth among the nations, adorned with all the regal virtues, and achieving the most splendid victories.

6. *Thy throne is God's;* i.e., is upheld and prospered by God. God has placed thee upon it, and he will have it under his peculiar care. (Comp. ii. 6, 7; cxi. 2.) So, in Ps. civ. 16, *trees of the Lord* denote trees planted and nourished by God. This translation and exposition, as given by Gesenius in his Hebrew Thesaurus (p. 98) and his Hebrew Grammar (§ 141), I regard as on the whole the most probable. It is also the translation of the Jewish critic, Aben Ezra, who refers to Chron. xxix. 23, *Then Solomon sat on the throne of the Lord,* &c. That the term *God* should be applied to Solomon or a Jewish king is a supposition which is not wholly without support from Hebrew usage. Thus, when the witch of Endor sees Samuel, she says, "I see a God, אֱלֹהִים, rising out of the earth." But it seems to me more probable that it is used in the same sense as in ver. 7, and in the psalms generally. If any prefer the rendering of the common version, the meaning will be, "Thy throne, O mighty king!" &c. The supposition, that the king who is the subject of the psalm is addressed as the Supreme

* Porta Mosis, Pococke's Works, vol. i. p. 18; also Allen's Modern Judaism, p. 27

Being, is repelled by the connection in ver. 7,* where he is represented as *anointed*, &c., above his *fellows;* and by the whole contents of the psalm. Whatever may be the true interpretation, this cannot be. A translation of the line somewhat different is given by De Wette and Hupfeld; namely, —

"Thy throne of God shall stand for ever;"

i.e., thy throne, given and upheld by God, &c. Another well-known construction is that of Griesbach, in Heb. i. 8, and others, —

"God is thy throne for ever and ever;"

i.e., God is the support and foundation of thy throne. But as *sceptre* is the subject, not the predicate, of the proposition in the parallel line, it seems more natural to regard *throne* as the subject, not the predicate, in this. — *for ever and ever*. This is a common Oriental idiom to express long duration. (See lxi. 5, xxi. 4, with the note; 2 Sam. vii. 13; 1 Chron. xvii. 11–14.)

7. — *anointed thee with the oil of gladness;* i.e., has given thee great joy or prosperity. (Comp. xxiii. 5; Isa. lxi. 3.) The image seems to be borrowed from the use of fragrant oil at feasts and similar occasions. — *above thy fellows;* i.e., above other kings.

8. — *ivory palaces;* i.e., adorned or bordered with ivory.

9. — *thy chosen women;* literally, *thy precious* or *dear ones;* evidently in reference to other members of the harem, as distinguished from the queen.

10. — *Forget thy people;* i.e., dispel the regret which you may have on leaving your nation and the house of your father.

12. — *daughter of Tyre;* i.e., the Tyrians. (See the note on ix. 14.)

16. *Instead of thy fathers*, &c. As you part from royal parents, you shall be the mother of royal children.

Ps. XLVI.

2. — *though the earth be changed;* i.e., though the earth become sea, and the sea land.

4. *A river*, &c.; i.e., of Jerusalem, the city of God. We need not inquire what particular river or streams are meant. A gentle river with its streams seems to be used as an image to denote the peaceful state of Jerusalem, as contrasted with a condition of war and commotion.

5. — *full early;* literally, *before morning appears;* i.e., with the utmost readiness, as a person who means to accomplish a favorite object rises early for it. (Comp. Jer. vii. 13, 25.)

6. — *He uttered his voice*, &c. The meaning seems to be, that the inhabitants of the earth melted, as it were, with terror at the sound of his voice, and were wholly discomfited.

---

* This is admitted by Stuart on Hebrews, p. 294.

Ps. XLVII.

4. — *an inheritance;* i.e., the land of Palestine, called "the glory of Jacob" in the next line, and "the glory of all lands" in Ezek. xx. 15.

5. — *goeth up with a shout,* &c. This alludes, probably, to the carrying of the ark in solemn procession to Mount Zion, on its return from some war to which it may have been carried. (Comp. 1 Sam. iv. 3–5; 2 Sam. vi. 15, xi. 11.)

9. *The princes of the nations.* It seems most agreeable to the phraseology to understand this of the nations mentioned as subdued in ver. 3. Otherwise, leaders of the tribes of Israel have been supposed to be denoted.

Ps. XLVIII.

The most common and the most probable supposition respecting the occasion of this psalm is, that it was composed in reference to the victory obtained by Jehoshaphat over the combined forces of the Moabites, Ammonites, and Edomites, as recorded in 2 Chron. chap. xx. Others have referred it to the deliverance from the invasion of Sennacherib.

2. — *of the whole earth.* This must be regarded as the hyperbolical description of a Hebrew poet, ascribing his own patriotic feelings to the inhabitants of foreign lands. — *The joy of the farthest North.* This rendering is more favored by the parallelism than the translation commonly given to the line, and at least as much by the grammatical construction. It is adopted by De Wette, Tholuck, and Gesenius. (See Ges. Thesaur. on יְרֵכָה)

7. — *as when the east wind,* &c., referring to ver. 4–6. — *ships of Tarshish;* i.e., which, sailing probably from Phœnicia to so distant a place as Tarshish in Spain, would be the largest and strongest of ships.

8. — *have heard;* i.e., from our fathers.

10. — *of righteousness;* manifested in the punishment of the enemies of thy people; equivalent to *righteous judgments* in the next verse.

11. — *daughters of Judah.* It may be considered as doubtful, whether this phrase denotes the lesser cities of Judah in comparison with the metropolis, or the female minstrels who celebrated the victories of the Jews. (See lxviii. 11.)

Ps. XLIX.

The subject of this didactic psalm is substantially the same as that of Ps. xxxix., lxxiii., and in fact of the whole Book of Job. It is designed to meet the doubts which arise in the mind on the contemplation of the manner in which good and evil are distributed in the world; the wicked often enjoying prosperity, and the righteous suffering adversity. In this psalm, spiritual good, internal peace, a sense of the friendship of God, and confidence in his protection, are set forth as more than a balance for all the advantages of prosperous wickedness.

It is observable that wealth alone is mentioned as the evidence of the prosperity of the wicked. It is not improbable, therefore, that the poet was one of many who were suffering under the oppression and extortion of rich and powerful enemies; possibly foreign enemies, enemies of the Jewish nation.

1. *Hear this*, &c. The poet begins with the solemn dignity of a prophet summoning the whole world to listen to a lesson of religious wisdom which concerns every class of men.

4. — *incline mine ear*. This may mean that the poet would give close attention to what he was about to sing upon the harp; or that he would listen in order to receive what should be suggested to his soul, as other poets are said to listen to the Muse.

9. — *the redemption of his life;* i.e., from death. I have reversed the order of the eighth and ninth verses for the sake of clearness.

11. — *men celebrate, &c.*; more literally, *Men call upon their names*, &c.

12. — *man, who is in honor*, &c.; i.e., possessed of dignity, wealth, &c.

13. — *the way*, &c.; i.e., of thinking and acting. (See ver. 11.)

14. *Like sheep;* i.e., huddled together into the lower world, as sheep into a fold. — *Death shall feed upon them;* i.e., consume them; or *Death shall feed them;* i.e., be their shepherd, rule them. The term רָעָה admits of either rendering. — *trample upon them;* i.e., on the graves of those whom they feared when alive.

15. — *will redeem my life from the underworld*, &c. This language is in itself ambiguous; it being doubtful whether the meaning is, that God would lengthen out the life of the writer, and not suffer him to go down to a premature grave, while his insidious adversaries were cut off, like slaughtered beasts; or whether the meaning is, that God would restore him to life after he was dead and buried. Similar language is found in Hosea xiii. 14, —

> "I will ransom them from the power of the grave;
> I will redeem them from death;
> O death! where is thy plague?
> O grave! where is thy destruction?
> Repentance is hidden from mine eyes."

In this passage from Hosea, the meaning is, that God was willing to save the nation of Israel from temporal destruction. So in Ps. lxxxix. 48, we read, —

> "What man liveth, and seeth not death?
> Who can deliver himself from the underworld?"

In these lines, too, the meaning is, that no one can help dying and going down to the grave. These passages seem to favor the opinion, that by God's redeeming the poet's life from the underworld is meant, that God would not permit him to go down into it prematurely, and not that he would raise him from the dead. It appears, too, from ver. 5, that he was in danger from insidious foes; so that the thought is agreeable to the connection, that God would not suffer these foes to bring him to a premature grave. Hengstenberg says, "According to the connection and the contrast, the redemption of the soul of the righteous from Sheol can mean nothing but deliverance from immediate danger."

On the other hand, the course of remark which the poet pursues might lead us, from our Christian point of view, to the idea of immortal felicity, as the great distinction between the good and the bad. The poet himself says, in ver. 10, that the wise die some time or other, as well as the foolish. But we must remember, that thoughts which are familiar to us might not be in the mind of a Hebrew writer of that age. In the Book of Job, of Ecclesiastes, of Proverbs, and other books of the Old Testament, we might expect the doctrine of a blissful immortality to be brought in, to account for the sufferings of the righteous. But we do not find it. (See the Introductions to Job, Ecclesiastes, and Proverbs.) If the doctrine were known to the writers of the Psalms, we might expect it to be stated more distinctly, and to occupy an important place in the minds of the writers. On the whole, therefore, it seems most probable that faith in a happy immortality is not what is expressed by the writer in this verse, but only confidence of deliverance from the danger of death. Inward, spiritual good, the friendship of God, and trust in him at all times, appear to have constituted, in the mind of the poet, the distinction between the righteous and the wicked, however improbable it may seem at first view to a Christian that those who had attained such elevated religious sentiments in other respects should be destitute of faith in a desirable immortality of the human soul. (See the note on vi. 5. See also a good discussion of the subject in Hengstenberg on the Psalms, vol. iii. pp. lxxxi.-lxxxix., English translation.) — *take me under his care.* For a similar use of לָקַח, see lxxiii. 24; Deut. iv. 20.

17. — *carry nothing away.* —

> "Linquenda tellus, et domus, et placens
> Uxor; neque harum, quas colis, arborum
> Te, præter invisas cupressos,
> Ulla brevem dominum sequetur." Hor. Carm. ii. 11.

Ps. L.

The sublime theophany with which this psalm is introduced (ver. 1–6) is to be regarded as a poetical representation, the meaning of which is, that the sentiments, promises, and denunciations which follow have the sanction of Divine authority. The mode of representation is designed to arrest the attention of the reader.

1. — *calleth the earth;* i.e., summons the inhabitants of the whole earth as witnesses.

2. — *perfection of beauty.* See xlviii. 2; Lam. ii. 15. — *shineth forth;* i.e., appears in splendor.

3. — *will not be silent;* i.e., his approach is manifested by thunder. (Comp. Exod. xix.)

4. — *the heavens,* — *the earth;* i.e., calls the inhabitants of them to be, as it were, witnesses of proceedings in court.

5. — *my godly ones,* &c.; they who profess to be my *godly ones,* and have bound themselves to worship and serve me by a covenant confirmed

by the blood of sacrifices, wishing that they might be dealt with like the victims, if they did not fulfil their engagements.

11. — *before me;* i.e., I know them, as in the preceding line, and consequently have them ready at my service.

20. *Thou sittest;* i.e., in company with others, in public places. — *thine own mother's son.* Polygamy being allowed among the Hebrews, they who were born of the same mother were in a more intimate relation to each other than they who had only the same father.

21. — *I kept silence;* i.e., did not make known my displeasure by the infliction of punishment. — *set it in order;* i.e., the sin which God reproves.

Ps. LI.

The inscription assigns the occasion on which this psalm was composed; namely, the sin of David in relation to Bathsheba and Uriah. There would be no good reason for questioning the correctness of this inscription, were it not for the last two verses, which seem to imply a later age than that of David. Hence it becomes necessary to question the correctness of the inscription, or the genuineness of the last two verses. As these verses do not seem to have any connection with the general subject of the psalm, perhaps the latter alternative is preferable.

3. — *ever before me*, i.e., my guilt haunts me night and day, reproaching me with ingratitude to God.

4. *Against thee, thee only.* The writer, if David, had deeply injured his fellow-man. But he felt his guilt most deeply in relation to God, to whom, as being king, he was alone accountable. He had been guilty of ingratitude to his infinite benefactor, who had raised him from obscurity to a throne; so that his feeling of ill-desert in relation to man was, as it were, swallowed up by his sense of guilt in relation to God. In the hyperbolical language of strong emotion, he therefore says, "Against thee, thee only, have I sinned."

5. *Behold! I was born in iniquity,* &c. It has been doubted whether the iniquity mentioned in this verse was that of the writer, or of the writer's mother. Eminent critics are divided in opinion on the subject. In the Book of Job we read, —

"Man, that is born of woman,
Is of few days and full of trouble."

"What is man, that he should be clean,
And he that is born of woman, that he should be innocent?"

But, in these passages of Job, the being born of woman is mentioned by way of lightening human guilt, and showing that man was more worthy of Divine compassion on that account. But in this psalm the writer seems deeply humbled with a sense of his actual guilt, and ready to exaggerate rather than to lessen it. It seems better suited to this state of feeling, that the poet should be speaking of his own personal iniquity, rather than that he should be exaggerating his low condition by representing that he was born of sinful parents. This consideration would alleviate instead of increasing his guilt. It appears to me, therefore, rather more probable that to be born in iniquity, and conceived in sin, means to be born a sinner, but not in a strict metaphysical sense. The writer is a poet, using the hyperbolical language of strong emotion. Under a deep sense of guilt, he expresses the thought, that he had not only been a great sinner on particular occasions, but an habitual sinner; that he had sinned against God a long time, even from his youth, so that he might say that he was, as it were, born in iniquity and conceived in sin. (Comp. xxii. 9, 10, lviii. 3; Isa. xlviii. 8; Job xxxi. 18.) So when we hear it said that one is born a poet, an orator, a mathematician, &c., we do not think of understanding the language to the letter.

6. — *wisdom;* i.e., moral strength, moral and religious principle.

10. — *steadfast mind;* i.e., moral strength, fixed purposes in that which is good.

12. — *a willing spirit.* It seems to be doubtful whether this phrase denotes the Divine spirit freely bestowed, or the willing, ready, free spirit of David, when he should obtain forgiveness of sin, and relief from fear, anxiety, &c. I prefer the latter, as the term "willing" is nowhere else ascribed to the spirit of God, and as there is no pronoun or article prefixed to refer the term to God. So in ver. 10 he had asked for a *steadfast* spirit. (Comp. Exod. xxxv. 5.)

13. — *thy ways;* i.e., the ways which thou approvest; thy precepts.

Ps. LII.

1. *Why gloriest,* &c.; i.e., why do you anticipate success in your evil designs against me, from whom the favor of God is never withdrawn?

8. — *like a green olive-tree,* &c.; i.e., I shall flourish and prosper, and be under God's special protection, like an olive-tree planted in the courts of God's house.

Ps. LIII.

See the notes on Ps. xiv.

Ps. LV.

The occasion of this psalm is not indicated with any degree of certainty. It is most commonly referred to the rebellion of Absalom.

10. — *these;* i.e., violence and strife.

15. — *alive.* Comp. Numb. xvi. 33.

19. — *no changes;* i.e., because they have uniform success, they persist in their designs, without fear of God.

Ps. LVI.

The dumb dove, &c. This appellation was probably given to the Hebrew nation, while exiled in a foreign land; and may have been the title to a song. (Comp. lxxiv. 19, and the paraphrase of the Septuagint.) Some critics, not thinking the Jewish inscription of this psalm well suited to its contents, have supposed that it was composed by some exile in Babylon.

4. — *his word;* i.e., his promise.

8. — *my wanderings;* i.e., in order to escape my pursuers. (See ver. 1.) — *into thy bottle.* As this figure is rather harsh, in itself considered, some suppose that there is an allusion to a custom, similar to that which prevailed among the Romans, of collecting tears occasioned by the loss of a deceased person into a glass vial, which was deposited in the sepulchre of the dead. (See Adam's Antiquities, p. 483.) De Wette refers to the traveller Morier, as showing that traces of this custom exist among the Persians. — *in thy book;* i.e., as it were, in a register, for remembrance.

Ps. LVII.

— *to the tune of "Do not destroy;"* i.e., of some psalm which began with those words. There is much reason to doubt whether the Jewish inscription, assigning the occasion of this psalm, be correct.

4. — *whose teeth;* an expression suggested by the term *lions*, to which ferocious men are compared in the former part of the verse.

5. — *above the heavens*, &c.; namely, by displaying thy goodness in relieving me from my distress.

6. — *My soul is bowed down;* i.e., I despair of escaping the plots and snares of my enemies; or, perhaps, in a physical sense, "I am brought low" by their artifices.

7. — *is strengthened;* i.e., has gained courage, firmness, confidence, in contradistinction to a desponding, trembling heart. (See cxii. 7.)

8. — *my soul;* literally, *my glory;* i.e., my dearest, most glorious part; like *ἐμὸν φίλον ἦτορ* in Homer. Other instances of a similar use of the word are in vii. 5, xvi. 9; Gen. xlix. 6. — *wake with the early dawn;* otherwise, *wake the early dawn.*

Ps. LVIII.

If the Jewish inscription of this psalm be correct, it may be referred to the times of Saul. But the contents of it favor the opinion of several critics, that it is the production of some unknown author in private life.

1. — *mighty ones.* Disregarding the Hebrew points, I read אֵלִם or אֵלִים.

2. — *weigh out;* i.e., from what should be scales of justice ye weigh out violence instead of equity.

3. — *The wicked, — The liars.* The connection seems to show that the writer is speaking of particular persons; namely, of corrupt judges and magistrates, and not of the wicked and liars in general.

5. — *the voice of the charmer.* See the note on Eccl. x. 11.

8. — *the snail, which melteth away*, &c. Allusion is here made to the

slimy track which the snail leaves behind, and which the writer regarded as consuming its life.

9. — *feel the heat of the thorns.* This proverb seems to be borrowed from the fires which in the East used to be lighted in the open air for culinary purposes. The fuel would sometimes be blown away by a sudden gust of wind, before it had answered its purpose. The defeat of the plans of the wicked, before they were executed, would thus be represented.

Ps. LIX.

6. *Let them return at evening,* &c.; i.e., at the close of the day, which they have spent in vain in lying in wait for me, let them return from their employment. — *howl like dogs;* i.e., which in the East, often having no owner, go about the city howling with hunger for whatever may be cast about the walls of a city. (See ver. 15.)

7. — *who — will hear;* i.e., God will not hear, nor punish. (Comp. x. 11.)

11. *Slay them not,* &c.; i.e., put not an end to them by sudden destruction, but by lingering misery, so that they may be an example of infamy which may not be forgotten.

12. This seems to be a proverbial expression, denoting that all their words were sinful.

Ps. LX.

— *Shushan-Eduth.* This term seems to denote a musical instrument; but why it received its peculiar appellation, "lily of testimony," is a difficult question. The instrument may have been of the form of a lily, and called lily of testimony from its consecration to the testimony, or revelation, of God. — *Joab returned,* &c. See 1 Chron. xviii. 13. Dr. Geddes remarks on the Jewish title to this psalm: "Whoever undertakes to reconcile the title of this psalm to any part of David's history will find it a hard attempt. It is, indeed, by some [such as Venema, Dathe, and Houbigant] supposed to have been written by David, not during his war with the Syrians, but in the beginning of his reign. But this hypothesis to me appears at least equally unfounded. David was successful in all his wars, and never could say what is here put in his mouth. But when, then, was the psalm most probably composed? Plainly, after some great disaster had befallen the hosts of Judah; and I can find no period so proper as at the commencement of the reign of Hezekiah. See his speech to the priests and Levites, 2 Chron. xxix. 5." Others refer the psalm to the time of the Maccabees.

3. — *the wine of reeling;* a common image in the Scriptures to denote the reception of punishment from God, which causes him on whom it is inflicted to reel like a drunkard.

6. *God promiseth,* &c. "This is a beautiful transition. The psalmist is already certain that his prayer has been heard; and, instead of continuing his plaintive expostulations, breaks forth into joyful

exultation, in the hope that he shall not only be rescued from his present enemies, but shall also recover the ancient territories that had been wrested from the house of David, both within and without the limits of Israel." — Geddes. — *measure out;* i.e., as a conquered land, for distribution among his followers.

7. — *my helmet;* the chief defence of me and my kingdom. — *my sceptre;* i.e., the seat of my government, the sceptre being the badge of government.

8. *Moab shall be my wash-bowl;* i.e., shall be in the most abject subjection, and used for the meanest services. — *cast my shoe.* It was considered the lowest menial office of a servant to bear the shoes of his master, when he had taken them off. (Comp. Matt. iii. 11.)

Ps. LXI.

This psalm is usually referred to the time of the rebellion of Absalom. But it is doubtful whether the psalm was composed by David.

2. — *the rock that is high above me;* i.e., grant me safety and deliverance, greater than I can attain by my own strength.

5. — *And give me the inheritance,* &c.; i.e., a residence in, or dominion over, the holy land, the land of Israel.

7. — *before God;* i.e., under God's protection; as it were, under his eye.

Ps. LXII.

If this psalm be a composition of David, it may most probably be referred to the time of Saul's persecution.

3. — *Like a bending wall,* &c.; i.e., with rude violence, and with confidence of overthrowing one in so dangerous a condition.

9. — *are vanity,* — *are a lie;* i.e., they disappoint expectation; they cannot afford the help which one needs.

10. — *in extortion;* i.e., in what is obtained by extortion; viz., wealth.

11. *Once,* — *twice.* The Hebrew way of expressing that a thing is done repeatedly. The design is to impart solemnity and importance to the truth declared in the next line.

12. — *belongeth mercy;* i.e., not only power, as in the preceding line, but mercy or goodness in delivering and blessing those who trust in thee, and in punishing their wicked enemies.

Ps. LXIII.

2. *Thus,* &c.; i.e., with such earnest desire. — *thy power and thy glory;* i.e., the symbols of them.

10. — *a portion for jackals;* i.e., because they shall have no burial.

11. — *swear by him;* because it is implied that they who swear by the true God reverence and worship him.

Ps. LXIV.

4. — *without fear;* i.e., of God, or of punishment.
5. — *will see them;* i.e., the snares, and so escape them.
7. — *will shoot,* &c.; i.e., in the midst of their secret plans which no man can detect, God shall discover, disappoint, and destroy them.
8. — *flee away;* i.e., in horror of their exemplary punishment.

Ps. LXV.

This psalm contains nothing from which we can infer, with the least confidence, the author, the occasion, or the time of the composition. It is well suited for public worship on any occasion.

8. — *awed by thy signs;* i.e., the operations of God, which most clearly manifest his agency; such as are enumerated in the following verses. — *outgoings of the morning,* &c.; i.e., the east and the west, the places whence the morning and evening go forth. The inexactness in ascribing *going forth* to the evening arises from connecting morning and evening together.

9. — *The river of God,* &c.; i.e., the source whence God supplies the rain.

11. *Thou crownest;* i.e., makest it rich and beautiful. — *drop fruitfulness;* i.e., wherever thou goest, blessings spring up.

Ps. LXVI.

This psalm was evidently written after some great national deliverance. But whether it relates to the time after David's peaceable establishment on the throne, or to the time after the destruction of Sennacherib's army, or to the time after the return from the captivity at Babylon, it is difficult to decide.

3. — *are suppliants to thee;* i.e., to thy chosen people, of whom thou art the supreme king. (Comp. xviii. 44.)

11. — *a snare;* i.e., into danger or distress.

12. — *to ride upon our heads.* This image seems to be borrowed from a man riding at full speed upon a horse, who is supposed to lean forward over the head of the horse.

17. — *And praise is now,* &c.; i.e., on account of the deliverance which I have experienced.

Ps. LXVIII.

From the contents of this psalm, it seems probable that it was composed on the occasion of the return of the ark of the covenant from some victorious war, and its reconveyance to Mount Zion. (See xlvii. 5, and the note.) Dr. Geddes thinks that it may have been composed "after David's signal and repeated victories over the combined forces of the Edomites, Ammonites, and Syrians, when the ark was brought back in triumph to Jerusalem." (See 2 Sam. viii.–xii.) I cannot, with De Wette, see any decisive traces of a later period. It has been suggested that it may have been occasioned by one of the contests with nations east of the Jordan, in the time of Jehoiakim, mentioned 2 Kings xxiv. 2.

2. — *the wicked.* By this term are probably here denoted the idolatrous enemies of the Israelites, who were, in general, worshippers of the true God.

4. — *Prepare the way,* &c. See Isa. xl. 3, and the note. — *rideth through the desert.* See xvii. 10, and the note.

8. — *This Sinai,* &c. The pronoun is used for emphasis, as if the poet pointed to Sinai with his hand.

9. — *a plentiful rain.* This probably refers to the miraculous supply of manna. — *wearied inheritance;* i.e., the people of Israel.

11. — *the song of victory* (comp. Hab. iii. 9); i.e., occasion for it by giving victory. If it be objected, that it is incongruous that tidings should be brought to the conquering host, the answer is that the female minstrels *celebrated* the tidings of victory in song. In reference to the rendering of the common version, it seems to me improbable, that there should be a mighty *host,* צָבָא, of female messengers. (Comp. Exod. xv. 20; 1 Sam. xviii. 6.)

13. — *repose yourselves in the stalls,* &c. The meaning of this difficult verse, which seems as probable as any, is, that those who had been engaged in war might now, on their return, enjoy peaceful repose amid their flocks and herds, having enriched themselves with spoils of gold and silver. (Comp. Judg. v. 16; Gen. xlix. 15.)

14. — *like Salmon;* i.e., when this mountain was covered with snow.

16. *Why frown ye,* &c.; i.e., through envy on account of the peculiar honor conferred upon Zion.

17. *The chariots of God,* &c. A figurative description of the majesty of God, and his power to deliver his people. — *in the sanctuary.* The sanctuary is here regarded as a second Sinai.

18. — *on high;* i.e., upon Mount Zion. Comp. Ps. xxiv. in reference to the conveyance of the ark of the covenant to Mount Zion after a victory obtained by the Israelites. — *received gifts,* &c.; i.e., presents from conquered enemies, who were made to pay tribute. (Comp. 2 Sam. viii. 6.) — *even among the rebellious;* i.e., among the Israelites, who had often proved rebellious. (Comp. Numb. xxxv. 34.) Otherwise, Thou hast received *gifts among men, even the rebellious, that thou mayst dwell,* viz. in heaven, *as Lord God.* Otherwise, *and the rebellious shall dwell with thee, O Lord God!*

22. *I will bring them back;* i.e., the enemies, as the connection shows. (Comp. Amos ix. 1, 2, &c.)

26. — *from the fountain,* &c.; i.e., who originate from him.

28. — *Show forth thy might;* i.e., by continuing and strengthening the power of Israel.

30. — *wild beast of the reeds.* This, at first view, may seem most naturally to refer to the crocodile or the river-horse as the emblem of Egypt. But, as the Egyptians were not at war with the Israelites when the psalm was probably written, and as Egypt is mentioned in

the next verse as about to be a worshipper of Jehovah, Lowth and others have supposed the lion to be referred to, as the emblem of Syria. — *bulls with the calves*, &c.; i.e., powerful nations and those of inferior strength; or bulls may denote commanders, and calves common soldiers. — *masses of silver*, &c.; i.e., as a tribute.

31. —*outstretched hands;* i.e., either in supplication, or in bringing presents to the temple.

33. — *ancient heaven*, &c.; i.e., which he built and inhabited of old. (Comp. xviii. 10.)

34. — *Whose majesty*, &c.; i.e., who manifests himself as the mighty ruler of Israel, and who thunders in the clouds.

35. —*from thy sanctuary*. Comp. xx. 2.

Ps. LXIX.

From ver. 33–36, it seems highly probable that this psalm was written during the captivity at Babylon. From ver. 6 it may be inferred that the author was a prophet, or some person of great distinction. Some suppose that the whole Jewish nation is represented by the writer as an individual. It appears to me, that his language would have been different, had this been his design.

4. — *I must restore what I took not away*. This seems to be a proverbial expression denoting the infliction of a penalty, or extortion of property, in relation to the innocent.

5. — *thou knowest my offences*, &c.; i.e., that I am not an offender. This verse is not a confession of sin, but a protestation of innocence. The writer maintains that he is a sufferer, not for his sins, but for his piety. (See ver. 7, &c.)

6. — *through me*, &c.; i.e., when I, thy pious worshipper, am seen to be a prey to my enemies.

8. — *a stranger*, &c.; i.e., on account of being changed in appearance through grief and suffering.

9. — *consumeth me;* i.e., proves my destruction.

12. — *sit in the gate*. It is well known that the gates of cities in the East were places of public resort for business, conversation, &c. (See Jahn's Archæol., § 180.)

21. — *gall*. The meaning of the original term, ראש, is altgether uncertain. From the common meaning of the term, as denoting the head, Gesenius conjectures that it was the poppy, referring to *papaveris capita* in Livy. Others suppose it was the hemlock.

22. *May their table*, &c.; i.e., that in which they find their enjoyment.

26. — *talk of the pain*, &c.; in derision.

31. *bullock;* i.e., offered in sacrifice.

Ps. LXXI.

7. — *a wonder to many;* i.e., on account of my extraordinary calamities.

20. — *bring us back from the depths of the earth;* i.e., from the extreme miseries in which we are involved.

Ps. LXXII.

On account of the power and greatness ascribed to the king who is the subject of this psalm, some have supposed that the Messiah is denoted. It appears to me, that, if we make due allowance for the hyperbolical language of Hebrew poetry, and that which was and is applied to monarchs in the East, the psalm contains nothing that the poet may not have said in reference to Solomon, or any other Jewish king. (See note on ver. 8. Comp. what is promised to David in Ps. lxxxix.) The contents of the psalm agree very well with the Jewish conceptions of the Messiah. But there seems to be no evidence that the writer had him in view. If this had been the case, would he not, like the prophets when they speak of the Messiah, have introduced him in the beginning of the psalm as one who was to be raised up by the Deity at some future time? (Comp. Isa. ix. xi.; Jer. xxiii. 5, 6, xxxiii. 14, 15, 16.) Would ver. 1 have been what it is, if the king were already living and reigning? The most prevalent opinion in the Christian Church has been, that Solomon is the immediate subject of the psalm, and that only in a mystical or typical sense the Messiah is shadowed forth. Thus the caption of the common version is, "David praying for Solomon showeth the glorious and blessed state of his kingdom (as typifying Christ's) in its duration, largeness, and graciousness."

1. — *the king, — the son of a king*. The same person is denoted by both expressions. May the king, who is also the son of a king, &c. The repetition is agreeable to the nature of the Hebrew parallelism.

3. — *the mountains shall bring forth peace*, &c. Here the mountains and the hills of Palestine, i.e., the whole land, are said to bring forth peace like the natural productions of the earth; i.e., abundantly.

6. — *mown field*. See the note on Isa. xxvi. 19.

8. — *from sea to sea*; i.e., from the Mediterranean to the farthest known sea on the east; namely, the Indian Ocean. — *the river*; i.e., the Euphrates. The meaning of the verse is, that the dominion of the great king shall be unlimited. Burder quotes, from Mr. Hugh Boyd's account of his embassy to Ceylon, a passage which shows the adulation which is paid to an Eastern monarch, his courtiers addressing him in the language, "that the head of the king of kings might reach beyond the sun," "that he might live a thousand years," &c. He also quotes from Davy's Account of Ceylon the following language, as addressed to the king: "Increase of age to our sovereign of five thousand years! Increase of age, as long as the sun and moon last! Increase of age, as long as heaven and earth exist!"

10. — *Tarshish* in Spain is probably mentioned as the most distant place in the west, and *Sheba* in Arabia and *Seba* in Ethiopia as the most distant places in the east and south.

16. — *on the tops of the mountains*; i.e., where corn might be least expected to grow. — *shake like Lebanon*; be tall and luxuriant, waving with the wind, like trees on Mount Lebanon.

17. — *By him shall men bless themselves*; i.e., they shall say, May God make us as happy as that great king! "In thee shall Israel

bless, saying, God make thee as E hraim and as Manasseh!" (Gen. xlviii. 20.)

18. Ver. 18 and 19 do not belong to the psalm, but were probably added by the collector of Ps. xlii.–lxxii., as a doxology at the end of his book. Ver. 20 was without doubt added by the same person.

Ps. LXXIII.

The subject of this psalm is similar to that of Ps. xlix. It may also be compared with Ps. xvi., xvii., xxxvii., xxxix., and the whole Book of Job. It sets forth the exercises of a pious mind in view of the manner in which happiness and misery are distributed in this world, or in view of the prosperity of the wicked, when compared with the poet's own sufferings. Notwithstanding all the difficulties which the subject presents to the poet's mind, he begins with confidence in God, and ends with it. Spiritual good, fellowship with God, a sense of his favor, and confidence in his guidance and blessing, are to him more than a compensation for all the outward prosperity of the wicked, which is of short duration and ends in destruction. There is the same doubt, whether the doctrine of immortality be contained in this psalm, as in respect to Ps. xlix. It may be here observed, that this psalm, with Ps. xvi., xvii., xlix., contains the strongest intimations of the doctrine of immortality which can be traced in any of the psalms. If it be not found in these four, it is found in none of them.

This psalm, like Ps. xlix., may have been composed in a depressed state of the Jewish nation, perhaps during the captivity, when the author, with other pious Israelites, was suffering oppression from the enemies of his nation. It is true, that there was an Asaph, the contemporary of David. (See 2 Chron. xxix. 30.) But nothing obliges us to consider that Asaph as the author.

1. — *to Israel.* This term seems to be used here for the true Israel, the "pure in heart," mentioned in the parallel line. (Comp. Isa. xlix. 3; Rom. ix. 6.)

2. — *gave way;* i.e., I began to doubt respecting the goodness and justice of God.

6. — *as a collar,* or neck-ornament. A lifted-up or stiff neck was with the Hebrews a sign of pride. Hence pride is said to encompass their necks. (See lxxv. 5.)

9. — *to the heavens.* A strong hyperbolical expression to denote proud speaking. A similar one is found in the parallel line.

10. — *his people;* i.e., the people of God. — *drink from full fountains;* i.e., become corrupted by the evil ways of the prosperous wicked.

15. — *to the family of thy children;* i.e., the true Israel, the devoted worshippers of God, ver. 1.

17. — *the sanctuaries of God;* i.e., the holy places of the temple, where he sought the will and purposes of God, and learned them. Some suppose that by *sanctuaries of God* are denoted the sacred recesses of the Divine mind. This seems to me very admissible.

20. — *when thou awakest,* &c. The Hebrew verb, like the English, being used both in a transitive and intransitive sense, there is here

an ambiguity. The meaning may be, *when thou awakest* the wicked from their dream of uninterrupted prosperity and enjoyment, or, in the intransitive sense, *when thou awakest* to action or to judgment; as in xxxv. 23. — *vain show;* i.e., their unsubstantial greatness and prosperity. The original term is the same which is thus translated in xxxix. 6.

21. — *pierced in my reins;* i.e., pained and vexed, as in the parallel line, with the prosperity of the wicked.

24. — *receive me in glory;* i.e., receive me with honor under his protection, and set me free from reproach, danger, and distress. (Comp. xlix. 15.) Others understand it, Thou wilt receive me into heaven after death. But, if this were the writer's meaning, it is remarkable that it is not expressed more distinctly, and that the same sentiment is not expressed oftener and more prominently in other psalms. It is also to be observed, that temporal ruin seems in ver. 27 and other parts of the psalm to be contrasted with the blessedness of the righteous. If the psalm was written during the captivity, or in the Maccabæan age, one cannot be confident that the writer does not here allude to the doctrine of the soul's immortality; still less can he be confident that he does make such an allusion.

Ps. LXXIV.

It appears from the contents of this psalm, that it could not have been written before the desolation of the city and temple of Jerusalem by the Chaldæans; and of course it could not have had for its author Asaph, the contemporary of David. Some suppose that the psalm refers to the calamities occasioned by Antiochus Epiphanes, as recorded in 1 Macc. chap. i. So Venema and Rosenmüller. This seems the most appropriate reference on many accounts, nor do any considerations in relation to the completion of the canon of Scripture forbid it. It is also favored by ver. 9, where it is said, "There is no prophet among us." But Jeremiah lived after the destruction by the Chaldæans. On the other hand, if ver. 6, 7 imply that the temple was destroyed and burned, they are inconsistent with the supposition that the invasion of Antiochus is referred to. There is no reason to believe that he burned or destroyed the temple. Rosenmüller thinks that these verses only imply that the temple was injured by fire and profaned.

4. — *Their own symbols,* &c.; i.e., the symbols of their own religion, in place of the "signs" of the covenant between God and us; namely, the sacrifices and other religious symbols. (See 1 Macc. i. 43–59; Joseph. Ant. xii. 5, 4.)

9. — *our signs.* See the note on ver. 4.

11. — *from thy bosom.* "This word," says Roberts, "does not always, in Eastern language, mean the breast; but often the lap, or that part of the body where the long robe folds round the loins. Thus, in the folds of the garment, in front of the body, the Orientals keep their little valuables; and there, when they are perfectly at ease, they place their hands."

13. — *the sea-monsters,* &c.; i.e., Pharaoh and his hosts.

14. — *the crocodile;* the well-known emblem of Egypt.
19. — *wild beast;* i.e., the ferocious enemy.
20. — *thy covenant;* i.e., by which thou didst promise the land of Canaan to thy people. — *dark places,* &c.; i.e., caverns, probably, which abounded in Palestine.

Ps. LXXV.

1. — *and near is thy name;* i.e., upon our lips; we frequently praise it. Others understand "thy name" to be a redundant expression for "thou," and that the meaning is, Thou art near us, or helpest us.
2. *When I see,* &c. In ver. 2, 3, and 10, the Deity is introduced as speaking; the poet speaks in the remaining verses. What is represented as said by the Deity may have been sung by a different choir, in response to the remainder of the psalm.
4. — *horn;* a metaphor drawn from an animal which lifts up its horns when excited.
10. — *lift up their heads.* Literally, *their horns,* as in ver. 4–5.

Ps. LXXVI.

4. — *mountains of robbers,* &c.; i.e., Thou hast displayed thy power and glory, by enabling thy people to overcome the enemies which have occupied the fastnesses in the mountains, and there deposited their prey.

Ps. LXXVII.

3. *I remember God,* &c.; i.e., how kind he has been in former times; but I am troubled the more, when I compare his former favor with my present misery.
6. — *my songs in the night,* &c.; i.e., in commemoration of the former favors of God.
10. — *A change in the right hand of the Most High;* i.e., The right hand of the Most High, which has been exerted in my favor and against my enemies, has been withdrawn from me. Or we may translate, *A change is in the right hand,* &c.; i.e., the right hand of God can change my affliction into prosperity. But we might have expected some adversative particle before "A change," &c., if the latter were the meaning.
16–19. In these verses the passage through the Red Sea is poetically described.
17. — *thine arrows;* i.e., the lightnings.

Ps. LXXVIII.

In this didactic psalm, there seem to be no indications of the period in which it was written. Only from ver. 9 and 67 we may infer with considerable confidence, that it was not written till after the separation of the ten tribes.

25. — *the food of princes;* i.e., excellent food.

49. — *A host of angels of evil.* It seems doubtful, whether the plagues of Egypt are here personified as messengers of evil, or whether personal angels are represented as the ministers of God in producing these plagues. The latter supposition is most agreeable to the representation of the later Jewish writers.

50. — *made a way,* &c.; i.e., gave it free course.

57. — *like a deceitful bow;* i.e., which sends the arrow in a false direction, so that it does not hit the mark.

58. — *high places;* i.e., places of worship for idols.

61. — *his strength* — *his glory;* i.e., the ark of the covenant. (See 1 Sam. iv. 21, 22.)

63. — *did not bewail them;* i.e., in the midst of the general terror and calamity, they had no time to give to the customary lamentations for the dead.

72. *He fed them;* i.e., ruled over them.

Ps. LXXIX.

This psalm seems to have been written on the same occasion as Ps. lxxiv.

2. — *food for the birds,* &c. See ver. 3.

5. — *for ever?* See note on xiii. 2.

11. — *appointed to die;* i.e., destined to death by their enemies; literally, *sons of death.*

Ps. LXXX.

This psalm seems to contain nothing which determines the calamitous time in which it was composed.

Shushan-Eduth. See note on the caption of Ps. lx.

1. — *sittest between the cherubs.* This may mean that God sits or rides on a throne borne by living cherubs. (Comp. xviii. 10 and the note.) Or it may refer to the images of cherubs which were over the ark of the covenant, where God was supposed to manifest himself. (See Exod. xxv. 22.)

5. — *bread of tears;* i.e., grief comes daily, while in consequence of our affliction we forget to take our ordinary food.

11. — *the sea;* the Mediterranean. — *the river;* the Euphrates.

13. *The boar,* &c. This is to be considered as a part of the imagery. We need not inquire who is denoted by the boar.

15. — *madest strong for thyself;* i.e., raised up to be a great nation to accomplish thine own purposes.

16. — *they perish;* i.e., the Israelites.

17. — *over the man,* &c.; i.e., the people of Israel collectively. — *of thy right hand;* i.e., which thy right hand has established.

Ps. LXXXI.

— *the Gittith;* a musical instrument of the nature of the lyre, deriving its name from נָגַן, *to strike.*

5. — *language which he knew not.* (Comp. cxiv. 1.) In the original, there is a change in the pronoun, which it is not well to imitate in English. Otherwise, *The voice of one I know not I hear,* in reference to the following language of the Deity.

6. — *from the hod;* i e., something used in carrying bricks or mortar. But it appears, from the use of the word in other passages, to have been more like a basket than a modern hod.

7. — *in the secret place of thunder,* &c.; i.e., enveloped in the dark thunder-cloud. (Comp. xviii. 11; Nahum i. 3; Exod. xiv. 24, 25.)

10. — *Open wide,* &c.; i.e., I will satisfy your desires of good, however large they may be.

Ps. LXXXII.

1. — *God's assembly;* i.e., the assembly of Israel, of which God was the supreme king. Otherwise, the assembly of the angels. — *in the midst of the gods;* i.e., kings or earthly magistrates. Otherwise, angels.

2. — *favor the cause,* &c.; be influenced in your judgment by the outward condition of the parties rather than by the merits of the case.

5. — *foundations,* &c.; i.e., the land is threatened with ruin.

6. — *said, Ye are gods;* i.e., exalted you far above the condition of common men to one resembling that of God, by investing you with your dignity, as kings or magistrates.

Ps. LXXXIII.

1. — *keep not silence;* i.e., hear our prayer.

3. — *thy chosen ones;* literally, *thy hidden ones;* i.e., hidden, as it were, in God's house.

9. — *to the Midianites.* See Judg. chap. vii. — *Sisera,* — *Jabin,* &c. See Judg. chap. iv.

11. See Judg. vii. 25; viii. 5, &c.

12. — *God's habitations;* i.e., the land of Palestine.

Ps. LXXXIV.

This psalm, which bears considerable resemblance to Ps. xlii. and xliii., may have been composed on the same or a similar occasion.

3. *The very sparrow,* &c. By this language the poet expresses the hardship of his own condition, when prevented by exile or a similar hindrance from visiting the temple of God.

5. — *In whose heart are the ways,* &c.; i.e., who loves the ways which lead to the house of God.

6. — *through the valley of Baca,* &c. Baca was probably a dry, barren, desolate valley; a vale of tears, or of weeping, according to the primary meaning of the term. But they who had their hearts set on Jerusalem and the temple would pass through it as joyfully as if it were filled with streams. Or, Wherever they go, blessings accompany them.

7. — *from strength to strength;* i.e., they shall continually increase in strength.

9. — *of thine anointed;* i.e., the king of the nation. In praying for the nation, the poet does not forget to pray for the king.

Ps. LXXXV.

7. — *thy salvation;* i.e., thy help, which gives deliverance.

8. *I will hear,* &c. The poet, having made his prayer, represents himself as listening to the voice of Jehovah, as to an oracle, and receiving a favorable answer.

10. *Mercy and truth,* &c. The whole verse means, that mercy, fidelity, righteousness, and prosperity shall flourish and abound where they have been wanting; the representation being drawn from the meeting of friends who have been long absent.

11. *Truth shall spring out of the earth,* &c. The meaning of this verse is commonly supposed to be, that truth or uprightness shall flourish among men, like plants that spring out of the earth; and that the righteousness, i.e. the mercy, of God will be manifested in blessings upon the righteous community. But it may be doubted whether the poet intended to express any other idea than the universal prevalence of truth and righteousness, representing the one as springing ont of the earth like plants, and the other as showing itself in the skies like the sun.

13. — *go before him;* i.e., as the leader or forerunner in a military march. — *set us in the way of his steps;* i.e., the way in which God walks, and wishes man to walk. Hitzig, relying on an Arabic root, renders *points to the way,* &c., which gives the same general sense.

Ps. LXXXVII.

This psalm, which could not have been written before the time of Hezekiah, may be illustrated by those passages in Isaiah which predict a time when the religion of Jehovah, made known to the Israelites, shall be the religion of the world. (See Isa. chap. ii., xi., xix., xl.–lxvi.) Without predicting a personal Messiah, it may be called, in one sense, Messianic, setting forth in a highly lyrical spirit the glorious Messianic future which is described by the prophets.

1. *His foundation;* i.e., that which God has founded; namely, the city of God, Jerusalem (ver. 3), or that of Zion (ver. 1), regarded as the representative of Jerusalem.

4. *I name Egypt,* &c. Jehovah is here introduced as speaking. — *They also were born there;* i.e., The inhabitants of Egypt, Babylon,

&c., shall be regarded as citizens of Jerusalem, professing the religion and acknowledging the government of the nation chosen by God. The same thoughts are expressed in the next two verses, in which the poet is the speaker.

7. *Singers as well as dancers*, &c. The meaning seems to be, that all the ministers of joy, of which singers and dancers are mentioned as an example, and all the springs or sources of happiness, are to be found in Jerusalem, the capital city of the world, "the joy of the whole earth."

Ps. LXXXVIII.

This psalm is most generally supposed to have been written in the time of the captivity. But it does not seem to afford sufficient indication, that it was designed to express the afflicted condition of the whole Jewish nation, as some critics have supposed. The terms *Mahalath Leannoth*, which appear in the inscription in the common version, mean *to be sung to*, or accompanied with, *wind instruments*.

6. — *left to myself:* The common meaning of חָפְשִׁי, *free*, is not to be lost sight of. But the connection seems to demand the secondary sense, which I have given it; i.e., free from protection, or destitute of it. Otherwise, *free*, &c.; i.e., from the cares and troubles of life.

7. — *all thy waves.* Comp. xlii. 7, and the note.

8. — *I am shut up;* i.e., by calamity, distress, &c., as by prison walls.

10–12. The meaning seems to be, Do good to me now, while I am in life; for, after I am dead, there will be no opportunity for it. (Comp. vi. 5.) — *place of corruption*, — *land of forgetfulness;* i.e., Sheol, the common receptacle of all the dead. (See Job xxviii. 22.)

Ps. LXXXIX.

As this psalm contains no allusion to the destruction of the city and temple of Jerusalem, it was probably written in some calamitous period of the Jewish nation before the captivity. But whether it was written by Hezekiah or by some one for him, or after the defeat and death of Josiah, or at some other period, there seem to be no sufficient means of ascertaining.

5. *The heavens*, &c.; i.e., the inhabitants of heaven, the angels, as appears from the parallel line.

6. — *sons of God;* i.e., inhabitants of heaven, angels.

8. — *is round about thee;* i.e., encircles thee; is the element in which thou dost exist.

10. *Rahab;* a significant appellation of Egypt, referring to her pride and fierceness, as of a huge sea-monster.

12. — *Tabor and Hermon.* One being in the west and the other in the east from the place where the poet wrote, these mountains are probably used to denote the west and the east, as is made probable by the parallelism. — *rejoice in thy name;* i.e., in thee, as their Creator, according to the parallelism.

15. — *know the trumpet's sound;* i.e., calling them to the festivals, offerings, &c., especially the sabbath. (See Lev. xxiii. 24; Num. x. 10.) — *in the light of thy countenance;* i.e., shall enjoy thy favor. (Comp. iv. 6.)

17. — *our horn exalteth itself;* i.e., we are confident, courageous, victorious.

18. — *our shield;* i.e., our king, as in the parallel line. (Comp. ver. 3, 4.) Otherwise, *For to Jehovah belongeth our shield,* &c.

19. — *in a vision,* &c. See 2 Sam. vii. 4–17.

24. — *through my name;* i.e., through me. — *his head;* literally, *his horn.*

25. *I will extend his hand;* i.e., his power, dominion. By "the sea" and "the rivers," the Mediterranean and the Euphrates are probably denoted.

27. — *my first-born.* This phrase is well explained by the parallel line. All kings, according to the conceptions of the Hebrews, might be called sons of God. (See lxxxii. 6.) An eminent king of Israel, distinguished above other kings, would, according to the same phraseology, be called the first-born son of God.

37. — *Like the faithful witness,* &c.; i.e., the moon, as in the parallel line. The moon, by its everlasting duration, would be a good witness of the Divine fidelity in the performance of his promise. Others suppose the rainbow to be denoted.

38. The poet now contrasts with the great promises, which have been recited, the present condition of the nation, when its king, one of the successors of David, was deprived of his throne, or had lost his power.

47. — *To what frailty,* &c. The poet urges the shortness of life as a reason why God should show mercy speedily, before the opportunity should pass away.

50. — *the reproach of thy servants;* i.e., the Israelites.

Ps. XC.

If the title of this psalm be correct, it was written by Moses in view of the calamities, and especially the peculiar waste of life, in the passage through the wilderness; and is illustrated by Num. chap. xiv. But it is the opinion of some eminent critics, such as Grotius, Kennicott, Geddes, and others, that the psalm was rather composed in the time of the captivity. Whichever supposition be adopted, the reader must remember that it was written in peculiar circumstances of calamity, and that parts of it do not apply to all men in all conditions.

1. — *dwelling-place;* i.e., our home or refuge, to which we look.

2. — *art God;* i.e., mighty and wise to govern, protect, and bless by thy providence.

3. — *to dust.* See Gen. iii. 19.

4. — *a watch in the night.* The Hebrews in the more ancient times divided the night into three watches; in the time of Christ, into four. A watch in the night, therefore, denotes the space of three or four hours.

9. — *like a thought;* i.e., as swiftly as a thought passes the mind. A similar expression occurs in the Greek poet Theognis:—

Αἶψα ὥστε νόημα παρέρχεται ἀγλαος ἥβη.

10. — *the pride of them;* i.e., that of which they can be most proud; the best and most flourishing part of them, to which we attach the greatest value.

11. — *thine anger,* &c.; i.e., which is manifested in the vanity and shortness of life.

12. — *to number our days;* i.e., to consider how few they are.

13. *Desist;* i.e., from thine anger. (Exod. xxxii. 12.) — *How long* ——; i.e., wilt thou be angry? (Comp. vi. 3, and the note.)

16. — *thy deeds;* i.e., of mercy to us.

Ps. XCI.

2. — *sitteth under the shelter,* &c.; i.e., he who resorts to God by faith, trust, and holy communion. — *Maketh his abode,* &c.; i.e., shall find protection.

8. — *only behold;* i.e., thou shalt look on, in perfect security, while punishment is inflicted on the wicked.

9. — *thy refuge.* In the Hebrew, *my refuge.* Hence the Septuagint translates the line, *Because thou, O Lord! art my refuge;* supposing that a different person, or singer, was to recite it. I cannot think the couplet was intended to be divided in this way. Whether the conjecture of Lowth* is to be adopted, or some accidental change of the person of the pronoun on the part of the writer is to be supposed, I believe that I have given the true meaning of the verse. Hupfeld supposes an ellipsis of "thou hast said." *Because* [thou hast said,] *O Lord!* &c.

Ps. XCIV.

This psalm seems to have been composed in a season of national calamity. Some refer it to the time of the captivity; others, to that of the tyranny of Antiochus Epiphanes.

10. *He that chastiseth nations;* He that brings punishment and ruin on whole nations, shall he not punish your oppressors in particular?

11. *That they are vanity;* i.e., that *men* are vanity; i.e., weak, without power to accomplish their proud purposes.

15. — *judgment shall return to justice,* &c.; i.e., however much the judgments of God may seem to depart from justice, while the wicked prosper and the righteous are afflicted, they shall at last return to a strict conformity to it, so that all the upright shall approve of them.

20. — *throne of iniquity,* &c. Comp. 1 Macc. chap. i.

23. — *their own iniquity;* i.e., the destruction which they plotted against others.

---

* Lecture XXVI.

Ps. XCV.

This psalm seems to have been composed to be used in the public worship of God, and perhaps on some festival occasion, such as that of the feast of tabernacles.

3. — *over all gods;* i.e., all the pretended gods of the Gentiles.

7. —*flock of his hand;* i.e., which his hand leadeth.

8. The Supreme Being is now introduced as speaking. — *Meribah.* (See Exod. xvii. 7.) Probably both *Meribah* and *Massah* were intended as proper names, with distinct reference, however, to their signification as appellatives.

11. — *I sware,* &c. See Num. xiv. 21–23; xxxii. 10, &c. — *my rest;* i.e., the land which I had destined for their resting-place.

Ps. XCVI.

This psalm corresponds to a part of one which is recorded in 1 Chron. chap. xvi., as having been sung on a different occasion. Perhaps it was used on the dedication of the second temple, after the return from the captivity at Babylon. It is entitled in the Septuagint version, "An ode of David, sung when the house of God was built, after the captivity."

5. — *idols;* possibly *godlings, little idols.* See Fürst's Lexicon on אֱלִיל, a term of contempt.

6. — *his holy abode;* i.e., in heaven. (See cii. 19.)

11–13. The whole creation is called upon to rejoice on account of the coming of Jehovah to reign. But, as Jehovah is at all times the ruler of the world, his coming to reign must be understood in a peculiar sense; and this sense, according to the conception of a Jewish poet of that age, can be no other than that of the extension of the Hebrew theocracy over the heathen nations. God would judge the world, when the heathen nations were punished through the Jews, were brought under their dominion, and adopted their religion, having renounced their own false gods. (Comp. ii., lxxxvii., lxxxix., xcvii., cx., and various passages in the prophets.)

Ps. XCVII.

2. *Clouds,* &c. Comp. xviii. 11; lxxxix. 14.

6. *The heavens,* &c.; i.e., the whole universe, the heavens and the earth, acknowledge and proclaim him the righteous and terrible judge. (Comp. l. 6.)

7. — *all ye gods,* &c. The connection shows that heathen gods are denoted. Though they have no real existence, they are figuratively represented as bowing down before the majesty of Jehovah. (Comp. Num. xxxiii. 4.) The inability of the heathen gods to protect the nations which worshipped them is probably alluded to. (Comp. Isa. chap. xlvi.)

11. *Light is sown,* &c. Though prosperity may be absent for a time, like seed which is hidden in the ground, yet in due time it shall spring up like seed.

Ps. C.

3. — *It is he that made us,* &c. In this connection, these words probably refer not so much to the fact that God created all mankind, as to that of his having constituted the Jews a people, and framed their national polity. (Comp. cxlix. 2; Deut. xxxii. 6.)

Ps. CI.

1. — *of mercy and justice;* i.e., which it is my resolution to practise, rewarding the good and punishing the wicked.

2. — *When thou shalt come to me;* i.e., to prove me, or to aid me. Otherwise, *When wilt thou come to me?* i.e., to bless me.

3. — *before mine eyes,* &c. I will not propose to myself any wicked scheme.

6. — *dwell with me;* i.e., as my ministers and counsellors, as is intimated in the parallel line.

Ps. CII.

3. — *burn;* i.e., with pain.

6. — *like the pelican;* i.e., I take no delight in society, but seek for solitary places like the pelican. — *like the owl;* i.e., in my doleful lamentations. Some think the *pelicanus onocrotalus* is denoted; a meaning which is favored by the etymology of the Hebrew term.

7. — *a solitary bird;* referring probably to some bird of night, like the owl, in reference to the writer's sleeplessness, mentioned in the preceding line.

8. — *curse by me;* i.e., in imprecating curses either upon themselves or upon others, they refer to me, as an example of extreme misery. (Comp. Jer. xxix. 22; Isa. lxv. 15.)

9. — *ashes like bread,* &c.; through grief I lie down in ashes, and neglect to take my food. (See xlii. 3; Job ii. 8; Ezek. xxvii. 30.)

10. — *lifted me up,* &c. This may mean, that he was lifted up as by a whirlwind, in order to be dashed to the ground; or, that he was raised to an exalted station, and then cast down from his eminence. Perhaps the first is preferable.

11. — *a declining shadow;* i.e., which continually becomes fainter and fainter, and soon vanishes away. (Comp. cix. 23.)

13. — *the set time,* &c. Comp. Jer. xxv. 12, 13; xxix. 10.

14. — *in her stones;* i.e., her scattered stones and her solitary dust are more precious to thy worshippers than the goodliest palaces in Babylon.

16. — *in his glory.* The meaning may be, that he shall be worshipped with the ancient ceremonies upon Zion, which seems to be favored by the parallel line; or, that the glorious power and goodness of God shall be manifested in behalf of Israel.

17. — *the destitute;* i.e., the Israelites, as a people.

18. *This shall be written;* i.e., the interposition of God in delivering his people and building up Zion.

20. — *doomed to death;* a figurative expression, denoting the threatened extinction of the Jewish nation and name.

22. *When the nations are assembled,* &c. When the Jewish nation, after the return from exile, shall have extended its dominion and its religion over the nations of the world. (See the note on xcvi. 11, &c.; Isa. xlv. 14, lxi.; Joel iii.)

23. — *by the way;* i.e., of life, the passage through life.

24. — *Thy years endure,* &c. The unchangeableness and eternity of God seem to be introduced with reference to the thought expressed in ver. 28; namely, that Israel should yet abide before God in the promised land.

Ps. CIII.

5. — *like the eagle's.* "It has been a popular opinion, that the eagle lives, and retains its vigor, to a great age; and that, beyond the common lot of other birds, it moults in its old age, renews its feathers, and is restored to youthful strength again. Whether the notion is in any degree well founded or not, we need not inquire. It is enough for a poet, whether sacred or profane, to have the authority of popular opinion to support an image introduced for illustration or ornament. See Isa. xl. 31. Aristot. Hist. Animal., lib. ix. c. 33. Plin. Nat. Hist., lib. x. c. 3. Horus Apollo, lib. ii. c. 92." — Harris.

12. — *our transgressions;* i.e., the punishment due for our transgressions.

14. — *our frame;* i.e., of what materials we are formed.

21. — *Ye, his ministers,* &c.; i.e., his ministering spirits in heaven, angels.

Ps. CIV.

1–4. The imagery is borrowed from the splendor of Oriental monarchs, setting forth how far Jehovah surpasses them in those things in which their magnificence is usually displayed; namely, in robes, tents, palaces, chariots, and servants.

3. — *in the waters;* i.e., the waters above the firmament, and which rest upon it as a solid support. (See Gen. i. 7.) These waters above the firmament are, as it were, the foundation of the dwelling-place of God. — *clouds his chariot.* Comp. xviii. 11; xxix. 3.

4. —*winds his messengers,* &c. He makes the winds and lightnings, which bid defiance to human control, to obey and serve him, as if endowed with intelligence. (Comp. cxlviii. 8; Job xxxviii. 35.)

6, 8. Comp. Gen. i. 2, 9. — *The mountains rose, the valleys sank,* &c.; i.e., in consequence of the receding of the waters, the mountains are poetically represented as rising out of the waters, &c. So Luther, Hupfeld, and Hitzig. Otherwise, *They go up the mountains, they go down the valleys,* &c.; i.e., The waters, excited by thy rebuke, dash up the mountains, and again sink powerless into the valleys.

11. — *the wild asses;* i.e., which, being very wild, and living in the most solitary deserts, might be thought specially liable to suffer from the want of water

13. — *fruit of thy works;* i.e., of the clouds.
16. *The trees of the Lord,* &c.; i.e., the wild trees of the forest, which were not planted by man, and receive no culture from him.
18. — *the conies.* See the note on Prov. xxx. 26.
19. — *to mark seasons,* &c. See Gen. i. 14; Ecclus. xliii. 6, 7.
26. — *the leviathan,* &c. In Job xli. 1, &c., the leviathan denotes the crocodile. But the term was probably applied to other huge sea monsters.
30. — *thy spirit,* &c. Comp. xxxiii. 6; Gen. ii. 7; Eccl. xii. 7; Job xxxiii. 4.
32. — *it trembleth,* &c. Earthquakes and volcanoes may be alluded to in this verse.

Ps. CV.

The first fifteen verses of this psalm are a part of the hymn said to have been given by David to the singers, on the removal of the ark to Zion, which is contained in 1 Chron. chap. xvi. It is the conjecture of Dathe, that some poet, after the return from the captivity at Babylon, adapted these fifteen verses, with an addition of his own, to the dedication of the second temple; as the same or some contemporary poet had adapted another fragment of the same hymn, namely, Ps. xcvi., to a similar purpose. De Wette supposes the hymn in Chronicles to have been compiled from the two psalms.
11. — *the lot,* &c.; i.e., the assigned portion of the earth.
14. — *rebuked kings,* &c. See Gen. xii. 17; xx. 1-7.
15. — *anointed,* — *prophets,* &c.; i.e., Abraham and the patriarchs.
19. — *the word of the Lord,* &c.; namely, that which Joseph uttered respecting the future.
25. *He turned their hearts,* &c. The more God blessed the Israelites and increased their numbers, the greater was the jealousy of the Egyptians, which at length settled into confirmed hatred. The Hebrews were accustomed to attribute to the direct agency of God what took place under his permission, foresight, and providence. (Comp. Matt. vi. 13.)
32. — *flaming fire;* i.e., lightning.
34. — *Destructive locusts,* &c. Undoubtedly a species of locust, different from that in the preceding line, is denoted. The Hebrew term comes from a root signifying *to lick up,* or *devour.*
37. — *silver,* &c. See Exod. chap. xii.
40. — *bread of heaven;* i.e., the manna.
44. — *the labor;* i.e., the fruits of the labor.

Ps. CVI.

3. — *practise righteousness at all times.* The general sentiment of this verse is probably expressed with reference to the unhappy condition of the Jewish nation in consequence of their wickedness.
5. — *thy chosen;* i.e., the Israelites, called the inheritance of God in the next line but one.
7. — *rebelled,* &c. See Exod. xiv. 11, 12.

12. — *sang his praise.* See Exod. xv. 1, &c.

13. — *waited not for his counsel;* i.e., did not wait patiently to see what were the designs of God, and how he would accomplish them.

14, 15. See Num. chap. xi. — *leanness.* This is probably a figure for want and misery in general.

16, 17. See Num. chap. xvi.

19. See Exod. chap. xxxii.

20. — *their God of glory;* literally, *their glory.*

23. — *in the breach.* This figurative expression refers to the breach made by an enemy in the walls of a fortified city. One stands in the breach for the purpose of opposing the enemy, and preventing the destruction of the city. (See Exod. chap. xxxii., xxxiii.)

24. See Num. chap. xiii., &c.

27. Comp. Num. xiv. 28–30; Lev. xxvi. 33; Deut chap. xxviii.

28. — *Baal-peor.* See Num. chap. xxv.

32. See Num. chap. xx.; Deut. i. 37.

36. — *they became;* i.e., the heathen. — *a snare;* i.e., caused their ruin.

37. — *to demons.* So the Septuagint translates the term שֵׁדִים, in this verse and in Deut. xxxii. 17. From the etymology of the term, we may infer, perhaps, that it denotes malignant spirits; but it is not necessary to suppose that precisely the same notions were entertained of demons in the time of this composition, as in that of the New Testament. The worship of Moloch is probably referred to.

39. — *played the harlot;* i.e., left the true God to worship false gods. — *with their practices;* i.e., the practices of the heathen.

Ps. CVII.

In this national psalm of thanksgiving, the reader will observe the art of the poet in dividing it into strophes, or divisions, closing with a form of thanksgiving as the burden of the song. In ver. 1–3 the subject is stated, and then follow the strophes, closing with ver. 8, 9; 15, 16; 21, 22; 31, 32; 43.

4. — *in a desert.* This may refer to the literal fact, that many of the Jews fled from the Chaldæans through the desert to Egypt, &c.; or it may be a figurative expression, referring to the miseries of exile.

10. — *darkness and the shadow of death;* i.e., in the profound darkness of a gloomy dungeon. — *in affliction and iron.* This may be a hendyadis for *afflictive iron;* or the meaning may be, that they were bound by their affliction, no less than by heavy chains. Perhaps the language of the whole verse figuratively describes the misery of the exile in Babylon.

20. — *sent his word;* i.e., commanded.

25–27. The classical reader may be pleased by comparing with this description of a storm that of Ovid, Trist. lib. i. Eleg. 2: —

> "Me miserum, quanti montes volvuntur aquarum!
> Jamjam tacturos sidera summa putes.
> Quantæ diducto subsidunt æquore valles!
> Jamjam tacturas tartara nigra putes.
> Rector in incerto est, nec quid fugiatve petatve
> Invenit; ambiguis ars stupet ipsa malis."

33–36. This language seems to have special reference to the depopulation of Palestine, and the subsequent restoration of the Jews.

Ps. CIX.

If this psalm was written by David, the curses contained in it have probable reference to his enemies at the court of Saul. (Respecting these imprecations, see pp. 19–21.) The following remarks of the Rev. Dr. French,* Master of Jesus College, Cambridge, England, and Mr. Skinner, a Fellow of the same college, agree very well with mine, though I cannot think that the spirit even of the Jewish religion fully justifies these imprecations: "It may be observed, with reference to the imprecations found particularly in this psalm and in Ps. lxix., that the morality which they breathe does not ill accord either with the general character of the Mosaic dispensation, or with the state of religious knowledge to which the Jewish nation had attained. The love of our enemies was a duty first distinctly and positively inculcated by the Divine Author of the Christian faith. This pure and sublime doctrine did not form a part of the law delivered to the Jews because of 'the hardness of their hearts.'

"Let it not be urged, that it would have been better, if the sacred volume had nowhere exhibited the 'holy men,' who were of old, thus betraying, even in their intercourse with God, a deep resentment of the unprovoked injuries which they were continually suffering from the wicked. These very passages of Scripture convey an useful and a very important lesson. For they teach Christians, in the most forcible manner, the value of those pre-eminent advantages which are enjoyed by them under the gospel."

6. — *a wicked man over him;* i.e., as a judge to hear his cause. — *over him.* This may refer to the principal enemy of David, or possibly to his enemies collectively; as the plural occurs in ver. 15. — *an adversary,* &c.; i.e., to accuse and plead against him in court.

7. — *his prayer,* &c. There is some doubt, whether this expression denotes a petition for pardon to a human judge, or prayer to God. The parallel line favors the former supposition; the use of the word, translated *prayer* in other passages, the latter.

8. — *take his office;* i.e., which is vacated by his death.

10. — *from their ruined dwellings;* i.e., going forth from them.

16. — *the poor man,* &c.; such as the poet.

20. — *wages.* Literally, *work,* and hence *wages,* the consequence of work.

23. — *shadow.* See the note on cii. 11. — *cast out as a locust.* An image of destruction, drawn from locusts, which are driven by winds, or by noises, fires, &c., made by men, from the fields into the water or waste places.

31. — *at the right hand,* &c.; i.e., as his advocate.

---

* See the note on this psalm in their "New Translation," &c.

Ps. CX.

The difficulties relating to particular portions of this psalm have been, in good measure, removed by modern investigation. But it is still an unsettled question among critics, who is the principal subject of the psalm, or who is meant by "my lord," in the first line, — "Jehovah said to my lord;" or, more literally, "The oracle," or "solemn declaration, of Jehovah to my lord." There are three opinions upon the subject.

I. Christian interpreters generally, until within a comparatively recent period, have supposed Jesus Christ to be the person addressed in the first line, and that the psalm predicts in figurative language his glorious condition after his resurrection, and the triumphs of him and his religion over all opposition. In favor of this opinion, it is alleged that David is said in the Jewish inscription to be the author of the psalm, and of course could not acknowledge a common Jewish king as his lord. But especially the use made of the psalm by our Saviour, in Matt. xxii. 43–45, and by the apostles, in Acts ii. 34, 1 Cor. xv. 25, Heb. i. 13, x. 13, is urged as decisive of the question. Some expressions in the psalm are also said to be more applicable to Jesus Christ than to a common Jewish king. In illustration of these views, see Christian commentators generally.

II. Some modern critics, such as Rosenmüller and Kuinöl, and some Jewish critics in ancient and modern times, have supposed the future Messiah, according to the Jewish conceptions of him, to be the subject of the psalm; while they maintain that its representation of him as a temporal king, a warrior, a conqueror, and shedder of blood, is inconsistent with any thing which we know of Jesus of Nazareth.

III. Other critics, such as Herder,* Geddes, De Wette, Ewald, Hitzig, and Bleek, maintain that the psalm relates to a Jewish king, living in the time of the writer, — either David or some other Jewish king; and that it expresses the sanguine hopes of some Jewish poet in favor of his sovereign, whom he is disposed to eulogize in the language of exaggeration which was commonly applied to Eastern monarchs. In behalf of this opinion, it is urged, that the ascription of the psalm to David, as its author, by some unknown hand, is of little or no weight, when it is considered that several of the titles of the psalms must be acknowledged to be erroneous; that the first line of it evidently supposes the person who is called "my lord" to be living on earth in the time of the writer, and cannot refer to the distant future, and, finally, that the attributes of a common Jewish king are all that the writer does in fact express in the language which he has used. In regard to the use made of the psalm by Christ and the apostles, it is also said, that they may have argued *ex concessis;* i.e., from the acknowledged opinions of their opponents or contemporaries, without vouching for their correctness; or that they may have made use of the psalm to express ideas for which it was not originally designed.

---

* Spirit of Hebrew Poetry, vol. ii. p. 282, &c., Amer. transl.

understanding it in a typical or allegorical sense, like portions of many other psalms.

Without going into a discussion of the difficult subjects connected with the question of the application of the psalm, I shall endeavor to give the meaning of its language according to what must have been the conceptions of the writer. (See the Introduction, pp. 9–11.)

1. — *Sit thou at my right hand;* i.e., Be associated with me in the government of my people; be next in honor to me. The language is borrowed from a king commanding his son to sit with him on his throne. (Comp. 1 Kings i. 13, 17.) Jehovah was regarded as the supreme king of the Jewish nation, and Mount Zion as the seat of his government. Thus, in cxlix. 2, "Let the sons of Zion be joyful in their king!" cxxxiv. 3, "May the Lord, who made heaven and earth, bless thee out of Zion!" cxxxv. 21, "Praised be the Lord out of Zion, he that dwelleth in Jerusalem!" cxxxii. 13, "For Jehovah hath chosen Zion; he hath desired it as his dwelling-place." Jehovah being thus, in a peculiar sense, the supreme king of Israel, the throne of Judea was called the throne of Jehovah (see 1 Chron. xxix. 23), and the human king of Israel is said to sit on the throne of Jehovah, i.e., at the right hand of Jehovah, the supreme king of Israel, as his vicegerent, participating in the government of his people. So in Zech. xiii. 7, "Awake, O sword! against my shepherd, even against the man who is my fellow, saith Jehovah of hosts." A common appellation of kings in ancient times was that of shepherds; and Jehovah being regarded as the supreme king of Israel, his shepherd or earthly king is styled the fellow or associate of Jehovah in the government of his people. To be the fellow or associate of Jehovah amounts to the same thing as to sit upon his right hand. In Josephus, vi. 11, 9, Jonathan is said to sit on the right hand of the king, and Abner on the left. Roberts, who was a missionary in Hindostan, says, "The host always places a distinguished guest on his right hand." Rosenmüller quotes from an ancient history of Arabia, "The Radaf," i.e., the one second in rank to the king, "sits at his right hand." The language, "Sit thou at my right hand," amounts to the same thing as that in ii. 7, "Thou art my son," &c., on which see the note. — *thy footstool;* i.e., completely subdue them. (See Josh. x. 24, 25.) The particle *until* does not imply that the king was not to sit at the right hand of God after his enemies were subdued. The expression is similar to that which we use when we say, "I hope you will be well, or behave well, till I return." (See 1 Tim. iv. 13.)

2. *Rule thou;* implying strong prediction. — *in the midst of thine enemies;* i.e., shalt control them, have them in subjection.

3. — *be ready;* i.e., willing and prompt to go to war with thee. — *when thou musterest thy forces;* literally, *in the day of thy host.* — *in holy splendor;* i.e., equipped in the best or choicest manner. So the Median soldiers are called "sanctified ones;" i.e., set apart for the war against Babylon, Isa. xiii. 3. So in Jer. vi. 4, "Sanctify war against her," li. 27. — *like dew,* &c.; i.e., numerous as the drops of morning dew. Perhaps at the same time their freshness may have been had in view.

4. — *a priest for ever;* i.e., during thy whole life. (Comp. Exod. xxi. 6; Deut. xv. 17; 1 Sam. i. 22; and the note on xlv. 6.) The

greatness of the promise consists in the circumstance, that the sanctity of the priest would be united with the dignity of the king in the great personage to whom it is given; thus making him in a higher degree the object of the divine care and favor. (Comp. Zech. vi. 13.) — *the order of Melchisedeck;* i.e., in the same way as Melchisedeck united the dignity of a priest and a king. (See Gen. xiv. 18.)

5. *The Lord is at thy right hand.* To be at one's right hand is not the same thing as to *sit* at one's right hand. It means, to be one's defender, ready to assist him. (See xvi. 8; cxxi. 5.) I understand, therefore, *The Lord,* as denoting the Supreme Being, and that the king who is the subject of the psalm is here addressed. Otherwise, with a change of the vowel-points, the line might be rendered, *My lord at thy right hand* [O Jehovah!] *shall,* &c.

7. *He shall drink of the brook,* &c. Here, I suppose, by a sudden change of person, which is not uncommon in Hebrew poetry (see civ. 9, 10), the king, who was addressed by the poet in ver. 5, is introduced in the third person, as pursuing his enemies, and as refreshing and strengthening himself for such pursuit by drinking water from a brook which he finds in the way.

I have thus, without entering into an examination of various opinions, given what seems to me the literal meaning of the language of the psalm. Whether the warrior-king whom it describes is to be regarded as a temporal king of Israel, or only as an image or type of Christ in his triumphant state in heaven, the language being understood in a figurative or allegorical sense, is a question which must be decided in view of all the considerations which were glanced at in the introduction to the notes on this psalm.

Ps. CXI.

This is one of the alphabetical psalms, in which each half-verse begins with a different letter, according to the order of the Hebrew alphabet. (See p. 47, &c.)

1. — *assembly,* — *congregation,* &c.; i.e., of righteous Israelites, assembled in the temple.

2. — *Sought out,* &c.; i.e., as being worthy of regard and admiration.

4. — *a memorial,* &c.; i.e., in his dealings with the Israelites, as recorded in their history.

9. — *redemption,* &c.; i.e., from Egyptian slavery.

Ps. CXII.

This is an alphabetical psalm of the same kind as the last. (See the remarks on Ps. i.)

3. — *His righteousness shall endure;* i.e., the consequences or reward of it.

4. — *He is gracious,* &c. It is doubtful, whether this is said of the righteous man, or of God. From ver. 4 of the last psalm, which seems to have had the same author as this, the last is the probable meaning.

6. — *be moved;* i.e., he shall stand secure from destructive calamity.

9. — *His horn,* &c. An emblem of power and authority, borrowed from animals whose strength was in their horns.

Ps. CXIV.

In this psalm, the subject of which is the deliverance of the Israelites from Egyptian bondage, the principal idea is, that all obstacles, even those presented by nature itself, must give way before the power of Jehovah. "This psalm," says Herder, "is one of the finest odes in any language. The abrupt brevity with which each particular is expressed, the astonished admiration ascribed to the sea, to the Jordan, to the mountains and hills, and repeated in the interrogatory form; the sublime explanation, that it all proceeded from a single glance of Jehovah, who looked upon them from the clouds, a look which converted rocks and stones to streams and living fountains, — all these give us, in the compass of this little ode, the substance of a long description." It may have been designed for the celebration of the feast of the passover.

2. — *his sanctuary;* i.e., the people set apart, and, as it were, consecrated, to be his peculiar people. — *his dominion;* i.e., the people of which he was king in a peculiar, theocratic sense.

Ps. CXV.

This psalm seems to have been composed when the nation was in distress, or in great danger, on account of foreign enemies. But it is idle to undertake to conjecture the particular occasion of it.

1. *Not unto us,* &c.; i.e., Help and deliver us, if not on our own account, yet on account of the honor of thy own name, and of thy promises to the patriarchs. (Comp. Ezek. xxxvi. 22.)

8. — *like unto them;* i.e., equally without power and worthless.

17. *The dead praise not,* &c. See the note on vi. 5.

Ps. CXVI.

There have been many conjectures in relation to the time and occasion of the composition of this psalm. On account of some Chaldee idioms which occur in it, I think the opinion of Dr. Hammond the most probable; namely, that it was written by some pious Israelite after the return from the captivity at Babylon.

3. — *pains of the underworld.* The literal meaning probably is, *straits of the underworld.* The meaning of the whole verse is, that the writer was in imminent danger of death.

7. *Return — to thy rest,* &c.; i.e., be again tranquil, after thy anxiety and agitation.

9. — *walk before the Lord;* i.e., aiming to serve him and do his will.

10. *I had trust,* &c.; i.e., I did not cease to place confidence in God. — *although I said;* or, *when I used to say.*

11. — *All men are liars;* i.e., disappoint the hopes that are placed in them. All reliance on human aid is vain.

13. — *the cup of salvation,* &c.; i.e., of thanksgiving for the deliverance which I have obtained from God. It seems to have been customary, after offering a sacrifice for some great deliverance, to make a feast, at which the host would take a cup of wine, and, having partaken of it, pass it round to his guests. (Comp. Matt. xxvi. 27.)

15. — *the death of his holy ones;* i.e., he preserves their lives. He considers their death too costly to be suffered for any light reason.

16. — *the son of thy handmaid;* i.e., thy servant or slave, as in the parallel line. The children of a female slave belonged of right to her master.

Ps. CXVIII.

This psalm was probably composed to be sung on the occasion of the deliverance of some king of Israel from the dangers of war. Different parts of it were probably to be performed by separate choirs of singers, representing the king, the priests, and the people. The author and the date of the composition, as well as the particular king who is the subject of it, are wholly unknown. It is probable, however, that it was composed after the erection of the temple, and of course was not a production of David. Some apply the psalm to Hezekiah, after his deliverance from sickness, and from the invasion of Sennacherib. Some suppose that it was sung at the dedication of the second temple, after the return from the captivity; some, that it relates to the time of the Maccabees, when Simon was made governor of the Jews. (See 1 Macc. chap. xiii., xiv.) Another opinion is, that it is not an individual, but the whole people of Israel personified, that is introduced as giving thanks for deliverance. We cannot find in the psalm sufficient reasons to justify this view. In the Lamentations of Jeremiah, and in Isaiah, chap. xl.–lxvi., there appears, however, to be such a personification of the Jewish people. But some indications in the particular passage in which such a use of language is alleged seem necessary to justify the opinion. Some of the ancient Jews, perhaps those who lived in the time of Christ, regarded the psalm as prophetic of the Messiah, and some suppose that Christ and the apostles regarded it as such. (See Matt. xxi. 42; Acts iv. 11.) But the most common opinion of interpreters is, that those verses are quoted only by way of accommodation, or rhetorical illustration; or, at least, are applied to Jesus in a mystical or allegorical sense.

13. *Thou didst assail,* &c. An address to his enemy.

19. — *the gates of righteousness;* so called because the righteous enter them for worship.

22. *The stone which the builders rejected,* &c.; i.e., he whose claims were disregarded and despised by the chief men of the nation has now attained to the highest dignity among his people. As was intimated in the introduction to this psalm, history does not seem to supply us with the means of determining who is meant by the stone which the builders rejected. Venema and Rosenmüller refer it to Simon, whose history is recorded in 1 Macc. chap. xiii., xiv.; De Wette and Tholuck, to the whole Jewish people.

24. — *which the Lord hath made;* i.e., so happy and distinguished.

26. — *that cometh in the name of the Lord.* This language seems to be more applicable to a prince than to the whole people.

27. — *to the horns of the altar;* i.e., in order to be sacrificed.

Ps. CXIX.

This is another of the alphabetical psalms, but of a different structure from any of the preceding. It is divided into as many sections, of eight verses each, as there are letters in the Hebrew alphabet; namely, twenty-two, — all the lines of the first section beginning with the first letter of it, Aleph; of the second with Beth; and so to the last in the order of the alphabet. From the structure and character of the psalm, it is generally supposed to have been written in the later period of the Jewish nation.

7. — *righteous laws.* The Hebrew term מִשְׁפָּט denotes sometimes *the law;* sometimes *the sentence* or *judgment* for or against; sometimes *the execution of the penalty, the bestowment of the reward.* In this psalm it is often difficult to decide which is meant.

19. *I am a stranger,* &c. As a stranger wandering in a foreign land feels the need of the guidance of friends, so man, a stranger in the earth, needs the guidance of God.

25. — *to the dust;* i.e., of death. (See the parallel line, and xxii. 15; vii. 5; xliv. 25.) — *thy word;* i.e., thy promise.

26. *I have declared my ways,* &c.; i.e., I have made known to thee my affairs, my purposes, my condition, and my dangers; and have sought thine aid.

27. — *thy wonders;* i.e., of thy love. (See ver. 18.)

32. — *enlarge my heart;* i.e., increase my intelligence (see 1 Kings iv. 29); or, grant me deliverance from trouble. (See Isa. lx. 5.)

42. — *him that reproacheth me;* i.e., on account of my reliance on thee.

43. — *take not the word of truth,* &c.; i.e., do not deal with me so that I shall be ashamed to mention thy word or thy promise, in which I have often gloried, respecting the deliverance which thou givest to the righteous, and the punishment which thou inflictest on the wicked.

54. — *have been my song;* i.e., the subject of my song or rejoicing. — *house of my pilgrimage.* This expression may refer to the exile in Babylon, or to human life in general.

56. — *as my own;* i.e., my peculiar happiness. (Comp. Rev. ii. 6.)

79. — *turn unto me;* i.e., unite themselves with me, and rejoice in my deliverance. (See ver. 74.)

83. — *a bottle in the smoke;* which, being made of skins, became shrivelled by smoke.

84. *How many are the days,* &c.; i.e., How short is my life.

89. — *like the heavens.* Comp. Jer. xxxi. 35, 36; Luke xxi. 33.

91. *They continue;* i.e., the heavens and the earth.

108. — *free-will offering,* &c.; i.e., my prayers which I freely offer.

118. — *their deceit is vain;* i.e., their deceitful plans shall be unsuccessful, and disappoint their expectations.

127. *Therefore;* i.e., because I am thy servant, ver. 125.

139. *My zeal consumeth me;* i.e., I burn with indignation.
142. — *everlasting righteousness;* i.e., never to be dispensed with, or made void.
148. — *anticipate the night-watches,* &c.; i.e., I am awake before the watchmen announce the night-watches, and need no warning from them.
175. — *thy judgments;* i.e., in my favor. (See ver. 149, 156, and the note on ver. 7.)

Ps. CXX.

It seems probable that this psalm was composed by one living in exile, though not in Mesech and Kedar; for these places were at an immense distance from each other. Mesech was a barbarous country in the North, between Iberia, Armenia, and Colchis; and Kedar was a district in Arabia. The terms are used figuratively to denote barbarous countries, as we should speak of living among Turks or Hottentots. For what may be said on the appellation, "*A psalm of steps,*" which is given to this and the fourteen following psalms, see p. 30.
3. — *what advantage,* &c. The sense of the verse is, that the deceitful tongue does not profit, but rather injures, him that employs it.
4. — *Like coals of the juniper;* which was thought by the ancients to have great heat, and to retain it long. (See Harris's Nat. Hist., p. 237, &c.) But there is great reason to doubt whether the juniper is the plant referred to in this passage. It is more probable that the broom is the plant denoted, the Arabic name of which, according to Dr. Robinson, is the same as the Hebrew, and the roots of which are regarded by the Arabs as yielding the best charcoal. (See Ges. Thesaur., on רֹתֶם, and Robinson's Biblical Researches in Palestine, vol. i. p. 299. I retain the term *juniper,* instead of *broom,* from rhetorical considerations. Ver. 3 and 4 may be rendered, *What will he* [God] *give to thee, and what will he do to thee, thou false tongue?* [He will give thee] *sharp arrows of the mighty man, with coals of the juniper.*

Ps. CXXI.

This psalm seems to have been composed by a poet who was exiled from Jerusalem, if not from Palestine. If written by David, it may refer to the time of the rebellion of Absalom.
1. — *to the hills;* i.e., of Palestine, on which God, as the king of Israel, was regarded as having his peculiar abode. (Comp. xiv. 7, cxxxiv. 3, cxxxv. 21; 1 Kings viii. 42–44.)
6. — *Nor the moon by night.* We have no evidence, except what is implied in this passage, that the Jews ascribed any noxious influences to the moon. Perhaps, therefore, the verse may mean nothing more than that no injury should be received by day or by night. It is not impossible, however, that injury received from passing the night in the open air may have been ascribed to the moon.

Ps. CXXII.

It is not probable that this psalm was written by David. (See ver. 3 and 5.)

3. — *joined together*; i.e., wholly built up, without vacant spaces.

Ps. CXXIV.

4. — *over our soul*; i.e., would have destroyed us.

Ps. CXXV.

It appears from ver. 3, that this psalm was composed at a time when Palestine was oppressed by foreign enemies, or in great danger from them.

3. — *the portion of the righteous*; i.e., the land of Israel. (See cv. 11.) — *Lest the righteous*, &c.; i.e., lest the Jews be tempted by idolatrous oppressors to renounce the worship and service of Jehovah.

5. — *their crooked ways*; i.e., of the heathen oppressors, or evil-doers, mentioned in the next line.

Ps. CXXVI.

1. — *that dream*; i.e., we could scarcely believe our senses, that so great and glorious an event had taken place.

4. — *Like streams in the South.* The streams in hot countries, especially in the southern deserts, dry up in the summer months, but return after the periodical rains. (See the note on Job vi. 15, &c.) The land of Palestine, deprived of its inhabitants during the captivity, might be compared to one of these deserts forsaken by its streams; and the return of the exiles in crowds to their native land might be compared to torrents of water returning in the season of rain.

5, 6. These verses are well paraphrased by Patrick: "Then this small handful of people, who are come to plant themselves here again, and have laid the foundation of the temple with a great mixture of sadness and tears (Ezra iii. 12), shall shout for joy to see so great an increase, and this pious work by their help brought unto perfection; just as we behold the poor husbandman, going to and fro with a little seed, which in a scarce year he throws with a heavy heart into the ground, returning again and again from the field with songs of joy in his mouth, when the harvest comes to reward his past labors with a plentiful crop of corn."

6. — *his seed*; Literally, *his seed-cast*; i.e., such a burden of seed as is fit to be *cast* or *scattered lengthwise.* In English, the idea is sufficiently expressed in *his seed.*

Ps. CXXVII.

1. — *build the house*, &c. There seems no good reason for referring this to the temple. The expression is rather proverbial, referring to houses in general.

2. — *bread of care;* i.e., earned by anxious labor. — *in sleep.* This is an hyperbolical expression to denote, that, what others aim to gain by wearisome efforts, God gives to the righteous without any such painstaking, as it were, while they sleep. (Comp. Matt. vi. 34.) Probably nothing more is expressed than the sentiment of ver. 1; namely, that without the blessing of God nothing prospers.

4. — *of young men.* In reference, not only to their vigor, but to their capacity to help their parents a long time.

5. — *speak with adversaries in the gate;* i.e., contend at law with them. Possibly, but not so much in accordance with usage: when they have something to say with their enemies in the way of fighting.

Ps. CXXVIII.

2. — *eat the labor;* i.e., the fruits of the labor, &c. Thou shalt not sow, and another reap. (Comp. Lev. xxvi. 16; Deut. xxviii. 33.)

3. — *fruitful vine.* The fruitfulness of the vine is the only point of comparison. — *within thy house;* where the customs of the East required the matron to be a great part of the time.

5. — *out of Zion,* &c. See the note on cx. 1.

Ps. CXXIX.

This psalm, which recounts the many past afflictions of the Jewish nation, and the deliverances which God had afforded it, and closes with imprecations against its enemies, was probably written soon after the return from the captivity.

2. — *from my youth;* i.e., from the time of the bondage in Egypt. (Comp. Hos. ii. 15, xi. 1.)

3. — *ploughed up,* &c. A figurative expression to denote stripes, and this to denote oppression in general.

4. — *cut asunder the cords;* i.e., delivered from servitude.

6. — *grass upon the housetops.* The roofs of the houses being flat and often covered with earth, grass would spring up on them, but would soon perish with the heat of the sun. (See Jahn's Archæol., § 34.)

8. — *The blessing,* &c. This appears to have been a usual salutation in time of harvest. (See Ruth ii. 4.)

Ps. CXXX.

This psalm appears to have been written by one who was suffering, in common with his countrymen, under the pressure of some great national calamity. No period seems more suitable for such a prayer than the time of the captivity.

3. — *treasure up,* &c.; i.e., in thy memory, for the purpose of strictly punishing them.

4. — *That thou mayst be feared.* Hope of mercy leads to the reverence and love of God. Despair would engage one for ever in a course of sin. Before the prodigal can return to his father, he must feel sure that he has a father to whom he can return.

8. — *From all his iniquities;* i.e., from the consequences, or punishment, of them.

Ps. CXXXI.

This psalm may have been composed by David, when he was accused of aiming to deprive Saul of his throne. On account of the accusations of Sanballat, it may have been used by the Jews after the captivity.

2. — *Like a weaned child;* i.e., I commit myself to thy care, acquiesce in my condition, and submit to be disposed of as thou pleasest, as a weaned child resting his head on his mother's breast.

Ps. CXXXII.

6. — *heard of it at Ephratah,* &c. *Ephratah* probably here denotes the country of Ephraim, in which was Shiloh, where the ark of God remained several years. *The fields of the forest* probably refer to Kirjath-jearim, where the ark was kept a long time. (See 1 Sam. vii. 1, 2.) The meaning, in connection with what follows, seems to be, that, having heard of the ark in different and distant places, and as removed from place to place, they might now rejoice that it had a settled abode.

15. — *bless her provision,* &c. To Zion, regarded as representing the nation, abundance and prosperity are promised.

16. — *clothe her priests with salvation;* i.e., cause them to give continual thanks for salvation granted to the people.

17. — *horn for David;* i.e., in his posterity. — *a light,* &c. This was an emblem of splendor and prosperity. (See xviii. 28; Job xxix. 3, and the note.)

Ps. CXXXIII.

2. — *precious perfume,* &c. (See the note on Eccl. vii. 1.) — *the border of his garments;* i.e., as seems probable, the upper border, which went round his neck.

3. *Like the dew of Hermon.* In a country where little or no rain falls, except at particular seasons, the dew is most grateful to the parched hills. It also descends in abundance. "We were sufficiently instructed by experience what the holy psalmist means by the dew of Hermon, our tents being as wet with it as if it had rained all night." — Maundrell's Journey, &c., p. 97, Amer. edition. — *life for evermore.* Here *life*, being parallel with blessings, signifies *prosperity, happiness.*

Ps. CXXXIV.

1. — *by night.* It was the duty of the priests and Levites to serve in the temple day and night. The service by night is mentioned in particular, as being more arduous. (Lev. viii. 35; 1 Chron. ix. 33.)

2. — *to the sanctuary.* See xxviii. 2.

Ps. CXXXV.

7. —*for the rain;* i.e., to accompany it.
13. —*memorial;* i.e., that by which God is brought to mind; namely, his perfections continually displayed in fresh deeds of omnipotence and love. (See Exod. iii. 15.)

Ps. CXXXVII.

This beautiful psalm was probably written very soon after the captivity in Babylon, while the memory of the sufferings and indignities connected with it was fresh in the mind of the author.
5. —*her cunning.* In this connection, skill in playing on the harp seems to be referred to. Otherwise, *Let my right hand forget me.*
6. —*my tongue cleave,* &c.; i.e., refuse its office in singing.
7. —*children of Edom;* who had shown great hostility to the Israelites, and joined with the Chaldæans in effecting the destruction of Jerusalem. (Comp. Ezek. xxv. 12; Obad. 10.) Respecting the imprecations in ver. 7–9, with which the patriotic can in some degree sympathize, but which the Christian can scarcely approve, see p. 9, &c.
8. —*thou destroyer!* I take שָׁדוּד to be a noun. (See De Dieu, in Poole's Synopsis.) Otherwise, *the desolated!* or, *who art to be destroyed!*

Ps. CXXXVIII.

This psalm is commonly supposed to refer to the circumstances of David, when, after the death of Saul, he was established on the throne. The term הֵיכָל, *temple* (ver. 2), seems to point to a later age than that of David.
1. —*Before the gods;* i.e., before the kings of the earth, or (see ver. 4) the angels of God; otherwise, *before God.*
2. —*thy promise above all thy name;* i.e., thou hast fulfilled thy promise, and more than fulfilled it; and hast done more than has ever been said or conceived of thee.
6. —*knoweth from afar;* i.e., takes cognizance of them for the purpose of punishment.
8. —*Forsake not the works of thine hands;* i.e., complete what thy hands have begun.

Ps. CXXXIX.

It appears, from ver. 19–24, that this admirable psalm, to attempt to set forth the excellence of which by descriptive epithets would be folly, was in some degree occasional. The author seems to have been led to the composition of it by false charges against the uprightness of his intentions, and the sincerity and purity of his course in respect to the worship and service of Jehovah. On account of the reference to idolatry, and certain Chaldaizing forms which occur in it, some critics refer the psalm to a later age than that of David.

4. *For before the word,* &c. So the Chaldee in Buxtorf's Bible. So Dr. Watts, —

"He knows the words I mean to speak,
Ere from my opening lips they break."

There is thus some expansion of the thought expressed in ver. 2 and 3. Otherwise, as in the common version, *For there is not a word,* &c.; i.e., thou knowest every word which I utter, as well as every act which I perform.

5. — *layest thine hand upon me;* i.e., hast me completely in thy power.

9. — *wings of the morning;* i.e., if I could move as swiftly as the rays of the morning sun, which in an instant go from one end of heaven to the other.

15. — *curiously wrought in the lower parts of the earth.* This language seems to amount to the same thing as that in ver. 13, *Thou didst weave me in my mother's womb;* i.e., in as dark a place as the lower parts of the earth. (See Ges. Lex. on סָכַךְ).

17. *How precious to me are thy thoughts;* i.e., How valuable in themselves, or how highly valued, precious in the contemplation, are thy purposes of wisdom and goodness, as displayed in the formation and care of man! It appears to me that De Wette and Gesenius unnecessarily depart from the common meaning of the term יָקַר, when they ascribe to it here the meaning *incomprehensible, inconceivable.*

18. — *When I awake, I am still with thee;* i.e., I am still engaged in meditating upon thee, and what thou hast done.

24. — *way of trouble,* &c. That עֹצֶב means *pain* or *trouble,* there can be no doubt. (See Isa. xiv. 3; 1 Chron. iv. 9; and Gen. iii. 16, without regard to the vowel-points.) That it may denote *sin,* or *idolatry,* cannot be proved. — *the way everlasting;* i.e., the way which does not end in trouble and ruin, as in Ps. i. 6. Or, *in the ancient way;* i.e., the good old way of the worship of Jehovah, sanctioned by the patriarchs Abraham, Isaac, and Jacob. (Comp. Jer. vi. 16.)

Ps. CXL.

This psalm is commonly supposed to have been composed by David in reference to the persecution of Saul and his courtiers.

3. — *sharpen their tongues like a serpent.* Perhaps there may be reference to the serpent's putting out his forked tongue, and moving it rapidly, so as to appear to sharpen it.

Ps. CXLI.

If this psalm was written by David, it may have had the same general occasion as the last. But it seems to contain no special allusions to the circumstances of David. It is most probable that the author and the occasion of the psalm are unknown.

4. — *eat of their delicacies;* i.e., associate with them at their sumptuous feasts, where their evil designs are discussed. Or, the expres-

sion may be a figurative one to denote participation in their cherished designs.

5. — *oil for my head;* as grateful as perfumed oil, which was poured on the head of guests. (See cxxxiii. 2, and the note. Comp. Prov. xxvii. 6; Eccl. vii. 5.) — *But now I pray against their wickedness;* i.e., but now, when I experience treatment the reverse of what is right and kind, I am impatient under it, and pray against my enemies who inflict it. (See Döderlein's Scholia ad loc.) The pronoun *their* refers to the enemies of the poet, whom he mentions in the next verse.

6. — *over the side of the rock;* according to an ancient mode of punishing malefactors. (See 2 Chron. xxv. 12.) — *Then let them hear my words,* &c. "But how," asks Rosenmüller, "could they hear his words, after being thrown from the rock?" But this question makes no allowance for the language of passionate emotion, which will not bear a strict analysis. St. Paul says that he delivered Hymeneus and Alexander to Satan, that they might learn not to blaspheme. An unpromising teacher! we might say, in the spirit of Rosenmüller's question. Besides, we suppose that the words, *let them hear,* refer to the survivors, the people warned by the fate of the judges or rulers.

7. *Our bones are scattered,* &c.; i.e., the bones of our countrymen, friends, or followers. This may be understood as a literal description of what had been done by the enemies of the writer, or as a metaphorical description of the low condition to which he and his followers were reduced.

Ps. CXLII.

According to the Hebrew inscription, this psalm was composed by David to express the feelings which he had while in the cave of Adullam (1 Sam. chap. xxii.), or in that of Engedi (1 Sam. chap. xxiv.). Some suppose this title to have been a conjecture of the person who placed it there, founded on ver. 7, *Bring me out of prison,* &c.

7. — *out of prison;* i.e., out of my distress.

Ps. CXLIII.

This psalm, if composed by David, may refer to his distress during his persecution by Saul, or during the rebellion of Absalom. This is one of the psalms which some Jewish and some modern critics suppose to be designed for the use of the whole people, personified as a single individual in distress. Without doubt, many of the psalms were designed for the use of the whole people of Israel, like Christian hymns for the use of a congregation. But whether there is a personification of the people in the psalms of complaint is very doubtful. Such a view needs more positive support than we find in those psalms.

3. — *in darkness;* i.e., in hopeless calamity. (See the next verse.)

Ps. CXLIV.

This psalm, if composed by David, seems to refer to a time when he was established on the throne, but was yet exposed to many dangers from his own rebellious subjects and from the Philistines and other foreign enemies. It contains so many verses borrowed from other psalms, that there is considerable plausibility in the conjecture of De Wette, that it was composed, or rather compiled, long after the age of David.

3. Comp. viii. 4.

5. Comp. xviii. 9.

6. Comp. xviii. 14.

7. Comp. xviii. 16.

12. — *Grown up in their youth.* It is somewhat doubtful, whether this line belongs to *sons* or to *plants*. The expression *in their youth*, in the Hebrew, is not applied to plants, but only to persons, and thus favors the former application. On the other hand, it may be said that the term *youth* may be used metaphorically. — *Hewn*, &c., probably elegantly sculptured, and possibly referring to *the Caryatides*, or columns representing female figures.

14. — *breaking in;* i.e., of enemies into the walls of our cities — *going out;* i.e., in flight, or into captivity; or, perhaps, sallying forth to attack an enemy.

Ps. CXLV.

This is another of the alphabetical psalms, constructed like the twenty-fifth and thirty-fourth. (See p. 47, &c.) The ancient Jews had so high an opinion of its excellence, that they used to say, that a man could not fail to be a child of the world to come, who would repeat this psalm three times every day.

1. — *the king;* i.e., the true king, the king of kings.

Ps. CXLVI.

This is a psalm of solemn praise to God, designed probably for public worship in the temple. It is a very ancient opinion, that it was composed after the return from the captivity, being ascribed in the Septuagint version to Haggai and Zechariah.

8. — *openeth the eyes of the blind.* This is probably a figurative expression, denoting that the Lord restores from distress to prosperity, when there are no hopes from human aid. (Comp. Isa. xxxv. 5; xlii. 7.)

9. — *he maketh crooked;* i.e., defeats their designs; prevents them from attaining the object at which they aim.

Ps. CXLVII.

This psalm appears, from ver. 2, in connection with 13 and 14, to have been composed after the return from the captivity.

3. — *the broken in heart;* an instance of which is his restoring those who were exiles at Babylon.

10. — *in the legs of a man;* i.e., not in infantry more than in cavalry He needs neither the one nor the other. Otherwise, *legs of a man* may denote swiftness of foot, which was considered a great accomplishment in an ancient warrior.

15. — *His word runneth very swiftly;* i.e., that which he commands is speedily effected.

18. *He sendeth forth his word;* i.e., gives command.

Ps. CXLVIII.

1. —*from the heavens;* i.e., ye angels who are from the heavens, in contradistinction from things on the earth, ver. 7. — *in the heights;* i.e., the heavens.

2. — *all ye his hosts;* i.e., of angels. (Comp. 1 Kings xxii. 19.)

4. — *Ye waters,* &c. Comp. civ. 3; Gen. i. 7.

9. — *all cedars;* which are mentioned in particular as representing all wild trees.

14. — *near to him.* Comp. Deut. iv. 7.

Ps. CXLIX.

This psalm contains no indications of the time when it was composed. The conjecture of Theodoret, that it was written after the return from the captivity, when the nation was established, and had obtained considerable success over their enemies, seems to be as plausible as any.

1. — *a new song.* The epithet *new* seems to denote nothing more than that the psalm had not been before sung, implying, perhaps, that there was new occasion to sing the praise of God.

2. — *in him that made him;* i.e., as a nation. (Comp. Deut. xxxiii. 6

4. — *with salvation;* i.e., deliverance from their enemies, or victory over them. The *distressed* probably denote here the people of Israel, mentioned in the parallel line.

5. — *in their glory;* i.e., the glorious condition in which God, their king, has placed them.

6. — *a two-edged sword,* &c. Comp. ii., cx., &c.; Neh. iv. 13, &c.

9. — *which is written.* This may refer to the command given to the Israelites to destroy the nations of Palestine, in Deut. chap. vii., or, more probably, to what is written in the book of the Divine Mind, and referred to in ii., cx., &c. (Comp. lvi. 8; cxxxix. 16; Jude, ver. 4; Rev. xiii. 8; xx. 15.)

Ps. CL.

It may be supposed that the first and last lines of this psalm were sung by the whole company of singers, and that the other lines were sung responsively by different portions of it.

1. — *in his sanctuary;* i.e., in the temple. — *in his glorious firmament;* i.e., in heaven, referring to the angels.

5. — *cymbals,* &c. For what information may be had respecting the musical instruments of the Hebrews, see Pfeiffer on the Music of the Ancient Hebrews, translated in the Biblical Repository for October, 1835; Jahn's Archæology, § 92–96.

NOTES ON THE PROVERBS.

CHAP. I.

1–6. These verses seem to be designed as a preface, pointing out the object and use of the Book of Proverbs.

2. — *wisdom* — *instruction*. It is impossible to give to these and similar terms a precise definition, which shall apply to all cases in which they are used. For their meaning is more or less extensive and general, according to the connection in which they stand. It may be said, however, that the term rendered *wisdom*, in its most common use in this book, denotes a general knowledge of all those subjects, divine and human, which ought to engage the mind of man; and especially that which may be applied to the conduct of life. It has so extensive a signification, however, as to denote the attributes of God manifested in the creation of the world. The term rendered *instruction* more commonly denotes that knowledge or education which relates to morals and manners; but the particular meaning and application of both these terms can be learned only from the context in the passages in which they occur. The same remark applies to the terms *understanding*, *knowledge*, and some others, which are sometimes interchanged with the terms above mentioned. Especially, the connection must show when any of these terms relate to religious subjects, when to moral conduct, and when to knowledge in general. — *words of understanding;* i.e., which come from the intelligent, and tend to make the hearer intelligent.

3. — *instruction of prudence;* i.e., such instruction as tends to make one prudent. — *justice, equity, uprightness.* These terms denote the same thing, and are heaped together in order to give weight to the sentiment.

4. — *to the simple;* i.e., to him who, by reason of inexperience, is liable to be imposed upon. We have an illustration of the kind of simplicity referred to in this proverb in the term *young man*, in the parallel line.

5. *The wise man*, &c. The maxims in this book are designed not only for the inexperienced and ignorant: he that is wise already will not lose his labor in reading it, but will become still wiser.

6. — *deep maxim* — *dark sayings;* i.e., such pointed, concise, figurative, or enigmatical sentences and maxims as are contained in the Book of Proverbs. The Hebrew term מְלִיצָה seems here to denote,

not *an interpretation*, but *a thing to be interpreted*, i.e., *a deep maxim*. The Septuagint has σκοτεινὸν λόγον. Hodgson renders the term *a mystery*.

7. *The fear of the Lord.* This expression, according to Scripture usage, evidently has no exclusive reference to the emotion of fear, but to all those sentiments which man ought to entertain towards God. — *beginning of knowledge.* The Hebrew term sometimes denotes the first of its kind, the most excellent part. Hence, the line may be rendered, "The fear of the Lord is the perfection of knowledge;" and so some critics have rendered it: but as in chap. ix. 10 a different Hebrew word is used, which must be rendered *beginning*, I prefer to understand the line as conveying the idea, that religion is the beginning or foundation of all valuable knowledge, without which men remain ignorant and foolish, however great their attainments in merely human knowledge. The religious man only will become wise. — *Fools;* i.e., impious fools. The idea of impiety was often associated with the Hebrew term.

8. *Hear.* This expression implies attention and obedience. It is the opposite of *neglect*, in the parallel line. — *O my son!* The Hebrews and other Orientals addressed their pupils, hearers, or readers, by the endearing appellation of *son.* The terms *dear reader, friend,* &c., in some modern books, correspond to it.

9. — *graceful wreath* — *a chain,* &c.; i.e., they shall, being followed, add more to thy beauty, and win more approbation and favor for thee from God and good men, than any ornaments which thy parents can place upon thy head or around thy neck.

11. — *innocent in vain;* i.e., to whom innocence is no protection.

12. *Let us swallow them up alive,* &c.; let us inflict sudden and unexpected destruction upon them, as surely as Sheol devours the unresisting dead.

14. — *thy lot;* i.e., though thou art young, thou shalt have an equal share in the plunder with us veterans of the trade. Thou shalt draw lots with us, whenever we determine, by casting lots, to whom any portion of the plunder we have gained shall belong. (See Ps. xxii. 18.) — *one purse;* containing the money we obtain, of which all shall have a right to the same share.

17. *For as the net is spread in vain.* Comparing vii. 23, the meaning may be, that it is spread in vain to the silly bird which sees the net, and does not take warning from it; and that the exhortation is, not to be so headstrong and incautious as the silly birds, who use to run into the net, although they see the fowler laying it before their eyes. Some, however, refer the words *in vain* to the fowler, and suppose the meaning to be, that the fowler loses his labor who sets his net while the bird is looking on, because the bird, perceiving the danger, will not come to the bait, but rather fly away; and that those who are not warned by the evil consequences of wickedness, which the writer sets forth, are even sillier than the birds. While plotting destruction for others, they are blind to the retribution which is sure to fall upon themselves.

19. *It taketh away the life,* &c.; i.e., it brings sudden and violent death upon those who have gained possession of it.

20. In opposition to the enticements of the wicked, wisdom is now

personified as a teacher, preaching to the sons of men. It is evident from this description, as well as from chap. viii. and ix., that a practical regard to God and duty, as well as a speculative knowledge of divine and human things, is included in the author's idea of wisdom. The circumstance, that wisdom, personified as a teacher, is represented as proclaiming her lessons in the streets, highways, &c., is supposed by some to denote, that in active life only is that rich fountain of experience from which wisdom is derived. But it may be doubted whether this particular idea was in the author's mind. I rather suppose, that, having personified wisdom as a teacher, he represents her as giving her lessons where it was customary for teachers and philosophers in ancient times to give their lessons. If the language implies any thing more, it is, that the lessons of wisdom are within the reach of all, presenting urgent claims to their attention. Bishop Patrick paraphrases ver. 20 thus: "Let me advise you, therefore, rather to hearken to the manifold instructions of wisdom, whose most excellent counsels you cannot but be as well acquainted withal as you are with that which is proclaimed in the open streets; for you hear them in the plain dictates of your own consciences, in the laws of God, in the mouth of his prophets and ministers, in the admonitions and examples of good men, and in the course of his providence and wise government, which call upon you more earnestly and loudly than these seducers to follow and obey them."

22. — *simple ones* — *simplicity* — *scoffers* — *fools.* If by these different terms the author refers to different classes of persons, — which may be doubted, — the first class may denote the wicked through inexperience, weakness, and credulity; the second, open scoffers at religion and virtue; the third, hardened, irreligious, and vicious men, who are yet self-satisfied, and regard themselves as wiser than persons of an opposite character.

23. — *pour out.* The mouth of wisdom is represented as a fountain copiously pouring forth its streams. — *my spirit;* i.e., my mind.

24. — *stretched out my hand.* It is more agreeable to usage to understand this as a beckoning gesture, inviting the hearer to come, than as one designed to enforce the language of the speaker, or to offer assistance. (See Isa. xiii. 2, and lxv. 2.)

28. — *early;* literally, in the morning; i.e., with great earnestness and diligence; as those who rise early in the morning for any object are in earnest about it. The meaning of the whole verse is, that the despisers of wisdom will not be able to escape from the calamity in which they are involved.

31. — *eat of the fruit,* &c. "Therefore, as it is just that men should reap what they sow, and eat such fruit as they plant, so these men shall suffer the punishments which their wicked doings naturally produce; nay, be glutted and surfeited with the miserable effects of their own counsels and contrivances." — Patrick.

32. — *the turning away of the simple;* i.e., from duty and wisdom. "For let them alone, and they need nobody but themselves to destroy them; their escaping dangers only making them more audacious to run into them." — Patrick.

Chap. II.

3. — *if thou wilt call aloud*, &c.; i.e., if thou wilt, as it were, give her a strong and pressing invitation to come and take possession of thy soul.

5. *Then shalt thou understand*, &c. In chap. i. 7, he represents religion as the condition of attaining true wisdom. Here he represents religion as the effect of a sincere and earnest search after wisdom.

6. *For the Lord giveth wisdom*. And let no one doubt that he will find true wisdom, if he seek for it in the right way; for God gives it to such as diligently seek for it. (Comp. Job xxxii. 8, xxxviii. 36; Dan. ii. 21; James i. 5, 17.)

9. *Then shalt thou understand*, &c. This verse is connected in sense with ver. 5; ver. 6–8 being parenthetic.

10. — *wisdom entereth — knowledge is pleasant*, &c. The language in this verse seems to be borrowed from the entertainment of guests. Wisdom then enters the heart, as her habitation, and is pleasant to one; i.e., is cherished by him as his dearest friend, when it is not merely speculative, but a living, practical principle.

16. — *wife of another;* i.e., the adulteress, who is here not a foreigner (comp. ver. 17). It is commonly said that the adulteress is called *a strange woman*, because that class of people were usually women of foreign origin. It is probable, however, that the term itself often denotes simply one of a strange family, one not belonging to the family of the tempted person.

17. — *friend of her youth;* i.e., the husband to whom she was united when young. — *covenant of her God;* i.e., the marriage covenant, in contracting which, God was called to witness by the parties. (Comp. Mal. ii. 14.)

18. — *shades of the dead*. רְפָאִים, literally, *the weak;* the shades or ghosts of the dead, which the ancient Hebrews represented as dwelling together in Sheol, destitute of blood and animal life, and therefore weak and languid, like a sick person (Isa. xiv. 10), but yet having some faculties, such as perception and memory.

19. — *return again; — paths of life*. The image of the preceding verse seems to be continued; and the representation is, that it is as difficult for one who has become intimate with an adulteress to recover from the moral and temporal ruin in which he involves himself, as it is for one who has gone down to the place of the dead to return to the land of the living.

21. — *dwell in the land*. To dwell till death in the land of Israel, the glory of all lands, the land of many promises, and not to be driven from it into a foreign country, was considered an inestimable blessing by every true Hebrew. Hence, it was used as an image of the highest good. It is often difficult, as in this passage, to decide whether the expression is to be understood in a literal or a figurative sense. In Matt. v. 5, occurs the figurative use of the expression.

Chap. III.

2. — *peace;* i.e., prosperity, satisfaction, that which is the object of every one's desire and pursuit, and that which he wishes for his friend.

3. — *kindness and truth.* On account of the latter clause of the verse, I understand these words as denoting the duties of humanity, sincerity, and justice in man. Others, on account of the use of the terms in other passages to denote the favor of God, and his faithfulness to his promises, understand them in the same sense here; and suppose the pronoun *them,* in the next line, to refer back to *precepts* in ver. 1. — *around thy neck;* i.e., let them never be forgotten or neglected, as you cannot fail to see and care for the ornamental chains which you wear around your neck.

5. — *lean not,* &c.; as one leans upon a staff. The precept in this line is limited and explained by the preceding parallel line. It is, that no one should trust to gain the ends which he seeks, or to obtain happiness, by his own sagacity and wisdom, without the Divine blessing; that the favor of God is more essential to a happy life than any labored plans which the human understanding can devise.

8. — *thy muscles;* which, with the bones mentioned in the next line, were meant to denote the whole body. — *moisture to thy bones;* the bones being supposed to be dried up in sickness. (See xvii. 22; Job xxi. 24; Ps. cii. 3.)

9. *Honor the Lord,* &c.; i.e., obey the directions of the law by bringing thy oblations to the house of God, and offering the first-fruits of the harvest and the vintage, in token of thy gratitude and dependence.

18. — *tree of life;* i.e., a tree, the fruits of which lengthen life. It is also probable that the expression has reference to the tree of life in paradise (Gen. ii. 9, iii. 22), here used as the emblem of constant and durable happiness.

20. — *deep waters were cleft;* i.e., separated into two masses, one above and the other beneath the firmament, according to the account in Gen. i. 6, 7. With the mass of waters above the firmament were supposed to be connected the clouds which drop down the dew.

22. — *life to thy soul;* i.e., these precepts, being observed, will give thee animation, cheerfulness, and vigor, when other things fail thee. — *grace to thy neck;* i.e., they shall be ornamental to thee, and secure thee favor and admiration more than the neck-chain which is worn to adorn the body. (Comp. i. 9.)

25. — *storm;* the same word which is used in chap. i. 27.

34. — *treateth scornfully.* I suppose this means simply, that God will punish the *scorners,* without reference to any particular mode of punishment. So, in the New Testament, we read, "If any man corrupt the temple of God, God will corrupt him;" as it stands in the original. (1 Cor. iii. 17.) The particular expressions used, having reference to the sin which is punished, are merely for strength and emphasis. A similar use of threatening language is very common in conversation.

35. — *bear off;* i.e., they shall take it up, and bear it off, as their portion. Otherwise, *shame shall bear off fools;* i.e., sweep them away like chaff.

CHAP. IV.

1. — *of a father.* See the note on i. 8.

4. — *and live.* An emphatic expression, and sufficiently agreeable to the English as well as the Hebrew idiom, for "thou shalt live," i.e., live happily.

7. — *principal thing;* i.e., the most excellent of all possessions.

9. See the note on i. 9.

12. — *goest,* — *runnest;* "if thy actions and designs have no other rule, thou shalt be at ease, and free from those straits and difficulties which others meet withal; and, in case thy business shall require haste, this will be the safest, as well as the most inoffensive (if not the shortest), way to accomplish thy ends."

13. — *thy life;* i.e., thy most precious treasure, — that upon which all happiness depends.

16. — *caused some to fall;* i.e., to stumble and fall over the stumbling-blocks set in their path. The expression in this verse may denote that the wicked rest not till they have brought some one to ruin by plunder, &c.; or till they have seduced some one to become a partaker of their wickedness. The former meaning seems to be most favored by the connection.

17. — *bread of wickedness,* — *wine of violence;* i.e., obtained by dishonesty and rapine, and not by honest labors. Others understand the verse as denoting, that it is very agreeable to the wicked, like bread and wine to them, to do mischief.

18. — *light of dawn;* i.e., it is full of brightness and joy. Their way shines to themselves, in the joy and comfort of it; before others, in the lustre and honor of it. It is a growing light: it shines more and more, not like the light of a meteor, which soon disappears, or that of a candle, which burns dim and burns down; but like that of the dawn, which is soon followed by that of the rising sun, which will arrive, in the end, at the perfect day. The light of the dayspring will at length be noonday light, and it is this to which the righteous are pressing forward.

19. — *at what they stumble;* i.e., like travellers in a dark and dangerous road, they are in constant danger of falling into ruin.

21. — *in the midst of thy heart;* i.e., as a most precious treasure, which is kept, not in an outer apartment, but in the innermost recesses of the house.

22. — *health;* more literally, healing.

23. *For from it goeth forth life.* I understand this line to mean, that as natural life, man's most precious possession, depends upon the heart, so his true happiness, his well-being, depends upon a well-regulated mind and well-regulated affections. (See ver. 13.)

25. *Let thine eyes look straight forward.* The phraseology of this verse is borrowed from a traveller who keeps fixed in the direction of the road, and does not allow his eyes to wander on one side and the other, lest by so doing he should stumble over a stone, or fall into a hole. The precept points out the necessity of being on our guard against the seductions of the wicked, of directing all our actions by a good intention to a right end, and of not allowing the mind to be diverted from it by any temptations.

26. — *be steadfast;* i.e., not turning, now in one direction, now in another. The thought is expressed more clearly in the next verse

Chap. V.

2. — *lips may preserve knowledge;* i.e., not only lay up wisdom for thyself, but be ready to impart it, as thou shalt have opportunity.
4. *But her end is*, &c.; i.e., the end to which she leads her victims.
5. — *the underworld.* The meaning is, that the harlot, quickly and surely, leads those who follow her to death.
6. — *ponder the way of life;* and so turn to it from the way to Sheol. Her paths are unsteady and vacillating, while she is unconscious of it; i.e., she is so absorbed and bewildered in her vacillating course of life, that she fails to ponder the path of safety and happiness.
9. — *thy bloom;* i.e., the beauty and strength of thy body. — *thy years;* i.e., thy life. — *others*, &c. The plural may be used as referring, not only to the harlot, but to her base attendants and children. — *a cruel one.* This may refer to a cruel master to whom he might be sold for the crime of adultery.
11. — *thy flesh and thy body are consumed;* i.e., well-nigh consumed; when thou art reduced to a mere skeleton.
14. *In the midst of the congregation*, &c.; i.e., so as to be a public example and a shameful spectacle to all men. Some suppose that the line has reference to condemnation for adultery in court, or to stoning in the midst of a multitude.
15. *Drink water*, &c.; i.e., be faithful to thine own marriage bed. Similar images occur in Num. xxiv. 7; Ps. lxviii. 26; Cant. iv. 12; Isa. xlviii. 1; Hos. xiii. 15; Sirach xxvi. 12.
16. — *thy fountains*, &c.; i.e., thy children which shall be numerous. (Comp. Num. xxiv. 7; Isa. xlviii. 1.) I see no sufficient reason for altering the Hebrew text by conjecture, so as to make another meaning, by the insertion of a negative, according to a few manuscripts of the Septuagint.
17. — *thee alone;* i.e., thou mayst be confident that the children of your wife are truly yours; whereas the children of harlots are of uncertain paternity. (Comp. Sirach xxvi. 19–21.)
18. — *thy fountain;* i.e., thy wife. — *shall be blessed;* i.e., have a numerous offspring. (Comp. Ps. cxxviii. 3.)
19. *A lovely hind, a graceful doe.* The Arabs have the proverbial expression, "More beautiful than the ibex, or mountain-goat." (See Bochart, tom. ii. p. 899.) It appears also from Bochart, that the ibex was domesticated for amusement, as a lovely creature which they delighted to adorn with chains, garlands, &c. Roberts, ad loc., says, "The hind is celebrated for affection to her mate; hence, in the East, a man, in speaking of his wife, often calls her by that name." (Comp. Cant. ii. 9, &c.)
21. — *the eyes*, &c. The most secret sins, such as that condemned in this chapter, are known to God, as well as the most public transgressions.
22. — *ensnare* — *cords*, &c. The image is borrowed from the condition of a wild beast or bird, caught in the nets of the hunter. The inevitable miseries or punishment of transgression are set forth. It brings a man into captivity to misery.

CHAP. VI.

1. — *stricken hands.* This expression denotes the same thing as the expression *become a surety*, in the parallel line. If, by giving thy hand to a creditor in presence of the debtor, thou hast become responsible for the debt of the latter.

2. — *ensnared.* Comp. ver. 5.

3. — *fallen into the hands*, &c. This may denote that the surety has placed himself at the mercy of the debtor, who, by neglect or misfortune, may expose him to the payment of the debt; or at the mercy of the creditor. From what follows, the first seems the more probable explanation. — *prostrate thyself*, &c.; i.e., earnestly entreat the debtor, for whom you have become bound, to pay the debt, and thus release you from the obligation which you have assumed.

5. — *as a roe.* The comparison may refer to the anxiety and the efforts of the roe or gazelle to extricate itself, or to the speed with which it runs away. The fleetness of the animal is proverbial in the countries which it inhabits. (See Robinson's Calmet, art. *Antelope.*)

7. — *overseer*, &c. The diligence of the ant is the more remarkable, as it has no overseer to exact its labor. It is worth mentioning, that Aristotle, having spoken of cranes, bees, and ants as living in a political state, says that the two former lived under a ruler, the latter not.

8. — *in the summer her food;* as a provision for winter. The illustration is borrowed from what was a universal notion in ancient times respecting the ant. But the ant is now supposed to pass the winter, in cold climates, in a torpid state.

10. *A little sleep*, &c. This verse is to be regarded as the expostulation of the sluggard, when called upon to leave his bed.

11. — *like a robber;* i.e., swiftly, unexpectedly, irresistibly. (Comp. ver. 15.)

12. *A worthless wretch;* literally, a man of Belial. An expression denoting mingled abhorrence and contempt; the most reproachful epithet which one Hebrew could apply to another.

13. — *winketh with his eyes;* who intimates, by signs with the eyes, hands, or feet, the base designs which he is afraid or ashamed to express in plain words, or which he wishes to conceal from persons who are present. — *Speaketh with his feet, — teacheth with his fingers.* Roberts, in his Illustrations (p. 366), observes, "When the Easterns are in their houses, they wear no sandals, so their feet and toes are exposed. When guests wish to speak with each other so as not to be observed by the host, they convey their meaning by the feet and toes. Does a person wish to leave a room with another, he lifts up one of his feet; and, should the other refuse, he also lifts up a foot, and then suddenly puts it down on the ground." — "When merchants wish to bargain in presence of others without making known their terms, they sit on the ground, have a piece of cloth thrown over the lap, and then put each a hand under, and thus speak with their fingers. When the Brahmins convey religious mysteries to their disciples, they teach with their fingers, having the hands concealed in the folds of their robes."

16. — *six* — *seven*. This mode of enumeration is found in other parts of the Old Testament, as also in the sententious compositions of the Arabs and Persians. (See Ros. ad loc. Comp. xxx. 18, 29; Job v. 19; Eccl. xi. 2.)

17. *Lofty eyes;* i.e., pride, haughtiness.

21. — *around thy neck*. See i. 9, iii. 3, and the note.

22. — *they shall guide;* i.e., the commandment and the precepts, ver. 20.

23. — *to life;* i.e., to true, solid, lasting happiness; so misery is expressed by the term *death*.

25. — *catch thee*, &c.; i.e., suffer not thyself to be caught in the nets of her wanton eyes. Perhaps the eyelids in particular are mentioned, because it was the custom in the East to paint them. (See note on Jer. iv. 30.)

26. — *precious life;* i.e., shortens life by starvation, in reference to the parallel line; or by the jealousy of the husband (see 33–35), or in some other way.

30. — *overlook;* i.e., do not let him go unpunished, though he may plead an excuse, which the adulterer cannot. The thief had no food, and stole some; the adulterer had a wife, or might have had, and yet corrupted his neighbor's wife.

35. — *content;* to remit the penalty of death. (See Lev. xx. 10.)

Chap. VII.

3. — *upon thy fingers;* like a ring, which is not out of sight, and which is kept with the utmost care.

4. *Say unto wisdom*, &c.; be as well acquainted, as familiar, with wisdom as with a beloved sister. (Comp. Job xvii. 14.)

8. — *her corner*. The expression here probably denotes the house of the harlot, as is suggested by the parallel line; and not merely her temporary station, as in ver. 12.

11. — *unruly*. The term is applied in Hos. iv. 16 to an untamed heifer.

14. — *have been upon me;* i.e., a vow to pay them has been upon me. These thank-offerings, or peace-offerings, consisted of oxen, sheep, or goats, which were offered in acknowledgment of some blessings received. Considerable portions of these victims used to be returned by the priests to those who offered them, and afforded materials for a feast, to which they used to invite their neighbors and friends.

17. — *sprinkled*, &c.; i.e., with the liquid extract of the spices mentioned.

22. — *as one in fetters to the chastisement of the fool*. "One in fetters" corresponds to the ox in the parallel line, and denotes the unresisting spirit and the forgetfulness, or disregard of consequences, with which the young man follows the allurements of forbidden pleasure. Otherwise, *as fetters*, &c. For a defence of the version which I have adopted, I refer to Buxtorf's Lexicon, or Gesenius's Thesaurus, on the term עֶכֶס.

Chap. VIII.

1. — *wisdom.* It is difficult to conceive that any one who attends to what is said of wisdom in the Book of Proverbs, and compares this chapter with chap. i. 20, &c., iii. 13, 20, and ix. 1–6, should fail to perceive that the author personifies the attribute of wisdom; that he represents wisdom as a female and a queen, dispensing her rewards to those who gain her acquaintance, and the assistant of the Almighty in the creation of the world. Respecting the theory, that the author describes a real person, the Messiah, or Jesus Christ, it is sufficient to say, that there is no proof of it, either in this book or in any part of the Old or New Testament; and of course it devolves upon those who maintain that any thing more than the attribute of wisdom is described to prove it. For what the author professes to describe is *wisdom.* (Comp. Job xxviii. 25–28.) Adam Clarke remarks on this verse: — "Here wisdom is again personified; but the prosopopœia is carried on to a greater length than before, and with much more variety. It is represented in this chapter in a twofold point of view: 1. Wisdom, the power of judging rightly, implying the knowledge of divine and human things. 2. As an attribute of God, particularly displayed in the various and astonishing works of creation. Nor has it any other meaning in this whole chapter, whatever some of the Fathers may have dreamed, who find allegorical meanings everywhere."

2. — *top of the high places;* where heralds often made their proclamations. (Comp. Luke xii. 3.)

9. — *to the man of understanding;* i.e., who does not, like a fool, despise instruction.

12. — *dwell with prudence;* i.e., between wisdom and prudence there is an intimate union. Those who have wisdom will have sound discretion in the conduct of life.

13. In connection with the discourse in praise of wisdom, this verse seems to mean, that with true wisdom is connected that fear of God which leads to holiness of life; in other words, that the wise man will manifest his religion in his life. (Comp. 1 John iv. 20.)

14. *Counsel;* the capacity of managing difficult affairs, and bringing them to a successful issue. — *I have strength.* So Eccl. vii. 19, "Wisdom strengthens the wise more than ten mighty men," &c.

15. — *kings reign;* i.e., the thrones of kings can be securely established, and the regal duties successfully discharged, only upon the principles of true wisdom.

17. *I love them,* &c. The lovers and seekers of wisdom shall attain it, and the blessings which it confers.

18. — *are with me;* i.e., in order to be bestowed upon those who seek and find me. (Comp. iii. 16.)

22. — *created me,* &c. *Created,* or *formed,* is the primary meaning of the verb קָנָה. (See Gesenius's Thesaurus.) It is so translated by the Septuagint, Chaldee, and old Syriac versions. Thus also in Gen. xiv. 19, "The most high God, who made heaven and earth," the same word is used. So also in Deut. xxxii. 6, "Is he not thy father, that created thee?" So Ps. cxxxix. 13, "Thou hast created my reins."

The meaning *created*, or *formed*, seems also to be confirmed by ver. 25, "Before the hills, *I was brought forth*." (See also the Son of Sirach, chap. xxiv. 9.) At the time when *wisdom*, in this passage, was regarded as a real person, and not a mere rhetorical personification of an attribute, there was a controversy between the Arians and Athanasians, whether the term in question should be rendered *created* or *possessed*. Some of the latter contended, that ἔκτισε was a corrupt reading of the Septuagint for ἐκτήσατο; and some, that the passage related to the human nature of Christ. Since the true view has prevailed, that wisdom is only personified, the rendering *created*, or *formed*, has been regarded as more agreeable to the connection. — *the firstling of his way*; i.e., the first production of his operating, creative energy; i.e., when Jehovah *went forth*, or *proceeded*, to create the world, when he commenced his *way*, *course*, or *process* of creation, I was his first production. He caused me to proceed from himself to be his assistant in producing a well-ordered world out of chaos. In Job xxvi. 14, xl. 19, the term דֶּרֶךְ, *way*, in the plural, denotes *the works* of God. The term *first* has reference to time chiefly, but has connected with it the idea of superiority or excellence. It is the same term which is used in Gen. xlix. 3, "Reuben, thou art my first-born, the firstling of my strength." It is also the term which is applied to the *first-fruits* offered in the temple (Lev. ii. 12, xxiii. 10; Deut. xviii. 4, xxvi. 10). The term is also used to denote *the chief* of its kind, dropping the idea of priority in time. Thus, the river-horse is called *the chief* of the works (literally, *ways*) of God. As to the plain, literal meaning of the verse, and of the following passage, it is simply that wisdom was exercised, or put forth, as the antecedent condition of the production of the world, or that the world was made by the wisdom of God, as in Jer. li. 15, "He established the world by his wisdom, and by his understanding he spread out the heavens." (So Prov. iii. 19; Ps. civ. 24; Job xxviii. 25–28.) God's *putting forth* of wisdom being regarded as antecedent in time to the actual creation of the visible world, the author, who had previously represented wisdom as having length of days in her right hand, and in her left hand riches and honor, here, by a bold figure, personifies wisdom as being formed to be the assistant, counsellor, and, as it were, architect of the Deity, in the formation of the world out of chaos. This bold personification is perfectly agreeable to the genius of the Hebrew poets, who represent Zion as "stretching out her hands, having none to comfort her;" the inanimate ways which lead to the temple, as "mourning because none came to the solemn feasts," and the trees of the field as "clapping their hands," in token of joy when the ransomed of Jehovah returned to Zion. (See the note on ver. 1.) The design of the author is to give the very highest praise of wisdom, by representing it as not confined to common affairs, not even to the office of kings, and as not being of modern or human origin; but that it was older than the creation, and that without its aid the Almighty formed no part of his works. The eulogies upon law by Cicero and Hooker proceeded from a similar train of thought. See Cicero de Legibus, lib. ii. cap. 4, and Hooker's Ecclesiastical Polity, at the end of book 1, where we read, "Of law there can be no less acknowledged than that her seat is the bosom of God, her voice the harmony of the world: all things in heaven and earth do her homage, the very least as feeling her care, and the greatest as not exempted from her power; both angels and men, and creatures of what condition soever, though each in different sort and manner, yet all with uniform consent, admiring her as the mother of their peace and joy." The writer's idea of the *creation* of wisdom belongs merely to the rhetorical personification of it. Before we can conceive of wisdom as waiting upon the Deity as a person, we must suppose her created. But the simple idea on which the personification was founded is, that the exercise of wisdom by God preceded the creation of the world, as the condition of its order and beauty.

23. — *anointed.* Wisdom is the most ancient queen in the world. God himself anointed her as such, before the origin of the visible world.

27. — *drew a circle,* &c.; i.e., by causing the apparently concave surface of the sky to form a curved boundary to the waters which surrounded the earth, according to the opinion of the ancients. (Comp. Job xxvi. 10.)

29. — *border;* i.e., the shore of the sea. — *foundations.* The earth is here represented as a house or building having foundations, &c.

30. — *as a master-builder.* This meaning of the term אָמוֹן, I regard as, on the whole, better supported by usage (comp. Cant. vii. 2), and by the scope and connection of the passage, than the meaning *foster-child,* which is preferred by some critics. The termination of the Hebrew term is masculine, for which an obvious reason may be given, if it denotes *an artist* or *architect,* and none if it denote *a foster child.* It appears most consistent with the general design of the passage, or with what we must suppose to be its literal meaning, to understand wisdom to be represented as the counsellor, as it were, the architect of the Deity, in the formation and furnishing of the world. As to the term *exult,* which, according to a more literal translation would be *play, sport,* or *dance,* which is thought to be more favorable to the rendering *foster-child,* I suppose it refers to the exultation of wisdom in the abundant and, as it were, lavish manifestation of her skill, and the ease with which she exercised it; perhaps it may even refer to the pleasure with which the Deity is represented as looking upon the work of each day of creation. "And God saw that it was good." In the Book of Job, to denote the terrible nature of the crocodile, it is said, "In his neck dwells strength, and terror dances before him." The rendering *master-builder,* or *architect,* is favored by the Septuagint and Vulgate, *ἁρμόζουσα,* cuncta *componens.* Luther also renders the term *werkmeister, master-workman.*

31. *Exulting,* &c. This verse is well paraphrased by Patrick. "More particularly I displayed my skill in the vast variety of creatures wherewith I have beautified this earth wherein you dwell, which afford a most delightful spectacle unto me and unto all wise observers, who may see, that, above all the rest, my principal thoughts were fixed upon the children of men (Gen. i. 26), in whom I delighted exceedingly, beholding them made in the image of God and after his likeness, capable to converse with me."

34. — *watcheth day by day at my gates.* I suppose the language to be

borrowed from the practice of those persons in the East who waited at the doors of rulers or persons of eminence, in order to be admitted to their presence, or to speak to them as they came out, and thus gain the favors which they had in view. Others suppose the language to be borrowed from the case of a lover, waiting at the door of his mistress; or of scholars at the door of a school.

35. — *findeth life;* i.e., the greatest blessing, true happiness.

36. — *love death;* i.e., behave as though they courted their own destruction.

Chap. IX.

1. — *builded her house.* By a personification somewhat different from the preceding, wisdom is represented as a queen, having built a splendid palace, and prepared a rich feast, to which she invites the sons of men, who will receive no less life, vigor, strength, and joy from her instructions than the body does, when it partakes of a liberal and most delicious feast. — *seven pillars.* *Seven* was regarded as the full, perfect, and sacred number, not only by the Hebrews, but by the Arabians and Persians.

2. — *mingled her wine;* i.e., either with spices, to make it strong and well flavored, as in chap. xxiii. 30; or with water, to make it more refreshing and wholesome.

3. — *maidens.* Wisdom being represented as a female, of course her attendants are maidens. — *She crieth aloud;* i.e., by means of her messengers.

7. — *shame;* — *a stain;* i.e., by being the object of the scoffer's reproaches and maledictions. It is the part of an enlightened conscience and a sound judgment to decide when admonition may be offered with the prospect of doing good. (Comp. Matt. vii. 6.)

12. — *bear it;* i.e., the consequences or punishment of thy scoffing.

13. *The foolish woman.* This may be intended as a personification of folly, so as to form a contrast with the preceding personification of wisdom. But as the term *woman* is expressly mentioned, and as the description, especially in ver. 17, 18, compared with chap. ii. 18, v. 5, is that of a harlot, and as in this book the transition is frequent from discoursing of wisdom to warning against harlots (see chap. ii. 16; v. 3; vii. 5), it is more probable that a literal harlot, rather than a personification of folly as a harlot, may be here intended.

17. — *bread,* &c. Comp. chap. xxx. 20.

18. — *the dead are there;* i.e., the shades, or ghosts. (See chap. ii. 18, and the note.) The foolish man does not consider, that, by entering the house of the harlot, he joins himself to the company of the shades in the underworld; i.e., he brings destruction upon himself.

Chap. X.

1. *The Proverbs,* &c. With this chapter begins the collection of proverbs properly so called; i.e., aphorisms following each other without connection. Hence the new title, the preceding part being regarded as an introduction to the proper proverbs. Perhaps, too, they may have once existed in a separate collection.

2. *Treasures of wickedness;* wealth gained by unjust means. Ill got, ill spent. — *righteousness delivereth,* &c. Some, without necessity, understand this term as referring particularly to beneficence, as it sometimes does.

3. — *craving;* i.e., the avaricious desires of those who make haste to be rich, even by unjust means.

5. — *gathereth;* i.e., the fruits of the earth. — *son causing shame;* i.e., one who disgraces himself and his family by his folly, and the poverty and misery which are the consequences of it.

6. — *of the just;* i.e., on account of the good which is done by them. — *concealeth violence;* while the wicked, by hypocritical professions or studied silence, conceal the injury which they intend to inflict.

7. — *rot;* and, of course, be offensive and loathsome.

8. — *the foolish talker;* i.e., who is so full of his own talk as not to listen to the advice of the wise. — *falleth headlong;* i.e., involves himself in danger and trouble.

9. — *perverteth his ways;* i.e., turns aside from the right way into crooked by-paths; i.e., practises deceit and fraud.

10. — *winketh with the eye,* &c.; i.e., the silent language of knavery is as pernicious as the undisguised perpetration of it. (See chap. vi. 13, and the note.)

11. — *fountain of life;* i.e., utters what is useful and wholesome to himself and others. (See ver. 6, and the note.)

12. — *covereth all offences;* i.e., overlooks, puts them out of sight, or forgives them.

13. The drift of this proverb seems to be, that the wise man is prudent in his words, and receives no blows; whilst the foolish man, by imprudent speeches, provokes and receives chastisement.

14. — *treasure up;* i.e., do not let out every thing without regard to time or place, but reserve it for a fit opportunity; while the fool seldom opens his mouth but it proves a swift mischief to himself.

15. — *strong city;* i.e., in certain circumstances, wealth may purchase safety, while the poor man cannot avoid destruction.

16. — *to life;* i.e., to true happiness. — *to sin;* which implies guilt and punishment, or ruin.

18. — *hideth hatred;* i.e., by friendly deportment to the object of hatred. Disguised hatred and open slander are both condemned.

21. — *feed many;* i.e., strengthen and nourish them for the enjoyment of true happiness by their discourses.

23. — *hath wisdom;* i.e., which keeps him from mischief, and makes him rather find happiness in doing well.

24. *The fear of the wicked;* i.e., that which he fears.

25. — *When the whirlwind;* i.e., when the punishment due to the wicked comes like a whirlwind. — *everlasting foundation;* i.e., he is safe from the whirlwind: his happiness is secure.

26. — *sluggard;* a dilatory, faithless agent or messenger causes the utmost vexation, by keeping his employers in suspense and anxiety.

29. *The way of the Lord,* &c. By this phrase is commonly meant the way in which the Lord requires man to walk. But it also means the way in which God walks; i.e., his providence or government. Either meaning is admissible here. Perhaps the latter is preferable;

in which case, the second line might be rendered, *But destruction for them that do iniquity.*

30. — *the land.* See chap. ii. 21, 22, and the note.

31. — *yieldeth wisdom;* i.e., abundantly and constantly: therefore he shall not be cut down, but be cherished and prosper; while he who uses his tongue perversely shall be cut down like a tree that cumbers the ground.

Chap. XI.

2. — *humble is wisdom.* If we interpret this in connection with the parallel line, the idea is, that the humble man is wise, inasmuch as he escapes the pain and shame which often follow pride.

4. — *the day of wrath;* i.e., the time when God brings judgments or punishment upon men for their sins.

6. — *mischief;* i.e., which they design for others. Otherwise, *But the treacherous are ensnared in their own desires.*

7. — *the expectation,* &c.; i.e., death utterly destroys all his plans and projects; whatever he expected to accomplish.

11. — *blessing of the upright;* their words, their wise counsels and admonitions, which operate as a blessing.

12. — *despiseth his neighbor,* &c. "It is a great weakness to speak contemptuously of any man, or to render him ridiculous (for no man is so mean but he is sensible of despisal, and may find ways to show his resentment); therefore a thoroughly prudent person, whatsoever he thinks of others, says nothing to their reproach." — Patrick.

16. Beauty and gracefulness of manners are to women what strength and valor are to men.

17. — *He that doeth good to himself;* i.e., he who enjoys the bounties of Providence freely is likely to be generous to others; while he who denies himself the common enjoyments, and even necessaries, of life is likely to be cruel to others. (Comp. Sirach xiv. 5, 6.) On the ground of grammatical construction, either rendering is allowable. It is a proverb against asceticism.

18. — *deceitful wages;* i.e., which disappoint his expectations, or even bring pain instead of pleasure.

> "Ye plough wickedness, ye shall reap wretchedness;
> Ye shall eat unlooked-for fruit." — Hos. x. 13.

21. *From generation to generation;* literally, *hand to hand.* That I have given the true meaning is probable from the parallel line, and from the circumstance, that a similar phraseology is in use among the Persians, as has been shown by Schultens ad loc. See also Gesen. Thesaurus on יָד.

22. — *jewel of gold.* The Hebrew ladies wore rings suspended from the nostril by a hole bored through it; a custom which still prevails in the East. (Isa. iii. 21; Ezek. xvi. 12.) Paul Lucas, as quoted by Bishop Lowth, speaking of a village a little this side of the Euphrates, says, "They have almost all of them the nose bored, and wear in it a great ring." — *without discretion.* Probably a dissolute woman is intended. "She may have the ornament; her mien may be graceful, and her person attractive; but, without the matchless jewel

of virtue, she is like the swine, with a gem in his nose, wallowing in the mire. 'The most beautiful ornament of a woman is virtue.' Tamul proverb." — Roberts.

23. — *desire of the righteous*, &c.; i.e., the desires and expectations of the righteous shall not be disappointed, but shall terminate in good; while the expectation of the wicked shall end in their punishment or ruin. (Comp. Job xi. 20.)

26. — *keepeth back;* i.e., in order to obtain an exorbitant price for it in a time of scarcity. — *selleth it;* i.e., at a reasonable price, without taking advantage of the necessities of the people.

27. — *seeketh favor;* i.e., by seeking to do good, he shall obtain favor. — *seeketh mischief;* i.e., to do mischief.

28. — *shall fall;* as a withered leaf. — *as a leaf;* i.e., a verdant leaf, receiving its proper nourishment from the tree.

29. — *harasseth his household*, &c.; i.e., by exacting of them excessive labor, refusing them proper food, and treating them with unkindness and severity, thus alienating their affections, and rendering them careless of his interest. — *inherit wind;* i.e., find nothing but disappointment and vanity.

30. *The fruit*, &c.; i.e., that which a righteous man says and does, or the influence which goes from him, becomes a principle of moral life and happiness to others. — *winneth souls;* i.e., the wise man *captivates* others by his wisdom, and leads them to imitate him.

31. *Behold, the righteous*, &c.; i.e., they are punished for those occasional offences which through infirmity they commit: much more shall the habitually wicked be punished for the sins which they commit, not through infirmity, but with a high hand.

Chap. XII.

1. — *loveth correction;* he who is not only willing to receive instruction, but even admonition and rebuke, shows that he is a true lover of knowledge, by accepting the terms, however unwelcome, by which alone it can be obtained.

3. — *root of the righteous*, &c.; i.e., "But the righteous, like a tree that hath taken a deep root in the earth, though shaken by storms and tempests, shall remain unmovable, in a flourishing state." — Patrick.

4. — *virtuous woman*, &c. See chap. xxxi. 10–31. "A wife that strenuously employs herself in her domestic affairs, and can prudently command her own passions and desires, is a singular ornament and honor to her husband, who may well glory in his happiness; but she, whose laziness or lasciviousness or other infamous quality makes him hang down his head for shame, is an incurable grief and vexation, consuming him and all that he hath." — Patrick.

6. *The words of the wicked*, &c. This sentiment may have particular reference here to high dignitaries, attendants at the courts of princes, &c.

7. — *house of the righteous*, &c.; i.e., his family shall be established in durable succession.

9. — *demeaneth himself*, &c.; i.e., he is far happier who makes no show in the world, but has a competent estate, so as to be able to maintain a servant, than he who appears in great splendor and pomp

abroad, but wants bread to eat when he is at home. The first line may, though less probably, be rendered, *He that demeaneth himself, and is a servant to himself.*

10. — *the life of his beast;* implying that he attends to his food, rest, &c.; much more to the welfare of his servants, dependants, &c. — *tender mercies;* literally, *the bowels* of the wicked; i.e., which in others are the seat of pity, in him are hardened and shut up, and only stir him up to cruelty. Instead of that mercy which is natural to other men, he has nothing but cruelty. (Comp. 2 Cor. vi. 12.)

11. — *tilleth,* &c.; an example of any honest employment. — *followeth,* &c.; i.e., but he that is idle, falling into the company of loose and wicked persons, will find, at last, that he wants not only bread, but understanding.

12. — *prey of evil-doers;* literally, *net;* i.e., what is caught in a net, *prey;* here, such prey, or unlawful gain, as is obtained by evil-doers. — *yieldeth fruit;* both for his own use, and that of others.

13. *In the transgression of the lips is a dangerous snare;* i.e., he who seeks to injure another by false and malicious speeches will be sure to bring himself into difficulty and trouble by such a course; while the man of truth and sincerity escapes such evils.

14. *By the fruit,* &c.; i.e., he that employs his mouth with rectitude and benevolence shall be satisfied with the fruit or happy consequences of such a course; and, for whatever good a man effects with his hands, he shall receive an ample reward.

15. — *own eyes;* i.e., a fool is so conceited, that he consults nobody but himself; for, whatever he does, in his own opinion he is always in the right: but a wise man will not rely upon his own judgment alone, but, suspecting himself, will make use of the sound advice of other men.

16. — *instantly known;* i.e., he cannot defer showing his resentments; like a brute, he immediately manifests it by his looks, words, and actions. — *hideth insult;* i.e., overlooks it, bears it with patience, as beneath his resentment; or, as some suppose, seems to take no notice of it at the time, because he designs afterwards to revenge it.

17. *He that speaketh the truth,* &c.; i.e., he who is accustomed to speak truth in common conversation may be depended upon as a witness in court.

18. — *babbleth,* &c. This remark seems to refer to that sort of persons who deeply wound the feelings of others by thoughtless, unguarded remarks, without respect to persons, times, and places. — *is health;* i.e., tends to promote mental peace and happiness.

19. *The lip of truth,* &c. This verse probably denotes, not merely that falsehood is speedily detected, whilst the truth is established, but rather that the speaker of truth shall be established in peace and happiness, while the liar shall be brought to ruin. (See chap. x. 31.)

20. *Deceit,* &c. It has been inferred from the antithetic line in this verse, that by *deceit* is intended self-deception or disappointment. But, as the term is connected with the adjunct *in the heart,* I think it better to understand it in the most obvious sense, of deceit practised towards others, which will not terminate in the joy which is promised, in the next line, to those who counsel peace, but rather in vexation of spirit.

23. — *concealeth his knowledge;* i.e., is not ostentatious of it, displays it only at a proper season, is modest; but a fool publishes his ignorance, as if he were ambitious that every one should know how great a fool he is.

26. — *showeth his neighbor the way.* This reading was adopted by Geier, John Taylor in his Concordance, and some other of the older critics. Though not so strongly supported by usage as is desirable, it has as good a claim on this ground as the common version, and affords a better sense. It is adopted by Gesenius, De Wette, Ewald, Fürst in his Concordance, and Bertheau.

27. — *will not roast his game.* This is probably a proverbial expression, meaning that the slothful man will not enjoy the fruit of the labors which he does perform: less probably, that he will not catch his game, and so have none to roast.

28. — *life;* — *death.* It is evident that these terms are used metaphorically to denote *true happiness,* and *ruin* or *misery.*

Chap. XIII.

2. — *fruit of a man's mouth,* &c. He that makes a good use of his mouth in speaking of others, giving good advice, or making wise observations, will reap the benefit of it himself. — *appetite,* &c.; i.e., the wicked shall suffer the violence which they meditated against others.

3. — *openeth wide;* i.e., speaks rashly and inconsiderately; lets out every thing which comes into his head.

5. — *causeth disgrace and shame;* i.e., by uttering falsehoods, he often brings undeserved reproach and shame on others.

7. — *hath nothing,* &c. "You will be deceived, if you judge of men by the outward appearance; for there are those who have the vanity to make a great show in the world, when they are not worth a farthing; and others who are so cunning as to dissemble their vast estates under the garb of poverty."—Patrick. Under the despotic governments of the East, where property is insecure, there exist many motives for the concealment of it. (Comp. chap. xii. 9.)

8. — *the ransom of his life.* This line may be understood in different senses, as denoting either the inconvenience or the value of wealth. According to the first, the meaning will be, that wealth has not so great an advantage over poverty as is sometimes thought, since it sometimes exposes its possessor, by means of false accusers or thieves or tyrants, to the peril of his life, which he is obliged to redeem by the sacrifice of his riches, while no one thinks it worth while to bring accusations against the poor. Or the line may point out the value of wealth; namely, that it enables its possessor to preserve his life when in imminent danger. The parallelism seems to favor the first meaning.

9. — *shall rejoice;* i.e., shine with a bright, cheerful light, like that of the sun, as described in Ps. xix. 5; i.e., their prosperity shall be great and lasting.

10. *By pride,* &c. "They that have a high conceit of themselves, and will yield to none, declare their folly, in that they can do nothing without strife and contention." — Patrick.

11. *Wealth gotten by vanity,* &c.; i.e., without effort, by luck, irreg-

ularly. — *gathereth into the hand;* i.e., by regular labor gets it, as it were, by the handful.

12. — *tree of life.* See chap. iii. 18, and the note.

13. — *the word;* i.e., of God. But it is uncertain whether it refers to the written word, or to the admonition of the prophets of God. — *be rewarded.* Otherwise, *be in peace.*

15. *A good understanding;* i.e., manifesting itself in inoffensive words and virtuous actions. — *is hard;* i.e., instead of winning favor, it provokes the enmity and opposition of men, and thus leads to vexation and misery.

16. — *acteth with knowledge;* i.e., with due deliberation, undertaking only what he understands. — *spreadeth abroad his folly;* i.e., by rashly and inconsiderately undertaking things beyond his strength, which of course do not succeed. His folly is thus made known to all.

17. — *into trouble;* i.e., receives punishment for his perfidy or negligence. — *is health;* i.e., by accomplishing the objects of his mission, procures safety and benefit both for himself and for him that sent him.

19. — *an abomination,* &c.; i.e., this is the case, although the sure consequence of continuing in their wicked course is disappointment and failure.

22. — *for the just;* i.e., in the course of Providence is transferred from the families of the wicked to those of the good.

23. — *fallow-ground of the poor.* A poor man often grows rich by hard labor on new or fallow ground, which requires extraordinary tillage; and there are those who, despising labor, lose large estates by dishonest attempts to increase them.

Chap. XIV.

1. — *wise woman,* &c. "By a prudent wife, one pious, industrious, and considerate, the affairs of the family are made to prosper, debts are paid, portions raised, the children are well educated and maintained, and the family has comfort within doors and credit without. Thus is the house built. She looks upon it as her own to take care of, though she knows it is her husband's to bear rule in (Esth. i. 22); while a foolish woman, the reverse of her that has been described, will as certainly be the ruin of her house as if she plucked it down with her own hands." — Henry.

2. — *in uprightness,* &c. "By this we may know a man that has grace and the fear of God reigning in him; *he walks in his uprightness,* he makes conscience of his actions, is faithful both to God and man, and every stop he makes, as well as every step he takes, is by rule: here is one that honors God. But, on the contrary, *he that is perverse in his ways,* that wilfully follows his own appetites and passions, that is unjust and dishonest, and contradicts his profession in his conversation, however he may pretend to devotion, he is a wicked man, and will be reckoned with as a despiser of God himself." — Henry.

3. — *a scourge of his pride.* "A fool is so insolent, that he boldly calumniates and wounds the reputation of others, though it come home at last with a terrible back-blow upon himself; but wise men

are careful of their words, not to offend, much less abuse, the meanest person; and thereby they remain in safety." — Patrick.

4. — *no oxen;* i.e., employed in agriculture by the husbandman. — *the crib is clean.* This is a satirical way of saying that the barn is destitute of fodder; there is a scarcity of provision. So cleanness of teeth denotes a scarcity, in Amos iv. 6. "This shows the folly of those who addict themselves to the pleasures of the country, but do not mind the business of it; who, as we say, keep more horses than kine, more dogs than swine: their families must needs suffer by it."

5. *A faithful witness,* &c. "A person of integrity will not be prevailed withal, either for fear or favor, to justify the least untruth; but a man of no conscience, who hath accustomed himself to lying, cares not how many falsehoods he testifies, which he utters without any difficulty." — Patrick.

6. — *scoffer* — *man of understanding.* By *scoffer* seems to be denoted a frivolous, superficial, irreverent inquirer, one inclined to turn serious things into ridicule; and by *man of understanding,* a man who has correct feelings as well as a sound mind. In order to arrive at truth, we must seek it with right views, dispositions, and feelings.

7. Bertheau supposes the meaning to be somewhat sarcastic. When thou hast gone to a foolish man to learn any thing, thou hast gone to the wrong door. There is no knowledge there to be had.

8. — *his way,* &c. "The greatest cunning and subtlety that a truly wise and good man studies is to understand what he ought to do and what to avoid, upon all occasions; but all the skill of wicked men, such is their folly, lies in cheating tricks, and in devising arts of circumvention and deceit." — Patrick. Possibly the meaning may be, that the foolish man allows *himself* to be deceived.

9. — *make a mock,* &c. Bad men make no account of injuring their neighbors, and therefore incur general hatred; while upright men, by being careful not to do wrong to any one, obtain general favor. This proverb, like many others, is somewhat enigmatical; the evil consequence of the course of conduct mentioned in the first line being implied in what is said of an opposite course of conduct in the parallel line.

10. *The heart,* &c. Every one has griefs and joys, the causes of which he cannot make known so as to secure the complete sympathy of others. Men should be slow, therefore, in passing censure upon their neighbors on account of their feelings of grief or joy.

12. — *a way,* &c. "Examine every thing strictly and impartially, and be not led merely by the appetite; for that makes many actions seem innocent, which, in the issue, prove deadly destructive." — Patrick.

13. *Even in laughter,* &c. This proverb may denote that men sometimes put on the appearance of joy, while their hearts are full of pain, which still recurs after all the efforts to disguise it. Or, the meaning may be, that immoderate joy leaves the heart sad, and that sorrow treads so close upon the heels of joy, that it may be said to follow it immediately.

14. — *with his own ways;* i.e., with the fruit, or evil consequences, of his course of life. — *from himself;* i.e., from his works; from his temper of mind, course of life, and the natural consequences of it.

15. — *to his steps;* i.e., proceeds cautiously, examining before he trusts, and considering well before he does as he is advised.

16. — *feareth;* i.e., the consequences of transgression, especially when he is reminded of them by a friend. — *is haughty;* when he is warned, &c.

18. — *inherit folly;* i.e., they retain it as their inheritance or portion; that in which they delight.

19. — *bow before the good;* i.e., however prosperous and insolent for a time, they are often reduced to the necessity of seeking the favor of the good in a humble manner. — *at the gates;* i.e., as suppliants.

22. — *fail of their end?* literally, *go astray, wander.*

23. — *labor,* &c. Working without talking will make men rich; but talking without working will make men poor.

24. — *is folly;* i.e., their high honor or station is only a source of folly, or the means of making it more conspicuous.

25. — *lives;* i.e., which are endangered by false accusation. — *lies;* although they thereby endanger the lives of the innocent.

26. — *confidence;* ground of confidence, security; parallel with *refuge.* — *his children;* i.e., the children of him who fears God, the antecedent to *his* being implied in the expression, *the fear of Jehovah.* (Comp. chap. xix. 23.)

28. — *numerous people,* &c.; the true glory of a king consists not in his personal splendor, his palaces, treasures, pomp, &c., but in a numerous people, which he cannot have without good government.

30. *A quiet heart,* &c. "There is nothing conduces more to health and happiness than a quiet, gentle, and contented mind; but envy, and such like fretful passions, is as miserable a torment and consuming disease as rottenness in the bones."

31. — *reproacheth his Maker;* because he is alike the Creator of the rich and the poor. (Comp. Job xxxi. 15; Prov. xxii. 2.)

32. — *is thrust down;* i.e., is ruined, perishes. Or the phrase may figuratively denote the state of the sinner's mind, when he falls into trouble; that he is utterly cast down, or reduced to despair: while the righteous, in the deepest trouble, even in death, has hope in God.

33. — *it will be made known;* i.e., what little may be there, as it were by mere accident. "He that is truly wise hides his treasure, so as not to boast of it, though he does not hide his talent, so as not to trade with it. If fools have a little smattering of knowledge, they take all occasions, though very foreign, to bring it in by head and shoulders."—Henry. Jarchi quotes from the Talmud the proverb, "A small piece of money thrown into an empty pitcher makes a loud sound; while one that is full of money makes no sound."

34. — *is sin;* i.e., caused by sin.

35. — *causeth shame;* i.e., who by ill management brings reproach upon his prince.

Chap. XV.

2. — *knowledge pleasing;* by taking due care when and what, and to whom and how, he speaks. — *poureth forth;* i.e., inconsiderately and at random utters thoughts which amount only to folly.

4. — *tree of life.* See the note on chap. iii. 18. — *wound in the spirit;* i.e., breaks the heart, as we say.

6 — *much wealth.* "A truly just and merciful man is very rich, whether he has little or much, because he is well contented, and what he has is likely to continue in his family; but there is much disquiet and trouble in the greatest revenues of the wicked, which can neither stay long with him, nor give him satisfaction while he enjoys them."

7. — *is not sound* or *stable;* i.e., has not stability or strength enough to be relied on for good counsel.

8. *The sacrifice of the wicked.* "Even wicked men bring God sacrifices to stop the mouth of conscience, and to keep up their reputation in the world, as malefactors come to a sanctuary, not because it is a holy place, but because it shelters them from justice; but their sacrifices are not offered in sincerity, nor from a good principle: they dissemble with God, and in their conversations give the lie to their devotions; and, for that reason, they are an abomination to him, because they are made a cloak for sin." But "God has such a love for upright, good people, that, though they are not at the expense of a sacrifice, their prayer is a delight to him." The verse is a caution against resting in mere ceremonial worship without moral virtue. (Comp. Ps. l.)

10. — *forsaketh the way;* i.e., the way of rectitude; the way prescribed by God.

12. — *to the wise;* lest he should receive rebuke.

13. — *spirit is broken;* which will be manifested in a wo-begone countenance, as is implied by the parallel line.

14. — *feedeth upon folly;* vain and foolish things are meat and drink to them.

15. — *afflicted;* i.e., in spirit. A melancholy spirit renders the brightest day dark. The mind gives to outward objects their color and complexion.

19. — *the slothful,* &c. "A slothful man, when he has any thing to do, feigns to himself most grievous difficulties, which he fancies or pretends are impossible to be overcome; but those very things seem easy to the industry of honest-hearted men, who go on smoothly in their business, and conquer all impediments." — Patrick.

20. — *despiseth his mother;* and thus makes her sad, as is implied by its connection with the preceding line.

21. *Folly is joy,* &c.; i.e., it is his delight to do foolish and wicked actions. — *walketh uprightly;* and finds his joy in it, as is implied by the parallelism.

23. — *by the answer of his mouth;* i.e., by giving good advice, when asked.

24. — *is upward,* &c. The wise pursue a path insuring to themselves a continuance of life and happiness, which, being directly opposed to the path leading down to the grave, is said to be an upward path.

25. — *the proud.* Those who imagine themselves independent of Providence are contrasted with those who have no support but Providence.

26. — *pleasant words;* which aim at the benefit, not the injury, of others. — *are pure;* and therefore acceptable to Jehovah.

27. "He that is so greedy of money that he cares not how he gets it, instead of raising his family, confounds it; but he that hates bribes

and all unlawful ways of gain shall prosper and continue it."—Patrick.

28. —*poureth out;* abundantly, hastily, and without consideration of consequences.

29. —*far from the wicked;* i.e., so as not to listen to their cry, nor to afford them aid, when they call upon him.

30. —*light of the eyes,* &c. This may mean bright, smiling eyes, equivalent to the *light of the countenance* (xvi. 15; Job xxix. 24; Ps. iv. 6). Some suppose it to mean the sunlight, according to Eccl. xi. 7; others, that it denotes what is seen by the eyes, such as a beautiful garden, a flowing stream, &c. I hesitate between the first and the third meaning.

31. —*reproof of life;* i.e., reproof which leads to a happy life, salutary reproof.

33. —*guideth to wisdom.* Comp. chap. i. 7; ix. 10.

Chap. XVI.

1. —*preparation of the heart,* &c.; i.e., when man has thought what to utter and in what order, still, after all, it depends upon God what language shall come from his tongue. Man proposes, God disposes. Or, *the answer of the tongue* may denote the answer of God to the voice of prayer.

3. *Commit thy doings,* &c.; consider the event of every thing which you undertake as depending upon God's providence.

4. —*for its end;* i.e., object, or purpose. Otherwise, for *his* purpose; the pronominal suffix being applicable to *the Lord,* or to *every thing.* According to the rendering in the text, the meaning will be substantially the same as that assigned to the verse by Grotius: "God has ordained every thing to that which answers or is suited to it; and the wicked he has ordained for the day of evil, i.e., of punishment. There is not only a wise arrangement or correspondence in good things, but also in evil things; for the evil of punishment follows the evil of guilt: the evil day is appointed for the evil-doer." Some understand the last line as denoting that wicked men are appointed to punish others, as in Isa. x. 5, 6. The idea which some have drawn from the passage, that God makes men wicked on purpose to punish them, is too metaphysical for the writer, and too gross for any writer. God made man upright: he makes himself wicked, and is justly appointed to punishment for his wickedness.

5. *From generation to generation.* See Gesenius ad verb. יָד.

6. —*kindness and truth;* i.e., exercised by men (comp. chap. iii. 3; xx. 28), and here used in opposition to sacrifices and ceremonies, by which the corrupt Jews supposed they might secure the favor of God.

9. —*deviseth his way;* i.e., if a man lay his plans with never so much care, he cannot insure success to them. This is at the disposal of God. (Comp. ver. 1, and Jer. x. 23.)

10. *A divine sentence.* The writer's aim seems to be to procure a religious respect for the sentence of the king, as being the minister

of God, and as placed above ordinary motives to give a wrong judgment.

11. — *his work;* made by his direction and appointment, so that no man can corrupt or alter them without violating his authority and incurring his displeasure. (See the note on chap. xx. 10.)

12. — *to kings;* i.e., to those worthy of the name.

14. — *messengers of death.* The expression may be derived from the custom of Oriental despotism. "When the enemies of a great man in Turkey have gained influence enough over the prince to procure a warrant for his death, a capidgy, or executioner, is sent to him, and shows him the order he has to carry back his head: the other kisses it, and freely gives it up." — Thevenot. (Comp. 1 Kings ii. 25; Matt. xiv. 10.)

15. — *light of the king's countenance;* i.e., his smiling, favorable countenance refreshes and invigorates. — *latter rain;* which falls in the spring, not long before the time of harvest, in Palestine, and refreshes the parched fields, and brings to maturity the harvest.

17. *It is the highway,* &c.; i.e., in departing from evil, they find a smooth and pleasant path.

20. — *giveth heed;* so מַשְׂכִּיל is used in xxi. 12; Ps. xli. 2. This rendering is preferred by Mercier and several of the older critics in Poole's Synopsis. Otherwise, *he who is prudent in a matter,* &c. — *to the word;* the commands of God. (Comp. chap. xiii. 13; Ps. cxix. 105.) This rendering is made probable by the parallelism.

21. "He whose mind is well furnished with wisdom cannot but win a great reputation, and be highly esteemed for his prudent counsels and resolutions; but, if he have the powerful charms of eloquence also, to convey his mind delightfully unto others, it will add a greater value to his wisdom, and make it more diffusive and instructive unto the world." — Patrick.

22. — *their folly;* which brings its punishment with it, or close behind it. The painful consequences of their folly is the only way to correct them. Otherwise, *the instruction of fools is folly;* i.e., when they undertake to give instruction, they only teach folly. *Chastisement* is the primary, and *instruction* the secondary, meaning of מוּסָר. (Comp. xxiii. 13.)

23. *The heart;* considered as the seat of the understanding, as it was regarded by the Hebrews.

24. *Pleasant words,* &c. Agreeable discourse is both delightful and salutary.

26. — *his mouth;* i.e., the craving of his appetite. (Comp. Eccl. vi. 7.)

27. — *diggeth mischief;* a metaphor derived from the practice of digging pits to entrap wild animals. — *a burning fire;* which consumes the reputation of his neighbor. (Comp. James iii. 6.)

30. — *shutteth his eyes,* &c.; i.e., in order to think more intently and closely. Compression of the lips indicates firmness of purpose. — *hath accomplished,* &c.; i.e., he has as good as accomplished it, because it is certain that he will execute his purpose. The design of the proverb is to intimate, that such a shutter of the eyes and compresser of the lips is to be suspected and guarded against.

32 — *the mighty;* warrior, or hero.
33. *The lot,* &c. "Acknowledge the Divine providence in all things, even in those which seem most casual; for though men cast the lots into the lap of a garment or into a hollow vessel, and thence draw them out again, yet it is the Lord who directs entirely in what order they shall come forth, and so determines the matter in doubt according to his pleasure." — Patrick.

Chap. XVII.

1. — *flesh-banquets;* literally, *slaughterings.*
2. — *ruleth over,* &c.; i.e., is sometimes appointed by the father as the guardian of unworthy children, or placed at the head of the concerns of the household.
5. — *the poor.* See the note on chap. xiv. 31.
7. *Excellent speech,* &c. Perhaps, *lordly,* or *imperious.* — *the base;* נָבָל. This meaning seems more appropriate than *fool.* The same word is translated *vile person* in the common version in Isa. xxxii. 5. — *the noble;* i.e., in birth, manners, character. So in ver. 26.
8. — *precious stone,* &c.; i.e., "A gift is so tempting, that it can no more be refused than a lovely jewel by him to whom it is presented; and, such is its power, it commonly prevails over all men, despatches all business, carries all causes, and, in a word, effects whatsoever a man desires." — Patrick.
9. — *covereth an offence,* &c.; i.e., he that takes little notice of an offence against himself, or soon forgets it, seeks and courts the love of the offender. But he who continually recurs to an offence committed by a friend against himself alienates him.
11. — *cruel messenger.* See the note on xvi. 14.
12. — *a fool in his folly;* an unreasonable, bad man, when his ungovernable passions and appetites are most excited.
14. *The beginning,* &c. "One hot word, one peevish reflection, one angry demand, one spiteful contradiction, begets another, and that a third, and so on, till it proves like the cutting of a dam: when the water has got a little passage, it does itself widen the breach, bears down all before it, and there is then no stopping it, no reducing it." — Henry. — *rolleth onward;* i.e., like water from a breach in a dam. (See Fürst's Lexicon on גָּלַע.)
16. — *seeing that sense,* &c. The idea is, that wealth cannot obtain wisdom, when natural ability is wanting.
17. — *born a brother;* i.e., becomes a brother; a true friend will in adversity show himself to be as valuable and dear as a brother. (Comp. xviii. 24.) Otherwise, *a brother is born for adversity;* i.e., though a true friend shows his love in all circumstances, yet a brother is peculiarly to be relied on in adversity, when common friendship may fail.
18. — *striketh hands.* See the note on chap. vi. 1.
19. — *raiseth high his gate;* i.e., *the gate of his house;* i.e., is proud and ostentatious, carries his head too high, as we say. — *seeketh ruin;* because he thus makes himself odious to God and man; or, because he involves himself in ruinous expenses.

21. *The fool*, &c.; i.e., a son who becomes impious and wicked.
23. — *out of the bosom;* i.e., in secret (comp. chap. xxi. 14), being secretly conveyed from the bosom of the giver to his own.
24. *Wisdom*, &c. See chap. xiv. 6. — *ends of the earth;* i.e., wander far and wide without discovering wisdom.
26. — *to punish the righteous;* as was and is practised in the regions of Oriental despotism. — *for their equity*; it may be, in the administration of justice, or in suppressing disturbances. Some recent critics have rendered עַל יֹשֶׁר, *beyond right.* It seems to me very doubtful whether usage sanctions this meaning.
27. — *a cool spirit;* i.e., not easily excited, not forward and hasty to utter whatever comes into one's head.

Chap. XVIII.

1. — *He who separateth himself;* i.e., so as to despise the ways and opinions of others, or who lives a life of seclusion. — *seeketh his own desire;* i.e., indulges his own wayward fancy, and obstinately pursues his own way. — *rusheth on;* nothing is too wise and good for him to oppose; whatever any one may urge against his opinions and plans, with never so much reason, he opposes it, and obstinately maintains his own prejudices.
2. — *in understanding;* i.e., in acquiring sound knowledge. — *revealing*, &c.; i.e., in giving utterance to all his thoughts, and thus exposing his folly.
3 — *cometh also contempt;* i.e., contempt is the companion of the wicked man; he is treated with contempt. (Comp. chap. xi. 2.) Some understand the verse as pointing out the danger of bad company, and the reproach which a bad man brings upon those who admit him into their society.
4. — *man's mouth;* i.e., a wise man's, as is to be understood from the parallelism.
5. This proverb is directed against the venality of judges, which is common in the despotic countries of the East.
6. — *calleth for blows*; i.e., he invites blows upon himself by his rash and provoking speeches.
8. — *like sweet morsels.* This meaning, adopted by Schultens, Gesenius, and De Wette, seems to me rather the most probable. Fürst, in his Lexicon, on לָהַם, proposes *oracular*, mysterious words, like those of a magician. This proverb seems to point out the danger of slanderous stories, inasmuch as they are swallowed with avidity, and remembered by those to whom they are related.
9. Idleness is as bad as wastefulness.
13. — *hath heard*, &c. Comp. Sirach xi. 8.
14. — *his infirmity;* a manly spirit will sustain one under bodily infirmity; but when the mind itself has lost its courage, and is cast down and oppressed with grief, how hopeless is the case!
17. — *searcheth him through;* examines into the truth of his allegations. One tale is good till another is told.
18. — *parteth asunder the mighty;* i.e., mighty combatants, or liti-

gants, so that they shall no more contend, but go each to his own business.

19. — *bars of a castle;* i.e., it is easier to break the bars of a castle than to remove the obstructions which lie in the way of a hearty reconciliation.

20. "The tongue is so hard to govern, and so much depends upon it, that we ought to take as great care about the words we speak as we do about the fruit of our trees, or the increase of the earth, which we are to eat; for, according as they are wholesome and good, or unsavory and bad, so will the pleasure or the pain be wherewith we shall be filled." — Patrick.

21. — *love it;* i.e., love to talk much.

22. — *a wife;* i.e., a wife indeed, a good wife. — *from the Lord.* It is probably implied, that, in consequence of the difficulty of discerning the true character, human skill and care are of less avail in the acquisition of a good wife than of other blessings. (Comp. xix. 14.)

24. — *will show himself false,* or *base* (see Fürst's Lexicon, on רָעַע); i.e., he who professes to be the friend of everybody will be the true friend of nobody. No dependence can be placed upon him when tried. Otherwise, *will come to ruin;* i.e., he will be ruined in consequence of neglect of business, and of his expensive mode of living. (Comp. xxi. 17.)

Chap. XIX.

1. — *of false lips;* i.e., who has acquired wealth by falsehood and fraud.

3. — *destroyeth his way;* i.e., brings him to ruin. — *against the Lord;* as the cause of the evils which he has brought upon himself by his own folly.

4. — *is separated.* This is the literal rendering. The poor man finds himself solitary and alone, because he is forsaken by his neighbor.

7. — *runneth after their words;* he calls to mind the former professions and promises of his friends, and reminds them of them; but finds that words are wind, that leaves no trace behind.

8. — *loveth himself;* i.e., is a truer lover of himself, or promotes his true interest more, than he who is bent upon mere outward good.

10. *Luxury,* &c. Comp. chap. xxvi. 8; xxx. 22. This verse seems to denote that a noble mind is required in a noble condition. A foolish, knavish, ill-behaving person becomes more ridiculous, the more splendid the style of living which he adopts. — *a servant,* &c.; as sometimes happens under the despotisms of the East.

12. — *roaring of a lion;* i.e., inspiring terror. — *dew upon the grass;* i.e., refreshing and invigorating.

13. — *a continual dropping;* i.e., from the eaves of a house. Her contentions are continually renewing themselves; there is no cessation. (Comp. chap. xxvii. 15.)

14. See the note on chap. xviii. 22.

15. — *deep sleep;* makes a man neglect his affairs, as if he were asleep, so that he comes to want.

18. — *to slay him;* i.e., use moderate punishment. Punish to correct, not to kill.

19. — *again;* when you have helped him out of one danger, it will not be long before his violent temper will involve him in new trouble.

21. — *devices.* Understand, from the parallel line, "which are often disappointed."

22. *The charm of a man;* i.e., that which makes him loved. Otherwise, *The desire of a man,* &c.; i.e., the will is to be taken for the deed of kindness. — *a liar;* i.e., one who promises favors which he does not mean to bestow.

24. — *the dish;* i.e., he is too lazy to eat. Allusion is made to the manner in which the Orientals help themselves to their food. (Comp. Matt. xxvi. 23.)

25. *Strike the scoffer,* &c. Severe punishment may do no good to a derider of religion, but it tends to warn and reclaim the incautious persons whom he has injured. Reproof will be sufficient to correct those who are well disposed.

27. — *instruction.* Beware of those who, professing to instruct or reprove you, would draw you away from the plain, established principles of virtue.

28. — *swalloweth down,* &c.; i.e., it is agreeable and pleasant to them. (Comp. Job xv. 16.)

Chap. XX.

1. — *reeleth;* literally, *wandereth;* i.e., from the path.

2. — *terror of a king;* i.e., the terror inspired by the wrath of a king.

5. — *like deep waters;* i.e., hard to come at.

6. — *faithful man;* i.e., in connection with the parallel line, one who comes up to his professions of kindness; who will be true to a friend in his distress. (Comp. chap. xix. 22.)

10. *Divers weights,* &c.; i.e., one to show, another to weigh with.

11. — *will be pure,* &c.; i.e., when he becomes a man. "The man and child an individual make."

12. — *the Lord made them;* and of course can himself see the actions of men. (Comp. chap. xv. 3; Ps. xciv. 9.)

13. *Open thine eyes;* i.e., awake early.

15. — *gold,* &c.; i.e., the ability to discourse with true wisdom is more valuable than the largest treasure of gold or jewels.

16. — *garment,* &c.; i.e., trust no one who is so inconsiderate and rash as to make himself responsible for a stranger, but obtain from him immediate security.

17. — *of falsehood;* i.e., obtained by dishonest means. Figuratively, all things obtained by injustice may be here denoted, which, though they may please a man in the beginning, will bring pain and sorrow in the end.

20. — *His lamp,* &c. See the note on Job xviii. 6; xxix. 3.

24. — *his way;* to what the way which he takes will lead. A man's enterprises succeed not as he desires and designs, but as God disposes and directs. (Comp. chap. xvi. 9; Jer. x 23.)

26. — *the wheel*, &c. See Amos i. 3, and the note.
27. — *lamp of the Lord;* i.e., lighted up by him, which takes full cognizance of the most secret thoughts.
30. — *remedy for the bad man;* i.e., effectual means to reclaim him. — *reach to the inner chambers;* i.e., not mere superficial touches.

Chap. XXI.

1. *As streams of water;* which husbandmen or gardeners conduct over their fields or gardens. — *heart of the king;* not only the hearts of other men, but even the hearts of kings, who are more absolute and uncontrollable than other men. The application of this proverb seems to be uncertain. It may be designed to show that the power of kings to do evil is limited; that the people cannot be oppressed by them more than God sees fit; or to show that a religious reverence is due to the determinations of kings. Harmer and some others suppose the verse to relate particularly to the bounty of a king. "Which way soever the heart of a king turneth, it conveys riches, just as a watering canal doth plenty; and let it be remembered that the Lord turns it whithersoever he will, and makes whom he pleases the favorite of princes."
4. — *lamp.* This appears to be a metaphor, denoting the splendor and prosperity on account of which the wicked man has lofty looks and a proud heart. (See the note on Job xxix. 3.) — *ruin;* otherwise, *sin;* which implies guilt and ruin, so that the bad man will not long enjoy his splendor. (See xx. 20.)
5. — *the active*, &c. "He that to prudent counsels and contrivances adds an honest diligence is likely to grow rich; but he that acts inconsiderately in his business, or greedily catches at every advantage, whether by right or wrong, or undertakes more than he can manage, out of an eager desire to grow rich presently, is most likely to be a beggar." — Patrick.
6. — *fleeting breath;* which is breathed forth from the lips, and immediately disappears. (Comp. chap. xiii. 11.) — *seek death;* i.e., seek that which will prove their destruction. (See chap. viii. 36.)
7. — *snatch them away;* i.e., shall prove their own ruin. (Comp. Ps. vii. 16.)
8. — *guilty man.* See Gesenius on וָזָר. — *is crooked;* i.e., he uses immoral means for the attainment of his end.
9. — *a large house;* literally, *a house of fellowship;* i.e., large enough to contain more families than one. Or the meaning may be, *a common house;* i.e., one occupied by more than one family.
10. The design of this proverb seems to be to give a caution against having any close connection with a wicked man, since he will spare neither friend nor foe who stands in the way of his designs.
11. See the note on chap. xix. 25.
12. *He casteth*, &c. By the pronoun *He* we may, with the common version, understand *God.* I should think it contrary to usage (*usus loquendi*) to make צַדִּיק mean the righteous One; i.e., God. It seems, indeed, to belong to the Deity rather than to a man "to cast the wick-

ed headlong into ruin." But *the righteous man*, being regarded as a judge or magistrate, may possibly be said to do it.

16. — *the dead;* more literally, *shades*, or *ghosts*. "By the term רְפָאִים, which denotes *languid, feeble*, the ancient Hebrews refer to the *shades, manes*, or *ghosts* of the dead, whom they supposed to be destitute of blood and animal life, and therefore weak and languid, like a sick person (Isa. xiv. 10); but yet not wholly without some faculties of mind, as, for example, memory. Isa. xiv. 9; Ps. lxxxviii. 11; Prov. ii. 18, ix. 18; Isa. xxvi. 14, 19." — Gesenius.

18. — *ransom.* Comp. chap. xi. 8; Isa. xliii. 3, 4.

20. — *swalloweth them up;* i.e., wastes by extravagance and dissipation what he ought to reserve for a future day.

22. Comp. Eccl. vii. 19; ix. 18.

24. — *scoffer is his name;* i.e., he is deserving of the severest condemnation, and exposes himself to punishment from God.

25. — *destroy him;* i.e., his indolent wishes, which lead to no exertion, prey upon his health; or, his wishes for ease make him neglect the means of support, and thus cause his death.

26. *The covetous man;* literally, *covetousness.*

27. — *an abomination.* See the note on chap. xv. 8. — *with an evil design;* i.e., when he is meditating some particular evil design, and wishes to hide it.

28. — *that hearkeneth;* i.e., to wholesome admonition; or, possibly, that testifies to nothing which he has not heard or seen. — *shall speak for ever;* i.e., when liars are cut off, he shall live, and be allowed to deliver his testimony as long as he lives.

29. — *hardeneth his face;* "Here is, 1. The presumption and impudence of a wicked man. *He hardens his face;* brazens it, that he may not blush; steels it, that he may not tremble when he commits the greatest crimes: he will have his way, and nothing shall hinder him. (Isa. lvii. 17.) 2. The caution and circumspection of a good man: he does not ask, 'What *would* I do? what have I a mind to? and that I will have;' but, 'What should I do? What does God require of me? What is duty? What is prudence? What is for edification?' And so he does not force his way, but directs it by a safe and certain rule." — Henry.

Chap. XXII.

1. — *good-will;* an interest in the affections and esteem of all about us. (Comp. Luke ii. 52; Phil. iv. 8.)

2. — *meet together;* i.e., the world does not consist of all rich, or all poor; but they are mingled together as the members of the same civil community. — *the Maker of them all;* and therefore they are under obligation to exercise respect and good-will toward each other. (Comp. chap. xiv. 31; Job xxxi. 15; Mal. ii. 10.)

5. — *far from them;* i.e., from the society of the deceitful.

6. — *in accordance with his way;* i.e., the calling, trade, or business for which he has a turn or bent; possibly to which he is destined by his parents. This is the literal meaning of the Hebrew עַל־פִּי דַרְכּוֹ. One is loth to part with the familiar paraphrase of the common ver-

sion. But the difficulty is, that, though the Scriptures very often speak of *the way* of a person, the phrase never denotes the way in which he *ought* to go, as a matter of moral and religious obligation, but only that in which he goes, or chooses and delights to go.

7. *The rich*, &c. The point of this proverb, probably, is the unexpressed consequence which is to be drawn from it; namely, that a man should by industry and frugality acquire property, and thus possess the glorious privilege of being independent.

8. — *is prepared;* i.e., made ready for him. For this meaning of the Hebrew term, comp. 1 Sam. xx. 7, 9; xxv. 17.

11. — *loveth purity*, &c. He that has a sincere and upright heart will utter, not flattery, but his honest convictions; so that his discourse will be agreeable, and gain the favor of a good king.

12. — *watch over knowledge;* i.e., men of knowledge, in opposition to false pretenders. The providence of God watches over such men, and prospers the advice they give; whilst the words or vain and deceitful counsels of the dishonest will come to nothing.

14. *The mouth;* by which they allure and persuade the thoughtless to sin and ruin.

16. — *giveth to the rich;* either as a bribe or in expectation of receiving some return. Some other versions of the preceding verse have been given, thus: —

"There is that oppresseth the poor, — to make him rich;
There is that giveth to the rich, — only to his poverty."

i.e., the oppressor of the poor sometimes gathers property, which he loses, and which goes to the benefit of the poor. And so what is given to the rich is often lost by injustice or dissipation, leaving him poorer than before. (So Umbreit) Otherwise thus: *He who oppresseth the poor to increase his riches, giveth to the rich, only to his own want.* By *giving to the rich*, in this last rendering, is meant giving to himself, who is rich. (So Bertheau.)

17. The passage from ver. 17 to 21, instead of consisting of proverbs, is an exhortation to the study of wisdom, and is to be regarded either as an epilogue to the division from chap. x. to this place, or as an introduction to the collection from ver. 22 to chap. xxiv. 22. The proverbs from chap. xxii. 22 to chap. xxiv. 22 differ from the preceding in being more in the way of exhortation or admonition, and less sententious; most of them requiring more than one verse, and some of them, three, four, or more, for the expression of the sentiment.

18. — *established upon thy lips;* i.e., if they be, as it were, at your tongue's end, ready to be applied to the various exigencies of life.

21. — *that send thee;* i.e., show yourself capable and trustworthy to them that employ thee in any business of which they expect an account of thee.

22. — *because he is poor;* i.e., do not take advantage of his poverty and his inability to resist thee. — *at the gate*; i.e., in a court of law. (See the note on Job v. 4.)

25. — *take to thyself*, &c.; i.e., acquire such a disposition and character as shall involve you in difficulties. — *a snare*; i.e., that which will prove a snare.

26. See the note on chap. vi. 1.

27. — *thy bed,* &c.; i.e., why should you expose yourself to such a state of things, that, if you are unable to pay your bonds, the creditor may take from you every thing, so that you shall not even have a bed upon which to lay your head?

28. — *landmark.* Comp. Deut. xix. 14.

29. — *obscure.* This is the metaphorical term of the original to denote persons in humble station.

Chap. XXIII.

2. — *thou wilt put a knife to thy throat,* &c.; i.e., thou wilt bring thyself into great danger, if by thy unrestrained appetite thou seize upon every thing, even what may have been reserved for the particular use of the king, or if thou incur his displeasure by gluttony and intemperance.

3. — *deceitful meat;* i.e., the friendship of rulers and great men, however agreeable and flattering, is very uncertain and unstable, nay, even deceitful; since experience proves that they who are familiar with princes are in a situation of great danger.

4. — *thy wisdom;* i.e., that sort of wisdom which consists in laboring to be rich, and supposing that riches are all that is wanting to happiness.

6. — *that hath an evil eye;* i.e., an avaricious, sordid disposition.

7. — *as he thinketh in his heart,* &c.; i.e., his true character is displayed in what is passing in his mind, rather than in what he utters with his lips. — *is not with thee;* i.e., his invitation is not cordial. It was given from ostentation, or for ambitious and selfish purposes.

8. — *vomit up;* i.e., when you have discovered his illiberality and selfishness, or perhaps ill treatment, you will feel such disgust as to wish that what you have swallowed could be thrown up on his table. — *pleasant words;* i.e., whatever compliments, courtesies, or agreeable discourse you may have bestowed upon your entertainer.

9. *Speak not,* &c.; i.e., for the purpose of admonition or direction.

10. — *enter not;* i.e., either to reap their crops, or perhaps, rather, to possess their lands.

11. — *their avenger;* i.e., though they may have no human guardians or friends to oppose thee, they have in heaven a vindicator, or avenger, who is able and willing to defend their rights, or punish their infringement. On the term *avenger* or *vindicator,* see the note on Job xix. 25.

13. — *he will not die;* i.e., he will escape the ruin which is the consequence of wickedness.

17. — *envy,* &c.; i.e., let not the view of their present prosperity excite thee to envy them, and to approve and imitate their evil courses.

18. — *a reward;* i.e., for them that persevere in the ways of religion and virtue.

19. — *go forward in the way;* i.e., not follow devious and crooked courses.

20. — *riotous eaters,* &c. Otherwise, *prodigal of their flesh;* i.e., waste away their bodies by sensual indulgence.

23. *Buy the truth;* spare no pains nor cost to obtain the knowledge of what is true and right, and hold it fast.

27. — *deep pit;* — *narrow well;* from which one can with difficulty escape, when he has fallen into it.

28. — *lieth in wait.* See chap. vii. 12. — *increaseth;* i.e., to the number of those whom she has already made her prey.

29. — *without cause;* i.e., not in the just and necessary defence of himself or his country.

30. — *go in;* i.e., to the place where mixed wine is kept. — *mixed wine;* i.e., spiced, strong wine.

34. — *midst of the sea;* i.e., in a ship in the midst of the sea. — *top of a mast.* As the comparison holds good in several particulars, there is some doubt as to that which was intended by the poet; whether he refers to the stupidity and senselessness of danger which are the consequence of intoxication, or to the giddy feelings of the persons intoxicated, when their heads swim, and they feel as if they were tossed about by the rolling waves of the sea.

35. Here the drunkard is represented as using the language which corresponds to his senselessness and stupidity. "I cannot deny that I expose myself by my drunkenness to various abuses and injuries. But I was not sensible of them at the time, nor do I now feel much harm from them." — *When shall I awake?* i.e., oh that I could rouse myself from my state of languor and stupidity! I would again seek wine.

Chap. XXIV.

1. — *envious of wicked men;* let it not disturb thy tranquillity to see men thrive who are bent upon wickedness. — *to be with them;* i.e., as a companion and a partaker of their profitable crimes. (Comp. chap. xxiii. 17.)

5. — *is strong.* Comp. Eccl. ix. 14–16.

6. Comp. chap. xx. 18.

7. — *too high;* i.e., so that he cannot attain it, and is ashamed to speak *at the gate,* i.e., in the place of judgment, or in public.

8. — *deviseth to do evil,* &c.; i.e., a contriver of unjust, malicious plans shall be hated (comp. chap. xiv. 17), and branded with an odious name.

9. — *is sin,* &c. The meaning of this verse seems to be, that the purpose of evil, before it breaks forth into action, is sinful in the sight of God; but that the bold and obstinate offender is not only offensive to God, but odious to men.

10. — *faint,* &c.; i.e., when courage or hope is lost, all is lost.

12. — *we knew it not;* it is no excuse to say, that you are ignorant of the guilt or innocence of the accused, or that you knew not but that he was justly condemned, unless you have taken all possible pains to discover the truth in relation to the case.

13. *Eat honey;* this is said merely to illustrate the following verse by an implied comparison.

16. — *fall seven times;* i.e., though he repeatedly fall into calamities. — *fall into mischief;* and not rise again.

17. *Rejoice not,* &c. Comp. Job xxxi. 29.

18. — *turn away his anger*, &c.; perhaps, and inflict it upon thee.

20. — *lamp.* See chap. xx. 20, and the note.

21. — *and the king;* whom the Orientals regarded as the vicegerent of God, standing in a near and peculiar relation to him, called his son, &c. — *given to change;* fond of revolution, disobedient and rebellious subjects, disorganizers.

22. — *coming from both;* namely, God and the king. — *in a moment.* See the note on Job ix. 5; or Gesen. Lex. on רֶגַע.

23. *These also are words of the wise.* These words probably have relation to chap. xxii. 17, and intimate that the proverbs from ver. 23 to the end of this chapter are an appendix to those mentioned in chap. xxii. 17.

26. — *giveth a right answer;* i.e., the judge who gives correct decisions; perhaps, others who give a good answer. — *Kisseth the lips;* i.e., gains good-will, makes himself beloved.

27. — *build thy house;* "do every thing in order; and first mind those things which are most necessary, contenting thyself with a little hut in the field, till thou hast gotten an estate by a careful improvement of thy pasturage and thy tillage; and then it will be timely enough to build thee an house, and to bring a wife into it."— Patrick.

29. Comp. chap. xx. 22.

Chap. XXV.

1. — *men of Hezekiah;* i.e., literary men whom Hezekiah appointed for the purpose. The title in which these words are contained is prefixed to the collection of proverbs extending to chap. xxx., which the learned men of Hezekiah copied from larger collections, or from books in which they were scattered.

2. — *to conceal a thing;* to hide from human eyes the reasons of his purposes and proceedings. — *search out a matter;* i.e., when they decide and decree nothing until they have made the most careful examination, so as to be able to give the clearest reasons for their proceedings.

3. — *unsearchable;* men in general are unable to penetrate the purposes and designs of kings.

4, 5. "You cannot have a pure silver vessel, till you have purified the silver; and no nation can have a king a public blessing, till all bad counsellors, wicked and interested ministers, and sycophants, are banished from the court and cabinet."

6, 7. Comp. Luke xiv. 10.

8. *Go not forth*, &c.; i.e., to the gates where the courts of law were usually held.

9. — *another's secret;* not even the heat of contention with an opponent will justify the revelation of his secret which may have been intrusted to you.

11. — *in figured-work*, &c. The illustration seems to be borrowed from a rich garment, on which were embroidered apples of gold among silver figures. (So Bertheau.)

13. — *cold of snow*, &c. There can be little doubt that the use of snow in cooling drinks is referred to.

14. — *falsely boasteth of giving;* i.e., makes many promises of what he will give which he never performs.

15. — *breaketh bones;* i.e., melts the heart as hard as a bone; as we say, as a stone.

16. This verse may be regarded as a separate precept, inculcating moderation, especially in things which are pleasant, or merely as an illustration of ver. 17.

18. *A battle-hammer,* &c.; i.e., equally pernicious and destructive.

20. — *vinegar upon nitre;* which causes it to effervesce, and, as it were, irritates it. *Nitre* here probably denotes a mineral alkali, the natron of the moderns, or Egyptian nitre, which, being mingled with oil, is still used for soap.

22. — *coals of fire upon his head.* This expression seems most naturally to denote that which causes the most intense pain, that which is insupportable. The meaning seems to be, that, by returning good for evil, the evil-doer will be overwhelmed with remorse and shame.

23. — *bringeth forth rain;* covers the face of the sky with black clouds, full of rain; so a backbiting tongue causes indignation in him who is slandered, which may be the cause of punishment to the slanderer.

26. — *troubled fountain, — corrupted spring.* It is as melancholy and discouraging a circumstance to see a good man, who is the source of much good to his fellow-men, fall into ruin through the arts of the wicked, as it is to the weary, thirsty traveller to find a fountain or a spring trampled upon and polluted, so as to be unfit for use. It seems to be more agreeable to the use of the word מָט to understand it as denoting *falling into ruin* or *calamity,* not voluntarily succumbing, and yielding to the persuasions of the wicked. Possibly, however, it may mean *to vacillate,* in a moral sense.

27. — *So the search of high things is weariness. High things,* a rendering based on a disregard of the Hebrew points, may denote difficult questions respecting Providence, or other subjects of human investigation; in which case, the meaning will be similar to that of the observation in Ecclesiastes, that much study is a weariness of the flesh. Or, *high things* may denote worldly honors; in which case, the line will relate to the cares and vexations which attend the pursuit of honor. In the original, there is, I think, a sort of play upon words, using the same word twice in the line with an altered signification. The word rendered *high things* denotes *high, honorable, glorious,* and also *heavy.* An imperfect imitation of the line in English would be, The search of weighty things is weighty; *weighty* being understood, in the first case, in the sense of *important,* and, in the second, in that of *heavy.* The verse is rendered in the sense which I have assigned to it by Coverdale: "Like as it is not good to eat much honey, even so he that will search out high things, it shall be too heavy for him." The supply of a negative, as in the common version, appears to me to be inadmissible. Gesenius, transferring a Hebrew letter from the end of one word to the beginning of another, translates, *So the search of glory is without glory.* But this negative use of מִן *in such a position* is hardly justified by usage.

Chap. XXVI.

1. — *snow*, &c.; i.e., unseasonable and incongruous. — *fool;* i.e., one who by his folly or wickedness, or both united, makes a bad use of power.

2. — *shall not come;* shall not take effect, or fall upon him against whom it is uttered, but be dispersed into the air, as the birds mentioned fly away, no one knows whither.

4. — *according to his folly.* Some suppose the meaning of ver. 4 and 5 to be, that, according to circumstances and the nature of his folly, a fool should or should not receive any answer. It seems to me that the meaning is best elicited by understanding the phrase *according to his folly* in different senses. In the first case, *Answer not in the manner of the fool;* in the second, *Answer him in the manner which his folly demands.* "If the fool boast of himself, do not answer him by boasting of thyself. If he rail and talk passionately, do not thou rail and talk passionately too. If he tell one great lie, do not thou tell another to match it. If he calumniate thy friends, do not thou calumniate his. If he banter, do not answer him in his own language, *lest thou be like him.*" — Henry. But answer in such a manner as his folly demands, as is adapted to expose it and convince him of it, and leave him nothing to say for himself, *lest he be wise in his own conceit.*

6. — *he cutteth off the feet;* i.e., he fails in the object of the mission, as surely as if he should cut off the feet of the persons sent.

7. — *hang loose;* like a bucket in a well, and serve no purpose. The rendering which I have adopted seems best supported. (See Gesenius ad verb.) For a different rendering, see Fürst's Lexicon on דָּלָה.

8. — *bindeth a stone*, &c.; i.e., it is as absurd to expect any good consequence from bestowing honor on a fool as to expect a stone to do execution when it is bound to the sling. Otherwise, *as he who putteth a purse of gems on a heap of stones;* i.e., honor is as ill placed in his hands as gems upon a heap of common, worthless stones.

9. — *a thorn*, &c. He injures himself and others by the ill use he makes of it, as one would by brandishing a thorn-bush up and down, at random.

10. *As an archer*, &c. The meaning seems to be, that the man who hires fools or chance wayfarers does as careless and inconsiderate a thing as the archer who should shoot at random at everybody and every thing.

12. — *of a fool;* i.e., who may become sensible of his folly, and willing to receive instruction.

13. — *lion*, &c. He is frightened from real duties by fancied difficulties.

14. — *turneth*, &c.; i.e., backward and forward, without leaving them; so the sluggard lies in his bed on one side till he is weary of that, and then turns to the other, but still is in his bed.

16. *The sluggard*, &c. Taking no pains to inform himself, and of course ignorant of the difficulties which attend an opinion or a determination, he takes himself to be wiser than others.

17. — *a dog by the ears;* i.e., he incurs much danger, without neces-

sity, or the possibility of advantage. Travellers in the East speak of the wild and fierce character of the dogs in that region.

18. *As a madman;* as dangerous and as much to be shunned as a madman. Otherwise, *as a jester,* &c.

22. See chap. xviii. 8.

26. Though he may for a time conceal his malicious feelings, yet the time will come when his malice shall be publicly known, and receive the punishment which it deserves.

27. — *diggeth a pit;* i.e., lays a plot for the injury of another. The metaphor is drawn from the practice of hunters, who used to dig deep pits, and then cover them with bushes, earth, &c., that wild beasts might fall into them. — *rolleth a stone;* i.e., up a steep place in order that it may crush another.

28. — *those whom it woundeth;* i.e., because the slanderer is conscious of having incurred the enmity of the slandered.

Chap. XXVII.

3. — *a fool's wrath.* See chap. xvii. 12.

4. — *overwhelming;* literally, *an overflowing.* — *jealousy.* Comp. chap. vi. 34, 35. These proverbs apply with still greater force to Oriental countries than to our own.

5. — *love kept concealed;* i.e., which does not manifest itself in giving needful reproof, and in care for the moral welfare of a friend.

8. *As a bird,* &c. As a bird that forsakes its nest exposes itself to danger, and cannot easily settle again, so he whose levity or discontent makes him rashly leave his country or trade or office, wherein he was well placed, too often undoes himself, but rarely mends his condition.

10. *And go not into thy brother's house;* i.e., by fidelity in friendship, acquire such faithful friends, that it shall not be necessary to repair to a brother.

11. — *that reproacheth me;* i.e., with want of care for my child, on account of his unworthy conduct.

12. Comp. chap. xxii. 3.

13. See chap. xx. 16, and the note.

14. *To him;* i.e., who blesses his neighbor, &c. His neighbor will regard this kind of blessing as no better than a curse. He will suspect the sincerity of it. There is an Italian proverb, "He who praises you more than he was wont to do has either deceived you, or is about to do it."

15. Comp. chap. xix. 13, and the note.

16. — *oil,* &c.; which is too slippery to be held fast. So the quarrelsome wife cannot be restrained. קָרָא, *to meet, to come upon;* in this case, to take hold of.

17. — *sharpeneth the face;* i.e., the looks, the countenance. This may be understood as expressing the idea, that by conversation and discussion one man may quicken and invigorate the mental faculties of another. But there is considerable reason for supposing that the face is here regarded as the seat of *anger;* in which case, *to sharpen the face* will denote *to inflame the anger.* (Comp. Job xvi. 9, and the note.)

19. *So doth the heart of man to man.* These words have been understood in various ways. They are commonly understood as denoting, that as there is a resemblance between the face of a man and the reflected image of it in the water, so there is a resemblance between one man's heart and another's, so that in many cases we may judge of others by ourselves. Otherwise, as the water is a looking-glass, in which we may see our faces by reflection, so the heart or conscience is a mirror, in which the character of the man may be discerned. Otherwise, as every man will find reflected in the water such a countenance, whether sour or smiling, as he brings when he looks into it, so he ought to expect no other dispositions and feelings from others than those which he exercises toward them. Love wins love, &c.

20. — *the eyes of man. The eyes* here denote not merely curiosity, but the desires generally. (Comp. Eccl. i. 8; iv. 8.)

21. *So let a man be;* i.e., let him take care not to be deceived by flattery, but consider who it is that gives praise, what may be the motive, and how far it is deserved.

23–27. "These verses recommend the advantages of private life; and show that diligence in rural employments, and the plenty obtained by it, are more conducive to true happiness than the unstable and uneasy, though splendid, possessions of wealth and authority.

24. — *riches.* The term here seems to denote that kind of wealth which may be treasured up, such as money, garments, &c., in distinction from herds, lands, &c. — *the crown;* i.e., royal or princely dignity.

26. — *the price of thy field;* i.e., that with which you may purchase land.

Chap. XXVIII.

1. "An evil conscience makes men timorous and cowardly, like a faint-hearted soldier who runs away at the appearance of an enemy, and never so much as looks back to see whether he pursue him." — Patrick.

2. — *transgression;* perhaps *rebellion;* — *many are its rulers.* This may denote rulers following each other in rapid succession, and by continual revolution; or rulers exercising authority at the same time, in rebellion against the legitimate king. — *the prince.* This word is implied in the parallel line.

3. *Is a sweeping rain;* which, instead of refreshing the corn, as gentle showers do, beats it down and lays it flat, so that it can never recover, and a famine comes upon the land. "This is especially true in the East. There places are often sold by the needy government to the highest bidder, who, not knowing how soon another may bid higher for his place, makes the most of his time to remunerate himself, unscrupulous as to the means."

4. — *praise the wicked;* i.e., their conduct encourages and virtually commends the wicked.

5. — *understand not equity;* i.e., discern not, or feel not the force of, moral distinctions; their consciences are weak or dead; their corruptions blind their eyes, and fill them with prejudices; and, because they

do evil, they hate the light. — *all things;* i.e., relating to equity or moral conduct.

8. *Gathereth it for him,* &c.; i.e., by the wise retributions of Heaven, it passes into the hands of one who will make a good use of it. (Comp. chap. xiii. 22; Job xxvii. 17.)

9. — *turneth away his ear,* &c. He that refuses to hearken unto God and to obey his laws deceives himself, if he thinks by his prayers to please him, and make amends for his crimes; for God will be so far from hearkening to him, that he will abominate such prayers as tend to nothing but to make God a partner with him in his sins.

11. — *will search him through;* i.e., he look through all his vain show, and easily discover and make it appear what he really is.

12. — *rejoice;* i.e., in the possession of authority and high station, as is suggested by the antithetical line. — *great glorying;* i.e., instead of *hiding themselves,* as in the antithetical line, men go about exulting in their safety, wealth, and prosperity. — *hide themselves;* from a feeling of gloom, and from regard to their safety, they conceal themselves, their wealth, ornaments, &c.

13. — *covereth his sins.* See Ps. xxxii. 3–5.

14. — *feareth always;* namely, to displease God, or to incur the evil consequences of sin. (Comp. chap. xiv. 16.)

15. — *a needy people;* who have little to satisfy his cupidity, and from their weakness are sure to be oppressed by him.

16. — *great in oppression;* and thus has a short reign, as is to be understood from the antithetical line.

17. — *stay him;* i.e., to afford him aid, or prevent his fleeing into the grave. The idea seems to be that the murderer deserves death. — *the pit;* i.e., the grave.

18. — *at once;* i.e., suddenly and unexpectedly.

19. — *bread enough;* — *poverty enough.* This rendering imitates the pointed correspondence or rather identity of the Hebrew words.

20. — *faithful man;* i.e., to his promises, engagements, &c. — *maketh haste to be rich;* i.e., not being a faithful man, as in the antithetical line.

21. — *for a piece of bread,* &c. Though at the first the partial judge could not be bribed without a great sum of money, yet, when he has once vitiated his conscience and accustomed himself to take bribes, he will at last sell a decision for the smallest advantage.

22. — *evil eye;* i.e., a sordid, covetous, uncharitable disposition. (Comp. chap. xxii. 9; xxiii. 6.)

24. — *no transgression;* under the plea, perhaps, that all will be his at last. — *is the companion of a robber;* i.e., deserves to be classed with robbers.

25. — *strife;* which involves him in expense and losses, as is to be inferred from the antithetical line.

26. — *his own understanding.* Comp. chap. iii. 5–7. — *is a fool;* his self-confidence and rashness lead him into misfortunes, from which *he who walketh wisely* is delivered.

27. — *hideth his eyes;* i.e., turns them away from the petition and miseries of the poor. — *many a curse;* i.e., from God. (Comp. chap. iii. 33; Mal. ii. 2.)

28. Comp. ver. 12.

Chap. XXIX.

1. — *hardeneth his neck;* i.e., continues refractory or disobedient; a metaphor drawn from stubborn oxen, which refuse to submit to the yoke.

2. — *are powerful;* רָבָה, though it does not signify to be in authority in the sense of *ruling,* does sometimes mean to be great in power or influence. (See Job xxxiii. 12.) This meaning suits the connection better than the rendering *increase.* (Comp. xi. 10; xxviii. 12, 28.)

3. — *rejoiceth his father;* i.e., by his success in life, as is implied in the antithetical clause.

4. — *receiveth gifts;* i.e., as bribes.

5. — *for his feet;* i.e., of his neighbor.

6. — *there is a snare;* in which he will be caught, and brought to ruin.

7. — *discerneth not knowledge;* i.e., he has no true knowledge; he is not imbued with the principles of equity, and pays no regard to them in his decisions.

8. *Scoffers,* &c.; i.e., they who deride religion and positive laws. — *a flame;* excite tumults and commotions.

9. *Whether he rage or laugh,* &c.; i.e., whether he take the serious or the jocular way of dealing with him, whether he be severe or pleasant with him, there will be no end to the controversy; the fool will answer, object, excuse, &c., and have the last word. Or the meaning may be, that the fool may rage or laugh without coming to a settlement of the dispute.

10. — *hateth the upright;* who disapprove and oppose his evil designs.

11. — *his anger;* so the Septuagint, Syriac, and Chaldaic; more literally, *his spirit,* as it is rendered in chap. xxv. 28, where a similar sentiment is expressed.

12. — *listen;* i.e., lend his ear to calumniators and flatterers. This verse is well explained by Ecclus. x. 2: "As the judge of the people is himself, so are his officers; and what manner of man the ruler of the city is, such are all they that dwell therein."

13. *The poor man and the oppressor,* &c. Comp. chap. xxii. 2, which contains a similar sentiment. — *enlighteneth,* &c.; he is the author of light and life to both.

18. — *no vision;* i.e., prophetic vision, or all that instruction which it was the office of a prophet to give to the people.

19. — *by words.* "A slave, and he that is of a servile nature, is not to be amended by reason and persuasions, no, nor by reproofs or threats; for though he hear, and understand too, what you say, yet he will not obey till he be forced to it by blows." — Patrick.

20. Comp. chap. xxvi. 12. "Seest thou a man that is forward to speak to every matter that is started, and affects to speak first to it, to open it and speak last to it, to give judgment upon it, as if he were an oracle? There is more hope of a modest fool, who is sensible of his folly, than of such a self-conceited one." — Henry.

21. — *become a son;* he will presume upon the indulgence of his

master, take the liberties of a son, conduct himself as if he one day expected to be master.

23. Comp. chap. xv. 33; Matt. xxiii. 12.

24. — *hateth himself;* i.e., by bringing ruin upon himself, he acts as though he hated himself. — *maketh no discovery;* i.e., *he heareth the curse* imprecated upon him as a witness, if he do not speak the truth; but, rather than acknowledge his own participation in the theft, he incurs the guilt of perjury. (Lev. v. 1.)

26. — *every man's judgment,* &c. This may denote that the sentence which the ruler gives concerning any man's cause depends upon God, who turns the hearts of rulers as the rivers of water are turned. (Comp. chap. xvi 33; xxi. 1.) Or, more generally, that every man's condition and success in life depend more upon the favor of God than upon the favor of a ruler.

Chap. XXX.

1. "This chapter contains a new collection of pithy sayings, which some fancy to be Solomon's, and therefore translate the two first words thus: 'The words of the collector or gatherer.' But why Solomon should call himself by this name, and also, instead of the son of David, style himself the son of Jakeh, seems to me unaccountable. And therefore it is most reasonable to follow our translation, and to look upon this chapter as a fragment of some wise sentences delivered by one whose name was Agur, and his father's name Jakeh; unless we will conceive that this son of Jakeh (whoever he was) had gotten the name of *collector,* because, though he was a very wise man, yet he composed nothing himself, but only gathered out of other wise men's works such instructions as he thought most profitable, and comprised in a few words a great deal of sense." — Patrick. Or, if the name *Agur* be regarded as symbolical, like Koheleth, the Preacher, it may denote *an assembler, one of the assembly,* i.e., of wise men. (Comp. Eccl. xii. 11.) *Ithiel,* a name denoting *God-with-me,* and *Ucal,* denoting *powerful,* were, no doubt, sons or disciples of Agur.

Hitzig and Bertheau, who are followed by Professor Stuart, have adopted a new division of the Hebrew words of this verse, according to which the sense will be very different. Thus: *The words of Agur, the son of her whose domain is Massa. I have wearied myself for God; I have wearied myself for God, and have failed.* I cannot persuade myself, that בֶּן־יִקְהָה מַשָּׂא, literally, *the son, her obedience Massa,* could have been used by the writer to express the meaning, *the son of her whose domain is Massa.* In regard to the latter clause, which those critics read thus, לָאִיתִי אֵל לָאִיתִי אֵל וָאֵכֶל, and translate, *I have wearied myself for God; I have wearied myself for God, and have failed;* — I do not believe the writer would have used לָאִיתִי אֵל, without an intervening preposition to denote, *I have wearied myself for God.* It would rather be, *O God!* Neither does the phrase, *I have wearied myself for God,* appear to me a natural one to express the meaning, I have wearied myself in searching out the nature or providence of God. Neither is the meaning, *I have failed,* in the sense in which those critics understand the expression, well supported by Hebrew usage. (See the Lexicons on כָּלָה.) As to the rendering which I have adopted, it is indeed singular that the three expressions, "the words," "the prophecy," and "the inspired utterance," should be used to denote the same thing. Possibly מַשָּׂא or נְאֻם may be a gloss introduced into the text from the margin.

2. — *more stupid than any man*, &c. It has been supposed, that the professions of ignorance, in ver. 2 and 3, are by way of reply to his disciples Ithiel and Ucal, who may have ascribed to him extraordinary knowledge, or have come to him with hard metaphysical or theological questions. But it is quite as probable that Agur speaks of his acquired knowledge and attainments with such humility, by way of contrast with the word of God (ver. 5); i.e., that truth which comes by inspiration, or which God has spoken or may speak by his prophets. (Comp. Amos vii. 14, 15; Jer. i. 6; Job xxxii. 7, 8.)

3. — *wisdom;* i.e., philosophy; that wisdom that comes by study and by the instruction of the learned. — *knowledge of the Most Holy.* Comp. chap. ix. 10. The meaning seems to be, that he had not a knowledge of the deep things of God, his purposes, the ways of providence, &c. (Comp. Job xi. 7.) It may have been part of the design of this profession of ignorance to rebuke some of the author's contemporaries, who may have made great pretensions to knowledge of things human and divine.

4. The design of the questions in this verse seems to be to illustrate man's ignorance of the works and the ways of God; to show that God alone is wise, and that man must depend upon him for instruction. (Comp. Job xxxviii.–xli.) No one was entitled to trust or boast of his knowledge of God acquired by his own faculties, unless he could show that he had obtained it by ascending to heaven, &c.; or unless he manifested his wisdom and power by doing such wonderful things as ascending to the skies, holding the wind, &c. Roberts quotes as Orientalisms still in use, "Yes, you are quite sure; you know all about it! Have you just returned from the heavens?" — "Truly he has just finished his journey from above; listen, listen to this divine messenger!" — "Our friend is about to do wonderful things: he has already caught the wind; he has seized it with his hand." (See Roberts's Illustrations, ad loc.) — *What is his name?* i.e., by what name is the wise man, the philosopher called, who can do or explain these things? — *his son's name;* i.e., either, what is the name of one of his disciples, or of one of his kindred, — his son. It is an emphatic way of declaring that no one ever heard of such a person. (Comp. Amos vii. 14.)

5. *Every word of God;* i.e., every declaration, promise, and precept. — *pure;* i.e., free from error and imperfection.

6. *Add not*, &c. Comp. Deut. iv. 2.

8. — *falsehood and lies.* These words may refer to the errors of idolatry, and to false religious opinions, so as to have some relation to what precedes. (Comp. Jer. xviii. 15.) Others suppose the expressions to refer to the outside show, the deceitful promises, of mere wealth, station, pleasure, the "lying vanities of life," so as to have some relation to what follows respecting a state of mediocrity.

9. — *violate the name*, &c.; viz., by a false oath. (Comp. Deut. viii. 11, &c.) It has been observed that the danger of perjury was greater among the Jews than with us, as their custom or law tendered an oath to persons suspected or accused of theft, to clear or purge themselves. (See Exod. xxii. 8–11.)

10. *Lest he curse thee*, &c. The consideration of the temptations of poverty reminds the author of the condition of the poor slave, who was probably often accused upon light grounds, and thus tempted to perjure himself, or incur the vengeance of a too rigorous master. It is also intimated that the curse imprecated by the slave upon such a careless, inconsiderate informer might take effect, not being causeless.

11. In this and the following verses, the author points out four vices, which were probably the prevailing vices of his time, as especially to be detested and avoided; namely, ingratitude (especially filial ingratitude), hypocrisy, pride, and oppression or extortion.

13. — *lofty are their eyes*, &c. Comp. chap. vi. 17, xxi. 4.

15, 16. After the mention of four detestable things, four insatiable things are enumerated, either as curious in themselves, or as illustrating the insatiable desires of man. Gesenius, Fürst, and others suppose that an imaginary female spectre is here denoted, which sucks human blood and is insatiable, like *El Ghûle* of Arabian superstition in the Thousand and One Nights.

17. — *shall pick it out*, &c.; i.e., they shall come to an infamous and miserable end, their dead bodies being unburied, and left to be a prey to the ravens which frequent the brooks that run in the valleys; and to the young eagles, which shall pick out those eyes in which their scorn and derision of their parents were wont to appear. Roberts observes that the eye is the first and favorite part attacked by birds of prey, as is seen in the numerous bodies which various Eastern superstitions cause to be exposed to birds and beasts. "The crows shall one day pick out thy eyes," is no uncommon imprecation in the East.

19. — *track of an eagle*, &c. "As, when a bird hath flown through the air, there is no token of her way to be found, but the light air, being beaten with the stroke of her wings, and parted with the violent noise and motion of them, is passed through, and therein afterward no sign where she went is to be found." — Wisdom v. 11. — *upon a rock;* which receives no mark from the passing of a serpent over it. — *a ship*, &c.; that passes over the water, and leaves no trace of the keel in the waves. (See Wisdom v. 10.) — *track of a man*, &c. The first three things are designed as comparisons to illustrate or satirize the last; namely, criminal intercourse with a maiden, with which no one is acquainted but the lovers; while she is reputed a virgin, and conceals her wickedness with so much art, and assumes such an appearance of chastity and modesty, that it is as impossible to discover that a man has had an improper connection with her, as to discover tracks left by an eagle in the air, &c.

20. *Such;* i.e., to be discovered with equal difficulty. — *She eats*, &c.; i.e., she conceals her criminal intercourse by a ready falsehood, as one would do, who, desiring to conceal that he has eaten any thing, should wipe his lips and deny it.

22. — *a servant when he becometh a king*, as sometimes happens under

18*

the despotic governments of the East, is of all others most insolent, imperious, and cruel. There is a German proverb, "No razor shaves closer than when a boor becomes master." — *filled with bread.* This may refer to a conceited fool, whose manners in his prosperity none can bear; or to a bad man, in whose hands wealth is the instrument of oppression and mischief.

23. — *when she becometh a wife.* An ill-natured woman, when she gets a husband, being elated with her new dignity, displays all those ill humors which for her own ends she formerly concealed. She is then puffed up and imperious, and becomes intolerable to her own family, and to her relations and neighbors. — *heir to her mistress;* i.e., succeeds to the place of her mistress by the marriage of her master. This great and sudden change makes her intolerably proud, scornful, and insolent.

24–28. The four following animals may be mentioned merely as curious in natural history, as the three in ver. 29–31. Or, if they are designed to teach a moral lesson, it may be "that we should not admire bodily bulk or beauty or strength, or value persons for that; but judge of men by their wisdom and conduct, their industry and application to business, which are characters that deserve respect. 2. To admire the wisdom and power of the Creator in the smallest and most despicable animals, in an ant as much as in an elephant. 3. To blame ourselves, who do not act so much for our own interest as the meanest creatures do for theirs." — Henry. Umbreit supposes the verses to contain a satirical reflection upon the speculating philosophers of the time. Instead of *Yet are they wise, instructed in wisdom,* he renders, *Yet are they wiser than the wise;* i.e., the learned men.

25. — *their food.* See chap. vi. 8, and the note. Comp. Virg. Æn., iv. 402.

26. *The conies.* The *shaphan,* for which we have no English name, probably does not denote the *coney* or rabbit. The most satisfactory statement on the subject is in Wilson's Lands of the Bible, &c., p. 27, &c. Dr. Wilson gives what he says is an exact representation of it in the natural attitude. He says, "The preparer of the skin mistook it for a rabbit, though it is of a stronger build, and of a duskier color, being of a dark brown. It is entirely destitute of a tail, and has some bristles at its mouth, over its head, and down its back, along the course of which there are traces of light and dark shade. In its short ears, small, black, and naked feet, and pointed snout, it resembles the hedgehog." (See also Kitto's Cyclopædia on the word *shaphan.*)

27. — *go forth in bands;* i.e., as a well-ordered host to war. (See Joel ii. 4–8.)

28. — *lizard.* This small animal is mentioned as frequenting houses by several writers quoted by Rosenmüller. "Quid, cum me domi sedentem stellio muscas captans, vel aranea retibus suis implicans, sæpe intentum facit?" Augustin. Confess., lib. x. cap. 35. "Sub noctem conspicitur exigua quædam lacerta secundum muros reptans et muscas captans." Bellonius, Observ., lib. ii. cap. 15. — *seizes;* its prey, such as flies, spiders, &c. — *in kings' palaces;* in pursuit of its prey, it is permitted to go into the palaces of kings; or it has such ingenuity that it enters them with impunity.

31. *The loin-girded war-horse;* literally, *the loin-girded;* an epithet

which most probably denotes the horse, as equipped for war, with girths and buckles around the loins, a species of ornament frequently seen in the bas-reliefs of Persepolis, as Gesenius observes. By others, the epithet is supposed to refer to the greyhound, or the zebra, or the cock. — *who cannot be withstood;* i.e., marching forward like a hero, putting down all his enemies. By resorting to the Arabic sense of אַלְקוּם, we may obtain the meaning, *in the midst of his people;* i.e., surrounded by them, and surveying them with pride and confidence, and walking before them with an air of majesty. (See Ges. Lex. on אַלְקוּם.) But this resort to the Arabic word for "people," especially with the Arabic article prefixed, seems unjustifiable.

32. — *lifting thyself up;* i.e., either in pride or passion or preparation to do an injury. — *hand on thy mouth;* i.e., be silent; do not say a word, much less do any thing toward the accomplishment of it.

33. — *the pressing of anger.* This verse I have rendered literally. The design of it evidently is to inculcate forbearance, composure, quietness, in opposition to the hasty expression of anger, and the utterance of provoking language. Instead of giving way to anger, the effort should be to repress it. (Comp. chap. xvii. 14.) Or, instead of provoking the anger of another by reproaches, we should endeavor to repress it by mildness.

Chap. XXXI.

1. *Lemuel.* This may have been the name of some Arabian or Edomitish king. There is no evidence that it was one of the names of Solomon; nor has any good reason been assigned why his appropriate name should not have been given him, if he was intended. The name denotes either *God-with-them*, or *of* or *from God.*

2. — *son of my womb;* very dear to me, as my own son; not merely mine by adoption. — *son of my vows;* for whom I made so many prayers and vows, if I might but see thee come safe into the world, and grow up to be a man, and sit upon a throne.

3. — *thy strength.* The original term denotes, not only strength of body and mind, but resources, treasures, &c. — *thy ways;* i.e., thy course of life. — *that which destroyeth kings;* i.e., an improper and excessive intercourse with women, which has frequently led to the overthrow of the most powerful monarchs, especially in the countries of the East.

4. — *to drink wine;* i.e., to drink it to excess. It is of more importance for kings to be sparing in the use of wine than for the miserable; because by its influence the former forget justice to others, whilst the latter forget their own misery.

6. *Give strong drink,* &c. If the liberal use of wine and strong drink is to be allowed to any, it is to the poor and miserable rather than to rulers. — *ready to perish* is to be understood, not in a strict sense, but as denoting an unfortunate, poor, miserable man (see ver. 7); though the Jews say that on this verse was founded the practice of giving a stupefying drink to condemned prisoners when they were going to execution, as they did to the Saviour.

8. — *for the dumb;* i.e., for those who, through incapacity, like orphans, or through fear of powerful opponents, are unable to defend their own cause.

10–31. It seems probable that this description of a good wife is not a continuation of the discourse of Lemuel's mother, nor a description of the wife of a king, but rather a distinct composition, and perhaps by a different hand. It consists of twenty-two verses, beginning with the letters of the Hebrew alphabet in consecutive order; the first with Aleph, the second with Beth, &c., whence Döderlein calls it the golden A B C for wives. Henry calls it the looking-glass for ladies, into which they should look, and by which they should dress themselves.

10. — *capable woman.* The term *capable* expresses the idea of the original better than *virtuous.* A capable as well as a virtuous woman is denoted, as is evident not only from the original term חַיִל, *strength,* i.e., *capacity,* but from the description which follows. The objection to the term *virtuous* is, that it makes the idea of chastity too prominent. The passage is a delineation of the *ideal* of a Hebrew housewife.

11. — *trusteth,* &c.; i.e., for the prudent and faithful management of all his domestic affairs. — *of gain;* i.e., by her industry and economy her husband is enriched with provision for the family.

12. *All the days of her life;* i.e., not at first only, or now and then, by fits and starts, but constantly and perpetually.

13. — *wool and flax.* It is well known that the most noble females among the Hebrews, Greeks, and Romans were engaged in labors of this kind. — *worketh willingly,* &c.; more literally, *worketh with the delight of her hands;* she makes it appear that her work is not her drudgery, but her delight.

14. — *bringeth her food,* &c.; by the sale of her homespun commodities, she procures provision from distant places.

16. By her industry and economy, she not only provides for the household, but even adds to her husband's possessions.

17. — *girdeth her loins;* i.e., what she does she does with all her might. (See the note on Job xii. 21.)

18. — *her lamp is not extinguished,* &c.; she continues her labors beyond the close of the day. Of course the expression is not to be understood to the letter. (Comp. Virg. Æn. viii. 407, et seqq.) Umbreit, who often strains his ingenuity to find a new meaning, supposes the expression to be an image of prosperity, as in chap. xiii. 9; xx. 20.

19. — *the spindle.* It is said to have been common in the East to draw the thread from the distaff with one hand, and to twirl the spindle with the other.

21. — *clothed with crimson;* i.e., not only protected from the cold, but even splendidly arrayed. (Comp. 2 Sam. i. 24.)

23. — *known in the gates,* &c. This may mean that he is distinguished by the richness of his dress, which his wife has provided for him by her industry. (Comp. Hom. Odys., vi. 60, &c.) Or that the husband is freed, by the industry and good management of his wife, from all cares but those of public business.

24. — *linen garments;* probably a linen under-garment. Adam Clarke observes: "Some such garments as these are still worn by

ladies in India and China, and are so thin and transparent, that every part of the body may be seen through them. I have many representations of persons clothed in this way before me, both of the Chinese, the Hindoo, and the Malabar ladies." (See also Gesenius ad verb.) — *girdles.* Girdles were sometimes of so rich a texture as to be con sidered a valuable present.

25. *Strength and honor are her clothing;* i.e., her greatest ornaments, however, are her strong and active mind, her honorable conduct, and her good name. — *she laugheth,* &c.; i.e., she lives in tranquillity ot mind; she has no concern about want or trouble in future time.

26. — *with wisdom;* she is neither silent through ignorance or sullenness, nor yet full of vain and unprofitable gossip. Her conversation is wise and instructive. — *kind instruction;* she is ever ready to give instruction or advice, and that not with the authority of a dictator, but with the affection of a friend.

27. — *ways of her household;* she carefully oversees the domestics and laborers of her family, so that they shall have their allotted work, and attend to it with diligence. — *bread of idleness;* i.e., gotten without labor. In connection with the preceding line, the sense may be, that her living is earned by her domestics, whom her activity stimulates to diligence.

29. *Many daughters;* i.e., many women. (Comp. Gen. xxxiv. 1; Ezek. xxx. 18.)

30. *Grace;* i.e., gracefulness, elegance of form and manners. — *deceitful;* i.e., it disappoints expectation, being of short duration, or unable to give the permanent satisfaction which the husband promised himself from it. — *vain;* i.e., like a breath, a vapor, a mist, — perishing, soon gone.

31. — *fruit of her hands;* i.e., the praise which she has well earned by her labors. — *the gates;* i.e., the places of public concourse.

THE END.

www.ingramcontent.com/pod-product-compliance
Lightning Source LLC
LaVergne TN
LVHW011150110826
845150LV00006B/1209